P9-CJF-064

In Search of Your
Canadian Roots

In Search of Your Canadian Roots

Angus Baxter

MACMILLAN OF CANADA
A Division of Canada Publishing Corporation
Toronto, Ontario, Canada

FOR NAN
Who honours me with her love
every day of my life

Copyright © Angus Baxter, 1989

All rights reserved. The use of any part of this publication reproduced, transmitted in any form or by any means, electronic, mechanical, photocopying, recording, or otherwise, or stored in a retrieval system, without the prior written consent of the publisher is an infringement of the copyright law.

Canadian Cataloguing in Publication Data

Baxter, Angus, date
  In search of your Canadian roots

Includes index.
ISBN 0-7715-9201-9

1. Canada — Genealogy — Handbooks, manuals, etc.
2. Genealogy. I. Title.

CS82.B39 1989   929'.1'0971   C89-093116-X

  3 4 5 6 7 8 9 GP 96 95 94 93 92 91 90

Cover and text design: Marc Mireault
Cover photograph used with permission of the Ontario Archives
(Acc 6993 S 12907)

MACMILLAN OF CANADA
A Division of Canada Publishing Corporation
Toronto, Ontario, Canada

Printed in Canada

Contents

If we begin with certainties, we shall end in doubts: but if we begin with doubts, and are patient in them, we shall end in certainties.

Francis Bacon *(1561–1626)*

INTRODUCTION

Since my first genealogical book was published in 1978, there has been a world-wide explosion in ancestor-hunting. In every corner of the developed world there are new genealogical or family history societies, and from New Zealand to Norway, South Africa to Sweden, Canada to Czechoslovakia, tens of thousands of men and women are searching for their roots.

Nowhere is this growth more evident than in Canada. In the past ten years the number of genealogical societies has increased tenfold, and the effect on archives and libraries has been very great. Both have had to change their attitudes and systems to deal with the flood of inquiries. Libraries are no longer just places to borrow a book, and archives are no longer the preserve of academics preparing their theses.

Libraries are becoming local archives, with their own local genealogical sections. With volunteer help they are developing their own projects: abstracting names from local newspapers, indexing census returns, copying gravestone inscriptions, indexing church registers, taping the memoirs of older people in the area, and arranging lectures by visiting genealogists.

Genealogical societies, too, are putting their members' minds and hearts and hands to work with similar projects. They are issuing their own publications, and arranging seminars and conferences.

All these developments in the past ten years have increased the need for a comprehensive book about genealogical sources in Canada. In these pages I have tried to cover most of the records available to the ancestor-hunter or family historian. Whereas my previous books detailed the services available to those who were researching their British or European roots, in this book, for the first time, I have concentrated exclusively on the many sources available to Canadian genealogical research *within* Canada.

I take full responsibility for any errors and omissions. I have had to make arbitrary decisions as to what to include and what to omit, because of the need to keep the book to a reasonable size. However, I believe I have given good coverage to all provinces and the Yukon and Northwest territories, and have supplied Canadian genealogists with a reference book that will help them trace their ancestors in Canada. You will find it contains general information in the early chapters, followed by eleven chapters of details about sources in each individual province and territory.

Whether you are an experienced family historian or a beginner, you will know you have started on a magic and romantic journey that will bring you happiness and misery, exultation and frustration, anticipation and disappointment; but, putting the good hours and the bad together, it will be a period in your life that you will long remember, and for which your children and your children's children will always be grateful.

When you have traced your roots beyond Canada into the soil of a country over the ocean, then you will embark on an even more thrilling journey, because you will learn about the great events in history. These happenings changed the face of nations, affected the lives of millions, and provided the reasons for the emigration of your ancestors. Did they flee the pogroms and the Cossacks of Tsarist Russia? The bloodshed and misery of the Thirty Years War in Germanic Europe? The potato famines of Ireland? The Highland Clearances of Scotland? The barbarous regime of Bela Kun in Hungary? The forced displacement of Germans in Poland and Czechoslovakia? The massacre of the Armenians in Turkey, or the Ukrainians in their own land? The loss of liberty of the ancient Baltic countries? Religious persecution in England?

Your search overseas will tell you of your family's place in this tapestry of events that will unfold before your eyes. Your search in Canada is but the start of a voyage of delight and discovery!

Angus Baxter

ACKNOWLEDGEMENTS

Many people have helped me with this book by providing information about national, provincial, and local records; projects and publications of genealogical societies; the location of church registers; and details of genealogical collections in local libraries. To all these people I send my thanks for their patience and kindness.

I want to express my admiration for and gratitude to, above all, two kinds of people:

1. The librarians and archivists — all listed below — who went to enormous trouble to provide me with details of their genealogical and local-history collections. From coast to coast they answered my appeal for information with goodwill and enthusiasm, and I am more grateful than I can possibly say. I know how busy they are, but their dedication to their profession and their interest in genealogy led them to put urgent work on one side and sit down and write to me. There were a few librarians who ignored my letters, but the number was minute. I hope they will have second thoughts in time for the next edition of this book.

2. The members of the various genealogical and historical societies who spent endless hours in all sorts of weather transcribing cemetery records, indexing badly written census returns, and abstracting BMD notices from faded and fragile old newspapers. I am sure that at times they wondered if anyone really cared or really appreciated the dull monotony of what they were doing. I can assure them that people do care, do feel gratitude, do admire their efforts, and they can be sure that future generations of ancestor-hunters will bless their names.

ALBERTA
Dennis Anderson, Minister of Culture and Multiculturalism
Marlene Balser, Reference Librarian, Medicine Hat Public Library
Jennifer Bobrovitz, Local History Librarian, Calgary Public Library
W. A. de Nance, Public Trustee, Alberta
Peggy Franko, Secretary, Alberta Family History Society
Susan Kooyman, Archivist, Glenbow Museum, Calgary
Rita Laczkowski, Library Chairman, Alberta Genealogical Society

Jo Nuthack, President, Alberta Genealogical Society
Edith Pinder, Medicine Hat Branch, Alberta Genealogical
Society
Marcia Redford, Director, Fort Saskatchewan Municipal
Library
B. Smith, Librarian, Cardston Public Library
Keith Stotyn, Senior Archivist, Provincial Archives of
Alberta

BRITISH COLUMBIA
Anne Allgaier, Public Services Librarian, Prince George Public Library
Madeleine Alto, Chief Librarian, Greater Victoria Public
Library
Sue Babtie, City Archivist, Vancouver
Jessie Belcher, Secretary, Cowichan Valley Genealogical
Society
John A. Bovey, Provincial Archivist, British Columbia
Bernice Chong, Asst. Archivist, Richmond Township
Cathy English, Curator, Revelstoke Museum & Archives
Jamie Forbes, City of Trail Archives
Jean Giesbrecht, Quesnel Branch, British Columbia Genealogical Society
Paul Gutteridge, Manager of Technical Services, Surrey Centennial Library
Maureen Lawson, Head, Reference Division, Legislative
Library, Victoria
Larry Little, Asst. Librarian, Penticton Public Library
David Mattison, Library and Maps Division, Provincial
Archives
Joan Newman, Archivist, Diocese of Cariboo
Gloria Novak, Vancouver Island Regional Library
Betty Ozanne, Chase & District Family History Association
Diana Quant, Museum Division, City of Penticton
Muriel Roberts, Librarian, Burnaby Public Library
Denise St. Arnaud, Chief Librarian, Prince Rupert Public
Library
Barbara Sheppard, Archivist, Prince Rupert City and
Regional Archives
Doreen Stephens, Diocesan Archivist, Diocese of New
Westminster
John Stewart, Kamloops Museum and Archives
Shelley Tegart, Corresponding Secretary, British Columbia
Genealogical Society

MANITOBA

Vera K. Fast, Archivist, Manitoba Provincial Archives
Hazel Hopkins, President, Thompson Historical Society
Mavis Menzies, Co-ordinator, Manitoba Genealogical Society
Shirley Metcalfe, Librarian, Minnedosa Regional Library
Wendy Owen, Archivist, Manitoba Provincial Archives
C. Potyondy, Western Manitoba Regional Library
Marielle Romanchuk, South Interlake Regional Library
P. J. Sinnott, Director, Administration, Attorney General of
   Manitoba

NEW BRUNSWICK

Effie Dewar, Harvey Community Library, Harvey Station
Carolyn Earle, Acting Archivist, UC Maritime Conference
   Archives
Fred Farrell, Archivist, Provincial Archives of New
   Brunswick
Mary Flagg, Manager, Special Collections, Harriet Irving
   Library
James Katan, Librarian, Chaleur Regional Library
W. P. Kilfoil, Editor, *Generations*, New Brunswick Genealogi-
   cal Society
Dawn Kinnie, President, New Brunswick Genealogical
   Society
M. Robertson, Archivist, New Brunswick Museum
Jackson Ross, President, Restigouche Genealogical Society
Eunice Stringer, New Brunswick Library Service
Judy Tribe, Librarian, L. P. Fisher Library

NEWFOUNDLAND AND LABRADOR

C. J. Goodyear, Registrar, Supreme Court of Newfoundland
David Leamon, Newfoundland Public Library Services
Don Morris, Genealogist, Provincial Archives of
   Newfoundland
Catherine Power, Librarian, Public Libraries Board
Sheilagh Rahal, Secretary, Newfoundland & Labrador
   Genealogical Society
Patricia Warren, United Church Archives, St. John's
Lynne West, Cornerbrook City Library

NOVA SCOTIA

Frances Anderson, Librarian, South Shore Regional Library
Marjorie Bulmer, Co-ordinator, Colchester Historical Society
J. B. Cahill, Archivist, Provincial Archives of Nova Scotia

David Cumby, Eastern Counties Regional Library
Julie Morris, Archivist, Provincial Archives of Nova Scotia
Patricia Palmer, Asst. Librarian, University of King's College
Fred Popowich, Asst. Librarian, Pictou-Antigonish Regional
    Library
Terrence Punch, President, Genealogical Association of Nova
    Scotia
A. E. Rennie, Director of Field Operations, Department of the
    Attorney General
Evangeline Way, Secretary, Pictou County Genealogical
    Society

ONTARIO
Gloria Affleck, CEO, Lanark Public Library
Ferne Allen, Librarian, Stayner Public Library
Robert Appleton, Land Registrar, Peterborough
Phyllis Armstrong, Asst. Librarian, Markdale Public Library
Margaret Asbury, Librarian, Fergus Public Library
Donna Binsted, CEO, Meaford Public Library
Rita Bloch, Librarian, Dundas Public Library
Margaret Bushell, Supervisor, Goderich Public Library
Bonnie Callen, Archivist, Wellington County Museum &
    Archives
B. J. Carney, Reference Librarian, Parry Sound
Margaret Carrington, Reference Librarian, Markham Public
    Library
Dorothy Chisholm, Archivist, United Empire Loyalist
    Association
Barry Church, CEO, Grimsby Public Library
Judith Colwell, Librarian, Canadian Baptist Archives
Irene Cox, Librarian, Deep River Public Library
Carolyn Croke, CEO, Brantford Public Library
Marie Cruickshank, Local History Librarian, Collingwood
    Public Library
Faye Cunningham, Head Librarian, Perth Public Library
Glen Curnoe, London Room Librarian, London Public Library
Pamela Currie, Reference Librarian, Chatham Public Library
Julie de Martigny, Local History Librarian, Waterloo Public
    Library
W. Eisenbichler, Asst. Director, Sault Ste. Marie Public
    Library
Barbara Fazekas, Chief Librarian, Elliot Lake Public Library

Lynne Gibbon, Collection Development Librarian, Barrie
  Public Library
Linda Gula, Research Librarian, Niagara-on-the-Lake Public
  Library
Christel Haeck, Special Collections Librarian, St. Catharines
  Public Library
Margaret Hardie, Reference Librarian, Sudbury Public
  Library
Nancy Harsanyi, CEO, Cornwall Public Library
Leona Hendry, Chief Librarian, Belleville Public Library
Helen Hodgins, Supervisor, Exeter Public Library
Margaret Houghton, Archivist, Special Collections, Hamilton
  Public Library
Janet Iles, Materials Researcher, Owen Sound Public Library
Gwen Ing, Metropolitan Toronto Reference Library
Jill Jamieson, Archivist, Local History Collection, Woodstock
  Public Library
A. Johnstone, Librarian, Bayfield Public Library
Gail Juris, Head, Main Library, Windsor Public Library
Mary Karpinchick, CEO, Port Colborne Public Library
Linda Kearns, Archivist, Local History, Guelph Public
  Library
Jane Kirkpatrick, Librarian, Stratford Public Library
Sandra Lamoureux, Asst. Reference Librarian, Sarnia Public
  Library
Lynn Leu, Supervisor, New Hamburg Public Library
Mary Lloyd, Head, Genealogy & Local History Collection,
  Richmond Hill Public Library
Marion Locke, Reference Librarian, Midland Public Library
John Love, Librarian, Gananoque Public Library
M. E. Maclean, Reference Librarian, Cobourg Public Library
Ruby McCoy, Supervisor, Marmora Public Library
Terri McFadden, Information Assistant, St. Thomas Public
  Library
Subhash Mehta, Chief Librarian, Pembroke Public Library
Judith Mitton, President, Ontario Genealogical Society
Peter Moran, County Archivist, Simcoe County Archives
Donald Mutch, Asst. Head, Reference Department, Ottawa
  Public Library
Jill Nicholson, Chief Librarian, Leamington Public Library
Anne-Marie Peachey, Chief Librarian, Bracebridge Public
  Library

James Pendergest, Reference Librarian, Peterborough Public Library
Marilyn Pillar, CEO, Alliston Public Library
Genevieve Prentice, Librarian, Whitby Public Library
Pat Ramsay, Librarian, Rideau Township (North Gower)
Christine St. Jacques, Local History Co-ordinator, Oakville Public Library
Jack Schecter, Librarian, Upper Canada Village
Mrs. K. Schecter, Chief Librarian, Smiths Falls Public Library
Matthew Scholtz, Chief Librarian, Tillsonburg Public Library
Erich R. W. Schultz (Rev.), Archivist, Eastern Synod ELCIC
Reta Sporring, Librarian, Madoc Public Library
Sam Steiner, Archivist, Conrad Grebel College, Waterloo
Phyllis Strain, Librarian, Bath Public Library
Ryan Taylor, Librarian, Grace Schmidt Room, Kitchener Public Library
Naina Thatte, Local History Librarian, Brampton Public Library
Marguerite Urban, CEO, Huntsville Public Library
Dorothy Van Slyke, CEO, Niagara Falls Public Library
Leon Warmski, Archivist, Private Manuscript Section, Archives of Ontario
Sister Frieda Watson, Archivist, Archdiocese of Toronto
David Weismuller, CEO, Nepean Public Library
Laura Williams, Reference Librarian, Burlington Public Library
Ian E. Wilson, Archivist of Ontario, Provincial Archives of Ontario
Jane Zavitz, Archivist, CYM Archives, Pickering College (Newmarket)

PRINCE EDWARD ISLAND
Douglas Fraser, P.E.I. Museum & Heritage Foundation
Alison Heckbert, Library Assistant, Confederation Centre Public Library
Orlo Jones, P.E.I., Museum & Heritage Foundation
Don Scott, Provincial Librarian, Provincial Library
Jane Symmes, Secretary, Prince Edward Island Genealogical Society
Elinor Vass, Asst. Archivist, Public Archives of Prince Edward Island

QUÉBEC
Hugh M. Banfill, President, Québec Family History Society
Mrs. M. S. Cazes, Registrar, Church Society of the Diocese of
Québec
Diane Duval, Présidente, Société de généalogie de Québec
Cécile de Lamirande, Trésorière, La Société Généalogique
Canadienne-Française
G. Lebans, Archivist, Synod of the Diocese of Montréal
Daniel Olivier, Chief, Gagnon Collection, Central Library,
Montréal
Yves Renaud, Executive Assistant, Bureau de Sous-ministre
associé, Ministère de la Justice, Québec
Réjean Roy, Secrétaire, Société de généalogie des Cantons de
l'est

SASKATCHEWAN
Kenneth Aitken, Prairie History Librarian, Regina Public
Library
D. H. Bockney, Acting Provincial Archivist, Saskatoon
Anne Dawe, North Battleford Library
Muriel Dickson, Co-ordinator, Saskatoon Public Library
Maureen Fox, Staff Archivist, Saskatchewan Archives Board
Krzyszlof Gebhard, Reference Co-ordinator, Saskatchewan
Archives Board
Carolyn Graham, Asst. Head Librarian, Moose Jaw Public
Library
D'Arcy Hande, Saskatchewan Archives Board
Greg Hebert, Administration Manager, Property Registration
Branch
Lorne Hepworth, Minister of Education
Trevor Powell, Acting Provincial Archivist, Regina
Greg Salmers, City Librarian, Estevan
M. Thomas, Co-ordinator, Saskatchewan Genealogical Society

YUKON TERRITORY
V. Baggaley, Acting Director, Dawson Museum & Historical
Society
Rt. Rev. John Frame, Bishop of Yukon
Felicitas Tangermann, Research Assistant, Libraries &
Archives Branch
H. J. Taylor, Registrar General

ABBREVIATIONS

You will find various abbreviations throughout the book and in the various genealogical records you will encounter in your research:

The simple ones are:

B	Births or Baptisms
M	Marriages
D	Deaths or Burials
BMD	A combination of all three
MS	Manuscript

The more complicated ones are those used, particularly by census enumerators, to distinguish the extraordinary number of different churches, denominations, and sects:

A	Anglican
B	Baptist
BC	Bible Christian
BWM	British Wesleyan Methodist
C	Congregational
CA	Catholic
CS	Church of Scotland
DR	Dutch Reformed
EB	Evangelical Baptist
EL	Evangelical Lutheran
EM	Episcopal Methodist
EUB	Evangelical United Brethren
FB	Fundamental Baptist
FC	Free Church (Presbyterian)
FP	Free Presbyterian
L	Lutheran
LDS	Latter-Day Saints Church (Mormon)
M	Methodist
ME	Methodist Episcopalian
MEN	Mennonite
MNC	Methodist New Connection
MO	Moravian
P	Presbyterian
PB	Primitive Baptist

PC	Presbyterian Church
PFC	Presbyterian Free Church
PM	Primitive Methodist
PR	Protestant
Q	Quaker
RB	Regular Baptist
RE	Reformed Episcopalian
RM	Regular Methodist
SB	Southern Baptist
SF	Society of Friends (Quaker)
TB	True Baptist
TM	True Methodist
U	Unitarian
UB	Ukrainian Baptist
UC	United Church (may include C, M, and P)
UP	United Presbyterian
W	Wesleyan
WM	Wesleyan Methodist
WMNC	Wesleyan Methodist (New Connection)
ANG(C)	Anglican Diocese of Calgary
ANG(CA)	Anglican Diocese of Caledonia
ANG(K)	Anglican Diocese of Keewatin
ANG(M)	Anglican Diocese of Montréal
ANG(N)	Anglican Diocese of Niagara
ANG(NW)	Anglican Diocese of New Westminster
ANG(O)	Anglican Diocese of Ontario
ANG(Ot)	Anglican Diocese of Ottawa
ANG(T)	Anglican Diocese of Toronto

The various lists of church registers given in each provincial chapter show the location of the records in a particular archive, library, museum, university, or private collection. The abbreviations for these are listed below:

NAC	National Archives of Canada
AA	Archives of Alberta
ABC	Archives of British Columbia
ANB	Archives of New Brunswick
ANF	Archives of Newfoundland
ANS	Archives of Nova Scotia
AQ	Archives of Québec
PAM	Archives of Manitoba

PAO	Archives of Ontario
PAS(R)	Archives of Saskatchewan (Regina)
PAS(S)	Archives of Saskatchewan (Saskatoon)
PEA	Archives of Prince Edward Island
AAM	Archives Acadiennes
ACO	Archives des Châtelets
BAP	Baptist Archives (McMaster University)
CBA	Cape Bretonia Archives (St. Francis-Xavier University)
GLA	Glenbow Library & Archives
KKC	Knox Crescent & Kensington Church
LMH	London and Middlesex County Historical Society
LUC	Library of the University of Calgary
MA	Mennonite Archives (Waterloo)
MBA	Maritime Baptist Archives (Acadia University)
NBM	New Brunswick Provincial Museum
OCA	Ottawa City Archives
PAK	Presbyterian Archives (Knox College)
PTE	Private Collections
QU	Queen's University
UCA	United Church Archives (Toronto)
UCM	United Church Centre (Montréal)
UM	Université de Montréal
UNB	University of New Brunswick
UWO	University of Western Ontario
UW	University of Winnipeg

Postscript! When making requests for information to any source, *never forget s. a. e.* — stamped, addressed envelope. If you do not cover return postage, you may not get an answer to your query.

CHAPTER 1
Starting Off on the Right Foot

As you trace back your family, you must expect to run into difficulties—no one ever said ancestor-hunting was easy. That being so, it is important to make sure you do not create your own problems by making mistakes at the start of your search.

You will find the main official sources of information set out in detail in later chapters. However, your most vital source of information is within your own family—this is the fertile soil in which you will grow your family tree. Unless you clear away the stones and rubbish, your tree will not take root.

The most important rule is, *never* believe anything you are told about your family unless it can be proved, and *never* make an assumption unless it is backed up by solid evidence. The things you may be told by relatives or family friends may be absolutely true, but be a little "from Missouri" until you can be certain. I do not suggest you are descended from a long line of congenital liars, but there is always the possibility of exaggeration, or decoration, or "improvement"—either accidental or deliberate.

Be very cautious about any story that touches on the social standing of the family, because this is the most likely area of decoration. The farm worker becomes a farmer, the sergeant in the army becomes a captain, the cottage in the "old country" becomes a fifty-room mansion. This is not lying—it is an "improvement". It happens today: someone emigrates to Canada, makes new friends, and tries to impress them a little with stories of his or her family background.

Many years ago I knew a couple of English immigrants to Canada. The husband had told me how he and his wife had grown up in the same poor district of the East End of London. They had married, worked hard, and prospered to a limited degree. Then they decided to emigrate. He was an honest, down-to-earth man who was quite proud of his early struggles.

A couple of years later I happened to be within earshot of his wife at a cocktail party and was amused to hear her saying, "Of course, I was brought up in the country in England. My parents were independently wealthy, and we had a large house in Oxfordshire. It was an Elizabethan manor-house, actually. We entertained a great deal, and the local hunt always started the season with a meet at our house, when it was my job to give the Master his stirrup-cup." It was a charming story, and I am sure her listeners believed her, but of course it was a pack of lies!

Stories of royal or noble descent should always be very suspect. Ninety-five per cent of your ancestors and mine were connected with the land — they were farmers, blacksmiths, shepherds, ploughmen, thatchers, farriers, stonemasons, stablemen, or any of the other occupations connected with agriculture or the countryside. If they had moved into urban areas at the time of the Industrial Revolution, they were probably miners, mill-workers, weavers, house servants, bricklayers, glaziers, railwaymen, or any of the other jobs connected with industry.

They did not have titles or great wealth — they were honest, hard-working men and women. If you are descended from a king or a queen, or a duke or a duchess, the probability is that you will already have documentary proof within your own family. If you have not, work your way back in the normal way and perhaps you will discover you have blue blood in your veins after all!

My wife's mother always maintained she was a distant cousin of the Empress Eugénie of France (1826–1920). The family treated this as just another family story. However, when my wife and I traced her ancestry, we found that she was absolutely right. Both my mother-in-law and the Empress were descended from a Sir Thomas Kirkpatrick. So here is a case where a family story of royal connections was based on fact!

The other family story which you may have been told is that

"There is money tied up in court." The usual version is that one of your ancestors could not inherit a fortune because a baptismal entry in a church register could not be found. The story is widespread. I have heard it often from people at my lectures in Canada and the United States, as well as in such faraway places as Australia and New Zealand.

Unfortunately, unclaimed money is not left lying around forever. After a few years it passes into the greedy hands of the government of a country and that is the end of it. I have never met anyone who found wealth while ancestor-hunting. If you do as the result of reading this book, I will be delighted, and will, of course, expect the usual ten-per-cent commission!

Be sure you talk to *every* member of your family and *every* old family friend—it is amazing how often just one member of a family has vital information not possessed by anyone else.

If you have an elderly aunt, or great-aunt, this may be like finding the mother-lode. Women are the custodians of family history, the recipients of confidences, the recorders of names and dates and miscellaneous facts. They know far more than any man—they know when and where people were born, who married who, and, in some cases, who had to marry who! They know when people died, and where, and the cause of death. Remember, too, that they can tell you not only about the events of their own long lives, but also about the events they heard of from their grandparents. In the clear mind of an elderly person may be stored one hundred and fifty years of family history—a rich source of material just waiting to be discovered!

Never neglect this source of information; if you have such an elderly relative, go and see her *now*—don't leave it until it is too late. Nearly all of us who have traced our family can say, "If only I had started this when Great-Aunt Jane was alive! I never listened to the old lady's stories when I was younger, and now, when I need her, she is gone, and all her family knowledge has gone with her."

Please handle your elderly relative with tender, loving care—don't descend on her out of the blue, without advance warning, armed with a tape-recorder, and firing off a barrage of rapid questions. Don't expect equally rapid answers — the human brain doesn't function in that way. Simply chat away quietly and take notes in a small notebook. Leave the tape-recorder at home—older people don't like them and become self-conscious and reluctant to speak. Start off by talking generally, perhaps compliment her on her youthful appearance or outlook, and introduce the question of family history very gently. Once the conversation is started, let her take the lead, occasionally prompting her with a short question when there is a suitable pause. Take your notes but *don't* interrupt her—what seems to you to be a wandering monologue may be a valuable and detailed narrative following a pattern all its own.

Be prepared to let your relative wander a little, and don't overtire her by staying too long. Tell her how wonderful her help has been, say you would like to talk again in a couple of weeks, and ask her if, in the interval, she will jot down any other information she remembers. *Be sure you do go back*, because I can guarantee you will get more information on the second visit. If you have been kind and charming, and have made a good impression, she will have been flattered by your interest and pleased that someone has listened to her. You are probably the first person she has talked to about the family and herself for quite a long time.

When you get home, and while the conversation is fresh in your mind, go over your notes, expand them, and make sure you write down who gave you all the information. This is the time, too, to write down the questions you didn't get a chance to ask this time, so that you will be prepared for your second visit.

Two stories to illustrate the points I have just made about one family member having vital information, and about the memory of an elderly relative:

A few years ago, while my wife's mother was still alive, we were on a visit to her in Scotland. She was ninety at that time, and one day she asked to be taken on a visit to the family burial-grounds and kirkyards near Dumfries, in the south-west. We spent a day going up and down the lovely valley of the River Nith. In one kirkyard we saw the tombstone of a Marion Grieve (died 1834, aged 8 years). My mother-in-law said, "I know all about her. She was a lovely child with long golden hair down to her waist, but the puir wee lass was always a sickly bairn, and she just wasted away and died." "Margaret," I said, "that was fifty years before you were born. How can you know about her?" "My grandmother told me," she said. So there you have a clear picture and physical description of an ancestor who had died nearly a century and a half ago!

As far as one person having vital knowledge, I can best quote the case of my wife's grandfather. Before we started out to trace her ancestors, we knew four generations to start with. My wife was born in Scotland, and so were her family back as far as we knew. Eventually we traced back to an ancestor who had died in 1710. There we stuck, because, although he had been married and had fathered three sons in that place, he had not been born there. He was an incomer from somewhere else. At that point my wife remembered that when she was a child her grandfather had told her the family had originated in England two centuries earlier. The years passed by, and her grandfather died, and when she mentioned his remark to her father, she was told she must have misheard him — "There's no English blood in our veins" was the comment. You must understand that, in Scotland, if you have English ancestors you keep very quiet about it!

Anyway, to cut a long story short, that remark to my wife by her grandfather—a comment he had never made to anyone else in the family — led us eventually to the place in the north of England whence her ancestor had migrated to Scotland. What is more, it led us to a printed family tree that took the family back to the fifteenth century, and provided us with enough clues to take it back even further, to 1296!

You must be prepared to find that no one in your family shares your interest in ancestry, and you will find yourself ploughing a very lonely furrow. You will meet with comments like "Leave well enough alone" or "Why stir the pot?" or "The less you know about them the better." Some of these relatives may refuse to share their family knowledge with you. Often these remarks hide fear or taboo knowledge. Some may be afraid you will discover some dark secret, or they may know the secret. They may know that your great-grandfather spent a month in gaol for stealing the communion plate from the church, or—horror of horrors!—was born out of wedlock. I don't understand why anyone should be bothered by such fears. If he or she is, explain that anything you discover will be kept confidential and that, anyway, it is unlikely you will discover anything unsavoury about the character or reputation of an ancestor. You will know when and where the birth took place, the same with marriage and death, but unless your ancestor was written about in a book or a newspaper, you will know nothing more about him. I cannot give you a magic word to open a locked door—it will depend on *you*, and your charm, your tact, and your dogged determination.

Two items within your family will be very important to you if they exist: the family Bible and the family photograph album.

Up until about 1900, it was the custom to give a Bible to a newly married couple. In it were special pages on which they could record all the vital events in the family—births and baptisms, marriages, and deaths of children, etc. These pages were either in the front or back of the Bible, or in the middle between the Old and New Testaments.

The entries can be of great value to you *if* they were recorded as they occurred. Check the writing; if all the entries are in exactly the same handwriting, with no variation because of increasing age, it will mean they were all made at the same time *after* the events occurred, and therefore were probably made from hearsay. In that case, treat them as a guide but not as a fact.

The family photograph album is the most frustrating family memento you are likely to find. It will contain lots of photographs of men and women who are undoubtedly your ancestors, but no one has written the names below or on the back. Your elderly relative may be able to identify them for you, but if not, the only value is in the name of the photographer and his city, which you may find embossed on the front of the photograph or printed on the back. This place may well be the place of origin of your family overseas, or the place of settlement (or the nearest town) of your ancestor in this country. Your immigrant forebear may have brought some of them over with him or her, or they may have been sent by the family left behind. I know a number of cases where people have used this information successfully by writing a letter to the local newspaper either here or overseas for information about the family. In this way they have made contact with long-lost or unknown cousins.

Letters to newspapers asking for such information are usually printed in small-town or county newspapers, but not in those in big cities. You should also check with local archives and libraries, because there are cases where a photographer's plates and records have been handed over when he died or retired.

At this point, if your recent ancestor was an immigrant, you may well be saying, "My grandfather came to Canada in 1880 —who on earth will know anything about him now?" You will be astonished. When your ancestor emigrated, it was the most traumatic event ever to have happened to your family—a son or a daughter leaving home to go across the Atlantic, never to return! It was like a sudden death, and it has been remembered. When Canada is in the news, someone over there will say,

"Canada? Do you remember Grandfather had a brother who emigrated there? I wonder what happened to him? Maybe we have lots of Canadian cousins!" They will not try to find you, but your letter in the local newspaper will be read and your grandfather remembered. The odds are good that you will hear from someone.

There are other obstacles to be avoided in the early days of your search; even when you are searching for official records and not just depending on family stories, you can go wrong in several areas.

Names are one of the most common causes of obstacle-creation — both first names and surnames. Whatever you do, don't assume you must be related at some point in time to people with the same surname. Surnames have a variety of origins, but, generally speaking, they are based on occupations, location, personal appearance, a father or a mother's first name, or even an event occurring in the district at the time of birth.

Surnames rarely existed before 1300 in all western countries. In a village you could find John the baker, John of the wood, John of the church hill, John of the storm, and so on. By 1400, because of population increase this clumsy system was ended. The words "the" and "of" were dropped, and you then had John Baker, John Wood, John Churchill, John Storm, etc. You can see why similar surnames do not mean a relationship.

As you go back — even in comparatively recent times — you must be prepared to find variations in the spelling of your surname. It is most unlikely it has always been spelt the same way, unless it was a very simple name like Smith — and even then you may find Smyth, Smythe, Smithe, or Smitt. The further back you go, the greater the difference. Names were often spelt as they sounded in the days when our ancestors could not read or write, and when a clergyman recorded a baptism he often came up with some weird and wonderful spellings. I can give you fourteen ways of spelling Baxter. The most complicated was Bacchuster, but if you say it quickly it sounds like Baxter. I also found it spelt Bastar, and I didn't like that quite so much! You may even find the surname of your great-grandfather spelt one way, and the surnames of his brother and sister in the same church register spelt two other ways.

If your ancestral background is European, you should check to see if the spelling of your name has been simplified. Quite often, for example, a Polish immigrant would find his name almost unpronounceable by native-born Canadians of Anglo-

Saxon descent, and he would simplify it. In this way Pryzeborski could become Price. Even a move from Québec to Alberta could change Boileau to Barlo.

First names can produce other problems. If you are told that your grandfather's name was John Hammond, try to make sure that John *was* his first name. It is by no means unusual for someone to dislike his or her first name so intensely that quite early in life all use of it was dropped and a second name was used. The fictional John Hammond may have been baptized Zebediah John Hammond!

Make certain that the first name by which you know your grandfather or grandmother is not a diminutive or a pet name. If grandmother was Jenny, remember that her baptismal name could have been Jane or Janet. There are other examples: Fanny could be Frances; Sally could be Sarah; Betsy, Betty, Bessie, Beth, Lizzie could all be Elizabeth; Nellie could be Helen; Frank could be Francis; Fred could be Frederick, Alfred, or Wilfred. The same problem arises in Europe, particularly in German-speaking areas.

Sometimes ancestor-hunters will take the easy way out in trying to overcome an obstacle by making an assumption not based on facts. This is likely to create an obstacle even greater than the original one. Let me give you an example. I know someone who had traced an ancestor to the Kingston area of Ontario. The ancestor had been born there in 1824, and the church register in which his baptism was recorded referred to his father as "Mr. Thompson". (I have changed the surname.) The ancestor-hunter then looked back through the register and found the marriage of a John Thompson and an Elizabeth Weston (name changed) in 1823. He immediately made an assumption that these were the parents. He then tried to find details of the birth of the bride and groom and failed. There was no record of them, and finally he gave up the search. Many years later he looked at the tombstone of his ancestor for the first time and found the words "son of Joseph and Mary Thompson of Kingston Township". This led him to land records and census returns and eventually back to a United Empire Loyalist ancestor who had obtained a grant of land. From there he followed the trail to New York State and finally to England. If he had not made that assumption years before, he would not have delayed his eventual success by twenty years.

Before we leave family sources, I must warn you that it is possible to encounter a deliberate falsification of family records.

Many years ago, as the result of a radio phone-in show, a listener wrote to me and asked for help in a particularly difficult problem she had encountered. In those days I was not so fully occupied in writing and lecturing as I am now, so I was willing to see what I could do. I went to see her and she explained she was descended from the famous Dr. Samuel Johnson of dictionary fame; an aunt of hers had traced the descent some years before, and she showed me a copy of the complete family tree. She had been trying to find out if she had any living cousins and had run into quite unexplainable obstacles. The tree was very detailed, with exact dates and places of baptism, marriage, and death for seven generations back to Dr. Johnson. I made a few inquiries and quickly discovered something was very wrong.

Then I checked the information compiled by her aunt and I found the family tree was entirely fictitious—none of the events recorded had ever taken place, and to top it all, I then discovered that the Doctor had never had any descendants. The aunt, anxious to claim descent from a famous man with the same surname, had painstakingly concocted a family tree out of her own mind! I have never come across another case like this, but you never know what you will find—so check, check, check!

The next common obstacle is ascertaining place of origin. You may have the name of a place in Ontario, for example, as the place of settlement of your ancestor. You know that in 1838 he owned land in Nelson's Falls, near Scott's Mill. You look at a map and you can't find either place. Why? The answer is simple: the names were changed to Lakefield and Peterborough. Many places in Canada have had several names. You can usually get help from your Provincial Archives in cases like this.

A similar problem can be caused by the merging of one parish with another, or the splitting of a parish into two. So far as overseas is concerned, you may have an additional problem. Grandfather may have always said he came from Bristol, England. In actual fact he came from a small village on the outskirts of the city, but it was much simpler to say Bristol. This sort of thing happens today. If you live in Spruce Grove, Alberta, and when you are on vacation in California someone asks where you live, you will most certainly say "Edmonton"—after all, it's almost true, and it saves you the bother of explaining just where Spruce Grove is located.

Some countries overseas will confront you with greater problems when you start searching over there. In Germany's "lost territories" after 1945, the names of cities were changed to

Czech or Polish ones: Leitmeritz became Litomerice, Allenstein became Olsztyn, and so on. In Ireland there is a variety of different land divisions. You may know that your great-grandfather came from a place named Ballypenahay but you can't find it on the map or in a gazetteer—probably because it is too small to be a parish and is either a townland or a barony.

As you work your way into the past, you will be writing lots of letters — to distant relatives, parsons, priests, archives, libraries, cemetery offices, government departments, genealogical and family history societies, and so on. When you are doing this, remember two things—if you don't, you are unlikely to get a reply:

1. Write a nice, polite, and friendly letter, and don't be abrupt and demanding. No one *has* to answer you—there is no law to force anyone to do so. I can hear you saying, "That's a totally unnecessary piece of advice. I always write a polite letter." I am delighted to know that you do, but you should see some of the extraordinary letters people in Canada and overseas receive from ancestor-hunters. As you may imagine, with my books being published in four countries I get a great deal of correspondence asking for information or advice. I have my share of the kind I don't bother to answer. "My grandfather emigrated from the U.S.A. to Canada in 1855. Send me his family tree at once." "My grandmother—her name was Harris — came from Canada. Tell me what you know about her by return mail." "You make that priest at Upton answer me." On top of that, none of them covered the return postage.

2. *Always* cover return postage. You are not the only family historian writing a letter—there are tens of thousands of you! I know one County Record Office in England which, in 1986, received over ten thousand letters from overseas, and only five hundred contained return postage. That is why the general rule has become "No return postage, no reply." If you are writing to an address in Canada, the process is simple — just enclose a stamped self-addressed envelope. If you are writing to the U.S.A., get a quarter (U.S.) from your bank and tape it to your letter. If you are writing overseas, you will have to buy two International Reply Coupons from your local post office and send them with your letter and a self-addressed airmail envelope. Your recipient can then go into a post office "over there" and exchange them for stamps. The two coupons will cost you a little over $2. This is extortionate.

If you know you will be writing a number of letters to a particular country over the next year, you can save fifty per cent of your return postage costs quite simply. You write to the Head Postmaster, the Central Post Office of any major city of the country — or any small town for that matter — and say, "I attach a bank draft for five pounds [or ten marks or whatever]. Please send me the equivalent value in stamps of the right denomination for airmail postage between your country and Canada." (If you send cash, you avoid bank charges.)

When you are writing for information, be brief, be clear, and type your letter or write very plainly. Quote accurate dates, names, and places. List the sources you have already checked (this will save them from going over the same ground). Do not write a "long letter from home", telling every detail. Your own family is absolutely fascinating to you, but the person who reads your letter has heard a similar story many times before, and will become very impatient if he or she has to wade through pages of family stories.

Finally, you must be sure not to make the greatest mistake of all: failing to check whether someone else has already traced your ancestors. You can do this in a number of different ways. Although you can never be absolutely certain, you can greatly reduce your chances of discovering, three years from now, that your time and money have been wasted because you failed to check!

(a) Write to the public library in any place in Canada where your family settled. More and more libraries have family or local history sections. They have ongoing projects such as card-indexing and microfilming the various type of records I mentioned in the Introduction.

(b) Write also to the public library in the place overseas from which your ancestor emigrated. We discovered the value of checking with a library many years ago. We decided to trace a side of my wife's family that had been located in the Dumfries area of Scotland for many generations. When we arrived in the city, we went straight to the local library and asked if they had any information about the Copland family. They had: a detailed family tree compiled by some unknown member of the family fifty years before. This took us right back to 1135, and we had no searching to do! Yes, we did check the accuracy of the family tree, and all its documentation was accurate! If we had not checked with the library, we would have spent a lot of money and time on an unnecessary quest.

(c) Write to the genealogical or family history society for the same areas, both in Canada and overseas.

(d) Write to local newspapers in areas outside the major cities — the *Globe and Mail*, the Montréal *Gazette*, and the Vancouver *Province* are unlikely to publish your letter.

When you are writing to these four sources, ask if they have any record of your family (give names and dates of emigration or immigration) and if they know of anyone else searching for the same family.

(e) Write to the LDS Church in Salt Lake City or visit or write to your nearest LDS Family History Center. Check the indexes I mention in the chapter on the LDS Church.

In spite of all the above checking, there may be an unknown individual who is not a member of a family history society or the LDS Church who is quietly working away on your family and there is no means of making contact, but the odds are you have covered all the major possibilities for duplication.

There are two items I have not covered in this book, for several reasons:

1. *Adoptions*: I have not touched on this subject because each province has its own laws regarding access to information about natural parents. Organizations, such as Parent Finders, exist to help adopted people discover more about their background.

I have ambivalent feelings on this problem. If I were adopted, I would move heaven and earth to discover my natural parents, and my ethnic and medical background. However, there are also the feelings of the adoptive and the natural parents to be considered.

A search for an ancestral background, or an interest in a family medical history, is admirable, but a search motivated at best by idle curiosity, and at worst by a feeling of hatred or a desire for revenge, is quite another matter.

Unfortunately, a successful search does not always end with happiness and can cause disappointment, deep sorrow, and — sometimes — tragedy for all concerned.

2. *Divorce*: Each province has its own system of record-keeping, and its own laws regarding access to information. You should check in the first instance with the Department of Vital Statistics for guidance — you may find divorce records there, or in the provincial archives, or in the county courthouse.

CHAPTER 2
How to Start the Family Tree

Your main sources of information in Canada, apart from your own family, are civil registration, census returns, church registers, tombstones, and land records. There are, of course, other sources as well, and all of them will be explained in detail later in this book.

At this point I am assuming that many of you reading these pages are only just getting started on tracing your own family and its history, but even the experienced ancestor-hunter may learn a little. I think the best way to explain the use of the main sources is to create an imaginary family.

Then, together we will trace this family back from the present day, using sources available in Canada. Of course, you may not be as lucky in your search as the imaginary Charles Gibson. He may find his roots more easily than you, but Charlie, too, will have his problems, as you will see.

So, imagine you are Charles. What do you do? You take a large sheet of paper or Bristol board (about 2' × 3') which you bought at an art store or a business and office supply company. You write down *your* name and those of your brothers and sisters (if any) at the bottom of the sheet, reading from left to right in order of descending age. When you have the names down, add the dates and places of birth. Leave space below this line for you to add the names of your spouse and children. As your tree grows, you add the names of previous generations above your original line. The additions start, of course, with your parents, and in the beginning your family tree will look like this:

DAVID GIBSON   =   MARY ANDREWS
B: 3 September 1895   B: 4 August 1896
(Belleville)   (Kingston)
D: 2 January 1944   D: 5 May 1946
(Toronto)   (Toronto)
(Married in St. George's
Church, Kingston, 5 May 1918)

CHARLES   ROBERT   AGNES
B: 8 June 1920   B: 13 January 1922   B: 2 February 1924

You are now going to try to find out about your grandparents and any other relatives. You will also want to know where the family came from before Belleville. Maybe you have already collected all possible information from within your family. However, just for the exercise, let us assume you have the elderly relative I talked about in an earlier chapter. In this case she is your father's sister Helen, known in the family as Aunt Nellie. She was five years younger than your father, you think, and if this is so, she was born in 1900, so she is quite old. She never married, and now she lives in a retirement home in Brampton, a few miles west of Toronto. You know her quite well. She used to own a candy store in Brampton, and when you and your brother and sister were children, you used to be taken to stay with her by your parents on occasional weekends. She used to say you all came to take stock! You have never really talked about the family with her.

So you write to her in Brampton and ask if you can come and see her on a Sunday afternoon in two weeks' time. You explain that you are going to start to trace your ancestors and would like her help. She answers your letter and says, "I really don't know anything about the family. Your grandmother never spoke much about it, but I will be happy to see you. I don't get many visitors nowadays."

On Sunday week you go out to see Aunt Nellie. She is very bright and cheerful, with all her wits about her. You find you have to raise your voice a little—you can see a hearing-aid on a side-table, but you know she never wears it! You have a small

notebook with you, and you have already written down some
questions you want to ask her:
1. What was my grandfather's name?
2. Where was he born, and when?
3. Whom did he marry, and when, and where?
4. When did he die, and where is he buried?
5. What was grandmother's name?
6. Where was she born, and when?
7. When did she die, and where is she buried?
8. Did my grandfather have any brothers or sisters?
9. Were they older or younger than he?
10. What do you know about them?
11. Did any of them have children?
12. If so, where are they now?
13. Do you know if he left a will?
14. Is there a family Bible anywhere?
15. Is there a family photograph album?
16. Is there anything else you can tell me?

So, with all these questions waiting to be answered, you chat
away with Aunt Nellie about her health and her life, and then
start — very gently — to ask the questions and write down the
answers:

What was my grandfather's name?
William George Gibson.
Where was he born?
Oh goodness! I don't know. Maybe it was somewhere in the
Maritimes.
What was the date, d'you know?
I have no idea.
Do you know when he died?
It was just before I was born. I remember my mother often said,
"What a pity your father never saw you."
When were you born? 1900 wasn't it?
Yes, on June 4.
How old were you when my grandmother died?
I was thirty-eight by then. She was bed-ridden for years. It wasn't
easy running the store and looking after her. Anyway, you should
remember that — you and your father were at the funeral.
*I know, Aunt Nellie, but I couldn't remember the year. What was
her maiden name?*
She had been a Mary Evans.
Where were they married?

In Belleville, where your father and I were born. He was a
foreman in the railway yard there.
*Do you know where he was buried? I know Grandma was buried
here in Brampton.*
Oh, he was buried in the cemetery in Belleville. It was in 1920
that Mother came to live with me in Brampton.

At this point you have discovered the names of your grandparents. You know when they died and where, and you now
have enough information to find out their birth dates, even if
Aunt Nellie didn't know them. Though you know your grandmother's maiden name, you are wise enough not to be diverted
from tracing the Gibson family. It is better to concentrate on
one side at first.
What was their religion?
Well, Mother was a Methodist. I think Father was an Anglican
originally but he wasn't a churchgoer. Mother went to chapel
every Sunday until she was bed-ridden, then she used to listen
to services on the radio.
Did your father have any brothers and sisters?
Oh yes, he sure did. He had an elder brother, Thomas, who
worked for the CPR out west somewhere—Winnipeg, I think.
Then there was Margaret—she married some French fellow and
went to live in Québec. I don't know what happened to her. There
was your grand-dad's younger brother, Jimmy. I remember him
very well—he used to give me pennies and bars of chocolate when
he came to visit. That's all of them.
Did any of them have children?
Oh yes. Uncle Tom didn't, but Uncle Jimmy did. I don't know
about Margaret. Jimmy went to work in Alberta—a little place
named Brooks. I remember that because he married a local girl
there, Susan Brooks. I often wondered if the town was named
after her family.
Did you say they had children?
Several, I think, but I never met any of them. I know they had a
girl they named after me. Neither of the uncles came to Mum's
funeral. I suppose they couldn't afford the long journey—it was
still Depression time. I know your father wrote to the two uncles
and told them, but he never could trace Margaret.
Did he leave a will? Grandpa, I mean.
Not that I know of. It all went to Mother, anyway—what there
was of it. She made a will, though, and it came to me. She didn't

leave anything to your father. I guess she thought he didn't need
it. He had a good job and was doing all right for himself.
Have you ever seen a family Bible or a photograph album?
No, we never had a family Bible that I know of. I had a lot of old
photographs in envelopes, but I threw them all out when I moved
in here — just a lot of old junk, anyway.

At this point you realize you are probably tiring the old lady,
so you thank her, arrange to come back the next Sunday, go
home, and add to your family tree. Now it looks like this:

THOMAS	MARGARET	WILLIAM GEORGE	JAMES
B:	**B:**	**B:**	**B:**
D:	**D:**	**D:** 1900	**D:**
Lived in	Married and	(Belleville)	= Susan Brooks
Winnipeg.	went to Québec.	= Mary Evans	(in Alberta)
No children.		(**D**: 1938,	
		Brampton)	

DAVID	HELEN
B: 3 September 1895	(Nellie)
(Belleville)	**B:** 4 June 1900
D: 2 January 1944	(Belleville)
(Toronto)	Unmarried.
= Mary Andrews	
(St. George's Church,	
Kingston, 5 May 1918)	

CHARLES	ROBERT	AGNES
B: 8 June 1920	**B:** 13 January 1922	**B:** 2 February 1924
(Toronto)	(Toronto)	(Toronto)

You go back to see Aunt Nellie again and you learn a lot
more from her. Though it does not take you any further back,
it does give you a lot of interesting information about your
father's childhood. It is not information that will go into a family tree, but it will certainly be included in the family history
when you write it.

What do you do now? You want to find out where your
grandfather was born. "The Maritimes" covers a wide area,
and in any case your aunt was not certain about it. In addition,
you don't know his age when he died. He must have been quite
young — his widow survived him for thirty-eight years. There
are several sources of information about him which you must
check. There is his tombstone in the public cemetery in Belle-

ville. There is also the fact that his death in 1900 should have been registered, and in that case the civil registration records are in the office of the Registrar General in Toronto. This will give his age at death.

You live in Toronto, so it is easy for you to visit the office in the Macdonald Building in Queen's Park. You are not allowed to make your own search, so you fill out a form giving all the details you have about your grandfather, pay $15, and then go home to wait. A week later you get a copy of the death certificate. It tells you that he died on 14 May 1900, and was thirty-five years old. This means that he was born in 1865, but, of course, it does not tell you where.

At this point you decide you will go to the cemetery in Belleville and look at the inscription on his tombstone. Of course, you don't need to go—you could write to the superintendent of the cemetery and ask him if a member of his staff could copy the wording for you. However, you have the time, and you think it would be interesting to see for yourself.

At the cemetery you go into the office and give your grandfather's *full* name; this is important, because there could be two William Gibsons buried there, and his middle name, George, will allow him to be pinpointed in the cemetery records. Oh yes, there *could* be two William George Gibsons buried there, but let's not make life too difficult for you!

The office staff find the entry of his burial and the number of his grave. They give you a very-small-scale map showing the location of all the graves. Each one is numbered, and so is each row or road. His number is A48, Row 32. The location is marked for you on the map and off you go. It is quite hard to follow the winding paths on the map, and you take several wrong turns, but eventually you find the grave. The passage of the years and eighty-odd Canadian winters make it hard to read the inscription, but finally you make it all out:

Sacred to the Memory
of
WILLIAM GEORGE GIBSON
Died 14 May 1900
Born 10 June 1865

Well, the good news is that you now know the exact date of birth. The bad news is that there is no place of birth mentioned. All is not lost, though, because you know he was living in Belleville when he died. If you can find out exactly where he was living in the city, you can then check the census return for that address.

You go to the Belleville Public Library, and in the Reference Department you find several early directories for the city, including one for 1891 — nine years before your grandfather died. (Censuses are held every ten years, and this is the last one prior to his death.) You look up his name in the index and there is William Gibson living at 14 Locke Street. It does not give his middle name, but he is the only William Gibson listed.

Then you ask one of the librarians about census returns. You know they are in the National Archives in Ottawa, but you are told it is not necessary to go there because the library has microfilm copies of all the Belleville census returns for 1851 and every ten years up to and including 1891. You tell the librarian that your grandfather was living at 14 Locke Street and she produces the microfilm of the 1891 census for that part of the city. She takes you to a microfilm-viewer and shows you how to thread the film on the spool.

Then you sit down, peer into the viewer, turn the handle very slowly, and watch the pages pass by. You go on turning until Locke Street appears, and then you look down the page in numerical order of houses — 2, 4, 6, 8, 12 (there is no entry for No. 10; probably the house was empty at the time), but at No. 14 you are lucky:

GIBSON, William George, 26, foreman. Born Nova Scotia

GIBSON, Mary Elizabeth, 25, housewife. Born Nova Scotia

There are no children mentioned, because they were not born until a few years later.

You now know that Aunt Nellie was quite right about the Maritimes and your thoughts must now be centred on Nova Scotia. The librarian shows you a book called *In Search of Your Roots*, and you find there is a whole chapter about sources of family information in Nova Scotia. You realize you cannot borrow it, because you don't live in Belleville, but the librarian tells you that your local library is sure to have a copy. At this point you decide that you had better buy the book, because it contains a lot of information about ancestor-hunting generally, not just in Nova Scotia, and you will be able to refer to it constantly. You buy it from a local bookstore, take it home, and settle down to read about Nova Scotia.

You soon find you are very lucky, because civil registration there started in 1864, the year before your grandfather was born. You see that the records are in the office of the Registrar

General in Halifax. In order to obtain a copy of your grand-father's birth certificate, you write for a form to complete, and when it comes you find that you are asked to give the names of the parents. You explain that you do not have this information, but you hope there was only one William George Gibson born on 10 June 1865. You also have to spend $15 for the certificate.

In a couple of weeks you get a copy of the birth certificate, with a covering letter stating it cannot be guaranteed that this is the correct one for your grandfather because you did not supply the names of his parents, but this is the only William George Gibson born in the province on that day. You open up the certificate and there is the vital information you want:

WILLIAM GEORGE GIBSON. Born 10 June 1865, Shelburne. Father: Alexander Gibson. Mother: Agnes Gibson (née MacDonald).

You have just stepped back another generation, because you now know the names of your great-grandparents. Up to this point you have used three sources of genealogical information: civil registration in Ontario and Nova Scotia, census returns, and cemetery records in Ontario.

Your next task is to find a record of the marriage of Alexander Gibson and Agnes MacDonald. You know that William George Gibson had an elder brother and sister, and this means the marriage must have taken place before 1863 as a minimum. Civil registration is of no use to you now because it had not started in Nova Scotia until after that date. This means that you must turn to church registers — probably Anglican ones, because Aunt Nellie did tell you that her father was originally an Anglican. You cannot be certain about this, of course, and can only proceed by trial and error. First, try Anglican records, and if that doesn't work out, you will have to try either Catholic records or those of the many Nonconformist religions. You look at a map of Nova Scotia and find that Shelburne is a small town on the south-east coast. The book you have lists the various church registers still extant, and you find there is an Anglican one for Shelburne in the Provincial Archives in Halifax, and it started in 1783. There is also a copy on microfilm in the National Archives in Ottawa. This is fine, because it means you can request the loan of the microfilm from the NAC through your own local library (if it has a microfilm-reader; otherwise you will have to arrange the loan through a larger library). In your case, all is well, because your own local library has a reader, and so you put in your request. Three weeks later the librarian telephones to let you know the microfilm has arrived.

You go to the library that evening and settle down at the reader. You start at the date of birth of your grandfather (10 June 1865) and work back from there. Eventually the words spring out of the register at you:

ALEXANDER GIBSON and AGNES MACDONALD, 8 June 1861. Son of James Gibson.

Unfortunately, the bride's parents are not mentioned, but you leave this problem alone, because your main concern at this stage is the Gibson family. While you have the microfilm, you continue to search, this time for the marriage of a James Gibson —probably before 1840. You also copy down all Gibson entries —there are not that many—just in case you can fit them into the family tree later in your research. You are successful when you reach the year 1830 when you find that James Gibson married Alison Grant on 12 May 1830. Of course, this may not be your James Gibson, but there is no other one listed in the marriage register.

You now want to find the baptismal entry of Alexander to fill in more family background. As he was probably at least twenty-one years of age when he married Agnes MacDonald in 1861, you will be searching the period 1830–40. You will also want to check for any brothers or sisters of Alexander. You order the microfilm of the baptismal register of Shelburne for that period—in actual fact it runs from 1783 to 1855. You search in the usual way, writing down all Gibsons listed, as well as your own *certain* ancestors. You find the following information about Alexander and his family:

MARY. Born 23 July 1833
ALEXANDER. Born 29 August 1835
JAMES. Born 10 January 1837

You now have had the opportunity to use all the main sources of information, except wills and land records, and you have a very good family tree back to 1830—over a century and a half, and five generations.

Of course, you have some tidying up and filling of gaps to do. What happened to Alexander's brothers and sister? When and where did Alexander die? What happened to your great-uncle Tom, who went to Winnipeg? How did your great-uncle Jimmy get on in Alberta? (Maybe you have oil-rich cousins out there!) Some of these questions you will be able to answer, others you will not. Don't worry too much about offshoots of your family tree—they are just decorations. Concentrate on your direct line of descent. Later on, when you can get back no further, you can start worrying about the other odds and ends you want cleared up.

This means you can focus on the next major step. You know only that your great-great-grandfather, James, was married in 1830. You go back to the baptismal entries which you copied for all Gibsons when you had the Shelburne microfilm. You guess he might have been born between 1800 and 1810. More information falls into place—there is an entry for the birth of James, son of Alexander Gibson and Janet Thomson, on 6 October 1801 (baptism took place on 17 October). The parents were described as "of this parish". You also find the entries of two sisters and a brother:

MARY, 24 March 1803

ELSPETH, 3 July 1804

JOSEPH, 16 June 1806

So here you are back to 1801 and you know that Alexander Gibson and Janet Thomson were alive and producing children at that time.

Can you get back any further? Yes, you can, because a further search of the registers gives you the date of the marriage — 16 June 1799 — and it tells you that Alexander's father was James. Unfortunately, there is no record in the Shelburne registers of the marriage of James. The event must have taken place elsewhere (or occurred before 1783, when the Church record begins).

At this point you do some reading about Nova Scotia and its history, if you have not already done so. You know that Alexander Gibson (who was married in 1799) must have been born some time in the period before 1779. You also know that his father was James, and *he* was probably born about 1750, give or take ten years on either side of that date. Your research into the history of the province points you in two directions:

1. James could have been a United Empire Loyalist—one of the people on the losing side in the American Revolution who fled to Canada. Many UEL families, particularly those from the New England colonies, went to Nova Scotia and received grants of land in the general area of south-east Nova Scotia — this included Shelburne.

2. By their names, the family were obviously of Scots descent and could have arrived in Halifax, received a land grant, and settled in the Shelburne area. Although the great exodus from

JAMES GIBSON
B: About 1740–60
D:

ALEXANDER
B:
D:
= Janet Thomson
(16 June 1799
Shelburne)

JAMES	MARY	ELSPETH	JOSEPH
B: 6 October 1801	**B**: 24 March 1803	**B**: 3 July 1804	**B**: 16 June 1806
(Shelburne)	(Shelburne)	(Shelburne)	(Shelburne)
D:	**D**:	**D**:	**D**:
( )	( )	( )	( )
= Alison Grant			
12 May 1830			
(Shelburne)			

MARY	ALEXANDER	JAMES
B: 23 July 1833	**B**: 29 August 1835	**B**: 10 January 1837
(Shelburne)	(Shelburne)	(Shelburne)
D:	**D**:	**D**:
( )	( )	( )
	= Agnes	
	MacDonald	
	8 June 1861	
	(Shelburne)	

THOMAS	MARGARET	WILLIAM GEORGE	JAMES
B:	**B**:	**B**: 10 June 1865	**B**:
( )	( )	(Shelburne)	( )
D:	**D**:	**D**: 14 May 1900	**D**:
( )	( )	(Belleville)	( )
Lived in	Married and	= Mary Evans	= Susan Brooks
Winnipeg.	went to Québec.	(**D**: 1938,	(in Alberta)
No children.		Brampton)	Children.

DAVID	HELEN
B: 3 September 1895	**B**: 4 June 1900
(Belleville)	(Belleville)
D: 2 January 1944	**D**:
(Toronto)	( )
= Mary Andrews	Unmarried.
(St. George's Church,	
Kingston,	
5 May 1918)	

CHARLES	ROBERT	AGNES
B: 8 June 1920	**B**: 13 January 1922	**B**: 2 February 1924

Scotland because of the Highland Clearances did not start before the early 1800s, there was a considerable number of Scots immigrants into Nova Scotia in the latter part of the eighteenth century.

In the former case, Alexander's birth and the marriage of his parents could have taken place in the United States; in the latter case, in Scotland.

At this point we will leave the mythical Charles Gibson to check further. Records of land grants in the province are very good, and there are a number of books about Scots and UEL settlements. At any rate, he has done well: he has traced back for two centuries, and his spreading family tree now appears as shown on the preceding page.

CHAPTER 3
The Great Migrations

The period from about 1750 until the First World War saw one of the greatest movements of people in human history — the emigration of millions from Great Britain and Europe to the new lands of North America. Quite often they came in organized religious groups, or, for example, as Scots clansmen travelling together as a close-knit family. Sometimes they came as destitute Irish, with passages paid by governments to get rid of them, or as half-pay British army officers hoping to become "landed gentry". They came as convicts and black sheep and remittance men, and they came as individuals setting out with courage and tenacity to make a new life and a future for their children. Their reasons were diverse: religious persecution, economic disaster, wars and revolutions, romantic dreams, and practical ambitions. They were the victims of harsh social systems, vicious landlords, unscrupulous shipowners, lying land agents, and their own total ignorance of the hardships that awaited them in their new country.

In times of suffering there are always the vultures who are prepared to swindle and exploit starving and destitute people for their own personal profit. Many formed partnerships with other opportunists; others bought cheap land in Canada and resold it to gullible emigrants who also bought passage on their ships.

Emigrant vessels were described in glowing prose:

NOTICE TO PASSENGERS
to
NOVA SCOTIA AND CANADA

A substantial coppered Fast Sailing Ship will be ready to receive passengers at Fort William on the 10th of June and sail for Pictou and Canada on the 20th. All those who wish to emigrate this summer will find this an excellent opportunity, as every attention will be paid to the comfort of Passengers, and they may depend on the utmost punctuality as to the date of sailing. For further particulars application may be made to Mr. John Grant, Merchant in Fort William.

Naturally, there was no mention of death by cholera or dysentery, no warning that if landfall was delayed, there might be no food or water left aboard.

| The Scots and the Irish

The cost of passage from the British Isles varied over the years of emigration, from as little as thirty shillings to as much as thirty pounds. For that, the emigrant could find himself sharing a board 6 feet by 2 feet with another emigrant. One vessel in 1773 sailed from Scotland with 450 passengers in a hold measuring 60 feet by 18 feet by 6 feet.

I think the emigrants from the Highlands of Scotland suffered more than any other race. Their sufferings were not only physical, but spiritual as well, because side by side with their starvation and lack of shelter they had also been forcibly detached from a unique way of life. A bleak day in April 1746 saw the end of an era in Scots history. On that day, on a windswept moor in north-east Scotland, the dwindling forces of the Young Pretender, Bonnie Prince Charlie, were defeated by an English army led by "Butcher" Cumberland, a son of the English king.

As John Prebble wrote in his book *Culloden*:

Once the chiefs lost their powers many of them lost also any parental interest in their clansmen. During the next hundred years they continued the work of Cumberland's battalions. So that they might lease their glens and braes to sheep farmers from the Lowlands and England, they cleared the crofts of men, women, and children, using police and soldiers where necessary.

It is easy, from this distance in time, to forget the Highland Clearances, but the hills in the Highlands are still empty, and the ruins of houses and cottages still dot the landscape after two hundred years. In the late eighteenth and early nineteenth centuries, over 100,000 people left the Highlands for Canada. In 1772, over 100 settlers came to Nova Scotia from South Uist, Moidart, and Arisaig. In 1785, 600 left Glengarry in Scotland to settle in Glengarry, Upper Canada (Ontario). In 1801–3, over 5000 left Strathglass in Sutherland for Antigonish in Nova Scotia — including over a thousand Chisholms. In 1816, Scots immigrants settled Perth, Ontario.

In 1851, 58,000 Highlanders sailed for North America, and another 66,000 the next year. Most of the men and women who landed in Canada settled in Nova Scotia and Ontario. In 1852, 1500 immigrants from Barra, Benbecula, and South Uist settled in the Dundas area of Ontario. Another 4500 went to Nova Scotia and Glengarry.

The Irish suffered as much as the Scots on many of the 200-ton ships that sometimes took two months to cross the Atlantic. Few of the Irish could afford to pay their own passages, but landlords and various philanthropic organizations provided the fare for thousands of emigrants. In the 1770s, 20,000 persons a year were settling in Montréal and Québec, the majority of them coming from Ireland. In 1825, Peter Robinson brought over 2000 settlers from Ireland, and they received land grants in the area of Peterborough, Ontario. They are well documented by name, and in many other ways. They were more fortunate than most of the Irish immigrants into Canada. Peter Robinson had picked them from the 50,000 who had applied for passage. Each family received a cow, axes, an auger, a saw, a hammer, one hundred nails, two gimlets, three hoes, a kettle, a frying-pan, an iron pot, three bushels of seed potatoes, and one peck of seed corn. One pound of salt pork and one pound of flour per day were given to all settlers over the age of fourteen for the next eighteen months, with half-rations for those from five to fourteen, and quarter-rations for any of lower age. All the cost of settlement was paid by the government.

Generally speaking, the English and the Welsh did not come in organized parties, and their descendants are to be found in all provinces. Other organized parties, such as Ukrainians, Mennonites, Hutterites, Mormons, Scandinavians, and others, are discussed in the chapters devoted to the provinces.

| German-Speaking Settlers

The Germans, although they did not come in organized groups, tended to settle in four areas of Canada. They settled in Lunenburg, Nova Scotia, and in three areas of Ontario: the Niagara Peninsula, the Kitchener area, and the townships around Pembroke. German settlers first entered the province of Ontario from Pennsylvania in 1786, but there was no mass movement, and in the next twenty-one years only twenty-five families settled in Niagara and in the county of Waterloo. In 1803 — by which time the cost of land in Pennsylvania had become prohibitive — a major move to Canada was organized. Sixty thousand acres was bought in 1803, and a further forty thousand the next year, money for the purchase price being raised in the United States. The settlers poured in from Franklin, Lancaster, Montgomery, and Bucks counties. Many of them were descended from Swiss-German Mennonites. The influx from the United States ended by about 1828, but there was still a great deal of movement across the border in the form of family reunions and arranged marriages. By this time, large numbers of German immigrants were arriving from the Germanic area of central Europe (Germany as a unified country did not yet exist). Other areas of German settlement on a smaller scale were along the north shore of Lake Ontario, but these were the "Hessians" — German mercenaries who had served with the British army during the Revolutionary War. They fled to Canada with the United Empire Loyalists when the British were defeated, and received land grants. The term "Hessian" (after Hesse) is a misnomer, since they came from all parts of the Germanic areas of Europe. Many of them went back overseas, but several thousand settled in Upper Canada, and a few in Lower Canada, where several anglicized their names and others frenchified theirs — just to make life difficult for the ancestor-hunter!

By the mid-1830s, immigrants were arriving from all parts of Germanic Europe — Austria, Baden, Bayern, Hessen-Darmstadt, Elsass-Lothringen (Alsace-Lorraine), Holstein, Mecklenburg, Württemberg, and the German settlements in the Baltic states of Estonia, Latvia, and Lithuania — as well as from the Ukraine area of South Russia. No single religious group predominated, and the original Mennonites were soon outnumbered by Lutherans, Catholics, Baptists, Moravians, and Swedenborgians. By 1850, more than twelve thousand German settlers were in Upper Canada.

In 1857 the railway reached the town of Berlin (renamed Kitchener during the First World War), the main centre of Waterloo County, and immigrants landing in Québec were able to travel directly to their destination by train. At this time, German settlers were arriving in Renfrew County, west of Ottawa, and by 1901 there were nearly ten thousand people of German birth living in thirteen townships in the area. The difference between the Germans who settled in Renfrew and those in Waterloo is that the former assimilated and the latter maintained their own religion, customs, and ethnic inheritance. The result is that it is hard to find much obvious evidence of Germans in the first area, whereas their presence is obvious in the second — even though they are in a minority.

Next, let's look at another large-scale movement, this one from north-western Europe and the Lowland countries, which goes back to the sixteenth and seventeenth centuries.

The Huguenots

One of the great movements of people in history was that of the Huguenots — a migration known only to historians and to the descendants of these people persecuted because of their religion. The exodus from France took place between the mid-1550s and about the year 1700. At one time, one million Huguenots lived in that country, which had then a total population of fifteen million. It is estimated that more than 300,000 left France, and that another 200,000 were massacred on St. Bartholomew's Eve on 24 August 1572.

They emigrated to England, Ireland, the Netherlands, and German-speaking areas of Europe, Switzerland, and North America. Research in the German areas is difficult, because Germany as a country did not exist and so we have to contend with hundreds of independent kingdoms, principalities, grand duchies, and city states. Generally speaking, the southern areas were Catholic and the northern areas Protestant. Most

Huguenot refugees went to Prussia, Hanover, Mecklenburg, Nassau, and Westphalia. Switzerland was not unified until 1848; before that, each of the twenty-five cantons had its own government. The Protestant cantons were Aargau, Appenzell, Basel, Bern, Geneva, Glarus, Graubünden, Neuchâtel, Schaffhausen, Thurgau, Vaud, and Zürich. They were the preferred areas for the refugees to settle, and in particular Geneva, Neuchâtel, and Lausanne, because these three cantons are French-speaking.

The origin of the name Huguenot is not certain. It was originally either a term of abuse or a nickname. One theory is that it originated as Hugues—a reference to Hugues Capet, the founder of the French royal house, whose ancient tower in Tours was the site of secret Protestant meetings; another idea is that it was the result of French difficulty in pronouncing the German word Eidgenosse (a companion or confederate). In Swiss German it became Eignot and in French Huguenot; the third theory is that it derived from the archaic French word *huguon*, which meant someone who walked the streets secretly after dark. This latter idea seems the most logical, but your guess is as good as mine, and it is not very important, anyway. It would have been so much simpler just to call them Protestants.

In the early sixteenth century, persecution and martyrdom of the Protestants took place in widely separated areas of France, but particularly in the south. In 1535 an edict was published ordering the extermination of heretics. This was followed by the first wave of emigration to England, and in 1551 even more fled as the killing grew.

France was slow to accept the Reformation, but by 1560 it was estimated that forty per cent of the nobles were Huguenot, as were a large number of bishops and priests. Catherine de Medici, the widow of King Henry II of France, was regent for many years, and, although a devout Catholic, she was tolerant of Protestants, refusing to allow the Inquisition to operate in France.

In 1572, the St. Bartholomew's Eve Massacre led to further emigration of the survivors. Those Huguenots living on the coasts in the north fled to England, while those on the eastern borders escaped to the Netherlands, the Rhineland, and Switzerland. Those who went to England settled in the south-coast towns of Southampton, Portsmouth, and Rye, and in the London area. Later they went to Norwich, Canterbury, Bristol, and Plymouth, while others moved on to Dublin, in Ireland.

Increasing massacres and persecution eventually led to civil war. But in 1594 the Protestant leader, King Henry IV of Navarre, converted to Catholicism, saying, "Paris is worth a mass." Although this ended the civil war and led to his coronation as king of France, his conversion was only a political expediency. In 1598 he signed the Edict of Nantes, which gave the Huguenots the right to worship anywhere in France except in a few specified cities.

The king was assassinated in 1610, and within a few years civil war broke out again. Sectarian strife continued sporadically throughout the century. Many Protestant churches were destroyed; children of Huguenot parents had to be baptized by a Catholic priest; the property of Huguenots who left the country was confiscated. By 1685, the number of Huguenots who had emigrated passed the 300,000 mark.

Through all these years of persecution there was steady emigration to the United States, with Huguenot settlements at several places along the eastern seaboard from Florida to New England.

So far as Canada was concerned, the migrations indirectly from England and Ireland or directly from Europe were not organized. Families settled in various places in the Maritimes and in what is now Ontario, and were rapidly assimilated into various Protestant religions, mainly Lutheran and other sects such as the Baptists, Methodists, and Presbyterians. This lack of organized immigration into Canada and of specific areas of settlement makes it more difficult for people of Huguenot descent to trace their origins than it is for Mennonites, for example.

There is a very good book that goes into great detail about the Huguenots in Europe, and I have made use of it while writing this chapter. It is *Huguenot Ancestry* by Noel Currer-Briggs and Royston Gambier, published in 1985 by Phillimore and Co., Ltd., Shopwyke Hall, Chichester, England PO20 6BQ.

There are also four societies that may be able to give you information about a particular family — one in Canada and three in Europe:

The Huguenot Society of Canada, 10 Adelaide Street East, Toronto, ON M5C 1H5.

The Huguenot Society of Great Britain & Ireland, University College, London, England WC1E 6BT.

Deutscher Hugenotten-Verein, Postfach 35,3305 Sickte, BRD.

Deutsches Hugenotten Museum, An der Schlagd 2,3522 Bad Karlshafen 1, BRD.

(The second society above has published a great many indexed registers of Huguenot churches in the United Kingdom and Ireland. You can get more details from the Society and from Kraus Reprint, Route 100, Millwood, NY 10546.)

| The United Empire Loyalists

The large migration that every schoolchild learns the most about is the influx of United Empire Loyalists. Two hundred years ago the success of the American Revolution sent many thousands of people still loyal to the Crown fleeing north to Canada, south to the West Indies, and east over the Atlantic to Great Britain and Europe. Those who came to Canada became known as the United Empire Loyalists. They were a cross-section of a society of mixed ethnic and social backgrounds. Contrary to popular belief, they were not all of British stock; a very large percentage of them were from the Low Countries, the German-speaking areas of Europe, and France. With them came former slaves from the Southern plantations and some soldiers from a British all-black regiment, Indians, German mercenary soldiers, and Huguenots and Quakers who had already fled one form of persecution and were unwilling to face another. There were a few aristocrats and wealthy businessmen and plantation owners, but the great majority were farmers and craftsmen.

Although the vast majority of the American colonists had very justifiable grievances against the British government in London, there was a hard core of resistance, probably ten per cent of the total population, that still supported the continuance of allegiance to the British king. When the rebellion started in 1776, many Loyalists became victims of the patriotic fervour of those fighting for freedom. They were harassed socially and politically, denied public office, and expelled from their land, and their property was seized. Some were conscripted into the Revolutionary Army, and some very militant ones, suspected of spying for the British, were tarred and feathered.

The first contingent of some 1000 men, women, and children left Boston in March 1776 and accompanied the British army as it retreated before the victorious revolutionary forces. During the next six years the trickle became a flood as the Loyalists in their thousands crossed the border and were allocated land in the Nova Scotia colony. There were still those who stayed behind in the American colonies, secure in the belief that, whatever the eventual result, their property would be secure. However, when the Peace Settlement was signed in 1782, no firm commitment was made to provide any protection.

There are a variety of estimates of the number of Loyalists who entered Canada, ranging from 50,000 to 100,000. It has also been estimated that 200,000 people in the American colonies opposed the Revolution, but all these figures are guesswork based on a great variety of unprovable statistics. It seems likely that some 100,000 Loyalists eventually accepted the establishment of the United States, and that a similar number fled the country. Many went back to Great Britain and Europe, and about 40,000 entered Canada. We had open frontiers by sea and by land, and no immigration records were maintained.

At that time, in what is now Canada, there were two colonies, Québec and Nova Scotia. The former included the area now divided between Ontario and Québec, and the latter the area of the present provinces of New Brunswick and Nova Scotia. The most informed estimates suggest that 30,000 went to the Maritimes and about 10,000 to Québec.

In 1783, after the British government, in the Treaty of Paris, recognized the United States, approximately another 30,000 Loyalists went to Nova Scotia: 14,000 settled in Sunbury County (which became the province of New Brunswick in the following year) and 16,000 in what is now Nova Scotia proper. A few hundred settled in Prince Edward Island, but they only stayed a year because of the impossibility of obtaining title to any land.

The 10,000 who settled in the Québec colony, which then stretched from Nova Scotia to Niagara, soon ran into difficulties with the French feudal system of seigneurial ownership of land and the unfamiliar French legal system. The Loyalists agitated for the creation of an English-speaking province, and, as a result, the Québec colony was divided in 1791 into Upper and Lower Canada, later to be known as Ontario and Québec.

Most of the refugees who settled in the Maritimes came by sea from the New England ports, and had originally settled in New York, New Jersey, and Pennsylvania, but some smaller groups came from as far away as Maryland, Virginia, and the Carolinas. The refugees initially concentrated in Annapolis Royal, Digby, Guysborough, Halifax, Parrsboro, Ramsheg, Shelburne, and Wilmot. Others bought farms or went into business in other more settled areas.

The social and political impact of the arrival of the Loyalists upon the Nova Scotians was tremendous, and is the root cause of the deep-seated and unreasoning anti-American feeling that permeates many areas of eastern Canada. The population of Halifax jumped from 2000 to 6000, that of Annapolis Royal from 200 to 600. Substantial settlements appeared almost overnight in Antigonish and Yarmouth. Though the newcomers were by no means all Southern aristocrats or rich plantation owners, they certainly included a good many who considered they had the experience and the breeding and the right to take an active part in the government of the colony. This led to increasing difficulties with the original settlers, and a movement soon started to create a new and Loyalist colony out of Nova Scotia — and the birth of New Brunswick took place in June 1784.

Such men as Edward Winslow saw the future of New Brunswick as a colony ruled by a landowners' elite for the benefit of the masses. Unfortunately for Winslow, the masses wanted to be property-owners and not tenants. As he lamented later, "Our gentlemen have all become potato farmers, and our shoemakers are preparing to legislate."

Many died during the first winter in their new northern home when little shelter was available — some were less suited than others to adapting to the cruel Canadian climate. The farmers and tradesmen were strong, adaptable men with wives who had pioneered by their side, but many others who had lived on large estates with many servants suffered a great deal. Many left in the spring of 1784 — some going to Great Britain and Europe, some back to the United States, and others to the West Indies islands of Barbados and Jamaica.

In the new area of Upper Canada, some Loyalists arrived by ship from the southern ports of the Lake Ontario shore, and others came by land into the Niagara Peninsula. Those arriving by water settled in such places as Augusta, Cornwall, Fredericksburg, Kingston, Prescott, and Prince Edward County. Other areas of settlement were along the Thames and Detroit rivers, and the Lake Erie shore. Settlers in Lower Canada went mostly to the Montréal area and Longueuil.

By 1784 the United States government was firmly established, the hatreds between the Loyalists and the "rebels" had died down, and it was possible for a Loyalist to return to the United States without any fear of persecution or physical assault. At least ten per cent of the Loyalists in New Brunswick and Nova Scotia left the colonies behind and returned home. It is estimated that fifty per cent of the settlers had left the Nova Scotian colony by the end of 1785—some to New Brunswick and Upper and Lower Canada, some to England, but the majority to the United States.

The most valuable genealogical source for tracing your UEL ancestry is probably the Audit Office Series in the National Archives of Canada. This contains evidence in support of Loyalist claims for losses suffered during the American Revolution, but do remember that not all the settlers submitted claims. The Audit Office records give the location of original residence in the American colonies, the size of the family (often with all names), details of military service, and residence at the time of the claim. The records are on microfilm and completely indexed. There is also the list of Loyalists in Upper Canada kept in the Crown Lands Department, Queen's Park, Toronto.

The government granted land to the Loyalists under the following conditions: one hundred acres to each head of a family, plus fifty acres to each family member; fifty acres to each single man; three hundred to one thousand acres to army officers, depending on rank; two hundred acres to each non-commissioned officer (NCO), and two hundred to their wives if they applied; one hundred acres to every private soldier, plus fifty acres to each person in his family. The Loyalists drew lots for their locations, and when they had occupied the land for a year they received a permanent deed. At a meeting of the Executive Council in 1789 it was further ordained that sons, when they came of age, should receive two hundred acres, and daughters the same, except that, even if under age, they would receive the grant on marriage.

More information about Loyalist settlement will be found in the later chapters on the particular provinces in which they settled.

The United Empire Loyalist Association is located at 23 Prince Arthur Avenue, Toronto, ON M5R 1B2. It has an excellent library — open each day from 1000 hours to 1500 hours — which contains a great many books about individual Loyalists, and a number of unpublished manuscripts. If you are descended from a Loyalist (and can prove it), you are eligible to join the Association. It is not, perhaps, as active as it was, but there are still twenty-eight branches in operation. If you cannot prove your descent, it is always possible that the genealogical and historical records of the library will help you to do so. A good book on the subject is *The Loyalists* by Christopher Moore (Macmillan of Canada, Toronto, 1984).

As a descendant of those brave men and women you are entitled — if you wish — to write after your name the proud initials UE, so that all men and women may know your heritage.

There are UEL branches in the following locations, and up-to-date addresses of secretaries can be obtained from the UELA:

Alberta: Calgary, Edmonton
British Columbia: Vancouver and Victoria
Manitoba: Winnipeg
New Brunswick: Fredericton, Saint John
Nova Scotia: Halifax–Dartmouth, Shelburne
Ontario: Brockville, Cambridge, Cornwall, Hamilton, Kingston, Kingsville, Lindsay, London, Orono, Ottawa, Picton, St. Catharines, Toronto
Prince Edward Island: Breadalbane
Québec: Granby, Hudson
Saskatchewan: Saskatoon

| The Ukrainians

If you look at a map of Europe, you will have difficulty in finding Ukraine; that is because this ancient nation is now within the boundaries of Soviet Russia and is one of the fifteen republics that make up that enormous country. There are 40 million Ukrainians there, and over half a million Canadians are of Ukrainian descent. What brought so many strong and gifted people half a world away from the black earth of southern Russia? To answer this question we must take a quick journey back over the centuries and learn a little of the tragic history of these people.

The Ukrainians are the largest Slavic nation in the world, after Russia. They originated as Neolithic tribes along the great rivers of the area, but over the centuries they were invaded and conquered by a variety of tribes and nations: Scythians and Sarmatians; Goths, Huns, and Avars; Varangians and Kievian Russians; Lithuanians and Poles; and Turks, Germans, and Austrians. Through it all, the Ukrainian people survived, and preserved their language and their culture, in spite of efforts by Poles and Russians to obliterate their cultural inheritance.

They had brief periods of semi-independence over the centuries, but predatory neighbours, coveting the rich farmland, soon ended them, and the country was several times divided among the conquerors. The end of any semblance of Ukrainian independence came in 1764 when the last Hetman, or leader, of Ukraine was forced out by Catherine the Great of Russia. The country was divided into three provinces. In 1783 the Russians seized the Khanate of Crimea from the Ottoman Empire, and then the Polish partition treaties of 1793 and 1795 awarded Podolia and Volhynia to Russia, and eastern Galicia went to the Austrian Empire.

In the nineteenth century, despite all efforts by Russia to ban the Ukrainian language and "Russify" the country, Ukrainian nationalism flourished and plans were started to try and unite Galicia, Bukovina, and Ruthenia in a single state. Galicia, with Austrian tolerance, was the centre of the independence movement directed at Russian Ukraine. When the Tsarist regime collapsed in 1917, Ukraine was, for a short period, a republic within Soviet Russia, then, for an equally brief period, an independent republic. But in 1919 Soviet troops occupied Kiev. At this point there was a short four-way struggle between the Soviet Union, the Poles, the Ukrainians, and the anti-Soviet (or anti-Bolshevik) forces under General Denikin.

The Soviet army regained control over the whole country and formed the Ukrainian Socialist Republic in 1922. Lenin granted a considerable amount of cultural autonomy, but this was abandoned by Stalin, who collectivized the farms, seized Ukrainian grain for export, and let millions of Ukrainians die in the famine that followed.

After the Second World War, parts of Bessarabia, Moldavia, Bukovina, Galicia, Zakarpatskaya Oblast, Ruthenia, and Crimea were all realigned and reshuffled between Russia, Czechoslovakia, and Romania, at last, in 1954, completing the process by which all Ukraine lands were united in a single republic.

It is ironic that Ukraine, which had fought for its independence and unity without success since 1200, was to achieve unity without independence in 1945. Persistent attempts to Russify Ukraine have continued to the present day, but Ukrainian nationalism is alive and well, not only in the USSR but in the thriving Ukrainian communities in Western Canada, and in the hearts and minds of the hundreds of thousands of Canadians everywhere who can say with pride, "I am of Ukrainian descent."

With this chequered history and constant warfare it is no wonder that Ukrainians emigrated in such large numbers. Western Ukrainians were first attracted to Canada by the successful settlement of Germans and Hungarians in Manitoba during the 1880s. The leader of the initial migration was Ivan Pillipiew (or Pylypiw) from Nebiliv, in Galicia. He and another neighbour, Wasyl Eleniak, sailed from Hamburg in 1891 on a visit to inspect the country. The land company in Winnipeg provided them with free rail transportation. They visited a German settlement near Yorkton, Saskatchewan, then travelled to the Calgary area, and finally returned to inspect a German Mennonite settlement at Gretna, Manitoba, which had been in existence for fifteen years. They were both amazed by its progress and success, and decided to settle near by. Pillipiew went home to Galicia to bring back his family, and Eleniak remained in Gretna. When Pillipiew started spreading the word about the promise of a new and prosperous and peaceful life in Canada, and the fact that the Canadian government would provide 160 acres of free land (thirty times the size of the average peasant holding in Galicia), he was arrested for sedition. After a three-month-long trial he was sentenced to a month's imprisonment. The news of the verdict spread throughout the western Ukraine and gave added impetus to the idea of emigration to Canada. Twelve families left for Canada, settling near Edmonton, in Gretna, and in Winnipeg. A year later a small party from Pillipiew's home town of Nebiliv settled at Beaverhill Creek, east of Edmonton. In the following year Pillipiew and his family settled at Edna — previously named Beaverhill, and later to be known as Star.

The mass movement of the Ukrainians to Canada started in 1896; between that year and 1914 it is estimated that over 200,000 came to Canada. Accurate figures are difficult to obtain, because some called themselves Rusin (an ancient name for inhabitants of Ruthenia), and this was often entered in the records as Russian. Others were registered as Austrian, Bukovinians, Galicians, Hungarians, Poles, Romanians, and Russniaks. The term "Ukrainian" did not come into general use in Canada until the First World War.

Immigration slowed because of restrictions enacted by the Austrian authorities, and the outbreak of the war. Afterwards, the flow started once more, and by 1930 another 70,000 had arrived. A third wave followed after the Second World War — probably over 30,000—and a high proportion of these were from those parts of Ukraine included within the USSR.

There are ten colonies in Manitoba: Stuartburn, Whitemouth, Brokenhead, Red River, Mid-Lake, Glenella, Riding Mountain, Dauphin, Shell River, and Swan River. Others exist in Saskatchewan and Alberta, and more details of the settlements in these provinces will be found later in this book. The largest urban Ukrainian communities are in Edmonton (63,000), Winnipeg (59,000), and Toronto (51,000). There is the inevitable drift from the rural settlements into the larger cities, and Ukrainians are not unique in this respect.

You will find information about your Ukrainian ancestry in the Provincial Archives of Alberta, Manitoba, and Saskatchewan. However, the resources of the National Archives in Ottawa should not be overlooked. There is a Ukrainian Archives Program in operation in the National Ethnic Archives division. A brief summary of the main holdings is given below:

Dr. Vladimir J. Kaye (Kysilewsky) Collection: Dr. Kaye (1896–1976) devoted his life to the study of Ukrainians in Canadian society. He was recognized as Canada's leading authority on the subject. His books include *Early Ukrainian Settlements in Canada* (1964) and *The Dictionary of Ukrainian Canadian Biography— Manitoba Pioneer Settlers 1895–1900* (1974). This collection contains his notes on Ukrainian pioneer families in the three western provinces mentioned above.

The Li-Ra-Ma Collection of Russian Consular Records: This is described in Chapter 5 on the National Archives. Many of the 10,000 immigrants listed were Ukrainians from Volhynia and Podolia.

Gordon Panchuk Papers: These contain information about Ukrainian prisoners of war in Western Europe after the Second World War ended, and a little about Ukrainian refugees in China.

Ukrainian Canadian Committee Records: This collection contains a great deal of information about Ukrainian families who came to Canada after the Second World War.

The J. B. Rudnyckyj Collection: This contains a number of articles on Ukrainians in Canada and still has some 33,000 cards that were used for "A Dictionary of Canadian Surnames" and the 10,000 cards that were collated for "A Dictionary of Cossack Surnames".

There is also the National Photography Collection; some of the holdings of Ukrainian interest are:

Dragan, George E.: Over 300 photographs of various Ukrainian organizations and communities in Western Canada (1910–64).
Kaye (Kysilewsky), V. J.: Over 300 photographs of individuals and groups in Ukrainian settlements (1890–1975).
Perepeluk, W. J.: Over 4000 photographs of the Ukrainian community in Toronto, and of the celebrations of the sixtieth anniversary of Ukrainian settlement in Canada, held in Winnipeg in 1891.

The National Map Collection of the Archives has many very detailed and large-scale maps of Eastern Europe, Ukraine, pre-1939 Poland, and parts of western Ukraine. The scale is large enough for you to identify the locations of churches, cemeteries, and farms in even very tiny villages. There are also a number of high-definition aerial photographs taken by the Luftwaffe for the German army.

Biographies and Family Histories: Ancestor-hunters are encouraged to donate a copy of their family history to the archives, since these can provide vital information for posterity. Examples are:

The Panchuk Family. 106 pages
Memoirs of the Maksymetz Family (1865–1982). 119 pages.

Genealogical Society

There is now a Ukrainian Genealogical and Historical Society of Canada, 1530-23rd Avenue NW, Calgary, AB T2M 1V1. This was formed very recently and I have not been able to include any details about it.

The Jews in Canada

If you are of Jewish descent, you will have no great difficulty in tracing your ancestors in Canada—your problems will start over the ocean.

So far as Canada is concerned, you will be searching for your ancestors in civil registration records, census returns, and all the other sources mentioned in this book. Obviously, church records will not be of value unless your Jewish ancestor married a gentile. You will be interested in circumcision records available in various synagogues and Jewish archives.

Jewish settlement in Canada dates from about 1760 and coincided with the British conquest of New France. There were Jewish soldiers in the British army who took their discharges here and settled mostly in Lower Canada (Québec). Shearith Israel, the oldest Jewish congregation in Canada, was founded in Montréal in 1768. The congregation grew very slowly. In Toronto, Holy Blossom Temple was founded in 1854, followed by a second temple in Montréal in 1859 — Shaar Hashomayim. Then came Anshe Shalom in Hamilton in 1863 and Temple Emanuel in Victoria in 1863.

By 1881 the Jewish community was well established and numbered about 2500. There were large numbers of Jewish immigrants from Europe from 1880 up to the beginning of the Second World War. They settled mainly in Ontario and Québec. By 1931 the Jewish population had passed the 150,000 mark, and fifty years later it was 300,000 — mainly in Ontario and Québec, but with about 15,000 in Manitoba. At the present time there are about 150 congregations across the country.

I give below the addresses of the main Jewish sources of genealogical information in Canada and the United States. For your further reading you should obtain a copy of *Archival Sources for the Study of Canadian Jewry* by Lawrence Tapper, published by the National Archives, 395 Wellington Street, Ottawa, ON K1A 0N3. It lists a large number of books and records in the custody of the archives.

There are a number of very useful books for Jewish research in Canada and the United States; remember that many Canadian Jewish families are descended from ancestors who originally settled in the United States and later moved north to Montréal, Toronto, Winnipeg, and many smaller places:

Belkin, Simon: *Through Narrow Gates (1840–1940)*. Montréal, 1966.

Chiel, A.: *The Jews in Manitoba*. Toronto, 1975.

Fishman, P.: *The Jews of the United States*. New York, 1973.

Gottesman, A.: *Who's Who in Canadian Jewry*. Montréal, 1965.

Hart, A. D.: *The Jew in Canada*. Toronto, 1926.

Howe, I.: *World of Our Fathers*. New York, 1976.

Hyamson, A. M.: *The Sephardim of England*. London, 1951.

Kaganoff, B.: *Jewish Surnames Through the Ages*. New York, 1956.

Kurzweil, A.: *From Generation to Generation*. New York, 1982.

Rosenberg, L.: *Canada's Jews*. Montréal, 1939.

Rosenberg, S. E.: *The Jewish Community in Canada.* Toronto, 1970.
Roth, C.: *History of the Jews in England.* London, 1951.
Rottenberg, D.: *Finding Our Fathers.* New York, 1977.
Sack, B. G.: *History of the Jews in Canada.* Montréal, 1965.
Stern, M.: *Americans of Jewish Descent.* Cincinnati, 1960.
Vigod, B.: *The Jews in Canada.* Ottawa, 1984.

Further information about Jewish ancestry in Europe can be found in two books of mine:

In Search of Your British and Irish Roots. Toronto, 1982.
In Search of Your European Roots. Toronto, 1985.

The following Jewish organizations in Canada may be useful in providing information for you. Be sure you cover the return postage:

MONTRÉAL: Jewish Immigrant Aid Services, 5151 Côte Ste. Catherine, H3W 1M6
Jewish Public Library—same address.
OTTAWA: Jewish Historical Society, 151 Chapel Street, K1N 7Y2
TORONTO: Canadian Jewish Congress, 4600 Bathurst Street, M2R 3V3
Jewish Immigrant Aid Services—same address
WINNIPEG: Jewish Public Library, 1725 Main Street, R2V 1Z4
Jewish Historical Society, 365 Hargrave Street, R3B 2K3
Canadian Jewish Congress, 370 Hargrave Street, R3B 2K3
VANCOUVER: Jewish Historical Society, 950 West 51st Avenue, V5T 2N7

There are two Jewish Genealogical Societies: Montreal: c/o Raymond Whitzman, 5787 McAlear Avenue, Cote St. Luc, PQ H4W 2H3; Toronto: PO Box 446, Station A, Willowdale, ON M2N 5T1.

Finally, when the time comes for you to research your ancestry further back than in Canada, do not overlook the Yizkor Books in the Robarts Library at the University of Toronto. They have over 300 of the 700 published so far. As you will know, these are also known as the Memorial Books, and each one tells the story of a Jewish community in one town. Each book is the product of a number of people who met together

after the Holocaust and talked together about their memories. Most are written in Hebrew or Yiddish, but translations can be arranged, and some do have English sections. The indexes are generally unreliable.

| Note on Passenger Lists

The greatest obstacle in our search for our ancestors who came from over the ocean is the rarity of records of immigration and the almost total absence of passenger lists. I suppose if every ancestor-hunter had three wishes, they would be for a discovery of such lists in some hitherto unknown hiding-place, the retrieval of family papers thrown away as garbage, and the magical appearance of a name below every photograph in the family album. Oh well, dream again, because what is lost is lost.

The keeping of regular passenger lists began in 1855 in Canada, although a few earlier records are available in the National Archives in Ottawa, and in some of the Provincial Archives. However, in most cases it is necessary to know the name of the ship, the port of arrival, and the date. These records are mostly from 1745 to 1752, 1810 to 1811, and 1817 to 1831. Even after 1855 the records are very scanty until 1865. From the latter year, lists are complete for the official ports of Halifax and Québec. Other ports became "official" later on: Saint John, N.B. (1900), Victoria and Vancouver, B.C. (1905), North Sydney, N.S. (1906), and Montréal (1919). There are no records of arrivals at unofficial ports. Arrivals in Québec from May 1865 to April 1900 are on microfilm at the National Archives, as are those in Halifax from January 1881 until December 1899. A nominal listing of passenger-ship lists for 1900–08 is also on microfilm.

In addition to these official lists, there are also records available of various organized parties of immigrants, and you should check with the Provincial Archives in your area of interest. Some examples taken at random are:

> Immigrants from Ireland settled in Peterborough, Ontario, by Peter Robinson in 1823 and 1825.
> The settlers who came with Governor Cornwallis to Halifax, N.S., in 1749; the Lunenburg settlers in the 1750s; the Yorkshire settlers in Cumberland County in the 1770s; and the passengers on the *Hector* to Pictou in 1773.

The Provincial Archives of Nova Scotia have scattered records of arrivals from Great Britain and the Netherlands from 1749. There are also a few lists in the Provincial Archives of British Columbia.

It should also be borne in mind that many emigrants to Canada landed at U.S. ports such as New York, Baltimore, Philadelphia, and Boston, as well as at much smaller and less-well-known ports such as Hartford, Wilmington, Bangor, Kennebunk, Marblehead, and so on. All the lists are in the National Archives in Washington and cover a high percentage of the arrivals at U.S. ports in the period from 1820 to 1945, although there are scattered records dating back to the late 1700s. In addition many, many books have been written listing passengers arriving at various ports; examples are: *Swedish Passenger Arrivals in New York 1820–50* by Nils Olsson (Chicago, 1967) and *Passenger Arrivals at the Port of Baltimore 1820–34* by Michael Tepper (Baltimore 1982).

This chapter has given a summary of the great historical migrations that populated our land. There was, of course, tremendous immigration into Canada after the Second World War, especially from central Europe. That immigration continues today, often for the same reasons, but now from Asia, Latin America, and elsewhere. I have not attempted to chronicle this because it is too recent to need genealogical research.

CHAPTER 4
The LDS Church

When Joseph Smith founded the Church of Jesus Christ of Latter-Day Saints (also known as "the Mormons") in the early years of the last century, he could not have foreseen that his teachings would benefit ancestor-hunters around the world. The Church now possesses the greatest single source of genealogical information in existence. No one starting to trace his or her ancestors in Canada or anywhere else should do so without checking all the information available from the Church and its branch Family History Centers (previously known as Genealogical Branch Libraries). There are no strings attached to the facilities which can be used by those of us who are not members of the Church. No one will try to convert you, no elder will arrive on your doorstep. The Church members are extraordinarily nice people; anyone who has used their records knows this, and is grateful they are prepared to share their knowledge—free, or for a small fee. Over many years I have learned to appreciate their good qualities and the help I have received from them.

The interest of the Church in genealogy stems from its belief that family relationships are intended to be eternal, and not limited to a short period of mortality, or "till death us do part". It is believed that a husband and wife and their children remain together throughout eternity as a family unit with all their ancestors and descendants. Members trace their ancestors in order to perform "sealing" ceremonies in temples erected for

the purpose. Before the families can be sealed together, as many ancestors as possible must be traced.

The Family History Department of the Church is engaged in the most active and comprehensive genealogical research program ever known. Microfilming and computerization are at the heart of the operation, and every day records are being copied and microfilmed by specialist workers in some thirty-eight countries around the world, including Canada, the United States, and most European countries. The records being copied include civil registration, census returns, church registers, wills, land grants, military and naval records, marriage bonds, tombstone inscriptions, passenger lists, guild membership lists, funeral sermons, cemetery records, school attendance lists, etc. There are more than 1.4 million rolls of microfilm in the Family History Library in Salt Lake City, and another 50,000 rolls are added each year. Over 200,000 books line the library shelves, and more than 400 new volumes are placed there every month. There are records of 10 million families in the archives, and nearly 100 million names appear in the International Genealogical Index (IGI). This latter figure grows by 7 million each year. These figures are all astronomical, and the growth is so fast that they will be out of date by the time you read this.

All these microfilmed records may be consulted either by contacting the Family History Library, 35 North West Temple Street, Salt Lake City, UT 84150, or your nearest Family History Center (FHC); there are 650 of these in the world, including 28 in Canada. You can order a particular microfilm or microfiche at the FHC and when it arrives from Salt Lake City you will be able to read it on a viewer in the library.

There are two indexes that may be of great help to you. There is the Family Group Records Archives (FGRA). This contains what are called family group sheets. They are submitted by Church members and are the result of their own personal research. They are further divided into two sections: main and patrons. The main sheets have been checked for accuracy, the patrons have not. All the sheets from both sections give the same type of information as in the IGI, plus dates of death and burial of parents, and the names of the grandparents.

The other index is the IGI mentioned earlier. This is built up, in the main, from church register entries and is updated every two years. It is printed on small sheets of film called microfiche and can be read with a microfiche-viewer. It is quite simple to use—the surname is on the left, followed in horizontal

order across the page by the first name; the name of the wife or husband (if the entry is a marriage) or the names of the parents (if it is a baptism); the sex (M for a man, F for a woman); H for husband, W for wife; then the letter B for birth or C for christening, M for marriage, N for a census, and W for a will. Finally, you arrive at the date and place of the event.

The main library in Salt Lake City has thousands of family histories, both bound and unbound, and others on microfilm or microfiche. To discover if the library has a history of your family, you must search both of the library catalogues: the Family History Library Catalog (FHLC) and the Microfilm Card Catalog (MCC).

The original master microfilms are stored under ideal conditions in an area giving protection from earthquakes and nuclear explosions. High in the Rockies a storage facility has been built with 700 feet of granite above the storage vaults. The total vault capacity is the equivalent of over 26 million 300-page volumes and can be expanded when necessary by further excavation.

You must bear two things in mind when using the IGI:

1. It is based on external records which Mormon researchers have copied. Very many church and civil authorities are not prepared to co-operate with the LDS workers, and therefore much material has not been made available to them and is unindexed for that reason.

2. Copies are only as good and accurate as the copier. Although the Church has a double-check system in operation, it is not one hundred per cent effective. Workers have been known to miss several complete pages of a church register or a census return. Other mistakes have been made in the copying of a first name or a surname.

I should, perhaps, give an example of this. A good many years ago I was tracing my Caley ancestors in the northern part of the county of Lancashire. This was in the days before the IGI and I was searching individual church registers myself in the original churches. I got back to a Henry Caley who married an Ellen Webster in a village named Cockerham in 1778. I could not get back any further because Henry had been an incomer into the village, and the Caley name did not exist there before his arrival—nor did it exist in any village around.

Over the years since, I had made sporadic searches of all known records: land, wills, taxes, deeds, censuses, manorial rolls, etc., without any success. A few years ago I noticed that the LDS Church had copied forty-eight per cent of the church registers of the county (including Cockerham), and so I bought a print-out of the Caley entries for the county. This produced no entry of birth for a Henry Caley which could by any stretch of the imagination be my Henry Caley. I was back to square one.

However, quite casually I looked through the marriage entries and found that the marriage of Henry and Ellen in 1778 was not listed! I knew this was wrong because I had seen the entry in the church register with my own eyes. I looked further down the list and found an entry of the marriage of a *Thomas* Caley to Ellen Webster on the same date and in the same place! I thought, "Could I possibly have made a stupid mistake?" and so I wrote off to the County Record Office in Lancashire (which now held the register) and asked for the entry to be checked. The reply confirmed that I was right and the IGI wrong. I notified Salt Lake City and in the answer I was told I was right, and the error would be corrected. In due course the new edition of the IGI appeared and there was Henry's marriage. There was only one snag—the marriage entry of the fictitious Thomas was still there. I wrote again and pointed this out and was assured it would be corrected. It wasn't, and the last time I looked, there was Thomas Caley married to Ellen Webster! As I had obtained my information from the original register, this comedy of errors was not important, but if I had been dependent on the information in the IGI, my research would have been really fouled up.

This is not a criticism of LDS records in general, or of the IGI in particular. I tell you about it to make the point that mistakes are made, the IGI is not infallible, and you should always check the information by going back to the original source.

If you are able to visit the Library in Salt Lake City in person (3000 people do so every day), you will find that more than 500 microfilm- and microfiche-viewers are available, all the printed volumes are on open shelves, and the very helpful staff will point you in the right direction with kindness and courtesy. The Library staff will not undertake searches for you, but you can obtain a list of approved researchers with whom you will make your own financial arrangements. When asking for this list, be sure you specify your particular area of interest; you will then

CHAPTER 5
The National Archives

Archives hold the memory of a nation. The National Archives of Canada (previously known as the Public Archives) were established in 1872, five years after Confederation. The main building is located at 395 Wellington Street, Ottawa, ON K1A 0N3. Its holdings grow almost hourly, and no one with Canadian roots can go far in his or her search without using this great source of information. Family historians are *welcome* at the National Archives, and that is almost something for the Guinness Book of Records, since too many archivists treat their holdings as if they were their own personal property and rather resent the interruption of the even tenor of their lives by bothersome people trying to find their forebears.

When writing for information, it is not necessary to cover return postage, or to prepay for any photocopies you may require. You will be billed for this service. There is no fee charged for providing basic information. The telephone number is 613-995-5138. Other numbers of value to you are:

Manuscript Division: 995-8094
Cartographic Records: 995-1077
Genealogical Services: 996-7458

Genealogists should consult the NAC publication *Tracing*

Your Ancestors in Canada. This 21-page booklet may be obtained free of charge from Publication Services at the above address.

Ancestor-hunters now account for forty per cent of all visitors and fifty-five per cent of all letters received. Most records of interest to you are on microfilm or microfiche; therefore you do not have to visit the NAC, because you can borrow microforms through your own local library if it has microfilm- or microfiche-readers. If not, your request must be sent through the nearest public library with these facilities.

In addition to its collection of public records, the NAC holds private correspondence, family trees, histories, family Bibles and albums, diaries, recorded family histories, passports, and birth, marriage, and death certificates. You will find it fascinating to skim through the family records of both the famous and the infamous, the known and the unknown — politicians and pioneers, writers and farmers, parsons and felons, sailors and steelworkers — the people who made us and made this nation.

It is not possible to list all the available records and sources of information in the National Archives, but I give below the details of the holdings most likely to be of help to you in your ancestor-hunting:

| Family Histories

The NAC is actively collecting such histories by purchase or donation. If you have already traced your pioneer or UEL family, do please give a copy of your research to the Archives — you will be helping to build the history of our country. The family histories in the National Archives are both in print and in typescript, published and unpublished. All are indexed by family name and cross-indexed by geographical location. Many also have an index listing people mentioned in the text, apart from family members. Always check with the Genealogical Services Division to find out if your family is already mentioned in their records.

If you will let me digress for a couple of minutes, may I suggest you be even more generous with the results of all your labours. Send a copy of your family tree or family history, or both, to the archives of the province in which your ancestor(s) settled; send copies to the local public library of the actual place of settlement; send copies to the library of the place from which your ancestor came in the old country. In this way, not only are you contributing to history, but you may also be blessed by posterity a century hence when someone among your descendants may be trying to trace back to you.

| Parish Registers

The earliest church registers in Canada are those of some Catholic churches in the province of Québec which date back to the 1620s. The earliest Anglican register is that of St. Paul's, Halifax, which dates from 1749. The Archives hold several hundred microfilms of church registers and these are listed in this book later under each separate province.

| Census Returns

Details of the NAC holdings are given in later chapters under each province.

| Passenger Lists

Few of these have survived. By all means check available ones in the NAC and in the Provincial Archives in Halifax, but do not raise your hopes high. Many searches have been made in archives and government offices in Canada for records without success. Some arrivals were recorded in newspapers in Halifax, Québec City, Montréal, and other port cities, but, generally speaking, any names mentioned were those of cabin passengers, while those travelling steerage—as most did—were dismissed with the words "there were also 385 immigrants in steerage." The *Quebec Gazette*, indexed from 1764 to 1825, is in the NAC on microfilm, but only cabin passengers are listed. Lists of assisted emigrants from the United Kingdom between 1817 and 1831 are indexed and on microfilm. Scots settlements in Ontario—which I mention in Chapter 3—were established under such schemes (Lanark, Perth, and Carleton).

Recording of immigrants did not start officially until 1865 for Québec City and 1881 for Halifax, the two main ports of entry. They are not indexed, and searches can only be made if your ancestor's date of arrival and name of port are known. Our borders by sea and land were wide open. Immigration from the United States and emigration to the United States went unrecorded.

Quarantine Records

In the early 1800s cholera and typhus were rampant on the "coffin ships" that brought people across the Atlantic. There are instances where as many as twenty per cent of a ship's passengers died during the voyage or shortly after arrival. Most ports had special areas where those suffering from such diseases could be kept until they died or recovered — usually the former. The NAC has a few scattered records of some of these people.

Naturalization Records

British subjects were automatically regarded as citizens on settlement. Immigrants from other countries had to take out naturalization papers, and records for the period 1828–50 are in the NAC. Those from 1865 onwards are with the Citizenship Registration Branch of the Secretary of State, and are fully indexed. The records from 1850 to 1865 have disappeared.

Passports

The first passports were issued by local mayors or reeves. In 1862, special local agents were appointed for this purpose, and from 1867 all passports were issued by the Secretary of State. From 1882 to 1895 the provincial governments took over the task, and then the Secretary of State took over again until 1909. After that date, passports were issued — as they still are — by the Department of External Affairs. Records exist from 1862 to 1882 and from 1894 to 1937 in the NAC. Some of the records between 1882 and 1894 are in some of the provincial archives.

Land Records

Applications for land grants for the period 1764–1842 are in the Archives and are indexed. Other applications and correspondence can be found in the various provincial archives. In the Ontario Provincial Archives, for example, you will find the Township Papers. These are not indexed, but there is a separate file for each township. They contain the original letters written by early settlers if they had cause to complain about their land grant. There are similar files in a few of the other provincial archives.

| Military Records

These cover the South African (Boer) War at the turn of the century, and later wars up to and including the Korean War. There are no records of enlistment in the War of 1812, the Rebellion of 1837, and the Fenian invasions. However, there are some muster rolls and pay lists in the NAC. Records of the First and Second World Wars and the Korean War are not open to public search, but questions from descendants of individual soldiers, as well as those from soldiers themselves, will be answered. This applies, of course, to navy and air force records as well.

There is a great deal of information in the Archives about military land grants, bounty awards, and disability and other pensions. When inquiring about these, be sure you supply all the information you have about the full name, dates of service, name of unit, and home address of the person concerned.

| School Records

Many public school attendance records from Québec and Ontario are in the Archives. They date from 1768 for Québec and 1841 for Ontario, and continue up to the middle of the last century.

| Newspapers

Canada's earliest newspapers were the *Halifax Gazette* (1752) and the *Quebec Gazette* (1764). The NAC has the latter, and it is indexed for the period of 1764–1825. It is an excellent source of information about people and places in both Upper and Lower Canada. It contains many references to ship arrivals, names of immigrants, and persons involved in public affairs in both provinces.

| Orphans

Between the 1870s and the 1930s over eighty thousand boys and girls were settled in Canada by various British organizations, headed by such people as Dr. Thomas Barnardo, Maria Rye, John Middlemore, and Annie Macpherson. Most of them were between eight and ten years of age, and not all were orphans. Many had been abandoned by their parents, others handed over to one of the philanthropic organizations by parents who loved them but were starving themselves and unable to provide for the large families of the era. Many of the children who came to Canada and were placed on farms to work were treated with love and adopted into the family; others were ill-treated and regarded as slave labour. If you talk to survivors today, you will hear both sides of the story.

The Barnardo files have been microfilmed by the NAC and often contain the names of the parents (if known) and the home address when the child was taken into Dr. Barnardo's care. However, there are great restrictions on access to the files in order to protect personal privacy. If your relationship to a Barnardo child is not sufficient to have the files opened to you, you should write to Dr. Barnardo's Homes, Tanners Lane, Barkingside, Ilford, Essex, England. One additional advantage in writing here is that they have on file the photographs that were taken of each child before he or she was sent across the Atlantic.

| Métis Land Claims

In the period from 1870 to 1924 there was a complicated series of land claims, legislation, committees of inquiry, and arbitration awards all arising from aboriginal rights to land in Western Canada and the Northwest Territories. All this material is on microfilm in the NAC, and it contains a great deal of genealogical information about Métis families. All are available through inter-library loan.

| Russian Consular Records

Although this book is concerned only with Canadian sources, this account of the records in the National Archives of Canada would not be complete without giving details of the Li-Ra-Ma Collection of Russian consular records. Do not be misled by the word "Russian". The information contained in them is invaluable for Canadians whose ancestral roots are Armenian, Byelorussian, Cossack, Estonian, Finnish, Georgian, German (Mennonite), Jewish, Latvian, Lithuanian, Polish, Russian, and Ukrainian.

For years there were rumours that a great hoard of genealogical material existed in Washington, D.C., consisting of the records and files of the Tsarist Russian consulates in Halifax, Montréal, and Vancouver, in Canada, and in Boston, Chicago,

Honolulu, New York, Philadelphia, Portland, San Francisco, and Seattle, in the United States.

In Canada, at the time of the Russian Revolution of 1917, there were three Russian consuls: Serge Likacheff in Montréal, Constantine Ragosine in Vancouver, and Harry Mathers in Halifax. The first two letters of each surname make up the name of the collection in Canada. After the Revolution, the Russian consuls (if they were Russian) were ordered home. Some went, some did not.

The U.S. government, which did not recognize the USSR until 1933, took custody of the consular files, as did the Canadian government. The latter continued to pay the three consuls until 1922, when diplomatic relations were established between the Canadian and the Soviet governments. Meanwhile, in the United States the records of the various consulates were first of all transferred to the building that housed the Boston consulate, and eventually to the now vacant Russian Embassy in Washington. In 1922 the three consuls in Canada transferred all their records to the United States, where they joined the rest of the records in Washington.

The files contained records of immigration, settlement, military service in Russia, education, Russian police permits, details of place of origin, and family histories. There were hundreds of thousands of photographs, letters, certificates, passports, etc. The consuls, living up to the Russian passion for bureaucracy and record-keeping, collected everything they possibly could about everyone with whom they had dealings. For example, during the First World War the Russian government tried to get Russians living overseas to return home to fight in the army. If a man had already done his military service before emigrating, he was under no legal obligation to return. When he received his orders to do so, he would write to the nearest consulate and send his release papers, his police permit to leave Russia, and, often, a photograph of himself in his army uniform. The consuls would retain such information for their files.

You must remember, of course, that Russian immigrants who had acquired citizenship in Canada or the United States will not be mentioned in the records *after* the date of naturalization. However, also bear in mind that the majority of Russian immigrants did not acquire new citizenship at the earliest possible moment. It should also be remembered that many Russian immigrants into Canada came via the United States, so you should check the records on both sides of the border unless you know for certain that your ancestor came directly to Canada.

As time went by, all trace of the consular records was lost. They had last been seen in 1933 when Soviet representatives paid a visit to the old Tsarist Russian Embassy in Washington before officially taking over. When they saw all the thousands of cartons of records, they complained bitterly about "Tsarist rubbish" and demanded that they all be removed. During the next day or so, the U.S. army provided trucks and men and all the records were removed to an underground repository. The years passed, but in 1980 some very astute detective work by Canadian archivists led to the rediscovery of the records. Over a hundred large cartons were sent back to Canada. Some idea of the size of the collection becomes apparent when one realizes that they contain over a hundred thousand names and a hundred and fifty thousand photographs. You will find such items as cancelled passports, other travel documents, birth certificates, identity cards, military service records, school records, estate records, wills, work permits, certificates of nationality, and general correspondence.

The U.S. records are in the National Records Center, Suitland, Maryland, and all the records in both countries are on microfilm and are indexed. So far as the NAC is concerned, you should make contact with the Ethnic Archives, Manuscript Division.

CHAPTER 6
Censuses

Censuses — or counts of the population — date back to Roman and biblical times. You will recall that King Herod was enterprising enough to institute a census in Israel for his own purposes! Originally censuses were used for tax purposes, later for military conscription, and, more recently, for demographical statistics including such arcane data as the answers to, "Do you have an indoor toilet?"

Some early censuses were only head-counts and produced figures and not names. Others only mentioned by name the "Head of the household" — who in those days was always a man! The information you will find in a census return varies. The basic information remains the same: name, age, sex, religion, occupation, and place of birth. The latter item, probably the most vital for the ancestor-hunter, can be disappointing. It all depends on the curiosity of the enumerator, or the attitude of the person providing the information, or his or her lack of that information. You may find your ancestor's place of birth as Inverness, Scotland, or just Scotland, or simply NB (for North Britain). If it is the latter, you may be sure that the person giving the information was not Scottish — no Scot would describe himself as "North British"!

So far as Canada is concerned, the first census was ordered by Intendant Jean Talon in New France (Québec) in 1666, and he listed 3215 inhabitants. Various censuses were held in the area after this, but none have survived from before the nineteenth century. It was not until Confederation in 1867 that the taking of a census became a legal requirement; in 1871 the first Dominion census took place, and this has continued every ten years since then.

However, there are scattered returns available before this, and the details are given later under the various provinces. For example, in parts of Ontario there were censuses in some places in the 1840s, but they only listed heads of households; there are similar scattered returns for parts of Québec in 1681, 1811, 1813, and at irregular intervals up to the start of regular censuses in 1851; Nova Scotia and Newfoundland also had some returns in the eighteenth century.

The provinces are divided into census districts, and these, in turn, are divided into sub-districts. As a general rule, the districts are based on cities and counties, and the sub-districts on townships and city wards. Villages, small towns, parishes, and seigneuries were enumerated within the county in which they were located. However — just to confuse you a little — census districts and county boundaries were not always the same, and townships could be transferred from one census district to another. Also, names of places could change. In 1851 you cannot find details of a census for Ottawa but you will find them under Ottawa's original name of Bytown. You will not find Kitchener mentioned but you will find Berlin.

As the years went by, the census authorities grew more curious and eager for information — it was no longer sufficient to list the head of the household. With a few exceptions, after 1851 everyone in the house was listed. Census returns are in the public domain up until 1891; after that year, access is restricted to protect the privacy of the individual.

In order to borrow the correct microfilm reel from the National Archives (through your nearest library with a microfilm-reader), you will need to know the street address of your ancestor in a city, and the township in a rural area. If you do not have this information within your family records, you will probably be able to obtain it from an early directory of the area, or one of the county maps showing the names of settlers and the lot they occupied. You may borrow three reels at a time from the National Archives and make use of them for four weeks. You will have to research them in the library and not in your own home. Census returns have also been copied by the LDS Church and may be viewed at the nearest Family History Library. In addition, many libraries have census microfilms for the areas served by the library. In a number of places the library, aided by volunteer help or the local genealogical society, has indexed the census returns for the area. If this has been done in your particular area of interest, life has been made easier for you!

Be prepared for difficulty in reading the returns. Ideally the enumerator wrote clearly and boldly and used heavy black ink. Inevitably you will find that in your case he wrote very lightly, with poor ink which faded considerably before the return was microfilmed. You will suffer from eyestrain, and after an hour of running your eyes steadily down lists of thirty-odd names per page you should stop, have a coffee or a beer near by, or go for a walk in the local park and smell the flowers. If you don't take a break, you may very well miss the one entry you are looking for.

You will find a wide variety of abbreviations used to describe religions and places of origin. A fairly complete list of such abbreviations appears at the beginning of the book.

Before you settle down in a local library or archive to check a particular census return, be sure you arm yourself beforehand with a list of every possible spelling of your own surname. The enumerator was probably not a very well educated man and his spelling may have been phonetic — in other words, he spelt the name as it sounded to him. He may have asked the occupier of the house about the spelling, but there is no guarantee he received the correct spelling from him or her either. After all, what is "correct" spelling? My name, Baxter, has been spelt that way in all official documents since 1750, but an 1811 census return shows it as Bakster and an 1821 one as Bakester.

Usually, at the end of the census returns for a township you will find an agricultural census. This described the acreage under crops, the type of crops grown, and a few extra little goodies like a vivid description of a storm that washed away the corn crop, or a list of prices received per bushel, or the cost of cattle feed. None of this will help you with your family, but it will provide you with a background to the sort of life being led in a particular place at a particular time. Information about your family background should not consist of dates alone.

It is vital that you check with a local library or archive about the existence of an index to a particular census for a specific area. There is no centralized listing of such projects — except that later in this book, under each listing of a library and its holdings you will be given information about their census indexes, if they exist.

CHAPTER 7
Church Records and Registers

In many countries church records and registers are centralized; unfortunately this is not so in Canada, where they are scattered all over the place: in individual churches, church archives, libraries, museums, provincial archives, and the National Archives in Ottawa. There is no national policy, or even a nationwide church policy, governing the control and safekeeping of these irreplaceable records of our Canadian ancestry.

In other parts of the world where there is a greater regard for history and genealogy, church registers have been put on microfilm or microfiche, and only the copies are available for public search. In addition, many countries have allowed the Mormons to copy the registers.

In many areas of Canada there is little protection for the church registers against fire and water damage, or against theft and vandalism. With the growing interest in genealogy, theft is the greatest threat of all. It has been known for individuals searching a register without supervision to tear out and pocket any pages containing their ancestral entries. In the United Kingdom it is compulsory for Church of England parishes to lodge their registers in the County Record Offices in England and Wales — *unless* the parish can provide facilities for supervised searching, adequate heating, humidity control, and regular and frequent inspection. As a result, only a handful of parishes now keep their registers, and the CROs have an ambitious program of microfilming so that only the copies will be available for public search.

So far as Canada is concerned, we lag behind wiser and more progressive countries, not only in the preservation of our records, but also in our deep-rooted belief that everyone can be trusted. In one church not many years ago a clergyman offered to let me take home for the night his earliest register (dating from 1810). He had never met me before, and did not even know my name. When I showed my astonishment, he said, "Oh, you have an honest face." Naturally I refused his offer and suggested politely he should be more careful with precious records in his care.

Some church authorities in Canada — the *Catholic* Archdiocese of Toronto, for example — have arranged with the LDS Church to microfilm all records of baptism and marriage from the earliest date of entry in each parish (1833 in some cases) up to 1910. Where the registers contained death or burial entries, they were also copied. In addition, the Archdiocese has its own microfilming program which will shortly bring the records up to the present date. The microfilms are in the church archives and also in the parish if it possesses a microfilm-reader. In the *Catholic Church* generally it is left to the individual diocese to decide if the LDS Church can microfilm the registers; some allow this, some don't. Some insist the parishes hand-copy the registers and lodge the copies in the Diocesan Chancery Office.

Other denominations have their own policies. The *Anglican Church* "encourages" the parishes to lodge early registers in the Diocesan Office; the *United Church* has centralized many of its early registers and other records in eight locations across the country (details later in this book), but by far the greatest number of U.C. records of interest to the ancestor-hunter is to be found in the United Church Archives at the University of Toronto. The *Baptist Church* has concentrated its large collection of records and registers in two locations: the Canadian Baptist Archives, McMaster Divinity College, Hamilton (for Ontario, Québec, and the Western provinces), and the Baptist Historical Collection, Acadia University, Wolfville, N.S. The *Presbyterian Church* presents a much more complicated problem. When the United Church was formed in 1925 by a merger of Congregational, Methodist, and Presbyterian churches, nearly half the churches of the latter denomination rejected the merger. This means that you will find registers in a number of different places: the United Church Archives, the Presbyterian Archives, individual churches, the provincial archives, and the National Archives in Ottawa.

The *Lutheran Church*, both the Evangelical Lutheran Church in Canada and the Lutheran Church — Canada, generally speaking leaves the registers in the individual churches, and in any case very few of them pre-date civil registration. The *Mennonite Church*, in at least some of its branches, encourages the individual congregations to lodge registers in one of the four archives, or to microfilm them and give a copy to an archive. In this case, again, few church records date back to the nineteenth century. The *Society of Friends (Quakers)* have a number of early registers in their archives in Toronto, but others are still in the custody of the various meetings across the country.

Before referring to the church registers of the various denominations and sects listed under each province in Chapters 9–20, please make sure you understand these explanatory notes:

1. The church registers are listed alphabetically by name of city, town, village, or township. Those listed are either originals which are no longer in the particular church, or microfilm copies.

2. The locations shown are the archives in which the registers or copies have been lodged for safekeeping. The list is complete according to the information given to me by the archives. *However, additions are always being made.*

3. Very many original registers are still in the original church, and if the church in which you are interested is not listed, *it does not mean the register does not exist*. It simply means that the original or a copy has not been lodged in the archives. In that case, you must check with the church authorities to find out if the register is still in the church, or if it has been lost or destroyed. Until recently, the policy of the Catholic Church has been to leave the registers in the local church, but there are signs that this is changing. However, at the moment you will not find too many Catholic registers listed.

4. The registers listed cover the period up to the date of civil registration. There are many copies or originals *after* this date which I have not listed because, once registration started, a search of church registers is not so essential for your ancestral search.

5. The letters B, M, or D refer to Births or Baptisms, Marriages, and Deaths. The letters in the right-hand column are an abbreviation of the name of the particular archive; for example,

LUC for Library, University of Calgary, or UCA for United Church Archives. Details of these abbreviations appear on pages xvi–xviii.
6. Dates shown are the starting-date of the registers. B 1845, for example, means the entries start in that year and continue up to civil registration unless it is shown otherwise, as, for example, 1845–55.

As you search for church records, be prepared to find that denominations have merged or separated over the years, or even completely disappeared. The Methodist Church, for example, was rent asunder many times by splits and schisms and organized or spontaneous revolts. As some nineteenth-century wit remarked, "There is madness in their method." If you are tracing Methodist ancestry, you must look among the records of Wesleyan Methodists, Primitive Methodists, True Methodists, Regular Methodists, New Connection Methodists, and Bible Christians. If your ancestry is Baptist, you will find Evangelical Baptists, Southern Baptists, Ukrainian Baptists, Fundamental Baptists, Regular Baptists, and Primitive Baptists.

Whatever you do, don't start out with preconceived ideas or assumptions about the religion of your settler ancestor. Just because you are Anglican, as were your father and your grandfather, it is not at all certain that your great-grandfather was. People change their religion for a variety of reasons: marriage, a dispute with a minister, the lack of a church of their choice in the area in which they settled, or conversion.

Details of the organization of the churches of all major denominations in Canada are given below. The location of church registers will be discussed in the later chapters about each individual province or territory.

| Anglican

There are four Provincial Synods. They were formed as follows:

BRITISH COLUMBIA: This also includes the Yukon Territory and the Dioceses of British Columbia (1859), Caledonia (1879), Cariboo (1914), Kootenay (1899), New Westminster (1879), and Yukon (1891) (previously named Selkirk).
CANADA: Fredericton (1845), Montréal (1850), Newfoundland (1839) (now divided into three — Eastern, Central, and Western), Nova Scotia (1787), and Québec (1793).

ONTARIO: Algoma (1873), Huron (1857), Moosonee (1872), Niagara (1875), Ontario (1862), Ottawa (1896), and Toronto (1839). RUPERT'S LAND: Arctic (1933), Athabasca (1874), Brandon (1913), Calgary (1888), Edmonton (1914), Keewatin (1902), Qu'Appelle (1884), Rupert's Land (1849), Saskatchewan (1874), and Saskatoon (1874).

The addresses of the various dioceses and of their archives (where they exist) are:

Algoma: PO Box 1168, Sault Ste. Marie, ON P6A 5N7
Arctic: 1055 Avenue Road, Toronto, ON M5N 2C8
Athabasca: PO Box 279, Peace River, AB T0H 0X0
Brandon: 341-13th Street, Brandon, MB R7A 4P8
British Columbia: 912 Vancouver Street, Victoria, BC V8V 3V7
Caledonia: PO Box 278, Prince Rupert, BC V8J 3P6
Calgary: 3015 Glencoe Road SW, Calgary, AB T2S 2L9
Cariboo: 465 Victoria Street, Kamloops, BC V2C 2P5
Edmonton: 10033-84th Avenue, Edmonton, AB T6E 2G6
Fredericton: 115 Church Street, Fredericton, NB E3B 4C8
Huron: 220 Dundas Street, London, ON N6A 1H3
Keewatin: PO Box 118, Kenora, ON P9N 3X1
Kootenay: PO Box 549, Kelowna, BC V1Y 7P2
Montréal: PO Box 158, Station B, Montréal, PQ H3B 3J5
Moosonee: PO Box 841, Schumacher, ON P0N 1G0
Newfoundland (Central): 34 Fraser Road, Gander, NF A1V 2E8
Newfoundland (East): 19 King's Bridge Road, St. John's, NF A1C 3K4
Newfoundland (West): 311 Millbrook Mall, Corner Brook, NF A2H 2V3
New Westminster: 814 Richards Street, Vancouver, BC V6B 3A7
Niagara: 67 Victoria Avenue South, Hamilton, ON L8N 2S8
Nova Scotia: 5732 College Street, Halifax, NS B3H 1X3
Ontario: 90 Johnson Street, Kingston, ON K7L 1X7
Ottawa: 71 Bronson Avenue, Ottawa, ON K1R 6G6
Qu'Appelle: 1501 College Avenue, Regina, SK S4P 1B8
Québec: 36 rue Desjardins, Québec City, PQ G1R 4L5
Rupert's Land: 935 Nesbitt Bay, Winnipeg, MB R3T 1W6
Saskatchewan: PO Box 1088, Prince Albert, SK S6V 5S6
Saskatoon: PO Box 1965, Saskatoon, SK S7K 3S5
Toronto: 135 Adelaide Street East, Toronto, ON M5C 1L8
Yukon: PO Box 4247, Whitehorse, YT Y1A 3T3

In some areas Diocesan Archives do not exist, and, in that case, registers may be with one of the four Provincial Synod Offices, depending on the area covered. Their addresses are:

BRITISH COLUMBIA: Vancouver School of Theology, 6000 Iona Drive, Vancouver, BC V6T 1L4
CANADA: 5732 College Street, Halifax, NS B3H 1X3
ONTARIO: 135 Adelaide Street East, Toronto, ON M5C 1L8
RUPERT'S LAND: Provincial Archives, Winnipeg, MB R3C 1T5

| Baptist

The Baptist Church in Canada, like the other dissenting or Nonconformist denominations, has been divided and segmented a number of times by rebellious spirits within the church. In 1988, Baptist congregations in Canada were divided among ten different sects of varying sizes:

Baptist Federation, 1134
Baptist General Conference, 72
Canadian Baptist Conference, 60
Evangelical Baptists, 474
Fundamental Baptists, 16
North American Baptist Conference, 106
Primitive Baptists, 17
Regular Baptists, 8
Southern Baptists, 24
Ukrainian Baptists, 40

The total number of congregations has grown by ten per cent over the past twenty years.

If your Baptist ancestor came from an an area where splits occurred, you may have to search for registers and records in several different locations. It is also wise to remember that a split could take two forms:

1. The pastor and his entire congregation could move *en bloc* from one sect of the Baptist Church to another. In this case, the original church and its records would remain in the same place, but some slight change of name would be made to reflect its changed beliefs. In other cases, no change of name would be made, because the congregation would believe *it* had not changed its beliefs but everyone else had!

2. If the congregation itself split, the minority would stop attending that particular church and hold meetings in a barn or a private house until such time as a new chapel could be built. If the pastor himself left with the minority, he might take the church records with him.

You must also realize — as no doubt you do — that Baptist records and registers list marriages and burials, but not births. The church practises baptism of believers, and so only the believer (aged from about twelve years to infinity) will be listed in the registers. Burial entries are also rare, except in the province of Québec, where it is required by law.

Churches are "encouraged" to lodge their records in the Baptist Archives, but for the reasons set out above you will find them of limited value. However, the archives do have many other sources of information which may supply details of the life of your ancestor if he or she was prominent in the work of the church. These include minutes of meetings, membership lists, Sunday school attendance records, church histories, press clippings, church newspapers and magazines, and individual church histories.

One more discouraging fact to bear in mind is that before the Marriage Act of 1831 in Upper Canada, Baptist ministers were not allowed to perform marriages. An earlier Marriage Act of 1798 had allowed marriages to be performed by other denominations than Anglicans and Catholics. However, it very carefully described these other denominations as Church of Scotland, Presbyterians, Calvinists, and Lutherans. The Baptists were not mentioned, and this led to complications for your ancestors and for you. Your ancestors had to find a minister of another faith — usually Calvinist or Lutheran — who would be prepared to marry them, and you will have to search the registers of several churches in the area to find a record of the marriage. You are unlikely to find this in a Catholic church register, but all other denominations are possibilities. Some Baptist ministers were able to persuade local authorities they were Calvinists within the meaning of the Act, and obtained permission to perform marriages. Others tried this and failed. Still more refused on principle to forswear their Baptist beliefs in any way.

The first marriage by a Baptist minister that I have been able to trace took place in London, Ontario, in 1807. The number of such marriages increased steadily as the years passed, and the Act of 1831 really only legalized a situation that already existed.

As I mentioned earlier, there are two Baptist Archives, in Hamilton, Ontario, and in Wolfville, Nova Scotia. The former have some registers from Ontario and Québec, and you will find these listed under these provinces. The small staff of the archives are anxious to help ancestor-hunters but cannot undertake protracted searches. If these are required, you will be referred to a list of researchers from the local genealogical society.

The best collection of Baptist records is that in the Library of Acadia University in Wolfville. Quite apart from church records, the Library also has a number of books about Baptist history in the Atlantic provinces, where the church was once very active.

| Catholic

The Catholic Church in Canada is divided into seventeen provinces and sixty-four dioceses. The names and addresses of the dioceses are:

Alexandria–Cornwall: PO Box 1388, Cornwall, ON K6H 5V4
Amos: 450 rue Principale Nord, Amos, PQ J9T 2M1
Antigonish: 155 Main Street, Antigonish, NS B2G 2L7
Baie-Comeau: 639 rue de Bretagne, Baie-Comeau, PQ G5C 1X2
Bathurst: PO Box 460, Bathurst, NB E2A 3Z4
Calgary: 1916 2nd Street SW, Calgary, AB T2S 1S3
Charlottetown: PO Box 907, Charlottetown, PE C1A 7L9
Chicoutimi: 602 rue Racine Est, Chicoutimi, PQ G7H 6J6
Churchill–Hudson Bay: PO Box 10, Churchill, MB R0B 0E0
Edmonton: 10044 113th Street, Edmonton, AB T5K 1N8
Edmundston: PO Box 370, Edmundston, NB E3V 3L1
Gaspé: PO Box 440, Gaspé, PQ G0C 1R0
Gatineau–Hull: 119 rue Carillon, Hull, PQ J8X 2P8
Grand Falls: PO Box 771, Grand Falls, NF A2A 2M4
Gravelbourg: PO Box 690, Gravelbourg, SK S0H 1X0
Grouard–McLennan: PO Box 388, McLennan, AB T0H 2L0
Halifax: PO Box 1527, Halifax, NS B3J 2Y3
Hamilton: 700 King Street West, Hamilton, ON L8P 1C7
Hearst: PO Box 1330, Hearst, ON P0L 1N0
Joliette: PO Box 470, Joliette, PQ J6E 6H6
Kamloops: 635a Tranquille Road, Kamloops, BC V2B 3H5

Keewatin–The Pas: PO Box 270, The Pas, MB R9A 1K4

Kingston: PO Box 997, Kingston, ON K7L 4X8

Labrador–Schefferville: PO Box 545, Labrador City, NF A2V 2K7

London: 1070 Waterloo Street, London, ON N6A 3Y2

Mackenzie–Fort Smith: PO Box 25, Fort Smith, NT X0E 0P0

Moncton: PO Box 248, Moncton, NB E1C 8K9

Mont-Laurier: 435 rue de la Madone, Mont-Laurier, PQ J9L 1S1

Montréal: 2000 rue Sherbrooke Ouest, Montréal, PQ H3H 1G4

Moosonee: PO Box 40, Moosonee, ON P0L 1Y0

Nelson: 813 Ward Street, Nelson, BC V1L 1T4

Nicolet: PO Box 820, Nicolet, PQ J0G 1E0

Ottawa: 1247 Kilborn Avenue, Ottawa, ON K1H 6K9

Pembroke: PO Box 7, Pembroke, ON K8A 6X1

Peterborough: PO Box 175, Peterborough, ON K9J 6Y8

Prince Albert: 1415-4th Avenue West, Prince Albert, SK S6V 5H1

Prince George: PO Box 7000, Prince George, BC V2N 3Z2

Québec: 1073 boulevard St. Cyrille Ouest, Québec, PQ G1S 4R5

Regina: 3225 13th Avenue, Regina, SK S4T 1P5

Rimouski: PO Box 730, Rimouski, PQ G5L 7C7

Rouyn–Noranda: PO Box 1060, Rouyn–Noranda, PQ J9X 5W9

Ste. Anne–Pocatière: PO Box 430, La Pocatière, PQ G0R 1Z0

St. Boniface: 151 avenue de la Cathédrale, St. Boniface, MB R2H 0H6

St. Catharines: 122 Riverdale Avenue, St. Catharines, ON L2R 4C2

St. George's: 16 Hammon Drive, Corner Brook, NF A2H 2W2

St. Hyacinthe: 1900 rue Girouard Ouest, St. Hyacinthe, PQ J2S 7B4

St. Jean: 740 boulevard Ste. Foy, St. Jean, PQ J4K 4X8

St. Jérôme: 355 rue St. Georges, St. Jérôme, PQ J7Z 5V3

Saint John: 1 Bayard Drive, Saint John, NB E2L 3L5

St. John's: PO Box 37, St. John's, NF A1C 5H5

St. Paul: PO Box 339, St. Paul, AB T0A 3A0

Saskatoon: 106-5th Avenue North, Saskatoon, SK S7K 2N7

Sault Ste. Marie: PO Box 510, North Bay, ON P1B 8J1

Sherbrooke: 130 rue de la Cathédrale, Sherbrooke, PQ J1H 4M1

Thunder Bay: PO Box 756, Thunder Bay, ON P7C 4V5

Timmins: 65 Jubilee Avenue East, Timmins, ON P4N 5W4

Toronto: 355 Church Street, Toronto, ON M5B 1Z8

Trois-Rivières: PO Box 879, Trois-Rivières, PQ G9A 5J9

Valleyfield: 31 rue de la Fabrique, Valleyfield, PQ J6T 4G9

Vancouver: 150 Robson Street, Vancouver, BC V6B 2A7
Victoria: 4044 Nelthorpe Street, Victoria, BC V8X 2A1
Whitehorse: 5119-5th Avenue, Whitehorse, YT Y1A 1L5
Winnipeg: 1455 Waverley Street, Winnipeg, MB R3T 0P7
Yarmouth: 53 Park Street, Yarmouth, NS B5A 4B2

There are also dioceses of affiliated denominations:

Ukrainian Catholic Dioceses
Edmonton: 9645 108th Avenue, Edmonton, AB T5H 1A3
New Westminster: 502 5th Avenue, New Westminster, BC V3L 1S2
Saskatoon: 866 Saskatchewan Crescent East, Saskatoon, SK
   S7N 0L4
Toronto: 61 Glen Edyth Drive, Toronto, ON M4V 2V8
Winnipeg: 233 Scotia Street, Winnipeg, MB R2V 1V7

Greek-Melkite Catholic Diocese
Montréal: 329 rue Viger Est, Montréal, PQ H2X 1R6

Slovak (Byzantine) Catholic Diocese
Montréal: 12475 rue Grenet, Montréal, PQ H4J 2K4

| Lutheran

The Lutheran Council in Canada is the co-ordinating body of
the Church and it has two member churches:

   The Evangelical Lutheran Church in Canada (ELCIC)
   The Lutheran Church—Canada (Missouri Synod)

There are also some other branches which total one per cent
of the Lutheran population; these include the Danish Lutheran
Church Abroad, the Wisconsin Evangelical Lutheran Synod,
the Lutheran Brethren, and the Church of the Lutheran
Reformation.
   The details of the two main churches are:

The Evangelical Lutheran Church in Canada
1512 St. James Street, Winnipeg, MB R3H 0L2

The archives of the ELCIC are housed at the two seminaries of the Church, in Saskatoon, Saskatchewan, and in Waterloo, Ontario. The archivist at Saskatoon is Mrs. Jeanette Brandell, The Lutheran Theological Seminary, 114 Seminary Crescent, Saskatoon, SK S7N 0X3. The archivist at Waterloo is the Rev. Erich R. W. Schultz, The Library, Wilfrid Laurier University, Waterloo, ON N2L 3C5.

The Church has about 625 parishes and 225,000 members, and includes seventy per cent of Canadian Lutherans. There are five synods of the Church:

ALBERTA NORTH SYNOD: 10014-81 Avenue, Edmonton, AB T6E 1W8

BRITISH COLUMBIA SYNOD: 80 Tenth Avenue East, New Westminster, BC V3L 4R5

EASTERN SYNOD: 340 Queen Street North, Kitchener, ON N2H 6P4

MANITOBA-NW ONTARIO SYNOD: 201-3657 Roblin Blvd., Winnipeg, MB R3R 0E2

SASKATCHEWAN SYNOD: 707-601 Spadina Crescent East, Saskatoon, SK S7K 3G8

The Lutheran Church — Canada (Missouri Synod)
PO Box 55, Station A, 203-2727 Portage Avenue, Winnipeg, MB R3J 0R2

There are three district offices of the Church:

ALBERTA-BRITISH COLUMBIA: 35-9912-106 Street, Edmonton, AB T5K 1C5

MANITOBA-SASKATCHEWAN: 1927 Grant Drive, Regina, SK S4S 4V6

ONTARIO: 149 Queen Street South, Kitchener, ON N2G 1W2

Generally speaking, it seems clear from the information given to me by the two member churches that no early Lutheran records exist in the various archives, and that few of the registers still in the churches pre-date civil registration in the provinces.

| Mennonites

The Anabaptist movement started in Switzerland in 1525. Anabaptists taught that believers should be baptized only after they had reached the age where they intelligently consented to this religious ritual, and should not be unknowingly baptized as infants. A similar movement began in the Netherlands a few years later. Menno Simons, the main Anabaptist leader there, gave his name to the movement that became known as Mennonite. Religious persecution soon led to migration from both founding countries. From Switzerland the Mennonites moved to the Palatinate area of present-day Germany and into Alsace. In 1683, many of the "Swiss" Mennonites started emigrating to North America. The "Dutch" Mennonites emigrated east to Prussia. At the end of the eighteenth century, when Russia was engaged in populating its empty spaces, many "Dutch" Mennonites pushed east from Prussia to Russia, and descendants are often called "Russian" Mennonites.

Emigration to Canada came from three directions. In 1786, Mennonites from Pennsylvania settled in the Niagara Peninsula, and later moved on to Waterloo and York counties in Ontario. Amish Mennonites from Alsace settled in the western area of Waterloo County in the 1870s. The "Russian" Mennonites came to Canada in three separate waves: in the 1870s to Manitoba and further west; in the 1920s to Ontario and all the Western provinces; and after the Second World War to the same areas. The largest Mennonite population is now in Manitoba, and there are over 100,000 in Canada.

Various splits and schisms have occurred in the different groups and areas, and these make ancestor-hunting among the Mennonite records very difficult. In Ontario, schisms started in the 1840s and 1870s (between the Mennonite Church and the Mennonite Brethren in Christ — now the Missionary Church); in the 1880s the Old Order Mennonites and the Old Order Amish went their different ways; and as recently as the 1960s, a new grouping called the Conservative Mennonite Church was formed. Unlike the splits that occurred in other denominations such as the Baptists and the Methodists, the splits in the Mennonite Church were rarely caused by theological differences. For example, the Old Order Amish are opposed to having church buildings, and hold communal services in their homes. The Old Order Mennonites worship in plain meeting houses very sparsely furnished. The more progressive groups have modern churches with pipe organs and modern pews and carpets.

Some of the divisions among Mennonites in Western Canada occurred before they emigrated from Europe—between General Conference Mennonites, Mennonite Brethren, Evangelical Mennonites, and Evangelical Mennonite Missionaries. Among the "Swiss" and "Russian" Mennonites there are still more subfactions. Some of the latter came to Canada via Paraguay and Brazil, and others from Mexico (though they had gone there from Canada). All these small groups long separated from the mainstream developed their religion along different lines.

There are three major Mennonite centres in Canada:

The Conference of Mennonites in Canada, 600 Shaftesbury
Blvd., Winnipeg, MB R3P 0M4
The Canadian Mennonite Brethren Conference, 1-169 Riverton
Avenue, Winnipeg, MB R2L 0N1
The Mennonite Conference of Eastern Canada, 60 New Dundee
Road, Kitchener, ON N2G 3W5

Individual congregations are encouraged to lodge records or microfilm copies in one of the conference archives, and this is being done by an increasing number — though there is, of course, resistance from very conservative groups.

The major Mennonite libraries and archives in Canada are:

Mennonite Archives of Ontario: Conrad Grebel College, Waterloo, ON N2L 3G6. Phone: (519) 885-0220. The Archivist is Sam Steiner. It is advisable to telephone for an appointment. The collection includes a large amount of Mennonite material for this century; a limited number of records of baptism and marriage in the nineteenth century; and several hundred family genealogies, mostly Amish and "Swiss" Mennonite, but not exclusively; and a number of family Bibles. Old Order Mennonites and other conservative groups have not deposited their records, but some photocopies are available.

If you are descended from "Swiss" Mennonites, you should also contact the following:

Heritage Historical Library: Rte. #4, Aylmer, ON N5H 2R3. An appointment is essential (no telephone). It is operated by Old Order Amish and has a large number of Amish genealogies for both Canada and the United States.

Mennonite Heritage Centre: 600 Shaftesbury Blvd., Winnipeg,
MB R3P 0M4. This Archive specializes in "Russian" Mennonite
congregations and history. It has a number of family records dating
back to the immigration of the 1870s.
Center for Mennonite Brethren Studies in Canada: 1-169 Riverton
Avenue, Winnipeg, MB R2L 0N1. It specializes in Mennonite
Brethren congregations and history. These are mainly "Russian"
Mennonite, and though some of its records may overlap with those
of the Heritage Centre, if you are descended from "Russian"
Mennonites you should check both archives.
United Brethren Archives, Richlyn Library, Huntington College,
Huntingdon, IN 46750 USA

| Presbyterian

When the United Church was formed in 1925 by a merger of
Congregationalists, Methodists, and Presbyterians, about
forty per cent of the Presbyterian churches refused to join the
new church. This did not make life easy for Presbyterian ancestor-hunters, because you will have to look for Presbyterian
Church registers in five different places:

1. The United Church Archives
2. The National Archives of Canada
3. The Archives of Ontario
4. The Presbyterian Church Archives
5. The individual United Church or Presbyterian churches

The Church is organized into eight Synods, and these in
turn are divided into Presbyteries. Within each Presbytery
there is a number of individual churches. Each church is independent and not subject to outside control. The Archives of the
Church are located at Knox College, 59 St. George Street,
Toronto, ON M5S 2E6, but additional material can usually be
found in the various Synod Offices, in the Presbyteries, or in
the individual churches. You will find more details about these
holdings under the various provinces later in the book. You
will also find listed those registers that have been given to the
National and Provincial Archives. In other words, the records
are badly organized and widely scattered. The Church has neither the people nor the money to organize good archives in a
central location, or even to microfilm the registers on a
national basis.

The information I have obtained from the Synods and Presbyteries is included in the listings for each province. If a particular church in which you are interested is not mentioned, you should write to the Presbytery for the district. To obtain the name and address of the Clerk of the Presbytery, write first to: The Clerk of the General Assembly, 50 Wynford Drive, Don Mills, ON M3C 1J7. Be sure you enclose a stamped, self-addressed envelope for your reply.

Synods	*Presbyteries*
Atlantic Provinces	Cape Breton, Newfoundland, Pictou, Halifax and Lunenburg, Saint John, Miramichi, Prince Edward Island
Québec & Eastern Ontario	Québec, Montréal, Glengarry, Ottawa, Lanark & Renfrew, Brockville
Toronto & Kingston	Kingston, Lindsay & Peterborough, East Toronto, West Toronto, Brampton, Barrie, Temiskaming, Algoma & North Bay, Waterloo & Wellington
Hamilton & London	Hamilton, Niagara, Paris, London, Chatham, Sarnia, Stratford–Huron, Bruce–Maitland
Manitoba & NW Ontario	Superior, Lake of the Woods, Winnipeg, Brandon
Saskatchewan	Assiniboia, Northern Saskatchewan
Alberta	Peace River, Edmonton, Red Deer, Calgary–Macleod
British Columbia	Kootenay, Kamloops, Westminster, Vancouver Island

When searching for your roots among Presbyterian records, it must be remembered that, apart from the obvious BMD registers, some information can also be found in communion rolls and Sunday school lists. These are more plentiful in the Archives than the registers themselves. They will not give you information about specific dates, but they may help you in filling some gaps.

| The Society of Friends (Quakers)

The Society first held meetings in Canada towards the end of the eighteenth century. The archives are located at 60 Lowther Avenue, Toronto, ON M5R 1C7, but are of limited value. There are records of meetings, some books, and a few registers from meetings in Ontario:

> Norwich, BMD, 1842–
> Pelham, BMD, 1790–1867
> Pickering, BMD, 1845–74
> West Lake, MD, 1829–66
> Yarmouth, M, 1859–1974
> Yonge Street, BD, 1803–66, M 1804–40, 1859–97 (including
>   Hicksite marriages, 1828–51)

A visit to the archives is essential because records and registers for various Meetings are intermingled. There were also many schisms, and the records of one schism may include BMD in the "records" while in another they may be in the "registers". These complications are not exactly hunter-friendly!

At the present time, Meetings of the Society of Friends are being held in the following places in Canada:

Annapolis Valley, NS	Lucknow, ON	Thousand Islands, ON
Calgary, AB	Revelstoke, BC	Toronto, ON
Greely, ON	Sackville, NB	Vancouver, BC
Guelph, ON	St. John's, NF	Vernon, BC
Halifax, NS	Sault Ste. Marie, ON	Victoria, BC
Hamilton, ON	Simcoe, ON	Winnipeg, MB
Kitchener, ON	South Shore, NS	Wolfville, NS
Lobo, ON	Sparta, ON	Woodstock, NB
London, ON	Stratford, ON	

(Genealogical queries — initial fee $5.00 — should be sent to Friends Historical Collection, Pickering College, Newmarket, ON L3Y 4X2)

Remember, because of schisms in the past and separate meetings, burials took place in two separate cemeteries.

A sect called the Hicksites split off in 1828, and in 1880 the Fast Friends broke away and held their own meetings. These splits were caused by divisions of opinion between conservatives and liberals. The three sections were eventually reconciled and today there is only one Society of Friends. A number of meetings have been discontinued during the past ten years, and you should check at the above address as to the location of the registers. It has not been possible to obtain more detailed information.

| United Church

The Church was formed in 1925 by the merger of the Congregational, Methodist, and Presbyterian churches (except that forty per cent of the congregations of the latter church, and a few from the other two, did not enter the merged United Church).

Before the merger, not much had been done by the three churches so far as the establishment of archives was concerned. All three had started, in a very haphazard way, to collect odds and ends of material between 1917 and 1919, but practically no funds were allocated for this work. The collections continued over the years on a very hit-and-miss basis.

When the United Church came into being, the situation did not change very much, and in the general confusion following the merger a great deal of valuable material was lost. When local churches were merged, many elderly ministers retired, and some took the registers with them. Some were later recovered, but others simply disappeared after the death of the minister.

After the merger, attempts were begun to bring all the records and registers of the three churches into one archive, but this took a great deal of time, and there was also a great deal of opposition. The situation was further complicated by the refusal of the authorities of the dissident Presbyterian Church to hand over records. It was not until 1946 that this particular hurdle was overcome. The intervening twenty years since the unification had witnessed the disappearance of more records. By 1953 the Central Archives of the United Church were established at the University of Toronto (73 Queen's Park Crescent, Toronto, ON M5S 1K7).

The staff at the Archives emphasize that they are concerned with all aspects of Church work, and are not a centre for genealogical research, but they encourage genealogists to visit the premises to do their research. The staff do not answer queries by mail or by telephone, but if you ask a specific question such as "Do you have the church registers of the Presbyterian Church in Fountainhead, in Ontario, for 1877?" they will give you an answer. If it is "Yes," you will be welcome to visit the

Archives without any appointment and do your own searching. (The office is open from 0900 hours to 1700 hours Monday to Friday. The telephone number is [416] 585-4563.)

Strangely enough the Archives cannot supply a list of the church registers in their custody, but will provide brief information about a particular community. Dr. Neil Semple, the United Church Archivist, speaking in 1984, said, "Concerning local church records, most records are either no longer extant or are held in local congregations. We have the records of the churches that chose to send them to us. We have no way of knowing what records are still in the local congregations." So now you know.

Among the holdings at the Central Archives are:

1. The central baptismal register of the Wesleyan Methodist Church indexed by township. A similar register on a more limited scale is available for the Methodist Episcopal Church, which was largely centred in south-western Ontario.
2. The Perkins Bull Collection, which includes details of cemetery records in Peel County, Ontario.
3. A large number of histories of local churches and the leading members of the congregation.
4. A number of complete runs of church newspapers and magazines. There is an ongoing project to abstract names mentioned and index them. Quite a number of births, marriages, and deaths of members were recorded in these publications, which include the *Christian Guardian* and the *Canada Christian Advocate* (both Methodist publications).

The Archives do not have cemetery records for the nineteenth century, any nominal lists of individual church members, or any records outside Ontario.

If your ancestors are Methodist, you must be prepared to check the available records of the different sects, such as the Methodist Episcopal Church, the British Wesleyan Methodist Church, the Wesleyan Methodist Church in Canada, the Methodist Episcopal Church in Canada, the Methodist New Connexion Church of Canada, the Canadian Wesleyan Methodist Church (this is different from the Wesleyan Methodist Church in Canada), the Protestant Methodist Church, the Bible Christian Church of Canada, and the Primitive Methodist Church in Canada.

There are also eight United Church Conference Archives across the country, and some of these have custody of early registers, as well as miscellaneous information about churches and church members in the areas served by each Conference:

NEWFOUNDLAND: Mr. Burnham Gill, 320 Elizabeth Avenue, St. John's, NF A1B 1T9.

MARITIMES: Mrs. Carolyn Earle, Atlantic School of Theology, Halifax, NS B3H 3B5

MONTRÉAL-OTTAWA: Ms. Susan Stanley, Special Collections, Bishop's University, Lennoxville, PQ J1M 1Z7

ONTARIO (from Montréal–Ottawa Conference): Donald McKenzie, City of Ottawa Archives, 174 Stanley Avenue, Ottawa, ON K1M 1P1

MANITOBA: John H. Baillie, Manitoba Conference Archives, University of Winnipeg, Winnipeg, MB R3B 2E3

SASKATCHEWAN: Dr. Charles Johnston, St. Andrew's College, 1121 College Drive, Saskatoon, SK S7N 0W3

ALBERTA: Keith Stotyn, Alberta Conference Archives, 12845-102 Avenue, Edmonton, AB T5N 0M6

BRITISH COLUMBIA: Bob Stewart, B.C. Conference Archives, School of Theology, 6000 Iona Drive, Vancouver, BC V6T 1J6

CHAPTER 8
Coats of Arms

Have you ever received a letter in the mail offering you "a family coat of arms"? I expect you have, and I hope you did nothing whatever about it, because there is no such thing as a *family* coat of arms. All you will get for your money, at best, is a coat of arms granted at some time in history to someone who had the same surname as you have. At worst, you will receive a coat of arms created for you and to which you have no right.

I must admit I don't really understand this fascination that coats of arms hold for many people. I suppose they think a coat of arms will help them trace their ancestors, or they may think it means they are of royal or noble blood.

Heraldry has no connection with genealogy, and, quite frankly, I had no plans to include a chapter on the subject, but a recent lecture tour showed me that many people do not know anything about the subject and, as a result, are easy prey for get-rich-quick artists in this particular field of human endeavour.

So far as any ancient country is concerned—whether it be England, France, Prussia, Hungary, or Spain, for example—the right to use a particular design as a coat of arms was granted by the ruler of the country to someone who had done him a great service. This service could have been any one of a number of different things: raising a force of men to fight for the king in a rebellion, lending the king money so he could fight a war, providing willing and unwilling ladies for the king's bed, or other even more disreputable activities.

It is most unlikely that an ancestor of yours received such a grant, because the odds are that your ancestors and mine never came into contact with a king and were in no position to do him a favour. They were men and women whose work and life was closely associated with the land — farmers, hedgers, coopers, ostlers, carpenters, sawyers, etc. They had no titles, no great estates, and, certainly, no thoughts about a coat of arms.

How did it all start? The historian Herodotus, writing four hundred years before Christ, said, "The Carians seem to be the first who put crests upon their helmets and sculptured devices upon their shields." From that time on, there have been many references to shields and ornamentations and designs. Once a man had a shield to use in battle, it was a natural development for him to paint a design on it so that it was recognizable and other men would be able to identify him.

In the Middle Ages, everyone fought — the knight because knights were expected to fight, or because he owed allegiance to the king, or because he wanted the estates of his next-door neighbour, or even his neighbour's lovely daughter. The ordinary man fought because the knight owned him and told him what to do. When armour was invented, the knights wore it, and then came helmets, and finally a visor which covered the face but left slits through which the knight could see. The only problem about this development was that every knight looked like every other knight, since his face could not be seen. He then started to wear a linen surcoat over his armour, and his men wore the same thing over their suits of chain-mail. Originally, it was to prevent the armour from getting wet and rusty in damp climates, or too hot in hot climates. The next step was to decorate the surcoat with a symbol so that each man knew who was for him and who was against him. Usually the symbol was taken from the arms of the knight or earl or king who owned the soldiers. Thus the surcoat became the coat of arms.

This was the time when chivalry was in vogue, and there were tournaments and tilting and jousting and all the other knightly pursuits. The simple coat of arms worn by the simple soldiers moved up the social scale, and the right of anyone to have his own arms became the gift of the king. The right was granted to a particular individual and not to a family, and was for him and "his heirs in the male line". This means that this person, and his son, and his grandson, and so on, are the only ones with a right to use a particular coat of arms.

If your name is Adams and you send away for a "family coat of arms", you will probably get one that was granted to a man named Adams who owned vast estates in the Middle Ages, or who might have sold inferior uniforms to an army in a war and been knighted for his services to his country. In any case, they almost certainly were not ancestors of yours in the direct line.

There are all sorts of by-products that will be offered to you. You can buy a 48-piece dinner service, or a tastefully designed shield, or book matches with your coat of arms, or lampshades, book-plates and bookmarks, and notepaper, or wineglasses, and silverware, and tankards, and decals for the car and the boat, and flags and pennants, and lots of other items. You name it — they have it!

Of course, you may have a similar experience to one lady who spoke to me at one of my lectures. She sent off for a shield and in due course it arrived. Varnished wood, about 15 cm × 8 cm, with the coat of arms and above it a scroll with the words "The Blank Family". She was delighted, and she wrote to her two brothers — one in Calgary and one in California — and told them about it. They both sent off their twenty dollars and both received shields with the Blank Family coat of arms. There was only one problem — as they later discovered. They had three totally different coats of arms among the three of them!

However, if you are of English descent and want to have a genuine coat of arms created for you personally, and absolutely genuine, you can arrange this with the College of Arms in London, and it will cost you about $3000. If your ancestry is Scots or Irish, similar arrangements can be made with the Lord Lyon and the Ulster King of Arms. I regret that Wales does not have its own heraldic official, but your problems — if you are of Welsh descent — will be dealt with by a Pursuivant in the College of Arms called Rouge Dragon.

As you trace your ancestry back, it is just *possible* you will discover that a direct male ancestor was granted the right to a coat of arms, so I had better tell you a little about heraldry.

In England the College of Arms is responsible for proving the right to a coat of arms, and also for granting it. The office is headed by the Duke of Norfolk, who is hereditary Earl Marshal. Employment at the College is in great demand among those interested in heraldry, although the rate of pay is nominal. Of course, members of the staff can also obtain income from the tracing and proving of the right of your ancestors to have a coat of arms—proving your descent from an armigerous family, as it is called.

The more important officials have some romantic and almost fairy-tale names; the origin goes back into the mists of the Middle Ages when knights were bold and all ladies were fair. In the hierarchy of the College, the Earl Marshal is followed by the Kings of Arms, the Heralds of Arms, and the Pursuivants of Arms. There are three Kings: Garter (who is the Earl Marshal's deputy), Clarenceux (who is responsible for heraldry in the area south of the River Trent), and Norroy (whose area is north of the river). There are six Heralds—Chester, Windsor, Lancaster, York, Richmond, and Somerset—and four Pursuivants—Rouge Croix, Blue Mantle, Rouge Dragon, and Portcullis.

In Scotland the equivalent of the Earl Marshal is the Lyon King of Arms, known as the Lord Lyon, or "The Lyon". His office is not hereditary and the appointment is made by the Crown. There are three Heralds—Ross, Rothesay, and Albany —and three Pursuivants—Unicorn, Falkland, and Carrick.

The Office of Arms in Ireland is headed by the Ulster King of Arms. Under him are a Pursuivant, named Athlone, and two Heralds, Dublin and Cork.

In Europe, although coats of arms go back as far as or further than they do in the United Kingdom, no institution similar to the College of Arms exists. However, in Austria, Belgium, Germany, the Netherlands, Norway, Spain, and Sweden there are various non-governmental offices that regulate the use of coats of arms.

A coat of arms consists of a shield bearing the heraldic device of the family. It can be divided into quarters, and still further subdivided to include the arms of families whose daughters married into the family. All these divisions are called quarterings, and there is at least one family in England whose shield bears no fewer than 356 quarterings (the Lloyds of Stockton-on Cherbury, Shropshire).

Above the shield is the Helmet, or Helm, and that is surmounted by a Wreath (or Torse) and a Crest. The latter is often something like a mailed fist clutching a sword, or a boar's head. A kind of drapery, called the mantling, comes out from the helmet and hangs down on each side of the shield. Below the shield is the motto, usually in Latin. This can be a play on words that includes the name of the family, or some worthy expression of opinion, such as *In Recto Acer* (Vigorous in pursuit of the right).

If you can find no mention of a coat of arms in your ancestral research, but still want to make sure, you can write to one of the heraldic offices I have mentioned in the appropriate country and ask them what it would cost to check their records for you. You will be charged a fairly large fee. I think you will be spending your money on something very unimportant in modern life but to each his or her own fetish!

CHAPTER 9
Alberta

The foregoing chapters have outlined the process of genealogical research, described the primary sources, and generally
pointed you in the right direction. With this chapter, we begin
a detailed, province-by-province listing of sources that you can
use—a reference manual that should take you about as far as
it's possible to go in searching for your roots in Canada.

The early history of the province, which was originally part
of the enormous territory granted to the Hudson's Bay Company in 1670, was dominated by the fur trade. The traders
arrived from the upper Great Lakes long before Sir Alexander
Mackenzie crossed the region in 1793 on his epic journey to the
Pacific. As a matter of fact, in 1794 the Company built a fort
on the site of what is now the capital city of Edmonton. It was
destroyed by the Indians in 1807 and rebuilt in 1819. It served
traders and missionaries until 1857.

The area remained under the control of the HBC until 1870,
when it and the other areas which are now Manitoba and
Saskatchewan were sold by the Company to the Canadian government. In 1872 the North West Mounted Police established
Fort Macleod in southern Alberta, and in 1873 the force built
a log fort on the site of present-day Calgary.

In 1882 an Act of Parliament created four administrative
divisions from the Northwest Territories, and one was named
Alberta. The railway came through in the mid-1880s, opening
up the area to settlement. Europeans and Americans began the
invasion. Edmonton boomed during the 1898 Klondike gold-

rush, when it served as a supply base for the prospectors heading north.

This was the period of Alberta's greatest expansion of settlement. In 1886 the first Mormon settlers, led by Charles Card,
arrived in what is now the Cardston area. They had come from
Utah and were followed by others over the next few years; by
1901 over three thousand Mormons were settled in Alberta. In
1889 parties of Germans settled in Medicine Hat. Their ancestors had left Austria after religious persecution and had settled
in Galicia, but eventually they moved to Canada. They were
followed by many other groups and most settled in the areas
near Stony Plain, Horse Hills, and Fort Saskatchewan.

In 1892 there was a considerable influx of settlers from various areas: Moravians from Volhynia; Norwegians and Swedes
from Minnesota and the Dakotas; Danes and Icelanders from
Europe; Ukrainians from Galicia and the Bukovina; French
from Québec and France; and the "Parry Sounders" from
Ontario—fleeing not persecution but poor soil.

The vast, unsettled lands of Alberta were filling up as the
immigrants spread out from the railway tracks into land that
had hitherto been trodden only by nomadic Indians. The Peace
River district was first settled in 1903, and by 1906 — a year
after Alberta entered Confederation — such settlements as
Lethbridge, Wetaskiwin, and Medicine Hat were thriving
cities.

The population of 30,000 in 1895 had reached 73,000 by 1901,
and 185,000 by 1906. Alberta was the fastest-growing area in
the West.

| Civil Registration

The official recording of births, marriages, and deaths in what
is now Alberta started in 1897, but these records are not complete before 1905. In the very early days of civil registration
there were omissions caused by isolation from centres of population, and resistance to the legislation—"What has it to do
with the government?" This resistance was not peculiar to
Alberta—it existed right across the country.

There are a few birth records dating back to 1853 and deaths
to 1893. All the records are in the custody of the Director of
Vital Statistics, Texaco Building, 10130-112th Street, Edmonton, AB T5K 2K4. For genealogical purposes, birth records are
available to members of the subject's family, and marriage

records to the persons mentioned in the registration; there is no restriction on death records. Descendants of persons mentioned can obtain certificate copies by proving descent. A fee is payable.

| Provincial Archives

These are located at 12845-102nd Avenue, Edmonton, AB T5N 0M6 (telephone [403] 427-1750). The Archives are open Monday to Friday, 0900 hours to 1630 hours (until 2100 hours on Wednesday). Owing to space limitations, all records are not available immediately—some have to be transferred from storage in other parts of the city and it may take as long as two days to produce them. An advance letter or telephone call is advisable.

The Archives contain a great deal of material, but it is not all of value to the ancestor-hunter. The main genealogical documents are listed below:

Homestead Records

These files from various government departments contain information about every homesteader in the province. The ledgers list the location of the first settlers in each quarter section from 1883 to 1930. Records since that year are still with the Department of Energy and Natural Resources, but they may have been transferred by the time you read this. The records are on microfilm and are arranged numerically, with an alphabetical name guide to land location.

Land Transaction Records

These date from 1884 to 1912 and contain a record of all property transfers within the province.

Dominion Fiats

These cover the period from 1882 to 1930 and give details of notices from the various land title offices to the federal government. These notices advised which titles to homesteads could now be awarded to particular homesteaders.

Sheriffs' Summonses

These are listed chronologically and give details of all individuals in Alberta from 1923 to 1935 who were served by sheriffs on behalf of parties trying to clear a debt.

There are a number of other available records which are not of general interest but may be of vital importance to particular individuals:

Tax arrears, 1921–69
Foreclosures, 1918–54
Inquests, 1885–1928
Court records, 1881–1971
Divorce records, 1911–72
Changes of name, 1916–50
Disability pensions, 1870–1974
Indian annuity payments, 1910–80
Hospital registrations, 1921 to present date
Employment service papers, 1920–41
School attendance lists, 1913–19

The following records require more explanation:

Deceased soldiers' files, 1919–25
(These are in alphabetical order and refer to soldiers killed in the First World War. There is information about place of residence and family members.)
Proof-of-age records
(These refer to persons born outside the province who applied for pensions between 1900 and 1950. Given are place of birth, place of residence, occupation, and relatives.)
Alberta Golden Jubilee, 1955
(In this year illuminated scrolls were given to people who were residents of the province before 1905 and were still living there.)
Old-timers' clippings, 1956–59
(These are press references to Albertans who settled in the province before 1905.)
Vital-statistics registrations
(Official registrations of all marriages taking place in Alberta from 1895 to 1902. Ages, places of residence, occupations, and parents are listed. At the present time, this collection is restricted, pending written permission from the Director of Vital Statistics, but this may change at any moment. The Provincial Archivist has authority to acquire all marriage registrations 75 years and older, all registrations of birth 100 years and older, and certain death registrations. Transfer of these records to the Archives may have taken place by now.)

| The Glenbow Library and Archives

This superbly organized institution is located at 130-9th Avenue SE, Calgary, AB T2G 0P3. The genealogical holdings include the following:

Directories

North West Territories and rural Alberta for 1890, 1899, 1900, 1911, 1914, 1920, 1922, and 1928. City directories for Calgary from 1910; Edmonton from 1910; Lethbridge, 1948–57; Medicine Hat, 1913–25, 1952–55; Moose Jaw, 1939–53.

Homestead Maps

1917/18 to 1923, and 1927.

Local Histories

These are from many localities and contain mention of early settlers and families prominent in the development and settlement of the area.

Newspaper Clippings

These date back to the end of the last century and contain obituaries, awards, etc.

All the above items are located in the Library. The holdings in the Archives are:

Newspapers on Microfilm

These are mostly from major communities in Alberta, Manitoba, and Saskatchewan:

ALBERTA
Blairmore Enterprise, 1908–48, 1972–77
Calgary Daily News, 1907–18
Calgary Herald, 1883–1954
Calgary News-Telegram, 1907–18
Calgary Tribune, 1885–1906
Cardston News, 1925–49, 1952–72
Edmonton Bulletin, 1880–1923, 1947–51
Edmonton Journal, 1905–38
The Eye-Opener, 1902–22
Morning Albertan, 1906–38
Fort Macleod Gazette, 1882–1906, 1907, 1931–81
Hanna Herald, 1912–81

High River Times, 1905–41
Lethbridge Herald, 1905–45
Lethbridge News, 1885–1906
Medicine Hat News, 1894–1939
Medicine Hat Times, 1885–94
Pincher Creek Echo, 1906, 1915–80
Strathmore Standard, 1909–48
Victoria Daily Colonist, 1858–71

MANITOBA
The Nor'Wester (Red River Settlement), 1859–69
Winnipeg Daily Times, 1879–85
Winnipeg Tribune, 1890–1913

SASKATCHEWAN
Moose Jaw News, 1884–85
Moose Jaw Times-Herald, 1890–99
Regina Leader, 1883–1906
Regina Leader-Post, 1903–13
Saskatchewan Herald (Battleford), 1870–1900
Western Producer (Saskatoon), 1924–40

NORTHWEST TERRITORY
News of the North (Yellowknife), 1945–74

Directories on Microfilm
Henderson's Gazetteer & Directory
Manitoba and NWT, 1881–82, 1884, 1886–1901, 1905–08

Family Histories
Many of these, in published and MS form, have been deposited but are unlisted.

Canada Immigration Branch
Seventy-one microfilm reels of original records from the National Archives in Ottawa, detailing the operations of the Branch in the West from 1884 to 1952.

CPR Land Settlement Records
These are in manuscript form and in 229 volumes. They detail land sales in rural areas and in townsites. The rural volumes give area of land, payment due, and payments made. The townsite volumes include date, lot, purchaser, price, contract number, and deeds.

Cemetery Records
These are from the following places: Airdrie, Banff, Bergen, Big Prairie, Calgary (five locations), Camrose, Champion, Eagle Valley, Haneyville, Lille, Lobley, Morley, Okotoks, Pine Creek, Stony Indians (Wesley), Strathmore, Sundre, and T. Westcott United Church.

Photographs
Most of these are indexed and are of individuals, families, and Albertan scenes.

Oral History Interviews
These are with pioneers, mainly in the southern part of the province.

So much for the provincial and Glenbow archives—a great deal of material of vital importance. It seems a pity it is not all under one roof.

| Census Returns

Although censuses have been held in various parts of Canada since 1666 and nation-wide since 1851 (Upper and Lower Canada), they are not open to public inspection after 1891. Since Alberta was not in existence then, and the whole area was largely unsettled, there are very few census returns available. Those that are are on microfilm in the National Archives in Ottawa, and may be borrowed through your nearest public library with a microfilm-viewer. The places listed are:

Banff, Battle River, Calgary, Canmore, Coal Mine, Davisburgh, Edmonton, Fish Creek, Fort Saskatchewan, Gleichen, High River, Lac La Biche, Lethbridge, McLeod, Morley, Namaka, Pine Creek, Pincher Creek, Red Deer, Rosebud, St. Albert. (All these are for 1891. There are a few returns in 1881 for Edmonton and Peace River.)

| Wills

All wills probated in Alberta are retained in the Courthouse of the Judicial District in which probate was granted. For a small fee a search can be made in the office of the Surrogate Court. The offices are located as follows:

Judicial Districts	*Address*
Calgary	611-4th Street SW, Calgary, AB T2P 1T5
Camrose	5210-49th Avenue, Camrose, AB T5V 3Y2
Canmore	800 Access Road, Canmore, AB T0L 0M0
Drumheller	511-3rd Avenue West, Drumheller, AB T0J 0Y0
Edmonton	1a Sir Winston Churchill Square, Edmonton, AB T5J 0R2
Fort Macleod	PO Box 1360, Fort Macleod, AB T0L 0Z0
Fort McMurray	9700 Franklin Avenue, Fort McMurray, AB T9H 4E3
Fort Saskatchewan	10540-100 Avenue, Fort Saskatchewan, AB T8L 3S9
Grande Prairie	10260-99 Street, Grande Prairie, AB T8V 6J4
Hanna	Provincial Building, Centre Street, Hanna, AB T0J 1P0
High Level	PO Box 1560, High Level, AB T0H 1Z0
High Prairie	Sports Palace (2nd floor), High Prairie, AB T0G 1E0
Hinton	237 Jasper Street West, Hinton, AB T0E 1B0
Leduc	PO Box 430, Leduc, AB T9E 2Y2
Lethbridge	320-4th Street South, Lethbridge, AB T1J 1Z8
Medicine Hat	460-1st Street SE, Medicine Hat, AB T1A 7E9
Peace River	Bag 900-34, Peace River, AB T0H 2X0
Red Deer	4909-48th Avenue, Red Deer, AB T4N 3T5
St. Albert	3 St. Anne Street, St. Albert, AB T8N 2E8
Sherwood Park	190 Chippewa Road, Sherwood Park, AB T8A 4H5
Stony Plain	4711-44th Avenue, Stony Plain, AB T0E 2G0
Vegreville	4904-50th Street, PO Box 1812, Vegreville, AB T0B 4L0
Vermilion	4701-52nd Street, PO Box 149, Vermilion, AB T0B 4M0
Wetaskiwin	4605-51st Street, Wetaskiwin, AB T9A 1K7

(All letters should be addressed to the Courthouse at the above addresses, except for Edmonton, where it should be the Law Courts Building.)

| Land Titles

These can be searched at the Land Titles Offices in Edmonton and Calgary for the Northern and Southern Districts respectively. (The province is divided into two parts; that portion north of the ninth correction line is the Northern District, and that portion south of Innisfail is the Southern.) A small fee will be charged for a search for any document. The addresses are:

10365-97th Street, Edmonton, AB T5J 3W7
620-7th Avenue SW, Calgary, AB T2P 0Y8

Letters should be addressed to The Registrar, Land Titles Office.

| Genealogical Societies

There are two of these in Alberta, which seems a duplication of effort, but details of both and their activities are:

Alberta Family History Society, Box 30270, Station B, Calgary, AB T2M 4P1. This society has no branches in the province. It has published bibliographical guides to sources in Calgary libraries for English, Scottish, Irish, and German genealogy. Its major ongoing project is the copying and indexing of cemetery inscriptions for Airdrie, Banff, Beiseker, Bergen, Bergthal, Big Prairie, Blackie, Carstairs, Cochrane, Cremona, Didsbury, Eagle Valley, Hainstock, High River, Irricana, Lobley, Mennonite, Midnapore, Okotoks, Olds, Pine Creek, Strathmore, Sundre, Rosebud, and Westcott. (For a small fee a photo-copy of a burial record can be supplied, if you provide the surname and the name of the cemetery.)

Alberta Genealogical Society, PO Box 12015, Edmonton, AB T5J 3L2. This Society has seven branches, located in the following places:
Brooks: PO Box 1538, Brooks, AB T0J 0J0
Edmonton: PO Box 754, Edmonton, AB T5J 2L4
Fort McMurray: (in process of formation)
Grande Prairie: PO Box 1257, Grande Prairie, AB T8V 4Z1
Lethbridge: PO Box 1001, Lethbridge, AB T1J 4A2

Medicine Hat: PO Box 971, Medicine Hat, AB T1A 7G8
Red Deer: PO Box 922, Red Deer, AB T4N 5H3
Wetaskiwin: PO Box 84, Millet, AB T0C 1Z0

The Society publishes cemetery recordings made by its members; this is the major project at the moment, and it is now being expanded to include other vital statistics, such as baptisms and marriages, when they are available from the church to which a cemetery might be attached. It also has a quarterly magazine called *Relatively Speaking* which contains articles and information of great value to the ancestor-hunter with an Albertan background.

The Society, in its own library in Edmonton, has one of the best collections of any genealogical society I know. There are local histories covering such places as Battle River country, Bon Accord, Byley and district, Cadogan, Cairns, Camrose, Carbon, Delia, Farrell Lake, Glassford, Hillcrest, Lafond, Lethbridge, Majestic, Manyberries, Metiskow, Minda, New Home, Orion, Peavine, and Ranchville.

You will also find fairly recent telephone and local directories, and there are copies of cemetery inscriptions from such localities as Bruderheim Moravian Cemetery, Calgary Union Cemetery, and St. Paul's Church Cemetery at Agricola.

Best of all, there are over a hundred booklets and leaflets of cemetery inscriptions covering a wide area of the province. If you would like a complete list of these, you should send $1 to the Society to cover the cost of postage and photo-copying. If, for example, you are interested in Scandia (near Brooks), the cemetery leaflet will cost you $1.75, including postage. Perhaps you are interested in Bassano; that list is a much bigger one, with many more names, and this will cost you $8.40. In either case you may find it one of the best investments you have ever made.

The Church of Jesus Christ of Latter-Day Saints (the LDS Church)

As I mentioned in Chapter 4, the records and files of the LDS Church are an absolute essential for the ancestor-hunter. Access to all the material is as near as your nearest LDS Church Family History Library, and there are eight of these in Alberta; they are located at Calgary, Cardston, Edmonton, Grande Prairie, Lethbridge, Raymond, Red Deer, and Taber.

| Cemeteries

Nearly all the towns and villages in the province have municipal cemeteries in addition to church burial-grounds. There are also a number of small disused graveyards; these are the so-called homestead, or settlement, or pioneer cemeteries, and they were usually located where the boundaries of several farms met. Many of these have disappeared or have been ploughed under, but the Alberta Genealogical Society is working hard to list the inscriptions in the remaining ones before time and neglect mean they too will disappear.

The Cemetery Office in Edmonton (12420-104th Street) has burial records for the three Edmonton cemeteries, and there are also other cemeteries in the city, such as the Catholic Cemetery (11237 Jasper Avenue); the Jewish Cemetery (7622-101st Avenue); and the Ukrainian Cemetery (at 137th Avenue and 82nd Street). A letter to the superintendent of any of these cemeteries will give you information about the burial of a particular person. Remember to ask about any information given to them by the person arranging the burial. This is usually on record and can often include details such as address at time of death, cause of death, and name and address of next of kin. In Calgary the Cemetery Office is located at 3425-4th Street NW.

| Church Registers

The first missionaries—Catholics and Wesleyan Methodists— arrived in what is now Alberta in the early 1840s. Originally the main object of mission work was the conversion of Native peoples, but with the arrival of white settlers in increasing numbers the aims of the churches changed. As small urban settlements sprang up, churches and chapels were established. The earliest churches were soon followed by other denominations, including Anglicans, Congregationalists, Lutherans, Presbyterians, and Unitarians.

Realizing the importance of preserving church records — mainly for historical and social studies, and, to a lesser degree, for people tracing their ancestors—the government of Alberta entered into agreements with the various denominations. Under the terms that were negotiated, the denominations designated the Provincial Archives as the official repository for their records. However, you must understand that "records" may or may not include registers. In fact, the various churches seem to be more anxious to unload records than they do registers. The present position is as follows:

Anglican
The Archives hold *records* for three dioceses of this Church: Athabasca, Edmonton, and Mackenzie River (now incorporated in the Diocese of the Arctic). The University of Calgary has the *records* of the Diocese of Calgary in its Rare Books and Special Collections Library. Not all congregations are depositing records, and only a few of the registers deposited pre-date civil registration.

Catholic
A fair amount of record material has been deposited, but only one register.

Lutheran
Some records of disbanded congregations have been lodged in the Archives, and a few from existing congregations, but none pre-date civil registration.

Presbyterian
The Alberta Synod of this church was founded in 1925 by congregations unwilling to join the newly formed United Church. Some record material has been deposited, but no registers.

United
A number of registers are now in the Archives, but only a few pre-date the foundation of the province.

The church registers of the various denominations held in various archives and pre-dating civil registration are given below:

Church	Denomination	Dates	Archives
Athabasca (All Saints)	A	BMD 1893–1950	AA
Athabasca (St. Matthew)	A	BMD 1893–	AA
Banff (St. George)	A	BMD 1897–	LUC
Blackfalds	M	BMD 1903–33	AA
Bow River Circuit	M	BMD 1904–12	AA
Calgary (Cathedral)	A	BMD 1883–	GLA
Calgary (St. Dunstan)	A	B 1897– M 1901	LUC
Calgary (Knox)	P	BMD 1884–	GLA

Church	Denomination	Dates	Archives
Camrose	M	BMD 1904–	GLA
Canmore (St. Michael)	A	BMD 1892–	LUC
Clover Bar	M	BMD 1902–	AA
Cochrane (All Saints)	A	BMD 1892–	LUC
Davisburg	P	BMD 1890–	AA
De Winton (Sts. Philip/James)	A	B 1897–	GLA
Duffield Indian Reserve	M	BMD 1892–	AA
Edmonton (Knox)	P	BMD 1890–	AA
Edmonton (McDougall)	M	BMD 1855–73, 1879–94	AA
Edmonton (Grace)	M	BMD 1905–	AA
Edmonton (All Saints)	A	BMD 1893–1915	AA
Edmonton (Oblates)	CA	BMD 1842–	AA
Edmonton (Strathcona)	A	BMD 1895–1915	AA
Fort Chipewyan (St. Paul)	A	BMD 1871–1952	AA
Fort Norman (Holy Trinity)	A	B 1859– M 1882– D 1887–	AA
Fort Saskatchewan	M	BMD 1899–	AA
Fort Vermilion	A	BMD 1871–1949	AA
Fort Wrigley (St. Philip)	A	B 1881– M 1893– D 1900–	AA
Gleichen (St. Andrew)	A	BMD 1886–	LUC
Hay River (St. Peter)	A	BMD 1893–	AA
High River	P	BMD 1903–10	AA
Hobbema (Samson)	UC	B 1899– M 1903–	GLA
Lacombe (St. Cyprian)	A	BM 1901–	LUC
Lesser Slave Lake	A	BMD 1887–1941	AA
Livingstone (St. Martin)	A	B 1903– M 1899–	LUC
Midnapore (St. Paul)	A	BM 1895–	GLA
Millarville (Christ Ch.)	A	BM 1895–	GLA
Morley	M	BMD 1884–1906	AA
Namao	M	BMD 1900–08	AA
Okotoks	M	BMD 1895–1932	AA
Peace River (St. James)	A	BMD 1881–1936	AA
Pincher Creek	P	B 1889– MD 1905–24	AA
Priddis	P	B 1895–1922	AA
Red Willow	M	BMD 1905–31	AA
Tofield	P	BMD 1899–1907	AA
Vegreville	M	BMD 1901–40	AA
Wabamun	M	BMD 1904–55	AA
Wetaskiwin	A	BMD 1894–1925	AA

In addition to the above registers from specific churches, the Provincial Archives also have the personal registers of several travelling ministers:

McDougall (Methodist), 1855–73
McKitrick (Methodist), 1894–1927
Nicholson (Methodist), 1894–1910
Pow (Presbyterian), 1904–56
Schrog (Congregational), 1905–27

The under-mentioned parishes of the Anglican Church were in existence in Alberta before civil registration of births, marriages, and deaths:

DIOCESE OF ATHABASKA: Fort Chipewyan, Lesser Slave Lake, Smoky River, Vermilion, Wabiskaw, White Fish Lake.
DIOCESE OF CALGARY: Banff, Blackfoot Reservation, Blood Reservation, Bowden, Calgary, Canmore, Fish Creek, Gleichen, Innisfail, Lacombe, Lamerton, Lethbridge, Macleod, Mitford, Piegan Reservation, Pincher Creek, Poplar Lake, South Edmonton, Wetaskiwin.

The following parishes of the Catholic Church were in existence in Alberta before civil registration:

DIOCESE OF CALGARY: Banff, Canmore, Coalhurst, Cochrane, Fort Macleod, Lethbridge, Pincher Creek.
DIOCESE OF ST. PAUL: La Biche, Le Goff, Morinville, Saddle Lake.
DIOCESE OF EDMONTON: Beaumont, Hobbema, Lac Ste. Anne, Lamoureux, Leduc, St. Albert, Stony Plain, Wetaskiwin.

| Public Libraries

There are over 300 public libraries in the province of Alberta, but the resources of many of them are very limited because of lack of adequate funding on both the provincial and the municipal level. In many of the other provinces the local libraries have developed into local archives, with their own genealogical projects such as indexing census returns, listing local cemetery inscriptions, and abstracting and indexing names in local newspapers. In Alberta these activities seem to be left to the local branches of the Alberta Genealogical Society.

If your ancestors came from Alberta, you should certainly write to the public library in your ancestral place of settlement and ask what information it has about your family. Be sure you send a stamped, self-addressed No. 9 or 10 envelope with your letter, so that you are not a burden on the library funds.

The following libraries have supplied details of some of their books on local history and settlement, and other items of genealogical interest:

Calgary: The local-history collection contains more than 100 local histories of southern Alberta communities. The policy is to concentrate on materials for the city of Calgary, and to a lesser degree on those for the neighbouring areas of the province. Among the items in the collection you will find Calgary newspapers on microfilm (1880s to the present); the area census returns on microfilm; and a number of autobiographies and biographies of settlers in Calgary and district.

The library has on microfiche *Henderson's Manitoba and North West Territories Gazetteer and Directory*, 1881–1907 (this includes Calgary and other Albertan towns); *Gronland's Directory of the City and District of Calgary*, 1902; *Henderson's Calgary City Directory*, 1906–87; *Wrigley's Alberta Directory*, 1920 and 1922; *Henderson's Alberta Directory*, 1911; and the *Directory of Greater Calgary* for 1913. There is also *Henderson's Gazetteer and Directory for Alberta* for 1914, 1924, and 1929.

The emphasis of the collection is on pioneer life, homesteading, and ranching; the Riel Rebellion and the development of the West; missionaries; biographies; local histories; and genealogies.

The staff of the library will do all they can to assist ancestorhunters, but they cannot undertake long searches. They will answer a simple question like "Can you check Henderson's Calgary Directory for 1906 and tell me if you have an Andrew Telford listed, and if so at what address?" If you want a more complicated search of the records, your best course will be to contact the local genealogical branch and work out some arrangement for one of their members to do some research for you. If you visit Calgary, the library is open during normal hours; in addition, a local-history librarian is available for consultation at the following times:

Monday, 1730–2100 hours
Wednesday, 0900–1300 hours
Thursday, 0900–1300 hours
Alternate Saturdays, 0900–1700 hours

Cardston: The public library here is in the centre of a strongly Mormon area, and therefore is probably a little overshadowed so far as genealogical material is concerned. It does, however, have a number of local histories covering such places

as Coutts, Delbonita, Glenwood, Harrisville, Hartley, Hill-
spring, Mountain View, Standoff, and, of course, Cardston, and
also its founder, Charles Ora Card. If you are writing for information, my remarks above about return postage and simple
inquiries apply here as well.

Edmonton: This should be as good a centre as Calgary, but
it certainly is not. It has no archival collection of any kind,
and any requests for information by mail are answered by a
form letter saying, "The Edmonton Public Library is funded
to provide reference service to Alberta residents and we are
therefore returning your letter." So as far as Edmonton is concerned, you must depend for help on the LDS Church Family
History Library or the local genealogical society.

Fort Saskatchewan: Here in this most historic of towns
there is, as you may imagine, a deep sense of the past and a
determination to remember it. The library has, on microfilm,
41 rolls recording six local newspapers from 1903 to 1984, and,
in addition, many Alberta local histories, including a good
number that you are unlikely to find elsewhere and that refer
not only to Fort Saskatchewan but also to areas such as Lamo-
reux, Pakan, Josephburg, and Bardo.

There is also an Historical Society and Museum located at
10104-101st Street.

Medicine Hat: The holdings with the most genealogical
interest are a number of books on local history which give coverage of the district, including Lafond, Elkwater, Schuler, and,
of course, Medicine Hat itself; histories of two early churches,
Salem United and St. Patrick's; details of the Hillcrest Mine
disaster; and a series of newspaper articles and interviews
with senior citizens about the period of settlement from 1912
to 1963.

Be sure you write to the library in the area where your
great-grandfather or great-grandmother homesteaded — you
never know what information you will discover about your family. All libraries are not like Edmonton's!

CHAPTER 10
British Columbia

Both Great Britain and Spain were rivals for Vancouver Island and the mainland of what is now British Columbia. Their rival claims were settled by the Nootka Convention of 1790. Early in the next century, after Spain had withdrawn from the area, the first explorers from the North West Company reached the coast of what was then to be called New Caledonia and established trading-posts. After the merger of the company with the Hudson's Bay Company in 1821, the latter assumed control.

At this point the northern expansion of the United States became a threat to British interests in the area. The inclusion of California in the Union in 1848 created a flurry of activity further north. In 1849 Vancouver Island became British after a lengthy dispute with the United States and was declared a Crown Colony. Victoria became the capital, and the HBC was granted exclusive trading rights on the island. In return, the Company undertook to sell land to British colonists at a fair price and to devote a proportion of its profits to public works, including roads, bridges, and land clearance. The aim of all this was to build a strong British presence in the area and to stop further U.S. expansion.

In 1851 Sir James Douglas, the chief official of the Company in the West, was appointed governor of the colony and — on paper, at least — severed his connection with the HBC. However, the latter still maintained its dominant position on the island and on the mainland — which remained its property. By 1853 there were 450 settlers in the colony. They became increasingly frustrated by the total control of the HBC over their lives and agricultural production, to say nothing of their hunting and trapping.

The situation on the island changed suddenly in 1858 when gold was discovered in the Fraser Valley on the mainland. At this point Victoria became a centre of great activity as the "jumping-off" point for prospectors arriving from the south, and on the mainland there was a dramatic population increase as the newcomers pressed inland. The colony of British Columbia was officially proclaimed after the Company ceded the area to the Crown. Sir James Douglas became governor of both colonies, with New Westminster as the mainland capital.

By 1860 the prospectors had reached Quesnel, and the interior had been opened up by the construction of the Cariboo Road. In 1862 the settlement of Barkerville became the largest city north of San Francisco and west of Chicago! A year later the area of British Columbia had been extended to 60 degrees north latitude and 120 degrees west longitude. The expansion of the mainland colony continued rapidly.

In 1866 the two colonies were united, with Victoria as the capital, and in 1871 British Columbia joined the Canadian Confederation. The railway reached the coast in 1885, and a long-standing dispute with the United States over the border with Alaska was settled in 1903. British Columbia, as we know it today, had come of age, with firm boundaries, immense wealth, and a prosperous future.

| Civil Registration

This started in 1872, but early records are incomplete. The registers are in the custody of the Director of Vital Statistics, 818 Fort Street, Victoria, BC V8W 1H8. There are a few birth records dating back to 1849. A fee is charged for searching each three-year period, and this includes a certificate if the entry is found.

| Provincial Archives

These are located in the Parliament Buildings, Victoria, BC V8V 1X4. The Archives have not produced any booklet describing their holdings in detail; this is a pity, because they do have a considerable amount of material of value to the ancestor-hunter.

These include a few family histories; city and provincial directories from 1860; telephone directories; a few church registers (listed elsewhere in this chapter); provincial voters' lists from 1863; early newspapers (*Victoria Colonist*, 1858–99; *Cariboo Sentinel*, 1865–75; *Vancouver Daily World*, 1888–1900); indexed newspaper clippings; some family trees; a typescript MS listing farm settlers in the period 1858–71; and marriages by Rev. E. A. Robson from 1881 to 1911.

The staff will answer simple queries, but if a protracted search is required you will be referred to a list of researchers. The Archives are open from 0900 hours to 1700 hours and from 1800 hours to 2200 hours from Monday to Friday. The hours on Saturday and Sunday are 1300 hours to 1700 hours.

| Census Returns

Although censuses have been held across Canada since the last century, and, in Québec, very much earlier, only those of 1881 and 1891 are available for the following places in British Columbia:

1881: Alberni, Barkerville, Burrard Inlet, Cache Creek, Canoe Creek, Cariboo, Cassiar, Clinton, Coast of Mainland (New Westminster), Comox, Cowichan, Esquimalt, Highland, Hope, Kamloops, Keithley, Keithley Creek, Kootenay, Lightning, Lilloet, Lytton, Metchosin, Nanaimo, New Caledonia, New Westminster, Nicola, Noonas Bay North, Northern Interior, Okanagan, Omineca, Osoyoos, Richfield, Saanich, Salt Spring Island, Soda Creek, Sooke Lake, Spences Bridge, Vancouver, Victoria, Western Coast, Williams Lake, and Yale.

1891: These returns are available for the preceding places and for Alexandria, Alkali Lake, Big Bar, Bright, Cape Cook, Cedar, Chase, Cranberry, DeCourcey, Denman Island, Douglas, Douglas Lake, Englishman River, Fort St. John, Gabriola Island, Goldstream, Grand Prairie, Halls Island, Hornby Island, Institutions (in Vancouver, Victoria, and Yale), Kootenay, Kuper Island, Lac La Hache, Lake, Lightning Creek, Mackenzie River (Cariboo), Maple Ridge, Mayne Island, Merritt, Moresby Island, Mountain, Mudge, Naas, Nanoose, Nelson, North Arm, Okanagan Mission, Oyster, Portland Island, Port San Juan, Priest Valley, Prince Rupert, Princeton, Qualicum, Queen

Charlotte Islands, Quesnel, Richmond, Rocky Mountain Portage, Skeena, Sooke, Spallumcheen, Stickeen, Thetis Island, Trout Lake, Union Mines, Wellington, West Shore, and Coast A.

The returns are available on microfilm from the National Archives in Ottawa through the inter-library loan system to any public library with a microfilm-reader. There are also copies in the Provincial Archives and in major libraries such as Surrey, Vancouver, and Victoria. A number of smaller libraries have copies of the census returns for their own local areas; some have been indexed.

Directories

The Archives hold directories of British Columbia from 1889.

Wills

When searching for a will, bear in mind that the odds are your ancestor did not make a will, for a variety of reasons—he or she had no property, he or she died unexpectedly, or it was already known within the family who was to get what! If you do find a will, it may give you information about members of the family and their locations, and even a hint of a possible place of birth—"I leave my gold watch to my youngest brother George of High Spring Farm, Cirencester, England."

You will find wills — if they exist — in the Supreme Court Registry, Law Courts Building, Victoria, BC V8W 1B4; this is the main repository, but you should also check the Succession Duty Department, Parliament Buildings, Victoria, and the Division of Vital Statistics (address given on page 103). Some wills date back to 1867 and you can obtain a photo-copy for a small fee.

Land Records

For information about land records and titles, you should contact one of the seven Land Registry Offices listed below. Original Crown grants are retained by the Lands Branch, Department of Lands, Forests, and Water Resources, Parliament Buildings, Victoria, BC V8V 1X4. So far as the Registry Offices are concerned, it is essential, unfortunately, to provide the legal land description.

KAMLOOPS DISTRICT: 455 Columbia, Kamloops, BC V2C 6K4

NELSON DISTRICT: PO Box 290, Nelson, BC V1L 4E7

NEW WESTMINSTER DISTRICT: 625 Agnes St., New Westminster, BC V3M 1G9

PRINCE GEORGE DISTRICT: PO Box 1840, Prince George, BC V2L 4V8

PRINCE RUPERT DISTRICT: 730-2nd Avenue West, Prince Rupert, BC V8J 1H3

VANCOUVER DISTRICT: 160-800 Hornby Street, Vancouver, BC V6Z 2Z5

VICTORIA DISTRICT: 850 Burdett Avenue, Victoria, BC V8W 1B4

It may also be worth while to check the tax assessment rolls in the custody of the Surveyor of Taxes, Department of Finance, Parliament Buildings, Victoria, for details of land in unincorporated areas.

| Genealogical Societies

The British Columbia Genealogical Society (PO Box 94371, Richmond, BC V6Y 2A8) has only one branch, at Quesnel, but there are informal groups at Langley, Nanaimo, and White Rock.

The Society is among the most active of the Canadian societies. It has a great many publications, some of which are listed below, and a number of ongoing projects. There is a Newspaper Indexing Program which is indexing all the names found in British Columbia newspapers from 1858 to 1872 (up to the start of civil registration). This material has been microfilmed by the LDS Church. In addition, the index will probably be published by the time you read this.

A research group is also indexing parish registers and B.C. history books. Over 100 cemetery inscriptions have been copied — ten per cent of the 1000 cemeteries in the province. The Society also has a Pioneer Registry of people who were either born in, or arrived in, the province before 1900. In addition, there is a Surname Index based on the names of families researched or being researched by Society members. This is published every four years, with a supplement every two years.

The Society will undertake research on a fee basis for genealogists outside the province.

The publications include:

Heads of Households in British Columbia in 1874. This is compiled from early directories and lists names, addresses, and occupations of 15,000 men in that year.

Transcripts of British Columbia Cemeteries. These have been compiled as the result of the labours of many Society members and vary in size from one page to thirty-nine pages, and in price from 25¢ to $4.50. The following places have been covered so far, but the list grows all the time:

Abbotsford, Alexandria, Armstrong (Pelly Family, Lansdowne, Armstrong, and Spallumcheen), Blind Bay, Bridesville & Sidley, Burnaby (St. Stephens), Chase (Chase and Mattey Family), Donald, Edgewater, Fort Langley, Fulford Harbour (Salt Spring, St. Paul's Catholic, St. Mary's Anglican), Gibsons (Seaview, Mount Elphinstone, Cape Scott, and Gibson Family), Goldbridge, Golden (Municipal, Legion, and Henderson), Granite Creek, Greenwood, Harrison Mills, Hills, Lac La Hache (and Felker Family), Langley, Lone Butte, Midway (and Bubar Family), Pender Harbour, Rock Mountain, Rock Creek, Saanich, Soda Creek, Spences Bridge, Stanley, Surrey (St. Helens and St. Oswalds Anglican), Tulameen (and Rabbitt Family), Vananda, and Zeballos.

In addition to the provincial genealogical society there are also a number of other genealogical organizations that operate independently of the provincial society:

Abbotsford Genealogical Club, 1913 Westbury Crescent, Abbotsford, BC V2S 1B9

Chase & District Family History Association, PO Box 64, Anglemont, BC V0E 1A0

Cowichan Valley Genealogical Society, 7361 Bell–McKinnon Road, RR #4, Duncan, BC V9L 3W8

Kamloops Family History Society, PO Box 1162, Kamloops, BC V2C 6H3

Kelowna & District Genealogical Society, PO Box 501, Station A, Kelowna, BC V1Y 7A1

Langley Genealogical Society, 21107-88th Avenue, Langley, BC V3A 6X5

Nanaimo Family History Society, PO Box 1027, Nanaimo, BC V9R 5Z2

Powell River Genealogy Group, PO Box 446, Powell River, BC V8A 5C2

Prince George Family History Society, PO Box 1056, Prince George, BC V2L 4V2

Quesnel Branch BCGS, PO Box 4454, Quesnel, BC V2J 3J4
Revelstoke Genealogy Club, PO Box 309, Revelstoke, BC V0E 2S0
Vernon & District Family History Society, PO Box 1447, Vernon, BC
Victoria Genealogical Society, PO Box 4171, Station A, Victoria, BC V8X 3X8

Note: The addresses given are accurate at the time of writing, but experience has taught me that nothing stays the same with genealogical addresses. If you have difficulty in making contact with any of the above, I suggest you write to the local public library for information (be sure you cover return postage).

Some of the more energetic societies are highlighted below:

Chase and District Family History Association, PO Box 254, Sorrento, BC V0E 2W0. This association serves the areas of Chase, Salmon Arm, and Sorrento. It has local cemetery listings and indexes; copies of local newspapers such as the *Salmon Arm Observer* and the *Shuswap Sun;* and published local histories, such as *Centennial History of Salmon Arm (1885–1912), The Shuswap District, 1886–1969, Chronicles of Whitfield Chase, List of Residents of Chase and Grand Prairie* (now Westwold), 1912–24, and a Chase scrapbook.

Cowichan Valley Genealogical Society, 7361 Bell-McKinnon Road, RR #4, Duncan, BC. There are various publications available which describe this area and its settlement and history. These include *Water over the Wheel (A History of Chemainus);* a number of histories of the Valley by various authors; and histories of Duncan. Further information about them can be obtained from the Society — be sure you include return postage.

Kamloops Family History Society, PO Box 1162, Kamloops, BC. This society does not produce its own publications, but it works closely with the Kamloops Museum and Archives (207 Seymour Street, Kamloops, BC V2C 2E7), which does. These include *Kamloops,* Volume I (up to 1914) and Volume II (1914–45), *Place Names of the Kamloops District, Chase — The Man and the Village, Savona's Ferry, Heritage Kamloops,* and *The West End.* In addition, the Museum has early newspapers on microfilm:

British Columbian, 1861–69
Inland Sentinel, 1880–1916, 1924–87
Standard, 1897–1915, 1920–24
Standard/Sentinel, 1916–19
News, 1965–83
Chase Tribune, 1912, 1914 (a few copies)

The Museum also holds a collection of articles published in local newspapers from 1865 indexed by name; various published histories of local places such as Chase, Savona, Salmon Arm, Sicamous, Vernon, and other communities in the Okanagan and the Cariboo. There are other books, now out of print, that contain a great deal of information about early pioneers and their families; early directories dating from 1874; and a magnificent collection of 10,000 early photographs indexed by name. If your ancestors once lived in the area, you may be able to obtain copies of their photographs. People with roots here are more fortunate than most.

Nanaimo Family History Society, PO Box 1027, Nanaimo, BC V9R 5Z2. This society is recording cemetery inscriptions and death registers for Ladysmith and Nanaimo. BMD notices in the local newspaper from 1876–1900 have been indexed. Future projects include a pioneer registry, copies of church and school registers, and an index of current obituaries.

Quesnel Branch of the BC Genealogical Society, PO Box 4454, Quesnel, BC V2J 3J4. This growing and energetic society is busy compiling a Surname Index of members' interests, and although the membership is small, its holdings include an index of local cemeteries; extracts of BMD from local newspapers; school registers from 1894 to 1950; inscriptions from Barkerville Cemetery; old photographs and newspaper clippings; all back issues of the Society's newsletter; and a large collection of published books about the area held by both the branch and the local public library. These include many about the Cariboo area, Quesnel, Barkerville, Horsefly, and Chilako.

Revelstoke Genealogical Society. None of the members of this society are interested in Revelstoke research! Fortunately for those of you whose ancestors first settled in Revelstoke, there is the Revelstoke and District Historical Association, PO Box 1908, Revelstoke, BC V0E 2S0. The association has a BMD

Index from local newspapers 1894–1900; an index to many of the photographs in the local museum collection; indexes to published local histories; city directories for 1897–99; and a book of reminiscences by senior citizens. The association is anxious to assist researchers — but cover the return postage, please.

Victoria Genealogical Society, PO Box 4171, Station A, Victoria, BC V8X 3X8. This society is probably the least active of all the provincial-capital societies across Canada. It does not appear to have any ongoing projects, holds few meetings, and produces a Surname Index only at occasional intervals. It is explained that "this lack of activity is caused by the fact that only a handful of our 150 members have any British Columbia or Vancouver Island roots."

| Church Registers

Before reading this, please refer to Chapter 7. Listed below are the locations of registers that pre-date civil registration and are now in various archives.

Church	*Denomination*	*Dates*	*Location*
Barkerville	A	BMD 1869–1901	ABC
Bella Coola	UC	B 1880– M 1881–	UCA
Bella Coola	L	BM 1898–1946	ABC
Cedar Hill	A	BMD 1860–	ANG(NW)
Chilliwack	A	BMD 1872–	ANG(NW)
Cowichan	A	BMD 1866–	ABC
Derby	A	BMD 1859–81	ANG(NW)
Douglas	A	BMD 1862–	ANG(NW)
Fort St. James	A	BM 1873–1948	ABC
Fort Simpson	A	BMD 1857–	ANG(NW)
Fort Simpson	W	BMD 1874–1912	ABC
Fort Vancouver	A	BMD 1837–49	ABC
Hope	A	BMD 1861–	ANG(NW)
Kincolith (Indian Mission)	A	MD 1869–1914	ABC
Kuper Island Church	A	BMD 1831–1906	ABC
Lillooet	A	BMD 1861–1917	ABC
Lytton Mission	A	B 1867–1945	ABC
Metlakatla	A	B 1861– M 1863– D 1861–	
			ANG(CA)

Nanaimo	A	BMD 1865–	ABC
New Westminster	WM	BM 1859–96	ABC
New Westminster	A	BMD 1859–	ANG(NW)
Quamichan	A	BMD 1866–1950	ABC
Rupert's Land Diocese	A	BM 1813–90	ABC
Saanich	A	M 1863–80	ABC
Saint Joseph's Mission	A	B 1866–1923 M 1869–1943	
			ABC
Sandwick	A	BMD 1864–	ANG(NW)
Sapperton	A	BMD 1865–	ANG(NW)
Stuarts Lake	A	B 1867–70	ABC
Victoria (St. Andrews)	A	B 1849–99 M 1859–1903	
		D 1871–1924	ABC
Victoria (Christ Church)	A	B 1836–99 M 1837–1905	
		D 1837–1913	ABC
Victoria (Church of Our Lord)	RE	M 1847–1912 D 1874–1912	
			ANG(NW)
Victoria (St. Andrews)	P	BMD 1870–81	ABC
Victoria (First Presbyterian)	P	M 1865–	ABC
Victoria (St. Barnabas)	A	BM 1896–1936	ABC
Yale	A	BMD 1859–1900	ABC

Anglican Church

There are five Anglican Dioceses in British Columbia:

BRITISH COLUMBIA (1859): Holds registers up to 1915.
CALEDONIA (1879): Cannot supply a list of holdings.
CARIBOO (1914): Cannot supply a list of holdings.
KOOTENAY (1899): Holds no registers.
NEW WESTMINSTER (1879): Holds no registers.

As you will realize, only the Diocese of British Columbia was in existence before civil registration. Its parishes are Cadboro Bay, Cedar Hill, Chemainus, Comox, Cowichan, Craigflower, Esquimalt, Lake, Metlakatla, Nanaimo, Port Simpson, Quamichan, Saanich, Saanichton, Salt Spring Island, and Victoria. Other parishes in existence before civil registration but now part of the Diocese of New Westminster are Barkerville, Derby, Douglas, Hope, Lillooet, Lytton, New Westminster, and Vancouver.

Catholic Church

The following parish of this church was in existence before civil registration:

DIOCESE OF NELSON: Kelowna

The registers of the Catholic Church are still in the original parishes. For information about a particular register, write to the church concerned, or to the Archives of the Catholic Diocese of Vancouver, 150 Robson Street, Vancouver, BC V6B 2A7.

United Church

The registers — where they exist — are in the United Church Archives, Queen's Park Crescent East, Toronto, ON M5S 1K7. Inquiries should also be made to the Archives of the United Church (BC Conference), 6000 Iona Drive, Vancouver, BC V6T 1L4.

Other possible sources of information about various denominations are:

Jewish Historical Society, 950 West 41st Avenue, Vancouver, BC V5T 2N7
Baptist Theological College Library, 3358 SE Marine Drive, Vancouver, BC V5S 2H6
Archives of the Presbyterian Church, 59 St. George Street, Toronto, ON M5S 2E6

| Public Libraries

There are some seventy-five public libraries in the province, and, like libraries everywhere, they vary greatly in their genealogical collections — the low point being the Vancouver Public Library and the high point the Surrey Public Library with its quite extraordinary genealogical collection.

Burnaby Public Library, 7252 Kingsway, Burnaby, BC V5E 1G3. This library has some local newspapers on microfilm but they are of recent date, the earliest being the 1926–35 issues of the *Burnaby Broadcast* and the 1935–64 issues of the *Burnaby Advertiser*. The library also holds a number of local histories covering the period from the 1891 survey.

Matsqui–Sumas–Abbotsford Museum Society, 2313 Ware Street, Abbotsford, BC V2S 3C6. This library — part of the Fraser Valley Regional Library System — holds archival documents of local history; collections of MS and taped local histories and genealogies; and an index to the local newspaper — the *ASM News*—from 1923 to 1950 (this is being brought up to the present day).

Penticton Public Library, 785 Main Street, Penticton, BC V2A 5E3. The genealogical collection here consists of various books on local history, many of them containing references to early settlers, but without a combined index. The most valuable ones are the fifty volumes of annual reports of the Okanagan Historical Society. These books started in 1926 and are published each fall. They contain articles on many local subjects, list obituaries, and carry stories about "old-timers". The Penticton Museum has a number of obituaries.

Prince George Public Library, 887 Dominion Street, Prince George, BC V2L 5L1. It has a good local-history collection and a number of newspapers on microfilm: *Fort George Tribune*, 1909–15; *Herald*, 1910–16; *Post*, 1914–15; *Leader*, 1921–23; *Star*, 1916–17; and the *Citizen* from 1916. It also has cemetery inscriptions collected by the local Family History Society, and taped and printed interviews with pioneers of the area, mostly people who arrived in the early 1900s.

Prince Rupert Public Library, 101-6th Avenue West, Prince Rupert, BC V8J 1Y9. The only genealogical record here is the local newspaper (*The Daily News*) on microfilm from 1911 to the present day. It is indexed but includes very few personal names. The library is overshadowed by the City and Regional Archives, 424-3rd Avenue West, Prince Rupert, BC V8J 4H6. These archives include material from Prince Rupert and nearby places such as Port Edward, Port Essington, Metlakatla, Porcher Island, Digby Island, etc. There is a collection of 2000 photographs and 1000 negatives, indexed when the identity is known; city and telephone directories dating back to 1911; high school magazines from 1922; the Borden Street school register from 1913 to 1956; voters' lists from 1942 to 1954 and from 1970 to 1985; a 1909 list of owners of property; a few newspapers from the surrounding area; and records of all buildings and their owners for the years 1913, 1928, 1939, and 1954. The local-history books on the shelves include *Prince Rupert: The Gateway to Alaska* and the many local books of Phyllis Bowman.

Richmond Public Library has no genealogical material, but the *Richmond Municipal Archives*, 6911 No. 3 Road, Richmond, BC V6Y 2C1, have newspaper clippings, oral histories, and a collection of early photographs.

Surrey Centennial Library, Cloverdale Branch, Surrey, BC V3S 4G9. This library has the finest collection of genealogical material in the province — not only local but national — and serves as a model for any library anywhere. It is the work of one remarkable man, Paul Gutteridge, the Librarian. Oddly enough, he himself has no great interest in genealogy. "Most librarians are not interested in genealogists," he said. "It's a lot of bother to have a stream of inexperienced researchers who frequently want the librarians to do their work for them. But I concluded that genealogists were tax-payers, too." As a result of his efforts, the Surrey Collection is truly magnificent. If your ancestors came from Newfoundland or Québec or anywhere in Canada, you will find many items you need in the Surrey Library, in addition to local and provincial material.

I give below the most important local holdings:

Microfilm copies of census returns; passenger lists for Vancouver and Victoria for 1905; passenger-ship arrivals in B.C. ports from 1905 to 1907, including such well-known vessels as the *Empress of China*, the *Empress of Japan*, the *Empress of India*, the *Athenian*, the *Georgia*, the *Umtilla*, the *Indianopolis*, the *Tartar*, and the *Princess Victoria*.

There are Post Office Household Directories for areas in which a commercial directory was not issued. These date from 1972 to 1977 and cover such places as Capilano, Comox-Alberni, Esquimalt, Fraser Valley, Kootenay, Kamloops, Okanagan, and Prince George. There are also directories, maps, atlases, and many other items of lesser value.

City of Trail Archives, 1394 Pine Avenue, Trail, BC V1R 4E6. The Public Library here has no genealogical material, but these archives (which operate by appointment only) have all cemetery records from 1901 to date; Trail newspapers from 1895; voters' lists from 1902; recent city directories; and a very large collection of early photographs.

Vancouver Public Library, 750 Burrard Street, Vancouver, BC V6Z 1X5. Progress here is very, very, very slow. When I was writing my first book, *In Search of Your Roots*, in 1976, I was told by the Librarian: "We have no material of interest to the ancestor-hunter." Today, thirteen years later, the Library now has directories of Vancouver and British Columbia dating back to 1860, and some periodicals and newspapers. They state there is no obituary file, and all archival material is in the Provincial and City Archives and not in the library! Thank heaven for Surrey!

Vancouver Island Regional Library, 6250 Hammon Bay Road, Nanaimo, BC V9R 5N3. This is the headquarters for the thirty-six libraries on Vancouver Island. It holds about 3000 books on local history — too many to list, of course, but if your ancestor settled on the island or on the mainland, and you know the place, you should contact the Regional Library (don't forget the return postage!).

Greater Victoria Public Library, 735 Broughton Street, Victoria, BC V8W 3H2. The library does not have a large genealogical collection, but it has published (for $3 and postage) a bibliography of the holdings. These include Catholic Church records of the Pacific North West, and an Index of Surnames being researched by the British Columbia Genealogical Society.

Glenbow Library & Archives, 130-9th Avenue SE, Calgary, AB T2G 0P3. Although this institution is not located in British Columbia, it does have several items of interest, including the *Victoria Daily Colonist* on microfilm for 1858–71; directories covering the four Western provinces and dating back to 1881; land-settlement records of the Canadian Pacific Railway which include British Columbia.

Other possible sources of genealogical information in British Columbia are:
Special Collections, University of British Columbia Library, 1956 Main Mall, Vancouver, BC V6T 1Y3. The newspaper collection includes those from Chilliwack (1891–1968), from New Westminster (1861–1936, indexed), and the *Dominion Pacific Herald* (1880/81), *Mainland Guardian* (1869–89), *Vancouver News Advertiser* (1887–1917), *Vancouver Province* (1894), *Victoria Colonist* (1859–1912), and *Victoria Daily Chronicle* (1862–66). There are also school records dating back to 1900.

City of Vancouver Archives, 1150 Chestnut Street, Vancouver, BC V6J 3J9. These archives have not produced any booklet about their resources, but they do have card indexes on the premises. Primarily, their holdings date from the foundation of the city in 1886 and are concerned with city government, and not with any provincial or national records. They do have voters' lists on a ward basis and dating back to 1886—partly alphabetical. Other items include a very large indexed photographic collection of people and places; three collections of newspaper clippings which cover the period from 1930 onwards; a number of city directories and local-history books; and the papers of a number of families and Vancouver businesses.

Other sources of information are:

Simon Fraser University Archives, Burnaby, BC V5A 1S6
Victoria City Archives, 613 Pandora Avenue, Victoria,
   BC V8W 1P6
Port Moody Museum, 126 Kyle Street, Port Moody, BC V3H 3N7
Kamloops Museum, 207 Seymour Street, Kamloops, BC V2C 2E7

Finally, be sure you make full use of the records of the Church of Jesus Christ of Latter-Day Saints. Turn back to Chapter 4 and you will understand how essential its records will be for your search. There are six LDS Church Family History Libraries in the province, located in Cranbrook, Fort St. John, Kamloops, Vancouver, Vernon, and Victoria. You will find their full addresses listed in Chapter 4. Any one of these places will give you full access to all the millions (yes, millions!) of records held in Salt Lake City—brought to you by the magic of microfilm, microfiche, and computer.

CHAPTER 11
Manitoba

Originally the area we now call Manitoba (and also the provinces of Alberta, Saskatchewan, and part of British Columbia) was part of the grant to "the Governor and Company of Adventurers of England Trading into Hudson's Bay". The early visitors to the Bay were British sea-captains seeking the Northwest Passage to the Indies and far Cathay. They were followed by the fur-traders, and in 1670 the Company received its charter from Charles II. Manitoba is unique among the Canadian provinces in that it developed from the north down.

In its charter the HBC was given ownership of all the lands draining into Hudson Bay. This area was occupied by three major Indian tribes: Assiniboin, Cree, and Ojibwa. A trading-post was established at Fort Nelson, and operations were soon extended south into the Red River Valley. In 1717 Fort Prince of Wales was built at the mouth of the Churchill River and rebuilt in stone between 1732 and 1771.

Posts were established by both the French and the British, but French influence largely disappeared after the Treaty of Paris in 1763. The Scots took over most of the French fur trade and established the North West Company in competition with the Hudson's Bay Company. The two companies eventually merged in 1821 under the HBC name. From then until 1869 "the Bay" was in absolute control of the whole area. In that year it sold its vast land holdings to the newly formed Canadian government which had been established two years earlier. The sale created problems for the Indians and the Métis, who had enjoyed almost complete freedom under the HBC. Their grievances led to the Red River Rebellion in 1869.

Manitoba became a province in 1870, and in the same year the railway arrived. During the next twenty years the population doubled, with immigration from eastern Canada, the United States, and Europe. The area of the province was also increased.

During the latter part of the nineteenth century and the start of the twentieth, the federal and provincial governments were active in promoting emigration from Europe to Manitoba. Very large numbers of Russians, Ukrainians, Poles, Estonians, and Hungarians settled in the area, lured by generous land grants. There was further immigration in the First World War when Hutterites and Mennonites arrived from the United States and set up colonies in the province. Another estimated 30,000 Ukrainians came to Canada after the Second World War, and the majority settled in the Western provinces. In Manitoba many joined the earlier arrivals in such places as Winnipeg and Dauphin.

The name Manitoba was first used when the area entered Confederation in 1870; before that it was known as the Red River Settlement.

| Civil Registration

This started in 1882 after the area of the province had been extended northwards. In 1912 it was extended again, to the shores of Hudson Bay. The registers of birth, marriage, and death are in the custody of the Director, Office of Vital Statistics, 254 Portage Avenue, Winnipeg, MB R2M 1K3. This office is not among the most helpful in Canada. If you send a written application stating the purpose of your request and the relationship between you and the person about whom you are now inquiring (this is essential), and you write, "I am the great-granddaughter of Thomas Alexander Wilkinson, born in Winnipeg in about 1883, and I want a copy of his birth certificate," the odds are that you will not get it. According to the instructions of the Director, the application must give the full name of the individual whose birth certificate is requested, the full name of his or her parents, the exact address, and the place of birth and the exact date. All this, of course, is probably just the information you are trying to obtain from the birth certificate. Usually such an office is more reasonable, and all that is required is a city, town, or township, unless the first names and the surname are very common — then the need for exact information is obvious. The office staff will, if needed, search for thirty months before and after the date you give. A fee is charged for a certificate, but the fee is less if you only require verification of a date.

In Manitoba you can but try, and hope your application reaches the desk of someone kind-hearted and understanding if you cannot give every tiny detail. Failing that, you will have to try church registers and census returns. There you may discover an exact place and date for the Director.

| The Provincial Archives of Manitoba

These are located at 200 Vaughan Street, Winnipeg, MB R3C 0P8. There is no printed guide to the holdings of genealogical material, but they do have many very valuable records, including their greatest treasure — the archives of the Hudson's Bay Company! These we will talk about a little later. The other records include the following.

| Census Returns

They have early returns for the area for 1832, 1833, 1838, 1840, 1843, 1846/7, 1849, 1856, 1870 (incomplete). There is also the Red River Census of 1870, which is indexed, and, of course, microfilm copies of the Canadian censuses for 1881 and 1891. The earliest censuses — those for the period 1831–49 — name only the head of the household. Those for 1870, and the later country-wide ones in 1881 and 1891, contain the names of everybody in the house. Censuses after 1891 are not open for public search, in order to protect personal privacy.

Locations of places in Manitoba with early censuses are:

1831–35, 1838, 1840, 1843, 1846, 1849: Grantown
1835: Indian Village
1832–35, 1838, 1840, 1843, 1846, 1849: Lower Settlement
1831, 1835, 1838, 1846, 1856: Red River
1849: Royal Pensioners at Upper Fort Garry
1840, 1843, 1846, 1849: Saulteaux Village
1835, 1840, 1843, 1847, 1849: Swampy Village

1870: Headingley, High Bluff, Kildonan, Lake Manitoba, Long Lake, Near Pembina, Near the U.S. Line, Oak Point, Poplar Point, Portage la Prairie, Rat Creek Portage, St. André, St. Boniface, St. Charles, St. Clement, St. François-Xavier, St. James, St. John, St. Norbert, St. Paul (Lisgar), St. Paul on the Bay, St. Pierre, St. Vital, Ste. Agathe, Ste. Anne, Scander Berry, Scratching River, White Mud River, Winnipeg. (The 1870 returns are indexed.)

There was also a Catholic Census of Manitoba in 1870 and this is on microfilm in the Glenbow Museum and Archives, 130 Ninth Avenue SE, Calgary, AB T2G 0P3. It includes all the places shown under 1870 above. If you are living in Alberta, but are researching Manitoba records, it will be easier for you to contact Glenbow.

The 1881 Census has an alphabetical listing within each sub-district. The 1891 Census is not indexed, but by checking Henderson's 1892 Directory and land descriptions from the Historic Holders Land Index the Provincial Archivist says the staff can usually make a fairly well-informed guess as to within which census district an individual or a family is located. The Index is on microfilm and gives details of the first holders of land in Manitoba. It is indexed alphabetically by name, and also by legal land description. Each entry gives type of grant: i.e., half-breed, military bounty, homestead, transfer, sale, etc., with the date of entry and dates of sale and patent.

The land records in the Provincial Archives include the following:

Township Registers (land grants), 1871–1930
Parish Files (lot ownership), 1874–1959
Dominion Land Grants (half-breeds), 1873–83
Dominion Land Surveys, 1881–84

The remaining genealogical records of the Provincial Archives include Red River Genealogies (these are not reliable, and the information should not be accepted without further proof from your own research); the Alexander Ross Family Papers (1810–1903); the Gertrude A. Rhodes Papers (1813–94); a MS collection (Russenholt Family) that contains information about many Assiniboia families; and a number of local histories. However, the best collection of these is in the Legislative Library, 200 Vaughan Street, Winnipeg, MB R3C 0P8.

The following items on microfilm are from the National Archives in Ottawa and are available through inter-library loan:

Indian Affairs: Field Office records, Agency records, Land records, St. Peter's Reserve

Dept. of the Interior: Half-breed affidavits (giving parentage, age, and ethnic origin of spouse)

General Index to Manitoba and the Northwest Territories of half-breeds and original white settlers, with name of claimant, parents, date of birth, etc.

Applications made 1886–1901 and 1906 by half-breeds living in the Northwest Territories, 1870–85. These contain a great deal of genealogical information about the applicant.

| Wills

There is a Central Registry for Probate Matters in the province. It is the Court of Queen's Bench—Probate, located in the Law Courts Building, 408 York Avenue, Winnipeg, MB R3C 0V8. The records date back to 1879, and you will need to supply the approximate date of death, the last known address, and the name of the possible next of kin.

A division of the Public Trustee administers estates assigned for administration where there is no will, or when a will exists but the beneficiary is also dead or cannot be located. The official responsible is the Senior Trust Officer, Estates and Trust Division, 155 Carlton Street, Winnipeg, MB R3C 3H8. In the files that record investigations dating back to the 1880s you will find family records and lineages containing church records and early hospital records.

| Land Records

Land grants, land sales, and land transfers are all filed in the Land Titles Office for the area where the land is located. Records date back to the early 1800s and show the original grants from the Crown. The six offices are:

705 Princess Avenue, *Brandon*, MB R7A 0P4
308 Main Street South, *Dauphin*, MB R7N 1K7
351 Stephen Street, *Morden*, MB R0G 1J0
329 Hamilton Street, *Neepawa*, MB R0J 1H0
25 Tupper Street North, *Portage la Prairie*, MB R1N 3K1
405 Broadway, *Winnipeg*, MB R3C 3L6

(The former office at Boissevain has been merged with Brandon.)

| Genealogical Societies

The address of the Manitoba Genealogical Society is PO Box 2066, Winnipeg, MB R3C 3R4. It is a very active society with a regular newsletter, a number of projects in hand, and three equally energetic branches:

BRANDON: PO Box 1332, Brandon, MB R7A 6N2
DAUPHIN: PO Box 855, Dauphin, MB R7N 3B3
WINNIPEG: PO Box 1244, Winnipeg, MB R3C 0J0

The publications include:

A Surname Index of members' interests
A Cemetery Transcription List
An Index of Marriage and Death Notices from Manitoba
   newspapers, 1859–81

The on-going projects of the Society are:
1. Continuing to index BMD notices from newspapers.
2. Obituary Index from Winnipeg newspapers 1977 to the present date, plus some rural newspapers 1979–   .
3. Cemetery transcription program; nearly 300 have been completed so far (a list is obtainable from the Society).
4. An index of burials containing approximately 90,000 names.
5. List of locations of all cemeteries in Manitoba.
6. Index of Anglican baptisms and marriages from the Diocese of Rupert's Land 1820–1900.

| Newspapers

A considerable amount of indexing of newspapers has been done in Manitoba. I give below a list of the earlier ones and the organization responsible. In most cases the indexes are on microfilm and may be borrowed through inter-library loan:

Saint Boniface: Collège Universitaire de Saint Boniface, 200 Avenue de la Cathédrale, Saint Boniface, MB R2H 0H7 (*Le Manitoba*, 1881–1925; *Le Métis*, 1871–81).
Winnipeg: Legislative Library, 200 Vaughan Street, Winnipeg, MB R3C 1T5 (*Free Press*, 1884– ; *Sun*, 1886–90; *Telegram*, 1894–1920; *Tribune*, 1890–).
Manitoba Genealogical Society (address on page 122) (*Manitoban*, 1859–81; *Le Métis*, 1859–81; *Free Press*, 1859–81; *Sun*, 1978– ; *Times*, 1859–81; *Tribune*, 1978–).

| The Hudson's Bay Company Archives

The HBC records, which are housed at the Provincial Archives of Manitoba (address on page 119), are some of our nation's great treasures. The Hudson's Bay Company's trading-posts and forts dominated Canada from the Bay to the Pacific and from the Arctic Circle to the 49th parallel for more than three centuries. The Company established its archives in London, England, after the First World War. By 1922 many of the records from Canada had been sent over, although many of the earlier trading-post records had been either discarded or destroyed in fires. In the 1930s it was discovered that the estate of Lord Strathcona had handed over a great many records and Company documents to the Registry Office in Edinburgh. Lord Strathcona had originally been Donald Smith, a Company clerk in Canada. He played a leading part in the restoration of order in Fort Garry after the 1870 Red River Rebellion. He later bought stock in the Company, becoming its largest shareholder, and eventually deputy governor. Throughout his business career he squirrelled away hundreds of documents of interest to himself, in particular the records of the North West Company up to its merger with the HBC in 1821.

In 1951 the HBC started microfilming its records and, persuaded by the National Archives, undertook to film all of its records for the period 1670–1870. This task was completed in 1966. In 1970 the Company moved its headquarters from London to Winnipeg, and consideration was given to transferring the archives as well. Getting the records out of the United Kingdom was rather like pulling teeth, since the British government regarded them as part of the national heritage. Approval was finally given—provided that a complete copy was given to the Public Record Office. At this point microfilming was resumed to cover the period from 1871 to 1904, and this work was completed by 1983.

The records are still owned by the HBC but are on loan to the Provincial Archives. In 1986 the Archives announced that they were now available through inter-library loan. There are nearly 2000 reels of records available for you through your nearest library with a microfilm-reader. Requests for particular reels can now be made using the normal inter-library loan request form, or through the Envoy 100 Electronic Message System, Code HBCA.PAM.

If you are preparing to do your genealogical research through the HBC Archives, you should bear in mind that the records of the Company were not kept to provide genealogical information. They were a record of trade and company activities in various areas. So many people have worked for the HBC over the centuries that you need more information than just a name. You must be able to provide information about where your ancestor worked, the nature of his employment, and the date of his death. With this information you can make a start, but be prepared to get back no further than 1770—few earlier records survive.

In the later 1700s the rivalry with the North West Company led to an expansion of operations and more men were employed. One of the best sources of information for the 1780–1810 period is "The Lists of Servants in Hudson's Bay". These books record each employee's name, age, type of work, pay, address, and station. There are also many contracts of service. These had to be signed by the employee and give his original place of residence — usually in the United Kingdom, but occasionally in other parts of Canada.

In the main, the records were kept separately for each geographical department of the HBC. The Northern Department consisted of part of north-west Ontario, all the Western provinces, and the Northwest Territories. The Southern Department was made up of Québec and the shores of Hudson Bay—these were the two areas of Rupert's Land. The Montréal Department consisted of Labrador and that part of Québec not included in the Southern Department. The Western Department (previously known as the Columbia District) covered what is now British Columbia, the Yukon Territory, and operations in Washington, Oregon, Utah, and the Hawaiian Islands.

The HBC Archives also have some of the records of the North West Company, including employment records for the period 1811–21. When one realizes that in Manitoba alone the HBC owned seven million acres of land, it is easy to understand the range of activities within that area.

It is not possible to list all the holdings of the Company, but I give below just a sampling of the genealogical sources that you will find are available:

Officers and Servants Private Accounts, 1891–1919
Deaths of Pensioners, 1894–1918
Apprentice Clerks, 1891–1916
Pensions and Allowances, 1892–1920
Staff Files, 1890–1915
Lists of Servants, 1774–1841
Servants Staff Records, 1822–32, 1851–1927
Register Books of Wills, 1717–1903
Lists of Passengers, 1825–84
Lists of Servants Sent Out, 1823–76
Lists of Servants in Posts, 1800–70
Ships' Logs, 1751–1931
Red River Settlement BMD Registers, 1811–71
North West Company Servants Contracts, 1798–1822

If your ancestor worked for the HBC, you will have enough record-searching to keep you busy for quite a while!

| Church Registers

Before reading this, please refer to the paragraph about church registers on page 64. Listed below are the locations of parish registers which pre-date civil registration and are now in various archives:

Church	Denomination	Dates	Location
Baie St. Paul	CA	1874–82	PAM
Birtle	P	1881–1902	UW
Boissevain	M	1887–1981	PAM
Carman	WM	1882–95	UW

Church	Denomination	Dates	Location
Dugald	A	1880–1919	UW
Dynevor	A	1839–90	PAM
Emerson	P	1876–1908	UW
Headingly	A	1857–1928	PAM
High Bluff	A	1872–84	PAM
High Bluff	P	1873–76	UW
Kildonan	P	1851–1932	PAM
Little Britain	P	1884–1938	PAM
Little Saskatchewan	M	1878–79	UW
Manitou	M	1880–84	UW
Marquette (West Circuit)	P	1876–	NAC
Middlechurch	A	1850–1903	PAM
Minnedosa	M	1882–1920	UW
Morris	P	1879–1912	UW
Orrwold	P	1898–1904	PAM
Oxford House	M	1894–1975	PAM
Oxford House	A	1828–29	NAC
Palestine	P	1877–84	NAC
Poplar River	UC	1886–1962	PAM
Portage la Prairie	A	1855–83	PAM
Portage la Prairie	P	1884–1943	PAM
Portage la Prairie	M	1844–1944	PAM
Red River Settlement	A	1820–84	PAM
Ste. Agathe	CA	1872–1955	PAM
St. Boniface	CA	1825–34, 1860–1974	PAM
St. Charles Mission	CA	1868–1951	PAM
St. Eustache	CA	1874–1903	PAM
St. François-Xavier	CA	1834–1900	PAM
St. Jean Baptiste	CA	1877–1911	PAM
St. Lazare	CA	1885–1900	PAM
St. Norbert	CA	1857–1911	PAM
Winnipeg (Holy Ghost)*	CA	B 1850–1920 M 1901	NAC
Winnipeg (St. John)	A	1813–1901	PAM
Winnipeg (St. James)	A	1853–1908	PAM
Winnipeg (St. Clement)	A	1862–1928	PAM
Winnipeg (St. Andrew)	A	1835–1928	PAM
Winnipeg (St. Paul)	CA	B 1850 M 1853	PAS(R)
Winnipeg	M	1877–82	UW

*These registers are separated linguistically according to ethnic background:

Czechoslovakia B 1873–1918
Galicia   B 1861–98 M 1901
Hungary   B 1877
Poland   B 1850–1920
Russia   B 1869, 1884

The National Archives and the Hudson's Bay Archives also contain returns made to the HBC by its Anglican chaplains and other missionaries of the Church Missionary Society:

B 1820–51, MD 1820–41

The following parishes of the Anglican Church were in existence in Manitoba before civil registration of births, marriages, and deaths:

DIOCESE OF RUPERT'S LAND: Assiniboia, Birtle, Brandon, Chafyn-Grove, Devon, Dynevor, Emerson, Fairford, Fort Alexander, Fort Frances, Griswold, Headingly, High Bluff, Islington, Lac Seul, Lisgar, Mapleton, Minnedosa, Morris, Nelson, Pembina, Portage la Prairie, Pultney, Rapid City, Rounthwaite, Russell, St. Andrew's, Stonewall, Touchwood Hills, Turtle Mountain, Westbourne, Winnipeg.

The following parishes of the Catholic Church were in existence before civil registration:

DIOCESE OF KEEWATIN-THE PAS: Brochet
DIOCESE OF ST. BONIFACE: Cathedral, Letellier, Lorette, Ste. Agathe, Ste. Anne, St. Jean-Baptiste, St. Joseph, St. Labre, St. Norbert
DIOCESE OF WINNIPEG: St. Charles, St. Eustache, St. François-Xavier, St. Laurent, St. Lazare

Sources of further information about various church records and registers are:

Anglican Centre, 935 Nesbitt Bay, Winnipeg, MB R3T 1W6
Mennonite Heritage Centre, 600 Shaftesbury Blvd., Winnipeg, MB R3P 0M4
Jewish Historical Society, 402-365 Hargrave Street, Winnipeg, MB R3B 2K3
Catholic Archdiocese of St. Boniface, 151 Cathedral Avenue, St. Boniface, MB R2H 0H6

Catholic Archdiocese of Winnipeg, 1455 Waverley Street,
Winnipeg, MB R3T 0P7

United Church, Manitoba Conference Archives, Rare Book Room,
University of Winnipeg, 515 Portage Avenue, Winnipeg,
MB R3B 2E0

| Libraries

There are over one hundred public libraries in Manitoba, but
not very many appear to have genealogical holdings or projects. Those that do are listed below:

Minnedosa Regional Library, PO Box 1226, Minnedosa, MB
R0J 1E0. This library has a number of books and pamphlets
about the district, including *Lakelet School and Its Pioneers,
Minnedosa and Her Neighbors, They Called It Odanah, Min-
nedosa Valley News*, and *History of Minnedosa, 1883–1983*.
There are also several books about neighbouring areas such
as Eden, Birnie, Clanwilliam, Erickson, Cardale, Elton, and
Polonia.

South Interlake Regional Library, PO Box 908, Stonewall,
MB R0C 2Z0. The library has several printed histories of the
district, including such places as Grahamdale, Marquette,
Meadow Lea, Ossowa, Poplar Heights, Reaburn, Rockwood,
Rosser, Steep Rock, Teulon, Warren, Woodlands.

Thompson Historical Heritage & Museum Society, PO Box 762,
Thompson, MB R8N 1N5. The local library has no historical
or genealogical collection because Thompson is a very young
city—only twenty-nine years old. The Society is, however, publishing a book about its history so far.

Western Manitoba Regional Library, 638 Princess Avenue,
Brandon, MB R7A 0P3. The library holds Henderson's Directories for Brandon for the period from 1897 to the present; list-
ings of local cemetery inscriptions provided by the local
genealogical society; the *Brandon Sun* on microfilm from 1883
to the present (unindexed); and a number of local-history books
about places and families: Argyle, Arizona, Arthur, Ashern,
Austin, Basswood, Binscarth, Blanshard, Boissevain, Brandon,
Carberry, Cornwallis, Crandall, Dand, Darlingford, Dauphin,
Douglas, Eddystone, Elton, Glenboro, Hamiota, Hartney,
Kenton, Killarney, Marquette, Melita, Minto, Neepawa, Oak
Lake, Oakland, Parkhill-Cheval, Polonia, Rapid City, Reinland,

CHAPTER 12
New Brunswick

The earliest settlement in the area which is now New Brunswick was in 1604 when the French established a small colony
on an island in the St. Croix River. After one very severe winter they moved it across the Bay of Fundy to Port Royal (later
renamed Annapolis Royal by the British). Over the next
century many immigrants arrived from France, and lesser
numbers from Great Britain and Portugal. The French named
the area Acadie, or Acadia. Over the next century and a half
there was an almost constant state of war between Great
Britain and France, and the settlement and development of
the area were delayed. This was the story, too, of the whole
area of Atlantic Canada — Newfoundland, Prince Edward
Island, and Nova Scotia (of which New Brunswick was originally a part).

One-third of the present population of New Brunswick is
French-speaking — descendants either of the original Acadians
or of settlers from the neighbouring province of Québec. The
two warring powers had little regard for the inhabitants of the
contested areas. Some districts changed hands as many as ten
times in one century.

The Treaty of Paris in 1763 ended the French colonization of
North America, but even before that there had been massive
immigration into what is now New Brunswick. From 1759
a steady stream of settlers from the New England colonies
and New York established themselves in the area — over seven
thousand in all. In 1760, Pennsylvania Germans settled in the

Riding Mountain, Roland, Tremaine-Hunterville, Turtle Mountain, Virden, Westbourne, Woodlea (now Ingelow). About half of these have been published by local historical societies. I don't know of any other area in Canada with such an interest in history, and this promises well for the future of genealogical research in western Manitoba.

One of the branches within the library system also has its own genealogical collection: the *North Cypress Library*, PO Box 382, Carberry, MB R0K 0H0. Its holdings include the town of Carberry house list, 1890–1982; a list of inscriptions in the local cemetery at Carberry Plains; local newspapers on microfilm: the *Carberry News*, *Express*, and *News-Express* from 1889 to 1982, and bound copies from 1982 to 1988; minutes of Council meetings, 1902–84; and Council minutes of *North Cypress* from 1898 to 1984; tax rolls for Carberry, 1890–1983; school district registers for all the surrounding areas; and a number of local-history books.

Winnipeg Centennial Library, 251 Donald Street, Winnipeg, MB R3C 3P5. This library is not prepared to list its holdings or any details of its genealogical collection. Mr. R. Donner of the Reference and Information Section states that its holdings are made available to other libraries within the Winnipeg area. If you require any information from this library, I suggest you write directly to Mr. Donner.

However, all is not lost. Remember the resources and help-fulness of the Manitoba Genealogical Society and also the vast resources of the LDS Church, to which you have access through the church's Family History Library, PO Box 220, Winnipeg, MB R3C 2G9.

Petitcodiac Valley, and many of their descendants still live in Albert and Westmorland counties. Many of these new settlers occupied land seized from the Acadians at the time of the expulsion in 1755 (see Chapter 14).

In 1774 several hundred farming families from Yorkshire, in England, were settled in the Chignecto area, and they were followed by small settlements of Scots in the area of the Miramichi River.

In 1784, following the arrival of thousands of United Empire Loyalists, the Sunbury County area of Nova Scotia became the separate colony of New Brunswick. It entered Confederation in 1867 and, with Upper and Lower Canada and Nova Scotia, formed the new Dominion of Canada.

| Civil Registration

The history of civil registration in New Brunswick is more than a little complicated. In 1888 a law came into force which compelled clergymen of all churches to report baptisms, marriages, and burials. Unfortunately, the Baptists, for example, who do not baptize infants, left their births unrecorded. This also applied to others who for various reasons did not approve of baptism. In addition, the law was not enforced properly until after 1900. This very carelessly organized period means you may have problems in establishing a date of birth.

There is one possible means of establishing an approximate date and that is by checking a census return if you know the ancestral location. This usually gave the age of the inhabitants of a house, but in some of the early censuses the enumerator "rounded off" the age, so 75 might be entered as 70 and 76 might be entered as 80. But let us not complicate matters any further at this point. We will be talking about censuses later on.

From 1 January 1920, compulsory registration came into force, and entries are complete from that date. They are in the custody of the Registrar General, Department of Vital Statistics, Centennial Building, PO Box 6000, Fredericton, NB E3B 5H1. He also has custody of the incomplete records from 1888. You may be able to discover the birth date of an ancestor even if the department does not have any record. If you know the religion of his or her parents, you will be able to check the registers of the church or chapel. You may end up with the date of baptism only, but that is no major disadvantage. If you don't know the religion, you can probably find this out by checking the census records, which usually gave the religion of each person in the family. In this case you may find the religion is recorded with an initial or initials. If you find RE or WM, you must refer to the list of census abbreviations earlier in this book. You will then discover you are dealing with a Reformed Episcopalian or a Wesleyan Methodist.

The staff of the Vital Statistics Department will do a search for a fee, and they will usually cover a five-year period in case you are mistaken in the exact date. Be sure you ask for a "full" copy of the certificate; give details of your relationship, and explain that the certificate is required for genealogical purposes. If you don't do this, you will get a brief extract, whereas a full one will give all the details that appeared in the original entry, including addresses, ages, witnesses, officiating clergyman, and so on. All this extra information may speed you on in your search by solving problems of relationship.

A little later in this chapter we will be discussing the advantages of the emphasis placed on the county in the records of the province — one advantage being that each county maintained a Marriage Book, and this may solve many problems for you.

| Provincial Archives

These are located on the campus of the University of New Brunswick. The mailing address is PO Box 6000, Fredericton, NB E3B 5H1. The staff are particularly helpful to ancestor-hunters, with particular emphasis on helping those who visit the Archives to do their own searching. The records are extremely well organized and documented, and research there is a joy. In many ways the Archives are the best-arranged in Canada.

The Genealogical Section was specifically created to be of assistance to those tracing their New Brunswick ancestry, and you will find you are treated as one of the family coming home, rather than as a nuisance to be got rid of as quickly and quietly as possible. A great many of the records are on a county basis, and if you don't know the county in which your ancestors settled, your first action will be to check the land records (1784–1850) that may give you the vital information you need

—provided that the person in question applied for *or* received a grant of land. If not, there are other sources of information which will be mentioned in this chapter.

| Land Titles

These records are on microfilm and are indexed in two sections: Petitions and Grants. In other words, they are divided between people who applied for a grant and those who received one. The distinction is important, because a number of early settlers made a routine application for a grant but did not proceed any further — sometimes, if they could afford it, they made a private purchase of land, or, more often, they decided not to settle in the province and moved westwards to other pastures.

Once you know the county of settlement, you can ask the Archives to supply you with an information sheet for that county. At this point I had better describe these divisions of the province and the county records that are available. The province is divided into fifteen counties and these, in turn, are divided into parishes similar to townships. The counties are:

Albert	Kings	St. John
Carleton	Madawaska	Sunbury
Charlotte	Northumberland	Victoria
Gloucester	Queens	Westmorland
Kent	Restigouche	York

I will not set out every last detail of every record within each county—this you can obtain from the Archives—but I give below all the main items of county information available.
Albert: This county is located in the south-eastern corner of New Brunswick; to its north and east is Westmorland County, from which Albert was created in 1845; to the south is Chignecto Bay; and to the west are the counties of Kings and St. John. Two of the six parishes in the county—Hillsborough and Hopewell — were created as part of Westmorland County in 1686; Coverdale was created from Hillsborough in 1828 and Harvey from Hopewell in 1838. Elgin was part of Salisbury Parish in Westmorland until 1847, and Alma was created from Harvey in 1855. You must be careful about following these parish boundary changes, because otherwise you may be looking in the wrong place for the records you need.

The Provincial Archives have the land records for Albert

County, and reference maps that show the exact location of the grant. If you want a copy of the original land grant made to your ancestor, you can obtain this for a fee from the Department of Natural Resources, Lands Branch, PO Box 6000, Fredericton NB E3B 5H1.

The Albert County marriage records are on microfilm and date from 1845 to 1887. You can borrow them through the inter-library loan system. Marriage records before 1845 will be part of the Westmorland County records. Probate records and wills for the county are available from 1845 to 1900 and are located in the Office of the Registrar of Probate, PO Box 5001, 770 Main Street, Moncton, NB E1C 8R3. Records before 1845 are, of course, in the Westmorland County probate records. These may contain other documents besides the actual will, such as peti-tions, letters, real estate inventories, etc. Records since 1900 are also available.

Microfilm copies are available for the following church records:

Elgin Circuit Church, 1876–1948
Hopewell Anglican Church, 1884–1959

Census returns for the years 1851, 1861, 1871, 1881, and 1891 are available for most of the parishes of the county. They can be seen in the Provincial Archives or borrowed from the National Archives in Ottawa through your nearest library with a microfilm-viewer. There are also school records for the period 1877–1956. Other available records in the county are tax-assessment records from Alma, 1874; Coverdale, 1874–78; Elgin, 1874–78; Harvey 1874, 1875, and 1878; Hillsborough, 1871–78; and Hopewell, 1874–77.

Carleton: This county was created in 1832 from part of York County. It is located in the western part of the province, next to the state of Maine. To its north is Victoria County, and to the east and south York County. Five of the parishes—Wood-stock, Northampton, Wakefield, Kent, and Brighton — were created as parishes of York County in 1786, 1786, 1803, 1821, and 1830 respectively. Carleton County was separated from York in 1831, and Wicklow Parish was created in 1833 from Kent. Simonds was separated from Wakefield in 1842, and Rich-mond was established in 1853 from Woodstock. Peel was set up in 1859 from part of Brighton, and in 1863 Aberdeen was cre-ated from Kent. Two parishes, Perth and Andover, were part of

Carleton County until 1833, when they were transferred to Victoria County after its creation.

The information about land and probate records is the same as that for Albert County. The Carleton County marriage records are unindexed and are available from 1832 to 1888. Any marriages before 1832 will be found in the York County records. The probate records cover the period 1833–1947.

One record that may be of some interest is that of the school returns for 1877–1954. The census returns on microfilm are in the National Archives in Ottawa and cover the same five years as those for Albert County.

Census records for the county are available for every tenth year from 1851 to 1891 inclusive. The Provincial Archives have also published the 1851 Census for Carleton County, listed alphabetically within each parish. This can be bought. Unindexed censuses for all the years mentioned may be borrowed on microfilm from the National Archives, Ottawa, or searched at the Provincial Archives in Fredericton. The reels cannot be borrowed from the latter.

Charlotte: This county is in the south-western corner of New Brunswick. To the south is the Bay of Fundy, and to the west the state of Maine. Charlotte's northern and eastern boundaries are the counties of York, Sunbury, Queens, Kings, and St. John. The county was created in 1785. It has seven parishes: Pennfield, St. Andrews, St. Davids, St. George, St. Patrick, St. Stephen, and West Isles. The parishes of Campobello and Grand Manan were created from West Isles in 1803 and 1816 respectively. St. James was set up in 1823 from unassigned lands and a part of St. Stephen; a part of St. Patrick became Dumbarton in 1856; and Lepreau was created from Pennfield in 1859. Ten years later Clarendon was established; in 1873 Dufferin was set up from St. Stephen; and the parish of St. Croix was created in 1874. I hope you can follow all these changes; otherwise it is easy to go astray in your research.

The land and probate records are located in the same places as in the previous counties; the same remark applies to school returns (1877–1956). A number of church *records* (and some registers) have been microfilmed, and you will find details on the information sheet for the county, obtainable from the Provincial Archives.

Marriage records are available for the period 1806–87 and are indexed. There are also some early directories of the county in the Archives, a number of histories of the area, lists of ships and owners, and lists of Loyalist gravestones in St. Stephen.

There are also a number of family histories: Acheson, Armstrong, Caleff, Cockburn, Dibblee, Dunham, Foster, Getchell, Grimmer, Hachey, Hanson, Hill, Libby, Ludgate, Meloney, Moore, Owen, Pollard, Tilley, and Warren. Most of these are on microfilm and may be borrowed through the inter-library loan system.

Gloucester: This is in the north-eastern corner of the province. To the north is Chaleur Bay, and to the east the Gulf of St. Lawrence. To the west is Restigouche County, and to the south is Northumberland — from which Gloucester was created in 1826. The parishes of Saumarez and Beresford were created in 1814 as part of Northumberland County, while New Bandon and Caraquet were taken from Saumarez in 1831 to form separate parishes within Gloucester County. Shippegan, Inkerman, and St. Isidore were also formed from parts of Saumarez in 1851, 1855, and 1881 respectively. Paquetville was formed from part of Inkerman in 1897. When you are researching Gloucester County before 1826, remember that the area was part of Northumberland, and all the genealogical records before that date will be under the name of the original county.

Once again, note that the location of land records, wills, and census returns is exactly the same as for Albert County at the start of this chapter. Marriage records, available on microfilm, are for the periods 1832–60 and 1873–87. The first period is indexed. The usual school returns are available (1877–1956), as are some twenty church records and registers.

Kent: This county is situated along the eastern seaboard of New Brunswick. To the east is Northumberland Strait, to the south are the counties of Queens and Westmorland, and to the north and west is Northumberland, from which Kent was created in 1826. The two parishes of Wellington and Carleton were started as parishes of Northumberland County in 1814; Liverpool (renamed Richibucto in 1832), Dundas, Huskisson, and Harcourt were set up in 1826 when the county of Kent was established. Weldford was established from part of Richibucto in 1835, and the parishes of St. Louis, St. Mary's, Acadieville, and St. Paul were created in 1855, 1867, and 1883, respectively.

With this county, note again that land records, wills, and census returns are located exactly as described at the beginning of this section. Kent County marriage records are available from 1844 to 1887, unindexed, on microfilm. Incidentally, there are very few wills available before 1940 because of destruction by fire. School returns cover the usual period from 1877 to 1956. Some twenty church records have been microfilmed, most dating from 1800 or thereabouts. They are on microfilm, are available for inter-library loan, and are listed on the information sheet for the county.

Kings: One of the original counties established in 1785, it is bounded by Queens County to the north, Albert and Westmorland to the east, St. John to the south, and Charlotte to the west. The four parishes of Westfield, Sussex, Springfield, and Kingston were created in 1786; Norton, Greenwich, and Hampton were set up in 1785; Upham was taken from Hampton in 1835, and Studholm from Sussex in 1840. Havelock, Hammond, and Kars were established in 1858, 1858, and 1859 respectively. In 1870 Rothesay came into being, followed by Cardwell and Waterford in 1874.

The land records for 1783–1850 are in the Provincial Archives, as are marriage records for 1812–88 and probate records for 1787–1883. School returns cover the usual period (1877–1956). Census returns are in the Archives for the period 1851–91. The 1851 Census, alphabetized within each parish, has been published by the Archives. Some thirty church records have been microfilmed, and are listed in the county information sheet obtainable from the Archives.

Madawaska: The county is located in the north-western part of the province. To the north is Restigouche, to the south the state of Maine, to the west the province of Québec, and to the east Victoria County. Madawaska was created from the latter county in 1873. Don't forget that Madawaska records will be found under Victoria before that date. The parish of Madawaska was taken from Carleton County in 1833; St. Leonard and St. Basile were created in 1850; and in 1877 St. Francis, St. Jacques, St. Hilaire, and St. Ann were established.

The land records exist from 1783 to 1850, and the marriage records from 1792 to 1940, but there are problems about the probate records, most of which were destroyed by fire. Pre-1873 records are filed under Victoria County, but those since then have not been microfilmed, and many are missing. Further information can be obtained from the Archives. The school returns are available for the period 1877–1956, as are the census returns for the usual period of 1851–91. A few church records — mainly in the Edmundston and Madawaska areas — have been microfilmed.

Northumberland: This was created in 1785 and is in the centre of the province, with Gloucester and Restigouche to the north, Kent to the east, York and Sunbury to the south, and Victoria to the west. The parishes of Alnwick and Newcastle were set up in 1786, followed in 1814 by Chatham, Glenelg, Ludlow, Nelson, and Northesk. The parishes of Blissfield and Blackville were established in 1851, Derby in 1859, Southesk in 1879, and Rogersville in 1881.

The land records available are for the period 1785–1850, marriage records for 1806–87, probate records for 1872–85, school returns for 1877–1956, and census returns for the usual period. Some thirty-eight church records of various denominations are available on microfilm.

Queens: This was created in 1785. To the north of it lies Kent County, to the east Kings, on the south Charlotte, and in the west Sunbury. In 1785 the parishes of Wickham, Waterborough, Hampstead, and Gagetown were established, followed by Brunswick, Canning, and Chipman in 1816, 1827, and 1835 respectively. Petersville followed in 1838, Johnston in 1839, and Cambridge in 1852.

The land records cover the usual period applicable to the whole province, marriage records 1812–87, probate records 1788–1968, and census returns and school returns the same dates listed in previous counties. The records of some thirty-two churches are on microfilm.

Restigouche: This is in the northern part of the province, bounded to the north and west by Québec, to the south by Victoria, Madawaska, and Northumberland, and on the east by Gloucester — from which Restigouche was created in 1837. Addington and Eldon parishes were established in Gloucester in 1826, and in 1839 Durham, Colborne, and Dalhousie followed the setting up of Restigouche. Balmoral was created from part of Dalhousie in 1876. It is important to remember that before 1837 you will be researching Gloucester County.

Land records and census returns exist for the regular years, marriage records are on microfilm for the period 1838–78 and are not indexed, and probate records exist for the years 1838–1965. School returns are, of course, available in this county as in all others. A few church records have been microfilmed.

St. John: This was formed in 1785, with Kings County to the north, the Bay of Fundy to the south, and Charlotte on the west. The parishes of Portland, St. Martins, and Lancaster were set up in 1786, Simonds in 1839, and, finally, Musquash in 1877.

Land records exist for the usual period, but probate records are a different story—they start in 1785 and are indexed until 1912, though the records themselves continue to 1963. The census returns are fragmentary for the county for 1851 and 1861, but are more complete for 1871 and 1881, and there are no gaps in 1891. The marriage records run from 1810 to 1887. The school returns are for the usual period. The Archives have microfilmed over fifty church records, most of them in the Saint John area. There are other miscellaneous records, including assessment books for some parishes and early directories.

Sunbury: This county was created in 1785. It is south of Northumberland and north of Charlotte. Queens is on the east and York on the west. Four counties — Burton, Lincoln, Sheffield, and Maugerville — were created in 1786. Blissville, Northfield, and Gladstone followed in 1834, 1857, and 1874 respectively.

Land records, school returns, and census records follow the usual pattern. The Archives have published the 1851 Census for the county. It is in alphabetical order within each parish, and may be bought. The county probate records are available for the period 1786–1896 but have not been microfilmed. The marriage registers for the county have not survived, but there are a few marriage certificates for 1824–28, and 1812, 1816, and 1822. A few church records have been microfilmed.

Victoria: This is along the western border of the province. To the north is Restigouche, and to the east Northumberland. In the south are Carleton County and the state of Maine, and in the west is Madawaska. The county was created in 1844 from parts of York County. The parishes of Perth, Madawaska, and Andover were set up in 1833, St. Leonard in 1850, Grand Falls in 1852, Gordon in 1863, Lorne in 1871, and Drummond in 1872.

Land records and census records are available for the usual years, but probate records exist only from 1850 to 1976, and no marriage registers have survived. School returns are available from 1877 to 1956, and a few church records have been microfilmed.

Westmorland: This county was established in 1785 and is located in the south-eastern part of the province. To its north is Kent, to the east the province of Nova Scotia, to the south Albert, and in the west Queens and Kings counties. The parishes of Westmorland, Sackville, and Moncton were set up in 1786, and Dorchester and Salisbury in the next year.

Botsford and Shediac were established in 1805 and 1827 respectively.

Land records, census records, and school returns all exist for the usual dates. Marriage records cover the period 1790–1887, but are not indexed for 1875–85. Probate records are available for 1787–1885. About twenty church records have been microfilmed, and there are other miscellaneous records available, including the Dorchester Penitentiary Register for 1874–1930, some marriage bonds for 1798–1811, and the Dixon family papers (Sackville).

York: The county was created in 1785 and is in the centre of the province. Northumberland is to the north, Sunbury to the east, Charlotte and the state of Maine to the south, and Carleton to the west. The town of Fredericton came into existence in 1786, and in that year the parishes of Kingsclear, Prince William, St. Mary's, and Queensbury were established. Other parishes soon followed: Dumfries and Southampton in 1833, Stanley and New Maryland in 1846, Manners Sutton and Canterbury in 1855, Bright in 1869, North Lake in 1879, and McAdam in 1894.

Land records and school returns are available for the usual periods. Marriage records cover the years 1812–88, and probate records the years from 1794 to 1969. Census records are available for some of the parishes of the county for the years 1851, 1861, 1871, and 1881. That for 1891 is complete. The 1851 Census for the county has been published and is in alphabetical order within each available parish. Other censuses have been located by the Archives for 1851 for St. Mary's, Fredericton, and Dumfries. They are on microfilm and may be borrowed from the Provincial Archives.

Some fifty church records have been microfilmed, and other records on microfilm in the Archives include miscellaneous births (1887–1905) and deaths (1887–93), assessment books, court records, and the Charles Moffit family papers (1854–1905). The Fredericton Census of 1871 has been published with an index. It contains the names of some six thousand inhabitants of the city, and can be bought from the Archives for $4.

So much for the county records. Other general genealogical information at the Provincial Archives includes:

The Genealogical Card Index

This contains information from private sources, collections of church registers and records, cemetery inscriptions, lists of immigrants, town records and tax rolls, and local and family histories. There is no guarantee that your family will be mentioned, but it should be your first place to check.

The Family Histories Collection

This contains genealogical information about at least four hundred New Brunswick families—too many to list here.

The County Reference Collection

This contains records about individual counties, and is based on much of the information I have listed above under each county. You will find local histories, church histories, settlers' records, directories, etc.

Passenger Lists

Some ten thousand names have been taken from passenger and immigration lists, and are on microfilm. Unfortunately, the vast majority of passenger lists were lost when the Customs House in Saint John was destroyed by fire in 1877.

Saint John Burial Permits

There are thirty volumes of permits for over twenty thousand people from various parts of the province who died in Saint John between 1889 and 1919. The books are indexed and are on microfilm. There is also a Maiden Name Index containing some four thousand entries which should be checked in conjunction with the other list.

Late Registrations of Births

This may be the end of the mystery surrounding a particular ancestor. The index is based on proof supplied by individuals for legal or personal reasons and covers the years from 1810 to 1887.

Military Records

This is a small collection, but it does contain more than 180 reels of Loyalist military records in the National Archives, formerly kept in the Admiralty, War, and Audit Offices in

London. There are also another 140 reels of British military records dealing with New Brunswick and other British colonies. These reels can be used in Fredericton or ordered from Ottawa on loan.

Newspapers

The Archives have some newspapers on microfilm: *The Daily Gleaner*, Fredericton, 1889 to the present; *L'Évangéline*, Moncton, 1958–73; *Moncton Times*, 1877–1973; *Moncton Transcript*, 1882–1973; *Sackville Tribune*, 1902–72; *Daily Standard* (Saint John), 1909–22; *Saint John Gazette*, 1784–99; *Telegraph-Journal* (Saint John), 1924–75; *The Star* (Saint John), 1818–28, 1901–03; and the *Woodstock Bugle*, 1969–75.

The Bell Genealogical Collection

This includes genealogical information about at least fifty provincial families.

There is much more I could tell you about the wealth of information in these excellent Archives, but there are limits on space and so I have selected the most important sources of information; even so, I may be accused of leaving out items of importance. I suggest you ask the Archives for the leaflet *Genealogical Resources at the Provincial Archives of New Brunswick*, and try to buy or borrow an outstanding book by Robert F. Fellowes, *Researching Your Ancestors in New Brunswick*, privately printed in Fredericton in 1979, and obtainable from the author, % Historical Publications, RR #1, Mouth of Keswick, NB E0H 1N0.

There are several other sources of information in the province:

The Archives-Library Section, New Brunswick Museum, 277 Douglas Avenue, Saint John, NB E2K 1E5. The staff is small, and very little searching can be undertaken. The holdings include a General Card Index with over two hundred thousand names based on family histories, newspapers, diaries, various genealogical collections, etc. There are also the marriage registers for Saint John from 1812 to 1888, and marriage bonds (1830–32) for the counties of St. John, Kings, Queens, Charlotte, Kent, Westmorland, and York. There are also miscellaneous marriage records for Sunbury, Northumberland, and York. Some of these are also in the Provincial Archives, but by no means all. There are also many family histories, lists of Loyalist military men, and several early directories.

The Archives Collection, Mount Allison Unversity, Sackville, NB E0A 3C0. This is primarily a history collection rather than a genealogical one, but inevitably the two overlap, and when you are researching your family you will also want to research the history of the province and the particular area of settlement. There are a number of local and family histories, both published and in MS form.

Census Returns

Details have already been given of the census records in the various counties. They are all on microfilm and can be borrowed through the inter-library loan system from the National Archives in Ottawa. The available years are 1851, 1861, 1871, 1881, and 1891. There is no public access to returns of a later date.

There were censuses of the whole province in 1824, 1834, and 1840, but unfortunately these were head-counts and no names were recorded. The 1851 Census is the first one of use to you and it gives names, nationality, and date of entry into the colony. Later censuses give religion and place of birth (this can be simply a country or a province, but occasionally the exact place of birth is given).

Wills

Most of the early wills are in the Provincial Archives, and the years available appear above under each of the counties. They are all on microfilm. The odds are that you will not discover the will of an ancestor in early New Brunswick unless he was in business or the owner of considerable property. Many families simply arranged matters among themselves. In other cases, a will does not exist because the ancestor died suddenly or was killed in an accident early in life and long before he thought about making a will.

Land Records

Here, again, reference to the availability of these various records has been given under each county. Most of the records are in the Provincial Archives, but at the Lands Branch, Department of Natural Resources, PO Box 6000, Fredericton, NB E3B 5H1, there are copies of the original Letters Patent. The records at the Archives are of the greatest interest to the ancestor-hunter because the original petition quite often gave family details, such as, "I am of Scots birth (Aberdeen) and landed at Halifax from the ship 'Gabriel' on May 24, 1812, with my wife Mary (aged 24), and my children James (aged 3) and Elizabeth (aged 1). I am of good health, hard-working, and honest and can promise to work hard on any land granted to me, and to fulfill all my obligations thereon." This is an actual letter on file, but the names have been changed. You can see the value of this to anyone tracing back his or her family. The Provincial Archives have, on microfilm, the index to the land grants from 1765 to 1900.

| Genealogical Societies

The New Brunswick Genealogical Society is the parent body of various branches throughout the province. The mailing address is PO Box 3235, Station B, Fredericton, NB E3A 5G9. It has no projects, as such activities appear to be left to the branches. They are listed below:

BOIESTON: Wilmot Ross, RR #1, Nashwaak Bridge, NB E0H 1R0
CAPITAL: Clifford Marks, 145 Southampton Drive, Fredericton, NB E3B 4T5
CHALEUR: Kerry Price, 87 Lansdowne Street, Campbellton, NB E3N 1T1
GRAND MANAN: Mrs. G. Hettrick, Grand Harbour, Grand Manan, NB E0G 1X0
SAINT JOHN: Jim McKenzie, Comp. 7, Site 15, RR #2, Hampton, NB E0G 1Z0
SOUTHEAST: David Christopher, 160 Sussex Avenue, Riverview, NB E1B 3A7

These names and addresses were supplied by the Provincial Archives. As names and addresses of officials change quite frequently, it may be wiser for you to write to the particular Branch Secretary c/o The Provincial Archives, and your letter will be forwarded. The local branches have monthly meetings and are engaged in the cataloguing and collection of genealogical records. The NBGS has published several reference books, including *Vital Statistics from New Brunswick Newspapers (1784–1847)*, *New Brunswick Commissioned Officers Lists (1787–1867)*, and *Index of Surnames Being Researched by NBGS Members* (to 1986). As an example of projects of the branches, a recent issue of *Generation*, the magazine of the Society, contained lists of inscriptions from North Head (Grand Manan Island) and Campbellton cemeteries, and lists of St. John County marriages.

| Church Registers

As you will know by now, the Provincial Archives have microfilmed the *records* of very many churches in the province — mostly Anglican, but including some other denominations. These *records* as listed by the Archives may or may not contain registers of baptisms, marriages, and burials. Details of these churches can be found in the county information leaflets obtainable from the Archives. I suggest the following:

1. Get the leaflet for the county in which you are interested. If the church you want is listed, ask the Archives if the records for that church contain registers.

2. If so, apply for the microfilm through your local library, or your nearest library with a microfilm-viewer, but be prepared to wade through some very dull minutes, accounts, etc., before you reach the registers.

In addition to these *records*, the following church *registers* exist in various archives — either the originals or microfilm copies. Before referring to any of the registers listed, be sure you read the earlier chapter on the subject of church records.

Anglican

Church	Dates	Archives
Aberdeen	BMD 1929–34	ANB
Andover	BMD 1845–	ANB
Bathurst	BMD 1864–	ANB
Cambridge	B 1833– M 1885– D 1883–	ANB
Cambridge & Waterloo	BMD 1823–	ANB
Campobello	BMD 1830–	ANB
Canning & Chipman	BMD 1846–1914	ANB
Chatham	B 1822– M 1835– D 1833–	ANB
Douglas & Bright	B 1845– M 1843– D 1856–	ANB
Dumfries	BMD 1791–1816	NAC
Fredericton (Christ Church)	B 1816– M 1874– D 1859–	ANB
Fredericton (St. Mary's)	B 1843– MD 1846–	ANB
Gagetown	BM 1786–92	NAC

Church	Dates	Archives
Grand Falls	B 1882– M 1887– D 1883 only	ANB
Grand Manan	BMD 1832–	ANB
Greenwich & Westfield	BM 1801–1900 D 1822–1900	ANB
Hampton	BMD 1819–	ANB
Kingsclear	BMD 1791–1816	NAC
Kingston	B 1816–1900	ANB
Lancaster	BMD 1874–	ANB
Lepreau	BMD 1861–1970	ANB
Maugerville	BM 1787– D 1788–	ANB
Moncton	BMD 1843–	ANB
Newcastle	BMD 1843–	ANB
New Maryland	B 1836– M 1867– D 1860–	ANB
Northampton	BMD 1791–1970	ANB
Pennfield	BMD 1822–	ANB
Prince William	BMD 1792–1815	NAC
Richibucto	BMD 1815– MD 1825–	ANB
Rothesay	BMD 1870–	ANB
Sackville	M 1863–80	ANB
St. Andrews	BMD 1787–	ANB
Saint John (St. John's)	BMD 1852–	ANB
Saint John (Trinity)	B 1835– MD 1863–	ANB
St. Stephen (Christ Church)	BMD 1812–	ANB
St. Stephen (Trinity)	BMD 1870–	ANB
Shediac (St. Andrew)	BM 1825– D 1830–	ANB
Shediac (St. Martin) (including Richibucto & Buctouche)	BMD 1822–35	NAC
Simonds	BM 1846– D 1859–	ANB
Sussex & Norton	B 1817–44	ANB
Welford	BM 1848– D 1884–	ANB
Wellington & Buctouche	BMD 1868–	NAC
Woodstock	BMD 1791–1970	ANB
Westmorland (St. Mark)	BMD 1790–	ANS

Note: The Diocese of Fredericton, 115 Church Street, Fredericton, NB E3B 4C8, holds a number of registers which pre-date civil registration but unfortunately cannot list them. I suggest you write directly to the Diocesan Office for further information. If you refer to Chapter 7 you will find details of the various dioceses of

the Church. The churches in the Fredericton Diocese which were in existence before 1888 were:
Andover, Baie des Vents, Burton, Cambridge, Carlton, Chatham, Dalhousie, Derby, Dorchester, Douglas, Fairville, Fredericton, Grand Falls, Greenwich, Hampton, Johnston, Kingston, Moncton, Musquash, Newcastle, New Denmark, New Maryland, Norton, Petersville, Petitcodiac, Portland, Queensbury, Richibucto, Richmond, Rothesay, Sackville, St. Andrew's, St. David, St. George, St. John, St. Mary's, St. Martin's, St. Stephen, Shediac, Simonds, Springfield, Stanley, Studholm, Sussex, Upham, Waterford, Westmorland, Wicklow, and Woodstock.

Baptist

All the Baptist *records* listed below are in the Maritime Baptist Archives, Acadia University, Wolfville, NS B0P 1X0. It must be remembered that Baptists do not practise infant baptism, and that, generally speaking, the registers are not always separated from the general records of business of the particular church. You will find baptisms listed, but the age of the person baptized can range from six or seven up to ninety-six or -seven, depending on the age at admission to the Church. In some cases, too, marriages are recorded for a period, but not deaths — and vice versa. For this reason it is too confusing to list all the dates under each heading. The date shown below is the starting-date of the registers or records:

Church	Date	Church	Date
Avondale	1871	Keirstead Mountain	1838
Bayside	1838	Little South West	1845–81
Belle Isle Bay	1855	Lower Cambridge	1839–59
Belle Isle Creek	1888	Lower Queensbury	1841
Burtt's Corners	1812	McDonald's Corner	1839
Cambridge	1855–88	Nashwaak	1833–70
Canning	1800–73	Point de Bute	1850
Cape Tormentine	1892	Prince William	1800
Cookville	1896	Sackville	1808–83
Fredericton (Brunswick)	1814	St. Andrews	1865
Fredericton (George St.)	1845	St. Francis	1888
The Glades	1877	Saint John	1904
Hatfield's Point	1809–67	Scotchtown	1856
Jacksontown	1843	Tennant's Cove	1866*
Jemseg	1854–85	Upper Queensbury	1873

Church	Date	Church	Date
Victoria (Carleton)	1895	Wakefield (Rosedale)	1877
Wakefield	1804–10	Whitneyville	1819
		Woodstock	1857*

*Free Baptist

Catholic

The following parishes of the Catholic Church were in existence before 1888. They are listed alphabetically within each Catholic diocese:

DIOCESE OF BATHURST: PO Box 460, Bathurst, NB E2A 3Z4
Cathedral, Ste. Famille, Balmoral, Belledune, Campbellton, Caraquet, Charlo, Grand-Anse, Inkerman, Jacquet River, Lamèque, Miscou, Négouac, Paquetville, Petite Rivière, Petit Rocher, Pokemouche, St. Isidore, Shippegan, Tracadie.

DIOCESE OF EDMUNDSTON: PO Box 370, Edmundston, NB T5K 1N8
Cathedral, Grand Sault, Lac Baker, Red Rapids, Ste. Anne de Padoue, St. Basile, St. François, St. Hilaire, St. Jacques.

DIOCESE OF MONCTON: PO Box 248, Moncton, NB E1C 8K9
Barachois, Cap Pelé, Cocagne, Grande-Digue, Memramcook, Port Elgin, Richibuctou Village, Ste. Anne, St. Anselme, St. Bernard, St. Charles, St. Ignace, St. Louis, Ste. Marie, St. Paul, Shediac.

DIOCESE OF SAINT JOHN: 1 Bayard Drive, Saint John, NB E2L 3L5
Cathedral, Blessed Virgin, Bartibogue Bridge, Blackville, Boiestown, Chatham, Douglastown, Fredericton, Johnville, Loggieville, Milltown, Newcastle, Oromocto, Red Bank, Renous, St. Andrews, St. George, St. Margarets, South Nelson, Sussex, and Woodstock.

The following Catholic Church registers exist in various archives; abbreviations are as shown on p. xvi–xviii:

Place	Dates	Archives
Baie-Ste-Anne	BMD 1845–	NAC
Baie-des-Vents	BMD 1801–	NAC
Barachois	BD 1812– M 1820–	NAC
Bartibogue	BMD 1801–21	AAM
Bathurst	BMD 1798–	AAM
Botsford	See Cap Tourmentin	NAC
Buctouche	BMD 1800–70	NAC
Cap-Pelé	BMD 1813–	AAM

Cap Tourmentin	B 1839–53 M 1846–47 D 1839–48	NAC
Caraquet	BMD 1768–	NAC
Charlo	BMD 1853–	AAM
Cocagne	BMD 1800–70	NAC
Dalhousie	BMD 1843–	NAC
Fredericton	BMD 1806–59	NAC
Grande-Digue	BM 1800– D 1802–	NAC
Haute-Aboujagane	*See* Barachois	NAC
Hillsborough	*See* Acadie and Gaspésie, Nova Scotia	
		NAC
Hopewell	*See* Acadie and Gaspésie, Nova Scotia	
		NAC
Inkerman	BMD 1818–	AAM
Lamèque	BMD 1841–	AAM
Madawaska	BMD 1792–	AAM
Memramcook	BM 1806–70 D 1807–70	NAC
Moncton	BMD 1873–	AAM
Naboiyagan	*See* Barachois	NAC
Nash Creek	BMD 1867–	AAM
Neguac	BMD 1796–1848	NAC
Paquetville	BMD 1874–	AAM
Petitcodiac	*See* Acadie and Gaspésie, Nova Scotia	
		NAC
Petit-Rocher	BMD 1824–	AAM
Pointe-Sapin	BMD 1821–69	NAC
Pokemouche	BMD 1843–	AAM
Richibuctou	BD 1796–1871 M 1800–71	NAC
Robertville	BMD 1885–	AAM
Rogersville	BMD 1877–87	AAM
St. Anselme	B 1832– MD 1832–70	NAC
St-Basile-de-Madawaska	BMD 1792–1850	NAC
St-Charles-de-l'Ardoine	BD 1800–70 M 1801–70	NAC
St-Charles-de-Kent	BMD 1887–	AAM
Ste-Anne-de-Kingsclear	BMD 1767–	AAM
St-Ignace-de-Kent	BMD 1887–	AAM
St. Isidore	BMD 1876–	AAM
St-Louis-de-Kent	BMD 1800–70	NAC
St. Martins	BD 1876– M 1877–	ANB
St-Paul-de-Kent	BMD 1883–	AAM
Scoudouc	B 1850–70 M 1852–70 D 1855–70	NAC
Shediac	BMD 1863–	AAM

Place	Dates	Archives
Shemogue (Chimogoui)	BD 1813– M 1818–	NAC
Shippegan	BMD 1824–	AAM
Tracadie (St. Jean)	BMD 1798–	AAM
Tracadie (St. Pierre)	BMD 1811–	AAM
New Brunswick (General)	BMD 1753–57	UM

United Church (including Methodist & Presbyterian)

The following United Church registers are in these three archives:

Place	Dates	Archives
Campbellton (UC)	BMD 1874–	ANB
Fredericton (UC)	BM 1794–	NBM
Newcastle (P)	B 1831– M 1830– D 1891–	ANB
Newcastle (M)	B 1882– M 1884– D 1893–	ANB
Sussex (UC)	BMD 1857–	ANB
New Brunswick (General)	BMD 1753–57	UM

The United Church of Canada (Maritime Conference), c/o The Atlantic School of Theology, Francklyn Street, Halifax, NS B3H 3B5, states it is unable to list its registers, but the majority of them are in the Provincial Archives of New Brunswick, Nova Scotia, and Prince Edward Island. If you want information on this subject, I suggest you contact the Maritime Conference directly at the address above.

Non-Denominational (town and civil registers)

Place	Dates	Archives
Chipoudy & Petitcodiac	B 1755 and 1756 M 1756	NAC
Jemseg (Rivière-St-Jean)	B 1681 only	NAC
Missions-de-N-Brunswick	B 1755–57	NAC
Petitcodiac (Hopewell)	BMD 1753–55	NAC
Sackville*	M 1748–1822	NBM
Sheffield	B 1750–1829 MD 1766–1845	NAC
Westmorland County	M 1790–1835	NAC

*In addition, the Provincial Archives of Nova Scotia, Halifax, NS B3H 1W4, have the township records of Sackville, 1760–1871. Sackville was originally part of that province. The records include land transactions, cattle marks, and BMD. Often children are listed who were born before their parents came to the township.

| Cemeteries

Over 300 cemeteries and their inscriptions have been recorded
— many on microfilm — and full information about them is in
the County Reference Section of the Provincial Archives.

| Libraries

As in the other provinces, genealogical information is not concentrated in two or three main locations but has spread into
specialized libraries and local public libraries. All this has happened within the past fifteen years.

The Harriet Irving Library, of the University of New Brunswick, is a case in point. Fourteen years ago, when I was
researching my book *In Search of Your Roots*, the librarian
there told me, "We have very little genealogical material in
our collections," and listed for me the names of a few families
described in some unpublished manuscripts: Beckwith, Chipman, Close, Glasier, and Ludlow.

How things have changed! The library now contains the histories of many more New Brunswick families, and there are
newspaper clippings, papers from various organizations containing biographical information about individuals, theses
completed by students, and copies or microfilms of early newspapers: the *New Brunswick Reporter*, 1844–1902; the *St.
Andrew's Standard*, 1836–80; the *Chatham Gleaner*, 1829–80;
and others.

If your ancestors were Loyalist, you will be able to obtain
by inter-library loan many records on microfilm, including
genealogical documents from the various Atlantic provinces,
as well as Québec and Ontario.

The staff cannot undertake detailed research but can supply
a list of qualified researchers for you. The mailing address of
the library is Box 7500, Fredericton, NB E3B 5H5.

The public library system of the province is divided into five
regional libraries and some sixty local libraries. If you are
interested in a particular locality, be sure you write to the local
library—it may well have information about your family if your
ancestors were early settlers. Remember to cover the return
postage! The amount of genealogical information varies, of
course, and depends on the size of the library, its financial
resources, and the enthusiasm and interest of the staff. Some
examples of the type of information available are given below:

Chaleur Regional Library, PO Box 607, Campbellton, NB E3N 3H1. A MS history of the French settlers in the area, with an index of names; a history of the Roy Family through eleven generations; inscriptions from the Old Athol House Cemetery; the Pioneers of Hopetown; Vital Statistics of Restigouche and Bonaventure counties, 1909–31, listing the names of everyone who was born, married, or died in that period. The important thing to note is that all these histories are in manuscript form, unpublished, and not in existence elsewhere.

Campbellton Centennial Library, PO Box 607, Campbellton, NB E3N 3H1. Indexed census records for 1881 (hand-written only); a history of the Presbyterian and Methodist missions of the Escuminac; St. François Xavier Church, Charlo, 1853–1920; the First United Baptist Church, Campbellton (1885–1986); the Loyalists of Gaspésie; Restigouche County Marriages, 1838–78; the Arran Clearances in the Restigouche area; Town Lots of New Carlisle, 1783–84, etc. Here again these manuscripts, documents, and papers have not been published, except in a couple of instances.

The library also holds records of BMD abstracted from the *Campbellton Graphic*, 1909–31, and it has records of the inscriptions of twenty-three local cemeteries, both Protestant and Catholic. There are a number of family trees, including those of Adams, Ahier, Beebe, Burton, Calder, Durette, Hall, Hocquard, Kierstead, McColm, McLean, McLellan, MacPherson, Scott, Sillars, Tozer, and Willett.

Dalhousie Regional Library, 405 Adelaide Street, Dalhousie, NB E0K 1B0. This library holds family trees for a number of local families, including Alexander, Archibald, Barthe, Cook, Crawford, Dickie, Elsliger, Guitard, Hamilton, James, Kennedy, LeCouffe, McLean, McNair, Miller, Murchie, Reid, St. Onge, Stewart, and Wood. There are also "bits and pieces" of another fifty families.

All this hidden information illustrates the point I make continually in books, articles, and lectures, and on TV and radio: "Check with a local library, make sure your family has not already been researched." I am always amazed at the number of people who say, "Oh, I never thought about doing that!" and I am equally amazed at the number who later write or say to me, "If only I had thought to do that earlier. I found out all sorts of things about my family."

Harvey Community Library, Harvey Station, NB E0H 1H0. Here is a small local library that contrasts with the bigger ones above. Limited resources, limited support, and yet an incipient genealogical collection starting with family histories of Cleghorn, Swan, and Wilson—and more to come.

L. P. Fisher Library, PO Box 1540, Woodstock, NB E0J 2B0. This is another local library, but famed in New Brunswick for its genealogical collection. I would like to list the holdings in detail but can only give a sampling of the wealth of information that awaits you if your family originated in the Woodstock area. You will find such items as the Muster Roll of the Carleton Light Dragoons, 1840; and the histories of the families of Campbell, Collicott, Dibblee, Dow, Faulkner, Feero, Fisher, Flowers, Fowler, Gallagher, Grant, Joyall, Kinney, Longstaff, Morehouse, Nicholson, Orser, Perry, Price, Raymond, Sharp, Shaw, Snow, Stoddard, Tompkins, Tomson.

There are early records and registers of the Anglican Church, 1791–1816; Baptist records, 1804–11; BMD of the Anglican church in Woodstock, 1791–1838; the Anglican church of Andover, 1846–1902; and lists of cemetery inscriptions from Victoria and Carleton counties, Florenceville, and northwestern York. You will find indexed censuses for Victoria and Carleton counties; the marriage records of Carleton County, 1832–88; and a number of books about early settlement and settlers in areas such as Argyle, New Denmark, Perth-Andover, Woodstock, and Carleton County itself.

The LDS Church

As I mentioned in Chapter 4, the full genealogical resources of this church are at your disposal through your nearest LDS Family History Library. In the case of New Brunswick, this is in Hampton, and the mailing address is PO Box 414, Hampton, NB E0G 1Z0. The information collected by the Church is available to those of us who are not members, and there are no strings attached! Use its vast store of information—which is essential to your research—and be grateful it is shared with us.

Historical Societies

There are also a number of these in the province, and although their interests are primarily with local history, they do inevitably collect a lot of genealogical information. They will be of particular value to you in areas where a branch of the New Brunswick Genealogical Society has not been established. They can usually be contacted through a local library:

Albert County: PO Box 39, Hopewell Cape, NB E0A 1Y0
Carleton County: Ross Memorial Museum, St. Andrews,
   NB E0G 2X0
Grand Manan: Castalia PO, Grand Manan, NB E0G 1X0
Kings County: Centennial Building, Route 121, Hampton,
   NB E0G 1Z0
Miramichi (Northumberland County): 225 Mary Street, Newcastle,
   NB E1V 1Z3
Queens County: Jemseg, NB E0E 1S0
Southern Victoria: Perth, NB E0J 1V0
York-Sunbury: c/o Provincial Archives, Fredericton, NB E3B 5H1

Note: There is also a Genealogical Society in Campbellton which is not, apparently, affiliated with the New Brunswick Genealogical Society. It works closely with the Campbellton Centennial Libary and is responsible for much of the good genealogical collection there (President: Jackson B. Ross, Restigouche Genealogical Society, 6 Chaleur Street, Campbellton, NB E3N 1T1).

CHAPTER 13

Newfoundland and Labrador

The origins of the area we now know as Newfoundland—the main island, several small ones, and Labrador—are clouded in the mists of history, mists as deep as those that often hide its shores today. The first inhabitants were the Red Paint People. This ancient race of seafarers is believed to have inhabited the Arctic Rim more than seven thousand years ago, and traces of their settlement have been found from Ungava to Maine. They were followed by Indian tribes — mainly the Micmac — and finally by adventurers from Europe. Leif Ericsson and John Cabot and Samuel de Champlain blazed the trail which others then followed from France, England, Wales, Scotland, Ireland, and Portugal.

Life has never been easy in the Atlantic provinces of Canada —first the constant struggle with the elements, and then some two centuries of fierce rivalry between France and Great Britain.

The first would-be settlers arrived in 1583 with Sir Humphrey Gilbert, but the West Country English merchants who dominated the island were determined to prevent permanent settlement, because increasing numbers of colonists would threaten their despotic control of the fishing industry and other trading activities. Some hardy souls persisted on the Avalon

Peninsula at Cuppers Cove (now Cupids) on Conception Bay. Very little further settlement took place until 1610.

The rivalry between France and Great Britain increased, and in 1660 the French occupied some parts of the island and established colonies at Placentia and near St. John's. By 1713 the British were back under the terms of the Treaty of Utrecht, but the persistent French recaptured and held it from 1756 to 1763, when they finally lost control of it forever. Only the offshore islands of St. Pierre and Miquelon remained under the French flag.

Newfoundland obtained representative government in 1832, and a parliamentary system of government was established in 1855. The idea of joining the Canadian Confederation was rejected in 1869 and the island remained a self-governing colony of Great Britain.

By 1929 economic collapse faced the colony, and the British government reassumed direct control by establishing government by a commission of three British and three Newfoundland officials. By 1949 the debts of the colony had been cleared and there was a $40 million surplus. At this point two referendums were held which resulted in a narrow margin in favour of Confederation. The British government relinquished control and the island became Canada's tenth province.

| Civil Registration

This started in 1891. Before that year, the clergy of the various denominations maintained records of birth or baptism, marriage, and death. The church registers containing this information are in the Provincial Archives. The official records since civil registration commenced are in the Vital Statistics Division of the Department of Health, Confederation Building, St. John's, NF A1C 2C9. These are not open to public search, but, of course, information and certified copies can be obtained for a fee. Always request a *full* copy. The Provincial Archives have microfilmed birth records from 1891 to 1923 and this material is open for public search.

The oldest parish registers in existence are those of the Church of England, the only official church in the early days of the colony. The registers date back to 1752. In 1784 other denominations began to establish churches: Catholic registers for St. John's start in 1798; Methodist registers at Carbonear in 1794; Presbyterian registers in 1842 in St. John's; and Congregationalist registers in the 1780s.

Provincial Archives of Newfoundland and Labrador

These are located in the Colonial Building, Military Road, St. John's, NF A1C 2C9. Note the full title of the province and always use it in correspondence — oh, you don't *have* to, but Newfoundlanders are always glad to have it emphasized, because Québec still claims most of Labrador!

The holdings of the Archives, apart from the church registers mentioned above, are wills, newspapers, directories, early court records, deeds of sale, registers of deeds, and early books and magazines; most of the records date back to the early 1800s. There are also personal papers from many well-known Newfoundland families such as Andrews, Calvert, Currie, Holdsworth, Oke, Pinsent, etc. There is also the Devine Collection — originally put together by P. K. Devine, of St. John's, and containing a mass of early papers, documents, records, books, clippings, diaries, and early newspapers.

Census Returns

These are maintained by the Department of Social Services, Confederation Building, St. John's, NF A1C 2C9. As Newfoundland did not enter Confederation until 1949, the law regarding census-information release did not apply. The result is that census returns in Newfoundland alone are available up to 1945, and not only up to 1891 as in the rest of Canada.

Early censuses include those for the Plaisance area in 1671, 1673, 1698, 1706, and 1711. There were general censuses for other parts of the colony in 1691, 1693, and 1704. However, any returns before 1698 gave only the head of the household. All are on microfilm. Province-wide censuses were held in 1911, 1921, 1935, and 1945, and, of course, after that in the same years as the rest of Canada. Only fragments of the 1911 census have survived.

The places covered by the censuses between 1921 and 1945 are listed below. They are on microfilm and are in both the National Archives in Ottawa and the Provincial Archives in St. John's. They may be borrowed through the inter-library loan system for your use in your local library (if it has a micro-film-viewer):

Bay de Verde, 1935, 1945	Humber, 1935, 1945
Bay de Verge, 1921	Labrador, 1935, 1945
Bell Island, 1935, 1945	La Poile, 1921, 1935, 1945
Bonavista, 1935	Mill Fortune, 1935
Bonavista North, 1945	Placentia, 1921, 1935, 1945
Bonavista South, 1945	Placentia West, 1945
Burgeo, 1921, 1935, 1945	Port au Port, 1921
Burin, 1921, 1935, 1945	Port-de-Grave, 1921, 1935, 1945
Carbonear, 1921	St. Barbe, 1921, 1935, 1945
Carbouer, 1945	St. George, 1935
Ferryland, 1921, 1935	St. John's, 1945
Fogo, 1921, 1935, 1945	St. John's East, 1921, 1935, 1945
Fortune, 1935	St. John's West, 1921, 1935, 1945
Fortune Hermitage, 1921, 1945	St. Mary's, 1921, 1935, 1945
Grand Falls, 1945	St. Mary's West, 1935
Green Bay, 1945	Trinity, 1921, 1935, 1945
Harbour Grace, 1921, 1935, 1945	Trinity North, 1945
Harbour Main, 1921, 1945	Trinity South, 1945
	White Bay, 1935, 1945

| Wills

The probate records of the province date back to the 1700s and are in three locations. Those from 1832 on are in the Probate Registry, Courthouse Building, Water Street, St. John's. Earlier ones are in the Provincial Archives and the Registry of Deeds, Confederation Building, St. John's (wills from the Burin area are all in the Provincial Archives). There are plans to index all wills and enter them into the computer.

| Land Records

A great deal of genealogical information can often be obtained from land records and conveyances of property. You may find references to wills, and to other members of the particular property-owner's family. The Registry of Deeds, in the Confederation Building, St. John's, is the main source for more recent land information. The earlier and original Crown Land Grants are in the Crown Lands Office, Howley Building, St. John's.

Genealogical Society

The five-year-old Newfoundland and Labrador Genealogical Society is located in the Colonial Building, Military Road, St. John's, NF A1C 2C9. At present there are no branches or chapters within the province. The Society maintains its own library, which includes family trees, directories, and a collection of cemetery inscriptions. This latter effort is the main ongoing project, and leaflets have already been published with details of cemeteries at Topsail (Anglican), Cupids (United), Labrador, the Northern Peninsula, and Fortune; several others are nearly completed and will be published shortly.

Church Registers

The following parishes of the Anglican Church were in existence in Newfoundland before civil registration of births, marriages, and deaths (1891):

Battle Harbour, Bay de Verde, Bay of Islands, Bay Roberts, Belleoram, Bonavista, Bonne Bay, Brigus, Brooklyn, Burgeo, Burin, Carbonear, Catalina, Channel, Exploits, Flowers Cove, Fogo, Fox Trap, Green Bay, Greenspond, Harbour Breton, Harbour Buffett, Harbour Grace, Heart's Content, Hermitage, Herring Neck, King's Cove, Lamaline, New Harbour, Port-de-Grave, Portugal Cove, Random, Rose Blanche, St. George's Bay, St. John's, St. Pierre, Salmon Cove, Salvage, Sandwich Bay, Spaniards Bay, Topsail, Trinity, Twillingate, Upper Island Cove, and White Bay.

The following parishes of the Catholic Church were in existence before civil registration:

DIOCESE OF GRAND FALLS: Baie de Verde, Brigue, Harbour Grace, Harbour Main, and Tilting.
DIOCESE OF ST. GEORGE: Harbour Breton, Port-au-Prince West, St. Bernard's, St. George's, Searston, and Stephenville.

DIOCESE OF ST. JOHN'S: Cathedral, Bay Bulls, Bell Island, Freshwater, Lamaline, Placentia, Renews, St. Joseph, St. Kyrans, St. Lawrence, St. Mary's, Trepassey, and Witless Bay.

As mentioned earlier in this chapter, the early church registers of the province are in the custody of the Provincial Archives, Colonial Building, Military Road, St. John's, NF A1C 2C9. I give below a complete list of these registers with starting and finishing dates. Please note this does not mean that every entry for every year between the two dates is available — there are gaps.

Anglican (Church of England)

Church	Dates
Bareneed Church (*See also* Port-de-Grave)	B 1839–63 M 1829–63 D 1828–69
Bay Roberts	B 1837–1907 M 1834–1907 D 1838–1907
Bay of Islands	B 1864–1961 D 1870–1980
Bay de Verde	B 1841–1900 M 1841–1900 D 1841–1900
Bay St. George (East End)	B 1880–1961 M 1880–1974 D 1881–1983
Bonavista	B 1786–1834 M 1786–1834 D 1786–1973
Bonne Bay	B 1870–1903 M 1870–1903
Brigus	M 1830
Carbonear	B 1834–1954 M 1859–1908 D 1849–1953
Catalina	B 1834–79 M 1833–79 D 1829–1942
Channel	M 1929–40
Cupids	D 1860–95
Fogo	B 1901–72 M 1841–1962 D 1879–1972
Fogo Island & Change Islands	B 1841–79 M 1912–72 D 1965–72
Fogo (Joe Batt's Arm)	B 1911–65 M 1889–1969
Harbour Grace	B 1775–1916 M 1776–1917 D 1775–1917
Heart's Content	B 1879–1903 M 1879–1960 D 1866–1973
Lamaline	B 1849–59

Old Garrison Church	M 1830–79 D 1865–1978
Port-de-Grave	B 1827–42 M 1828–39 D 1828–69
Portugal Cove	D 1830–38
Pouch Cove	B 1841–91 M 1841–1970 D 1841–1976
St. George's:	
(1) Bay St. George	B 1841–52 M 1841–70 D 1841–71
(2) Sandy Point	M 1871–96
(3) Mission Bay	B 1871–80
(4) Bay St. George	B 1921–74
(5) Barachois	B 1881 D 1882–1972
(6) St. George/St. Michael	M 1881–1928
(7) St. David's	M 1929–59
(8) St. George/Robinson	M 1930–66
St John's Cathedral (west coast, north peninsula Labrador, 1849)	B 1752–1906 M 1752–1879 D 1752–1906
St. John's	B 1810–70
St. Thomas	B 1830–68
Topsail	B 1860–1909 M 1860–85
Torbay (with Pouch Cove)	B 1879–1976 M 1879–1975 D 1879–1976
Trinity	B 1753–1826
Twillingate	B 1816–23
Trinity Bay (Random)	B 1880–1985 M 1880–1984 D 1880–1980

Catholic

Church	Date
Argentia	B 1835–96 M 1835–96
Bay Bulls	B 1830–1933 M 1876–1956 D 1911–1965
Bonavista	B 1842– M 1844–
Burin	B 1833–94 M 1833–1904
Burin (Bay Book)	B 1895–1955
Carbonear	B 1849–1901 M 1852–80
Conception Harbour	B 1884–1905 M 1884–1930
Conche	B 1873–1981 D 1902–81
Ferryland	B 1870–1910 M 1870–1910
Harbour Grace	B 1828–1945 M 1812–88
Harbour Main	B 1857–99 M 1857–1905
King's Cove	B 1838–1909 M 1815–1909
King's Cove (Trinity)	B 1838–57

Church	Date
Marystown (Bay Book)	B 1895–1922
Northern Bay	B 1838–71 M 1838–1914
Placentia	B 1846–1921 M 1822–1921 D 1896–1934
Portugal Cove	B 1844–93 M 1844–92
Renews	B 1857–1919 M 1838–1920
St. John's Basilica	B 1802–86 M 1793–1890 (indexed)
St. Mary's	B 1843–98 M 1843–98 D 1891–98
Tilting	B 1842–1904 M 1842–1904
Trepassey	B 1843–1909 M 1861–68 D 1856–1915
Whitbourne	B 1891–1916 M 1891–1921 D 1892–1921
Witless Bay (Tors Cove)	M 1901–51
Witless Bay (Mobil)	D 1901–08
Witless Bay	B 1830–1949 M 1830–80

United Church (Pastoral Charge)

Church	Date
Baie Verte (White Bay South)	D 1906–33
Bay Bulls Arm	B 1917–67 M 1917–68
Bay St. George's	B 1883–1969 M 1883–1969 D 1875–1915
Blackhead	B 1842–1970 M 1842–1970 D 1883–1943
Bonne Bay	B 1874–1936 M 1875–1952 D 1874–1978
Botwood	B 1889–1963 M 1890–1958 D 1890–1958
Brigus	B 1822–40 M 1823–49 D 1804–92
Britannia Cove	B 1883–1957 M 1883–1957 D 1884–1958
Burin	B 1816–26 M 1816–36 D 1816–96
Burnt Island Mission	B 1860–93
Carbonear	B 1817–34 M 1794–1967 D 1820–88
Change Islands	B 1917–33 D 1947–67
Channel	B 1862–1963 M 1857–1965 D 1862–1965
Cupids	B 1842–88 M 1837–1930
(Rev. Atkinson's Book)	B 1918–21 D 1916–21
Flowers Cove	B 1874–1942 M 1874–1942 D 1874–1964

Fogo	B 1863–1972 M 1890–1972 D 1890–1972
Fogo (Indian Islands)	D 1907–17
Fogo (Seldom Islands)	B 1906–17
Foster's Point	B 1928–57 M 1928–57 D 1928–57
Green Bay Circuit	B 1841–1853 M 1842–78
Greenspond Circuit	B 1862–70 M 1862–86 D 1862–1924
Hant's Harbour	D 1861–95
Harbour Grace (Wesleyan)	B 1883–1964
Little Bay (Green Bay Circuit)	B 1883–1964 M 1867–1967
Little Harbour Ease	B 1927–56
Lower Harbour Cove	B 1816–91 D 1838–94
North West River (Labrador)	B 1884–1950
Old Perlican	B 1853–1901 M 1816–1941 D 1816–1901
Pelley's Island	B 1909–32 M 1909–75 D 1909–78
Port-de-Grave	M 1879–1914 D 1903–16
Pouch Cove	B 1878–1917
Pouch (Circuit)	B 1892–1917 M 1879–1917 D 1893–1917
Random South Circuit	B 1890–1936 M 1910–69
Red Bay	B 1877–1973 M 1878–1973 D 1878–1972
St. Anthony	B 1873–90 M 1873–90
Topsail	B 1886–1973 M 1873–1982 D 1886–1982
Twillingate	B 1853–78 M 1853–76 D 1852–76
Western Bay	B 1817–1970 M 1899–1963 D 1908–70
Whitbourne	B 1892–1917 M 1893–1919 D 1893–1917

Presbyterian

Church	Date
St. Andrew's (The Kirk)	B 1842–1969 M 1842–1969 D 1892–1914

Vital statistics from:
Harbour Grace Standard, 1862–1894
Twillingate Sun, 1945–52

Weekly Herald, 1849–50
The Star, 1840–43, 1872–75
Harbour Grace Weekly Journal,
   1828–38

Salvation Army

Church	*Date*
All Districts	B 1886–1952 M 1921–43
Bonavista North	B 1920–75
Bonavista South	B 1920–71
Burgeo–Lapoile	B 1920–74
Burin	B 1916–76
Fogo	B 1918–19
Fortune–Hermitage	B 1956–71
Grand Falls	B 1918–76
Green Bay	B 1918–70
Harbour Grace	B 1896–1970
Harbour Main (Bell Island)	B 1953–71
Humber	B 1953–67
Placentia West	B 1918–75
Placentia St. Mary's	B 1918–57
Port-de-Grave	B 1896–1973
St. Barbe	B 1918–76
Trinity North	B 1919–74
Trinity South	B 1953–76
Twillingate	B 1918–76

There are other church registers in other locations:

Moravian Missions
(in the National Archives of Canada, Ottawa)

Hebron (Labrador)	M 1904–33
Nain (Labrador)	M 1904–33
Okak (Labrador)	BMD 1777–1919
Ramah (Labrador)	BMD 1874–1929
Zoar (Labrador)	BMD 1825–1939

Anglican Church
(in the National Archives)

St. John's Cathedral	BMD 1752–90
St. John's District	BMD 1784–1849
St. John's Congregational	BMD 1780–1844
Trinity (St. Paul)	BMD 1753–1867

United Church of Canada
(UC Archives, 320 Elizabeth Avenue, St. John's, NF A1E 1R1)
The holdings here include several registers pre-dating those in the Provincial Archives by a few years, or not in the latter archives. Details are below:

Anglican Reformed Church
(These are from communities in the province which then formed Methodist congregations):

B 1810–18 M 1812–19 D 1856–93

Other Methodist, United Church, and allied congregations:

Blackhead and Western Bay	B 1816–42 M 1816–1900 D 1816–1907
Bonavista	B 1817–1884 M 1836–93 D 1827–40
Carbonear	B 1794–1837 M 1794–1848 D 1820–55
Englee	B 1883– M 1883– D 1883–
Exploits	B 1860– M 1862–93 D 1875–
Grand Bank	B 1817–49 M 1817– D 1817–
Hant's Harbour	B 1842– M 1851– D 1861–91
Heart's Content	B 1878– M 1878– D 1878–
Little Bay Islands	B 1867–1948 M 1867–1949 D 1867–1949
Old Perlican	B 1816–1901 M 1816–1913 D 1816–1910
Port-de-Grave	D 1847–1910
St. George's	B 1883– M 1883– D 1883–
Victoria	B 1883– M 1883– D 1883–

| Libraries

The Provincial Reference and Resource Library is located in the Arts and Culture Centre, St. John's NF A1B 3A3. This is one of the best-organized and most valuable of the genealogical sources in the province. Its holdings include the following:

Newspaper Index

This includes personal names and communities. It is an ongoing project dating from 1978: entries from the *Evening Telegram*; indexes from a wide variety of local newspapers from the early nineteenth century up to 1963; BMD entries from local newspapers from 1825 to 1870—this is a four-volume collection of entries by Mildred Howard; names in the newspapers (1825–70); a ten-volume record of BMD by Gertrude Crosbie; a Card Index by P. K. Devine.

Cemetery Records

Inscriptions from Labrador, Topsail Anglican, Cupids United Church, Northern Peninsula graveyards, and the General Protestant Cemetery, St. John's (1889–1912).

Census Records

A miscellaneous collection that includes local censuses and inhabitant listings not included in the official records: Newfoundland from Cape Race to Cape Bonavista, 1675; inhabitants and their boats from Bonavista to Trepassey, 1677; Census of St. John's, 1794–95; houses and inhabitants of Trinity, 1800–01; inhabitants of Brigus in 1817.

Family Names

Records of the first settlers, 1654–85, and various early directories from 1864 to 1932. Histories of various families — Adams, Bowring, Butler, Butt, Coish, Crosbie, Delurey, Murray, Pratt, Windsor, etc.

Voters' Lists

Bay de Verde, 1913; St. John's East, St. Mary's, and Placentia for 1917; and the whole province from 1948 to 1979.

There are over a hundred public libraries covering all the settled areas of the province, but not many have genealogical collections. It is, of course, worth while to write to the local library anyway and find out what information it does have. Be sure you enclose a stamped, self-addressed No. 9 envelope when you write.

One library that does have an excellent genealogical collection is Corner Brook City Library, Sir Richard Squires Building, Corner Brook, NF A2H 6J8. Its holdings include

church registers on microfilm from the general area of the city
— mainly Anglican and Methodist registers, as listed below:

Anglican	*Methodist*
Badgers Quay	Bonavista
Battle Harbour	Burin
Bay of Islands	Channel
Bay St. George	Glovertown
Bonavista	Grand Bank
Burgeo	Musgrave Town
Change Islands	Nippers Harbour
Channel	Twillingate
Fogo Island	
Rose Blanche	
Trinity	

Note: Several of the above registers are not listed among those
mentioned by the Provincial Archives and the United Church.

The library also has the *Western Star* newspaper on microfilm since 1907; early directories of Newfoundland and Corner
Brook; and a good collection of books on local history in which
many families of the area are mentioned.

| Other Sources

There are a number of other sources of possible information
that should not be neglected: Maritime History Group
Archives (Memorial University); Memorial University Folklore Archives (these hold a collection of family trees compiled
by students; there is no guarantee of accuracy, but they do
provide information about nearly a hundred families); Newfoundland Historical Society, Colonial Building, Military
Road, St. John's; Bay St. George Heritage Association, PO Box
314, Stephenville, NF A2N 2Z5; Trinity Historical Society,
Trinity, NF A0C 2S0; and Twillingate Museum Association,
Twillingate, NF A0G 4M0.

The LDS Church does not appear to be active in the province, but do not neglect its genealogical records; these were
described in Chapter 4.

CHAPTER 14
The Acadians

The Acadians are people of French descent living in the Atlantic provinces, Québec, the New England States, and Louisiana. Their ancestors were the victims of one of the most brutal expulsions in history. It is believed that at least half the original Acadians — the settlers from France — originated from the area near Aulnay, in the Département of Vienne, France. Geneviève Massignon, author of *Les Parlers Français d'Acadie* (1962), reached this conclusion after an exhaustive study of Acadian records and family stories in Canada, and parish registers in France.

Their original area of settlement in Canada was in what is now New Brunswick and Nova Scotia. Emery LeBlanc, in his book *Les Acadiens* (1963), estimated there were then 350,000 people of Acadian descent in the Atlantic provinces, 300,000 in Québec, 75,000 in the New England States, and 600,000 in Louisiana (where they are known as Cajuns — a corruption of Acadians). It is estimated that at least thirty-five per cent of the population of New Brunswick is French-speaking.

The first settlement in what the French called Acadie, and which is now part of Nova Scotia, was begun in 1604 by Samuel de Champlain and the Sieur de Monts on a small island in Passamaquoddy Bay, but after one winter of great hardship there, the inhabitants moved to a more sheltered location on the mainland. The new settlement was called Port Royal—later changed by the British to Annapolis Royal. Over the next century, more settlers arrived from France, and they were joined by small numbers of Scots, Irish, English, and Portuguese. The later immigrants blended well into the French settlement, and that is why you will find names like Fisher, Foster, and McGraw among lists of Acadian family names!

English and Scots settlers arrived in other parts of the peninsula a few years later, and from this time on, the Acadians were the innocent victims of power politics and the constant rivalry between the British and the French. It was ironic that battles in obscure places in Europe could affect the lives of the Acadians in far-off Acadie. Neither the British nor the French showed the slightest regard for the settlers, and ownership of the area changed ten times between the early seventeenth century and the final Peace Treaty of 1763 which ended the French colonization of North America. It was only then that the Acadians, after years of deportation, starvation, loss of their farms, and the breaking up of their families, could be left alone to till their fields, raise their cattle, and rebuild their lives.

By 1750 the Acadians numbered 10,000, and since 1713 they had been under British rule. Their main concern, in those troubled times, was to be neutral. They made it clear to the French that, whatever their natural instincts might be, their precarious existence in what was an increasingly British area depended on neutrality. However, Charles Lawrence, the Lieutenant-Governor, was reputed to look under the bed for Acadians at night. He was very unhappy at the thought of holding Nova Scotia with ten thousand French in the middle in the event of another war with France. He bombarded the government in London with suggestions that the Acadians should be expelled from the territory and settled in small colonies along the New England coast. To its credit, the government refused permission for this drastic step, but did instruct the Lieutenant-Governor to obtain an oath of allegiance to the Crown from every Acadian.

To Lawrence's surprise, the leaders of the Acadians agreed to this, but insisted that, in the event of war, they be excused military service against their fellow-French in Québec. Lawrence refused to accept this reasonable proposal, and insisted they give the full, unconditional oath. The Acadians, who had already proved their loyalty by refusing to join a French attack on Nova Scotia, remained firm. Lawrence then gave instructions for the mass expulsion of every Acadian — men, women, and children — and the seizure of all their land, livestock, and houses.

The expulsion started in 1755 when hundreds of Acadians were forced on to three ships and put ashore at various places in New England. There they were surrounded by people who spoke another language and were also strongly opposed to the Catholic Church. Six thousand Acadians in all were rounded up, placed on ships, and then distributed down the eastern seaboard of the American colonies from Maine to Georgia. Meanwhile, back in Nova Scotia, many escaped into the bush with their families and lived a precarious existence amid great hardship and constant harassment by British soldiers. Their houses and settlements were put to the torch, and in 1759 Lawrence (by now promoted to governor by a grateful government in London) invited seven thousand settlers from New England to take over the vacant land.

Other Acadians were deported to England, where they were detained until 1763, when they were allowed to go to France. Many of those left in New England also made their own way to France, while others went by sea and land to Louisiana. The original deportees established themselves in small settlements in Massachusetts, Connecticut, Maryland, Kentucky, and South Carolina — but all this time there was a tiny trickle of brave men and women making the difficult journey back to their beloved Acadie.

Although the British government had not specifically ordered the expulsion, it certainly approved the end result. Lawrence received fulsome congratulations from London. The expulsions continued until the treaty in 1763. Those Acadians who had trickled back from the American colonies, and those who had been living in the bush, mostly settled in the Chaleur Bay area and started their lives again from scratch. From here they spread down the coast, and after the creation of New Brunswick in 1784 they were given grants of land and treated as British subjects with full rights and privileges under the law.

In the meantime, those who had gone to France — either directly or from detention in England — had settled near French ports and on a large tract of land twenty miles north of Poitiers, in the parishes of Archigny, Cenan, La Puye, and St. Pierre-de-Maillé. From time to time parties of them returned to Canada, while others went to the West Indies and to the offshore islands of St. Pierre and Miquelon. In 1785 the King of Spain financed the passage of a hundred or so Acadians from France to Louisiana — then Spanish territory — where they joined a thriving community of fellow-Acadians.

So far as Acadian records are concerned, it must be remembered that officially they were treated like any other inhabitants — you will not find separate vital statistics, census returns, or land records, and you will have to be guided by geographical location in your search.

There are three main sources of information: the National Archives in Ottawa, the Provincial Archives in New Brunswick, Nova Scotia, and Prince Edward Island, and the Archives Nationales de France, in Paris. However, almost all these records have been copied or microfilmed by the fount of all knowledge about the Acadians: the remarkable Centre d'Études Acadiennes at the Université de Moncton. Let us talk about the available records and where you will find them.

| France

The National Archives of France are located at 60 Rue des Francs Bourgeois, Paris 75000. You will find the following records:

1762–73, Censuses of Acadians in France. Names, dates, ages,
1783–84: and relationship to others in the family, names of deceased spouses and parents; some dates of BMD; areas of residence in France; occupations; maiden names of married women; and, very often, name of place of origin in Acadia. (There are copies of these records on microfilm in the National Archives of Canada (NAC) and Le Centre d'Études Acadiennes, Université de Moncton (CEA).)

1763–89: Censuses of Acadians in Normandy: names, dates, residences, and relationships. (These records are in the Archives Départementales de Calvados, Caen 14000.) (Copies in NAC and CEA)

1764–69: Arrival and establishment in Louisiana of Acadian families from New York, Santo Domingo, and Halifax. Names, dates, relationships, port of sailing, and place of settlement. (Copies in NAC and CEA)

1773–97: Financial assistance given to Acadians living in France. (Copies in NAC and CEA)

1775–76: Census of four Acadian convoys from Chatellerault to Nantes. Names of all family members, ages, and occupation of husband.

1785: Passenger list of Acadians sailing from France to Louisiana. (Location not known, but listed in *The Crew and Passenger Lists of the Seven Acadian Expeditions of 1785* by Milton P. Rieder (Metairie, Louisiana, 1965).)

1791: Census of Acadians still living in 1791 in Monthoiron, Pleumartin, etc., in Vienne. (These records in the Archives Départementales de Vienne, Poitiers 86000.)

| Canada

1687–1728: Notarial Records. Marriage contracts, wills, land grants, orphan records, apprentice records, and other legal documents. (NAC)

1695, 1729, 1730: Allegiance Lists. Names and residences of heads of families in Nova Scotia pledging allegiance to the British Crown.

1711–58: Court Records (Registres des Greffes), Louisbourg. Names, dates, relationships of plaintiff and defendants, residences. (NAC)

1720–42: Land grants and deeds—Louisbourg. (NAC)

1750–97: Correspondence and memoirs of Acadians in France. (NAC)

1754–58: Land grants and deeds—Ile Royale. (NAC)

1755: Names, dates, places of residence, and relationships of Acadians deported to the English colonies. (NAC and CEA)

1755–63: Petitions of Acadians in Massachusetts. Names, dates, residences, relationships, and places of origin in Acadia. (NAC and Massachusetts State Archives, Boston)

1756: List of fifty places in Connecticut where 400 Acadians were assigned in January 1756. (NAC)

1758–84: Lists of former inhabitants of Ile Royale (Cape Breton Island), Ile St. Jean (Prince Edward Island), and the Gaspé Peninsula who landed at Brest, France. Names, dates, places of origin in Acadia, ages, and relationships. (NAC)

1760–63: Names of Acadians imprisoned on the St. John River (New Brunswick) and at Halifax (Nova Scotia). (NAC)

1762–72:	La Rochette Papers (lists of Acadians who sailed from England to France). Names, relationships, places detained in England, destinations in France. (NAC and CEA)
1763:	Names of Acadians in Kentucky. (NAC)
1763:	Names of Acadians in Maryland on 7 July 1763. (NAC)
1763:	Names of Acadians in Pennsylvania on 20 June 1763. (NAC)
1763:	Names of Acadians in South Carolina. (NAC)
1763:	Names of Acadians in miscellaneous English colonies. (NAC)
1763:	Pension Lists of Acadian children in France. Names, ages, relationships, residences. (NAC and CEA)
1766:	Lists of heads of families in Boston, Massachusetts, who wished to go to Québec. Numbers in each family (890 in all). (NAC)

| New Brunswick

If you refer to Chapter 12, you will find full information about the records in the various counties. As I mentioned earlier, the counties of Gloucester, Kent, Madawaska, Northumberland, Restigouche, and Westmorland have large Acadian populations, and so you should concentrate on these first. The Provincial Archives in their general collections and statistics also have information about individual Acadian families. You should certainly check the name index at the Archives. In the Photograph Section you will find many photographs of Acadians.

Other places to check for information are: Société Historique de Madawaska, PO Box 474, Edmundston, NB E3V 3L1; the Société Historique de la Vallée de Memramcook; the Société Historique de Clair, PO Box 119, Clair, NB E0L 1B0; and the Société Historique Nicolas Denys, PO Box 6, Bertrand, NB B0B 1J0.

The latter organization has the best collection, which includes church records on microfilm for Ste. Famille, Bathurst, 1798–1884; St. Jean l'Évangéliste, Belledune, 1886–1920; St. Pierre-aux-Liens, Caraquet, 1768–1920; St. Simon et St. Jude, Grande Anse, 1890–1920; St. Michel, Inkerman, 1818–1920; and St. Urbain, Lamèque, 1840–1920. There are also some other church records for Néguac, Paquetville, Pointe-

Verte, Pokemouche, Robertville, St. Isidore, Shippegan, and Tracadie. It also has *Le Moniteur Acadien* on microfilm from 1867 to 1926.

The outstanding centre for anyone searching for his or her Acadian ancestors is, without any doubt, Le Centre d'Études Acadiennes at the Université de Moncton. The whole aim and object of the Centre is to collect in one place all Acadian documents and published books. It has spent years finding originals and copies of all obtainable sources of information. It is not just a genealogical centre, though genealogy is a major interest. It is a place for study of a whole people: their history, folklore, economy, language, and all aspects of their culture.

You will find extensive collections of original and microfilmed church registers and records, census returns, passenger lists, and, in fact, nearly all the records I have already listed. The Centre has cast its net wide: because many Acadians moved to Québec, and those who remained in Acadie have relatives there, there is a collection of marriage records from over two hundred parishes in that province. You will get some idea of the size of the holdings when I tell you there are over four thousand microfilm reels at the Centre.

There is a complete run of all Acadian newspapers since 1867; there are many family histories of both prominent and unknown Acadians; and an Index File with over four hundred families listed — you will find Albert, Bernier, Carré, De la Garde, Duon, Gautreau, Pothier, Troye, Vienneau, and hundreds of others. There is a collection of ten thousand books and periodicals.

Another organization of great value in New Brunswick is the Société Historique Acadienne, PO Box 2263, Substation A, Moncton, NB E1C 8J3. This has land, school, and church records, voters' lists, and passenger lists.

| Nova Scotia

The Provincial Archives have civil registers of BMD for Acadie and Gaspésie for 1679–1758, as well as Catholic Church registers for Annapolis Royal, Beaubassin, Grand Pré, Lorembec, Havre St. Esprit, Forchu, and Port au Basque. There are, of course, all the other records listed in Chapter 15 — both general, and also applicable to geographical areas settled originally by the Acadians.

Prince Edward Island

The first thing to do in this province is to check the Master Name Index at the Museum and Heritage Foundation, 2 Kent Street, Charlottetown. This, of course, includes names of every ethnic origin, but many of them are Acadian. You will find the index described in Chapter 17. The Acadian associations of the island are often overlooked, but once upon a time it was called Île St. Jean and its population was Acadian. The main areas of the settlement were Crapaud, East Point, Miscouche, Pinette, Pisquid, Roma, Rustico, St. Peters, Savage Harbour, Tignish, and Tracadie.

At the Provincial Archives there are four Catholic Church registers from Acadian areas:

Port La Joie (Charlottetown), 1721–57
St. Pierre du Nord, 1721–58
St. Augustine (Rustico), 1812–24
St. Jean Baptiste (Malpèque), 1817–35

The Acadian Museum in Miscouche has been collecting Acadian records for several years. They have a number of Catholic Church records for Prince County—an area of settlement. The Alberton Museum has the Tignish Church registers and a number of family histories from western Prince County.

If you know for sure that your Acadian ancestors were established on the island at an early date, the odds are that you will have the names Gallant and Hache in your family tree, and very comprehensive records exist for these two families. The families came from the Rustico area.

The Miscouche Museum has a number of Acadian church registers, including those for Bloomfield (1830–90), Charlottetown (1721–57), Egmont (1814–90), Miscouche (1817–90), Mount Carmel (1820–90), Palmer Road (1878–90), Summerside (1852–90), Tignish (1831–90), and Wellington (1884–90).

Other Sources

There are a few other sources that should not be neglected: *The National Archives* in Ottawa have several other records on microfilm: the Collection of Placide Gaudet, which covers the period 1610–1900 and contains names, dates, places of birth, marriage, and death, and family trees; the Godbout Collection, with genealogical information on Acadians in Acadia, England, France, Québec, and the United States, in alphabetical order; some information about Acadian families in Yarmouth, Nova Scotia; and details of Acadian families who settled on Belle-Ile-en-Mer, in the parish of Morbihan, France, based on parish registers. All the information mentioned in this paragraph is on microfilm.

The National Archives also have church registers on microfilm from Louisiana and other places in the United States where Acadians settled after the expulsion. The following registers from Louisiana are on microfilm and may be borrowed:

Atakapas, BMD 1756–94
Fort Biloxi, D 1720–23
Iberville, B 1773–4, M 1773–1859
La Fourche, BMD 1756–94
Natchitoches, BMD 1728–34
Nouvelles-Orléans, BD 1721–34
Opelousas, BMD 1776–1806

The Archives also have copies of Catholic records from the United States. Though not strictly Acadian, they exist in areas where Acadians settled and so are worth checking. They also are on microfilm.

St. Philippe, Arkansas, BMD 1744, 1761–5
Crown Point, New York, BMD 1732–60
Detroit, Michigan, BMD 1704–1800
Fort de Chartres, Illinois, BMD 1721–65
Fort Duquesne, Ohio, BD 1753–6
Fort Pontchartrain, *see* Detroit
Fort St. Frédéric, New York, BMD 1732–60
Michilimackinac, Michigan, BMD 1695–1799
Ouabache, Indiana, BMD 1749–86
Petersham, Massachusetts, M 1767–73
Prairie du Rocher, Illinois, BMD 1761–99

There is also the Acadian Genealogical and Historical Association of New England, PO Box 668, Manchester, NH 03105, which has a growing collection of information about the Acadian families who were expelled to various places in New

England—some to remain there and others to return to Acadie. Whichever decision was made by your ancestors, you will be likely to obtain information from the Association—particularly if you remember the return postage. You can always get a U.S. quarter from your bank and tape it to your letter!

CHAPTER 15
Nova Scotia

In one sense, Canadian history begins here, on the rocky Atlantic coast of what we now call Nova Scotia (New Scotland). John Cabot—sailing out of my home town of Bristol—may have landed in 1497 at the tip of Cape Breton Island. In 1621 Sir William Alexander obtained a patent from James I for the colonization of Acadie — as the French called the area around the Bay of Fundy and beyond. French explorers were led by Jacques Cartier, who landed in 1534, and much later — in 1604 — the Sieur de Monts and Samuel de Champlain began the first French settlement on an island in Passamaquoddy Bay. They moved it a year later to a better location on the mainland which they called Port Royal (later changed by the British to Annapolis Royal). Simultaneously English and Scots settlers established small settlements in other areas of what is now Nova Scotia and New Brunswick. Along with early settlements farther up the St. Lawrence, these were the first European settlements in Canada (ignoring, for convenience's sake, the legends of Norse landings on Newfoundland).

Until recent times the history of Nova Scotia was also that of New Brunswick and Prince Edward Island, since the latter two provinces were for many years part of it. Development and settlement of the whole area were delayed by the constant wars between France and Great Britain over nearly two centuries. Both countries sent explorers into the area, both coveted its natural resources, and both had little regard for the well-being of the hardy adventurers who settled the coves and bays that mark the rugged coasts of the three provinces.

Control of the area changed hands some ten times between Great Britain and France before the Treaty of Utrecht gave Nova Scotia to Great Britain in 1713. Cape Breton Island remained in French hands until 1763, when the Treaty of Paris finally ended all French control of the North American colonies. Of course, the departure of French government officials and soldiers did not end French settlement of Acadie, and you will find much more about the Acadians in Chapter 14, which tells about the history of these brave and persecuted people.

Prince Edward Island separated from Nova Scotia in 1769 and New Brunswick in 1784. The province entered Confederation in 1867. It had achieved responsible government in 1848 — the first British colony to do so. The time of greatest settlement from Scotland and Ireland was in the early nineteenth century, as it received many of the people involved in the great migrations described in Chapter 3.

| Civil Registration

In Nova Scotia we are faced with the same problems as in New Brunswick and Prince Edward Island. There are gaps in the registers when the law was not enforced, problems in establishing an efficient system, and a generally lackadaisical approach to record-keeping. The official recording of births, marriages, and deaths started in 1864. Although there was the usual period of adjustment at the start, the system limped along with some success until about 1874. The first couple of years met with the usual resistance to change, plus a suspicion that any information collected by the government would lead to higher taxation. An additional cause for the lack of enforcement was the scattered nature of settlement and the isolation of many small communities.

When Nova Scotia entered Confederation in 1867, one of the terms of the agreement was that civil registration would be taken over by the Dominion Bureau of Statistics in Ottawa, starting in ten years, in 1877. When that year arrived and no action was taken by the Canadian government, the provincial government just let the registration system lapse, except for that of marriages. Records of births and deaths were not kept again until October 1908.

So, in these years of troubled civil registration we are

dependent on other sources of information about the vital events of our ancestry: church registers, census returns, newspaper clippings, and so on. These we will talk about later, and, in particular, the marriage bonds.

Since 1908 the records of births, marriages, and deaths have been in the custody of the Registrar General of Nova Scotia, Provincial Building, PO Box 157, Halifax, NS B3J 2M9. I have heard many complaints about the department's rigid and frigid reaction to applications for certificates. I am sure there are two sides to the story. When an ancestor-hunter applies, for example, for a copy of a birth certificate, it is infuriating to be told he cannot obtain this unless he supplies full name, exact date, full place of birth, full name of father, and full name (and maiden name) of mother. If he (or she) had all this information, the application would not be made! On the other hand, the Registrar General and his staff have to make sure they are able to supply the right information to the right person. All the different provinces have similar regulations, but the other nine do not seem so unbending in their demands — an approximate date, a place, and the first name of the father and mother are usually sufficient. In Nova Scotia they appear to need more. As the Registrar General replied to one applicant, "There is no way this office can assist you in preparing a genealogy because the information for a genealogy is that which we must have to be able to locate a record on file."

| Provincial Archives

These are located at 6016 University Avenue, Halifax, NS B3H 1W4. Here you will get a totally different reception. The Provincial Archivist and the staff go out of their way to be as helpful as possible, and the material in the Archives is of very great value. It consists primarily of family records and histories, township records, directories, newspapers, census returns, church records and registers, poll-tax records, school records, land grants and petitions, passenger lists, militia muster rolls, marriage licences, BMD records, wills, probate records, assessment records, Loyalist records, and, of course, a master card index. There are a great many more items which refer to particular places in the province. I do not list them in any detail because they are not of general interest. However, if you know the specific area of settlement of your ancestor, you should check with the Archives and also with the local public library.

We will be dealing with censuses, church registers, land records, and wills later in this section, so at this point let us concentrate on the other records I mention above.

| Township Records

These are known as the Township Books. In the early days of settlement the province was divided into counties and townships. Originally the townships were carved arbitrarily out of largely undeveloped land. When the population of voting age had reached fifty, the township was entitled to send a representative to the provincial Legislative Assembly. This was not entirely satisfactory, since it tended to create what was known in England as "pocket boroughs", where one powerful landowner could influence voting. The system was abolished in 1859.

From a genealogical point of view, the township system is a gold-mine of information. The records list land transactions, cattle marks, and BMD. The records in the Archives and the dates covered are:

Annapolis (1783–1856)
Argyle (1702–1913)
Aylesford (1792–1855)
Barrington (1764–1958)
Barronsfield (1755–1837)
Chester (1762–1824)
Cornwallis (1760–1874)
Douglas (1784–1880)
Falmouth (1747–1941)
Fort Lawrence (1766–1891)
Granville (1720–1933)
Guysborough (1782–1869)
Horton (1751–1889)
Liverpool (1761–1870)
Londonderry (1780–1858)

Newport (1752–1858)
Onslow (1761–1841)
Parrsboro (1760–1882)
Rawdon (1810–97)
River Philip (1793–1928)
Sackville (1748–1871)*
St. Mary's River (1807–67)
Southampton (1761–67)
Stormont (1784–1877)
Truro (1770–1853)
Westchester (1782–1900)
Wilmot (1749–1894)
Windsor (1761–1819)
Yarmouth (1760–1811)

*Now in New Brunswick.

| Directories

There is a small collection of early directories dating back into the last century, and an early map collection that contains the names of the occupiers of the land sections recorded.

| Newspapers

The Archives have a good collection of early newspapers, including the *Halifax Gazette*, the *Halifax Journal*, the *Morning News*, the *British Colonist*, the *Weekly Chronicle*, the *Acadian Recorder*, *The Sun*, the *Nova Scotian*, and the *Free Press*. A number of these were short-lived publications in the 1800s. Because of the missing early vital statistics, a newspaper that published birth, marriage, and death notices can often provide the vital link for you.

There are also a number of newspapers with religious affiliations, and more information about these can be obtained from the Archives.

| Census Returns

The first censuses of Nova Scotia were carried out under the French occupation, and details of these are given in Chapter 14. The majority of those taken under British rule have survived and are in the National Archives in Ottawa or in the Provincial Archives in Halifax, or in both.

1752: A population return was made for Halifax and the immediate area. It gives the name of the head of the family, and the ages and sex of other members.

1770: This covered the area outside Halifax and included Amherst, Annapolis, Barrington, Conway, Cumberland, Falmouth, Granville, Hillsborough (now in New Brunswick), Horton, Londonderry, New Dublin, Onslow, Pictou, Sackville (now in New Brunswick), and Truro. This gave the names of the master or mistress of the family, numbers and sex of other members, country of origin.

1773: A similar count took place for Yarmouth Township.

1787: Same for Queens County.

1811: Census for Cape Breton Island (the first under British rule). It lists name, age, date of arrival, occupation, marital status, and number of children.

1817: A census was taken for the counties of Hants, Pictou, and Sydney. This gives the head of the household, number in the family, and country of origin for Sydney only. The other two counties list head of the household and sex and ages of the family.

1818: A second census of Cape Breton Island.

1818: At about this time, and in about 1840, a Catholic priest held an unofficial census for St. Mary's Bay. He also held one in the parish of St. Anne and St. Pierre, in Argyle, a couple of years earlier.

1827: A census was held in Annapolis, Bras d'Or and Louisbourg in Cape Breton, Cumberland, Digby, Halifax County, Liverpool, Shelburne, and Yarmouth. (The city of Halifax was not included in the census for Halifax County.) The townships of Argyle, Barrington, Clare, Clements, and Wilmot were also included in the census, and the returns for part of Antigonish County have survived.

1838: This is the first general census of the province to survive in its entirety—or almost, since Cumberland County is missing. Only the head of the family is named.

1851: Little remains of this census—only Halifax city and county and Kings County.

1861: This census covered the whole province and was the final one before Confederation. Only the head of the family is named.

The censuses since are complete; they give detailed information about each member of the family — name, age, sex, place of origin, etc.—and, like the other provinces that entered Confederation at this time, were held every ten years and are open to public search for 1871, 1881, and 1891.

The National Archives in Ottawa have on microfilm some other censuses dating back to the eighteenth century. These may be borrowed by the inter-library loan system and researched in your own local library if it has a microfilm-viewer. Details are given below:

Amherst, Cumberland County, 1770, 1791, 1792, 1793, 1794, 1795
Annapolis, Annapolis County, 1770, 1792, 1794
Antigonish, Sydney, 1791, 1793
Aylesford, Kings, 1792
Barrington, Queens, 1770
Canso (Gut of), Sydney, 1791, 1794

Chester, Lunenburg, 1791, 1793, 1794, 1795
Clements, Annapolis, 1791
Conway, Annapolis, 1770
Cornwallis, Annapolis, 1791, 1795
Country Harbour, Sydney, 1791, 1793
Crow Harbour, Sydney, 1794
Cumberland, Cumberland, 1770, 1785, 1791, 1794
Digby, Annapolis, 1795
Douglas, Hants, 1791, 1792, 1793, 1794, 1795
Economy, Halifax, 1793, 1794, 1795
Falmouth, Hants, 1792, 1793, 1794, 1795
Falmouth, Kings, 1770
Fort Lawrence, Cumberland, 1791, 1792, 1794
Granville, Annapolis, 1770
Guysborough, Sydney, 1792, 1793, 1794, 1795
Halifax, 1793
Halifax Road, Hants, 1795
Harbour au Bouche, Sydney, 1791
Hillsborough, Annapolis, 1770
Horton, Kings, 1770, 1791
Kings, 1792
Little Harbour, Halifax, 1791
Londonderry, Halifax, 1770, 1791, 1792, 1793, 1794, 1795
Lunenburg, Lunenburg, 1770, 1792, 1793, 1794, 1795
Maccan, Cumberland, 1791, 1792, 1793, 1794, 1795
Manchester, Sydney, 1792, 1793, 1794, 1795
Merigomish, Halifax, 1791
Musquodoboit, Halifax, 1791, 1792, 1793
Nappan, Cumberland, 1791, 1792, 1793, 1794, 1795
New Dublin, Lunenburg, 1770, 1791, 1793, 1794, 1795
Newport, Hants, 1791, 1792, 1794, 1795
Onslow, Halifax, 1770, 1791, 1792, 1794, 1795
Pictou, Pictou, 1770, 1793
Pomquet, Sydney, 1791
Queens, 1787, 1791, 1792, 1793, 1794, 1795
Ramsheg, Cumberland, 1791, 1792, 1793, 1794, 1795
Rawdon, Hants, 1791, 1792, 1793, 1794, 1795
River Hebert, Cumberland, 1791, 1792, 1793, 1794, 1795
River Philip, Cumberland, 1791, 1792, 1793, 1794, 1795
Sackville, Halifax, 1770
St. Lawrence, Sydney, 1793
Shelburne, Shelburne, 1791, 1792, 1794, 1795
Shubenacadie, Hants, 1795

Stewiacke (Lower), Halifax, 1795
Stewiacke (Middle), Colchester, 1794
Stewiacke (Upper), Halifax, 1791, 1792, 1793, 1795
Tatamagouche, Halifax, 1791, 1792, 1793, 1794
Tracadie, Sydney, 1791, 1794
Truro, Halifax, 1770, 1791, 1792, 1793, 1794, 1795
Wilmot, Annapolis, 1791, 1792, 1794
Windsor, Hants, 1791, 1792, 1793, 1794, 1795
Yarmouth, Queens, 1773
Yarmouth, Shelburne, 1793

Note: The National Archives also have microfilms of many census returns for the early years of the nineteenth century (between 1811 and 1838).

Poll-Tax Records

These almost unique Nova Scotia records can, to a small degree, fill in some of the gaps in the census returns for some of the localities. A poll-tax was a small sum of money payable by each adult male in a district. It is not a complete list of all men in the district, because there were large holes in the net — people lived in remote areas, or were missed by the tax-collector, or lied about their age to avoid payment. In addition, a great many lists have disappeared. Those that have survived are in the Provincial Archives and are listed below:

Amherst, Cumberland, 1791–95
Annapolis, Annapolis, 1792
Argyle, Yarmouth, 1791–95
Aylesford, Kings, 1791
Chester, Lunenburg, 1791, 1793–95
Clements, Annapolis, 1791
Cornwallis, Kings, 1791–95
Digby, Digby, 1795
Douglas, Hants, 1791
Economy, Colchester, 1793–95
Falmouth, Hants, 1791–95
Fort Lawrence, Cumberland, 1792–94
Halifax, Halifax, 1791–93
Horton, Kings, 1791

Liverpool, Queens, 1792–94
Londonderry, Colchester, 1791–95
Lunenburg, Lunenburg, 1793–95
Maccan, Cumberland, 1791, 1794
Musquodoboit, Halifax, 1791–93
Nappan, Cumberland, 1791, 1794
New Dublin, Lunenburg, 1791–95
Newport, Hants, 1791–95
Onslow, Colchester, 1791–95
Queens, Queens, 1791–95
Ramsheg, Cumberland, 1790–95

Rawdon, Hants, 1791–95
River Hebert, Cumberland, 1791–94
River Philip, Cumberland, 1791–95
Shelburne, Shelburne, 1791–94
Stewiacke (Middle), 1796
Stewiacke River, Colchester, 1795
Tatamagouche, Colchester, 1794–95
Truro, Colchester, 1791–95
Wilmot, Annapolis, 1791–94
Windsor, Hants, 1791–95
Yarmouth, Yarmouth, 1793

| Marriage Bonds

Another very valuable Nova Scotian record in the Provincial Archives is marriage bonds for the periods 1763–1854 and 1858–1871. Most marriages, of course, took place in a church after the calling of banns. However, for a variety of reasons—privacy, haste, illness—people could be married by licence and thus avoid the delay of waiting for the banns to be called. Before the licence was issued, a bond had to be given as security that there was no legal impediment to the marriage. The bond gave the name of the groom, the name of the bride, the groom's address, and, often, his occupation. It is important to understand that the granting of a licence was no guarantee that the wedding actually took place—there was "many a slip 'twixt the cup and the lip". It is vital, therefore, that you cross-check with other records, where possible, to make certain the marriage took place.

| Wills

These date back to 1749 and are filed in the Court of Probate in the capital of the county where the deceased lived or owned property. The Registrars of Probate are located in the following places:
Amherst, Annapolis Royal, Antigonish, Arichat, Baddeck, Barrington, Digby, Guysborough, Halifax, Kentville, Liverpool, Lunenburg, Pictou, Port Hood, Shelburne, Sherbrooke (St. Marys), Sydney, Truro, Windsor, and Yarmouth.

Requests for copies of wills, or other information, should be addressed to the Registrar of Probate in these places. The Department of the Attorney General, under whose jurisdiction probate is administered, is planning changes in this area, and so the above information may soon be out of date. Microfilm copies of all but the most recent wills are in the Provincial Archives.

In the 1750s there was a large influx of settlers from Germany and Switzerland. If your Germanic ancestors settled in Lunenburg County, you may be faced with the problem that the will of your ancestor was written in German.

Land Records

The Provincial Archives have an alphabetical file of the draft grants of the first time an area of land was granted by the Crown, and also of the settlers applying to the government for land. Once the grant had been made, all later transactions were recorded in the county registry of deeds for the area where the land was located.

The value to the ancestor-hunter of the land records, and, in particular, the applications, is that they often provide evidence of a place of origin. It was not unusual for the applicant to go into some detail about his family and background when he applied—this was in the belief that it improved his chances of obtaining the grant. There is also an alphabetical index in the Archives on microfilm, and on a county basis. This can often be helpful in tracing your family's movements within the province.

The Registrars of Deeds who hold the land records in their custody are located in the following places:

Amherst, Antigonish, Arichat, Baddeck, Barrington, Bridgewater, Chester, Guysborough, Halifax, Kentville, Lawrencetown, Liverpool, Pictou, Port Hood, Shelburne, Sherbrooke, Sydney, Truro, Weymouth, Windsor, and Yarmouth.

Side by side with your research into land titles, it is worth remembering that county maps, showing the location of most houses and the names of the heads of households, were published between 1865 and 1888. Copies may be bought from the Department of Lands and Forests, Torrington Place, Suite 100, 780 Windmill Road, Dartmouth, NS B3B 1T3.

Genealogical Societies

The Genealogical Association of Nova Scotia, PO Box 641, Halifax, NS B3J 2T3, has no branches and therefore there is no central organization; it is not easy to discover where local genealogical organizations are located, and some that were active are now in a state of suspended animation. Up-to-date information can be obtained from the Provincial Archives. According to the latest information I have been able to obtain, there are active organizations in:

CAPE BRETON: PO Box 53, Sydney, NS B1P 6G4
COLCHESTER: 29 Young Street, Truro, NS B2N 5C5
PICTOU: PO Box 1210, Pictou, NS B0K 1H0
SOUTH SHORE: PO Box 901, Lunenburg, NS B0J 2C0
YARMOUTH: PO Box 232, Yarmouth, NS B5A 4B1

There are also believed to be societies in Guysborough and North Cumberland. If there are others, I will be delighted to hear about them and will include them in the next edition of this book.

The publications of the Genealogical Association are:

Vital Statistics, 1813–22, 1769–1812, 1823–28, 1835–47
Published Genealogies
Nova Scotia, Surnames, 1864–77
BMD St. Paul's, Halifax, 1749–68
Vital Statistics, 1848–51

| Church Records

Details of the various church authorities with jurisdiction over, or interest in, Nova Scotia are given below:

Anglican

The Diocese of Nova Scotia is located at 5732 College Street, Halifax, NS B3H 1X3. The following parishes were in existence before civil registration:

Albion Mines, Amherst, Antigonish, Arichat, Aylesford, Barrington, Beaver Harbour, Bridgetown, Dartmouth, Halifax, Horton, Hubbard's Cove, Kentville, Liverpool, Lunenburg, Maitland, Manchester, Melford, New Dublin, Newport, New Ross, Pictou, Pugwash, Rawdon, River John, St. Margaret's Bay, Shelburne, Ship Harbour, Stewiacke, Sydney, Sydney Mines, Tusket, Weymouth, Wallace, and Yarmouth.

Baptist

The Baptist Archives are at Acadia University, Wolfville, NS B0P 1X0.

Catholic

The Diocese of Antigonish is at 155 Main Street, Antigonish, NS B2G 2L7. The following parishes were in existence before civil registration:
Antigonish, Arichat, Arisaig, Boisdale, Bras d'Or, Bridgeport, Broad Cove, Brook Village, Cheticamp, Christmas Island, D'Escousse, East Bay, Guysborough, Havre Boucher, Ingonish, Johnston, L'Ardoise, Main-Dieu, Mulgrave, North Sydney, Pictou, Pomquet, Port Felix, St. Andrew's, St. Margaret's, South West Margaree, Sydney, Tracadie, West Arichat.

The Diocese of Halifax, PO Box 1527, Halifax, NS B3J 2Y3. Many parishes preceded civil registration, but information was refused. Write directly to the Diocesan Office.

The Diocese of Yarmouth, 53 Park Street, Yarmouth, NS B5A 4B2. The following parishes were in existence before civil registration:
Cathedral, Annapolis Royal, Butte Amirault, Butte Comeau, Digby, Kentville, Meteghan, Plympton, Pointe-de-l'Église, Pubnico, Quinan, Rivière-aux-Saumons, St. Bernard, Ste-Anne-de-Ruisseau, and Wedgeport.

Presbyterian

Presbytery of Cape Breton, PO Box 184, Baddeck, NS B0E 1B0; Presbytery of Pictou, 139 Almont Avenue, New Glasgow, NS B2H 3G8; and Presbytery of Halifax and Lunenburg, 67 Russell Street, Dartmouth, NS B3A 3N2.

United Church

Maritime Conference, Pine Hill Divinity Hall, 640 Franklyn Street, Halifax, NS B3H 3B5.

| Church Registers

The following are listed by the Provincial Archives as *registers*, but a rough check suggests that in some cases they are not. They are, however, on microfilm and may be borrowed. Please note that the dates are for the start only, and no breakdown between BMD is available, nor are all the gaps recorded.

Registers Preceding Civil Registration

Anglican

Amherst, 1822
Annapolis Royal (St. Luke), 1782
Arichat (St. John), 1828
Aylesford, 1789
Aylesford (St. Mary), 1791
Baddeck (St. John), 1877
Barrington, 1861
Bear River (St. John), 1854
Blandford (St. Barnabas), 1859
Bridgetown, 1830
Bridgewater (Holy Trinity), 1854
Caledonia, 1856
Centre Rawdon, 1793
Chester (St. Stephen), 1762
Clementsport (St. Edward), 1841
Clements Township (St. Clement), 1841
Clements Township (St. Edward), 1841
Conquerall Mills (St. James), 1854
Cornwallis Township (St. John), 1775
Country Harbour (Holy Trinity), 1851
Dartmouth (Christ Church), 1793
Digby (Trinity), 1785
Falmouth (St. George), 1793
French Village, 1834
Granville, 1790
Green Harbour, 1885
Guysborough (Christ Church), 1786

Halifax (St. George), 1783
Halifax (St. John), 1839
Halifax (St. Luke), 1858
Halifax (St. Mark), 1861
Halifax (St. Matthias), 1888
Halifax (St. Paul), 1749
Halifax (St. Stephen), 1876
Horton & Wolfville (St. John), 1775
Hubbards (St. Luke), 1858
Jeddore (St. James & St. John), 1860
Joggins, 1898
Kentville (St. James), 1893
La Have (St. Matthew), 1884
Lakelands, 1858
Lawrencetown (St. Andrew), 1846
Liscomb (St. Luke), 1852

Liscomb (St. Marys), 1852
Liverpool (Holy Trinity), 1819
Lockeport, 1883
Londonderry, 1865
Lower Stewiacke (Holy Trinity), 1850
Lunenburg (St. John), 1752
McPhee Corner (St. Thomas), 1860
Mahone Bay (St. James), 1833
Maitland (Hants County), 1855
Manchester, 1847
Milton (Yarmouth County), 1890
New Dublin, 1821
New Germany, 1888

Newport & Walton (St. James), 1793
New Ross (Christ Church), 1822
Parrsboro, 1787
Port Dufferin, 1847
Port Morien (St. Paul), 1865
Ramsheg, 1832
Rawdon (St. Paul), 1793
Roseway, 1885
Sackville (St. John), 1813
Seaforth (St. James), 1865
Shelburne (Christ Church), 1783
Ship Harbour (St. Stephen), 1841

Springhill, 1881
Sydney (St. George), 1785
Sydney Mines (Trinity), 1848
Truro (St. John), 1824
Upper La Have, 1884
Upper Stewiacke, 1872
Westphal (St. John), 1889
Westville, 1897
Weymouth (St. Peter), 1823
Wilmot Township, 1789
Windsor (Christ Church), 1811
Windsor (Fort Edward), 1775
Yarmouth (Trinity), 1813

Baptist
Barrington, 1851
Cornwallis, 1804
Halifax (Central), 1848
Halifax (Granville), 1827
Halifax (Tabernacle), 1890
Liverpool, 1821
Lunenburg, 1795

Malvern Square, 1870
Milton (Queens), 1838
New Germany, 1864
Sable River, 1841
Sackville, 1832
Yarmouth (First), 1784

There are also *records* of Baptist congregations in the Maritime Baptist Archives at Wolfville (Acadia University).

Advoate Harbour, 1839
Antigonish, 1823
Avonport, 1876
Barrington (Providence United), 1859
Barrington (Second Free), 1878
Barrington (Temple United), 1841
Barrington West (Free Baptist), 1848
Barss' Corners, 1842
Bear Point, 1866
Bedford, 1899
Berwick, 1829
Bridgetown, 1838
Bridgewater, 1848
Canning, 1882

Canning (Free Baptist), 1850
Centreville, 1836
Chegoggin, 1892
Clementsvale, 1825
Falmouth, 1843
Gaspereaux, 1857
Greenfield, 1858
Guysborough, 1848
Halifax (First United), 1835
Hebron, 1837
Indian Harbour, 1843
Kentville, 1876
Londonderry, 1903
Lower Granville, 1832
Maitland, 1891
Milton (Queens), 1823
New Tusket, 1843

North Brookfield, 1828
Onslow, 1791
Onslow West, 1868
Paradise, 1827
Scotch Village, 1799
Smith's Cove, 1842
South Ohio, 1859
South Rawdon, 1823

Springfield, 1835
Springhill, 1904
Summerville, 1859
Upper Canard, 1816
West Bay, 1869
Wolfville, 1778
Yarmouth, 1767

Catholic
Annapolis Royal
  (St. Jean Baptiste), 1702–55
Beaubassin, 1712–48
Dartmouth, 1830–54
Enfield (St. Bernard), 1857–85
Forchu, 1741–49
Grand Pré (St. Charles),
  1707–48
Halifax (St. Mary), 1800–56

Ile Royale (Cape Breton)
  Lorembec, 1715–57
  Havre St. Esprit, 1728–37
  Port au Basque, 1740–57
  Louisburg, 1722–58
Minas, 1714–57
Prospect, 1823–35
Salmon River, 1849–1907
Sheet Harbour (St. Peter),
  1857–80

Lutheran
Baker's Settlement, 1899
Camperdown, 1889
Conquerall Bank & Mills, 1889
Feltzen South, 1887
Hemford, 1888
Lapland, 1903
Lunenburg, 1772
Middlewood, 1909

Midville, 1889
Newburn, 1888
Newcombville, 1908
New Germany, 1900
North River, 1899
Upper Northfield, 1889
Waterloo, 1889
West Northfield, 1889

Society of Friends (Quakers)
Dartmouth, 1786

United Church (including Congregational, Methodist, and
  Presbyterian)
Amherst (P), 1840
Annapolis (Circuit) (M), 1793
Annapolis Royal (M), 1875
Antigonish (Dorchester) (P),
  1821

Barney's River (P), 1812
Barrington (M), 1823
Blue Mountain (P), 1844
Bridgewater (UC), 1861
Canning (M), 1856

Canso (UC), 1854
Cape North (UC), 1854
Chebogue (C), 1767
Chester (C), 1762
Coldstream (P), 1833
Cornwallis (M), 1815
Dartmouth (P), 1835
Dartmouth (M), 1864
Dorchester (P), 1821
Earltown (P), 1782
Elmsdale (P), 1879
Falmouth (C), 1844
Folly Village (P), 1798
Gabarus (M), 1807
Glenholme (P), 1896
Grand Pré (Horton) (UC), 1819
Granville (M), 1824
Great Village (P), 1852
Greenhill (P), 1864
Guysborough (M), 1822
Guysborough (UC), 1845
Halifax (Brunswick St.) (UC),
   1784
Halifax (City Mission) (M), 1855
Halifax (Fort Massey) (M), 1855
Halifax (Poplar Grove) (P), 1843
Halifax (St. Andrew) (P), 1818
Halifax (St. John) (P), 1843
Halifax (St. Matthew) (P), 1769
Halifax (Salem) (C), 1868
Ingonish (M), 1874
Kennetcook (P), 1876
Kings County (M), 1819
Kingsport (C), 1819
Liverpool (C), 1843
Liverpool (M), 1795
Lochaber (P), 1811
Lunenburg (M), 1815
Lunenburg (P), 1770
McLellan's Mtn. (P), 1838
Middle Musquodoboit (M), 1860

Middle Musquodoboit (P), 1848
Middle Musquodoboit (UC),
   1860
Milton (Queens) (C), 1854
New Glasgow (P), 1801
New Harbour (UC), 1854
New Minas (M), 1819
Newport & Walton (UC), 1824
North Beaverbank (P), 1886
Northeast Harbour (UC), 1878
Oxford (M), 1879
Parrsboro (Circuit) (M), 1824
Parrsboro (Circuit) (P), 1858
Petite Rivière (UC), 1847
Pictou (P), 1824
Pictou (UC), 1808
Port Hastings (P), 1852
Port Morien (P), 1868
Port Mouton (UC), 1849
Pugwash (P), 1857
Pugwash (M), 1875
Ramsheg (M), 1831
Rogers Hill (M), 1855
St. Croix (P), 1873
St. Margaret's Bay (M), 1820
Salem (C), 1868
Sambro (P), 1820
Scotsburn (P), 1840
Shelburne (P), 1828
Shelburne (M), 1856
Shelburne County (M), 1790
Shubenacadie (P), 1817
Southampton (M), 1883
Stellarton (UC), 1851
Sydney (UC), 1865
Tatamagouche (M), 1855
Truro (M), 1834
Upper Canard (P), 1893
Upper Londonderry (UC), 1859
Upper Stewiacke (P), 1872
Valley (Harmony) (P), 1887

United Church — continued

Wallace (M), 1817	Windsor (UC), 1876
West Branch, East River (P), 1827	Yarmouth (M), 1846
	Yarmouth (P), 1848

| Civil Registers

Acadie and Gaspésie, 1679–1758

| Libraries

Colchester Regional Library, 754 Prince Street, Truro, NS B2N 1G9. This library has a very limited collection of genealogical material and refers inquirers to the Colchester Historical Society & Museum, PO Box 412, 29 Young Street, Truro, NS B2N 5C5. The latter organization is the main centre for genealogical research in Colchester County. Its resources include census returns on microfilm, local genealogies and family histories, a large number of scrapbooks and newspaper clippings, over thirty thousand transcriptions from tombstones in the county, a large collection of early local photographs, and files on most early settler families in the area. A great many of these records are indexed.

Eastern Counties Regional Library, PO Box 250, Murray Street, Mulgrave, NS B0E 2G0. This library has an outstanding collection of genealogical material since it serves the three counties of Guysborough, Inverness, and Richmond. The library has published a ten-page booklet which describes its holdings, and this can be supplied at a nominal charge to cover the cost of photo-copying. I think this is very generous, and I hope you will send a small donation over and above the small amount you will be charged. Because the booklet is easily available, I will not describe the holdings in detail but simply give you a brief outline.

The records include Nova Scotia census returns for 1871, 1881, and 1891; a census of Pictou County for 1827; an index of the heads of families in Guysborough County for 1838; county and local histories for some sixteen counties in the province; a number of family histories including those of Donald, Fraser, Giffin, Hart, Hingley, Jackson, MacDonald, MacMillan, MacNeil, McGillivray, Poirier, Smith; a collection of new and old maps; and an excellent library, with emphasis on Acadians, and Blacks in Nova Scotia, Great Britain, and Ireland.

Halifax City Regional Library, 5381 Spring Garden Road, Halifax, NS B3J 1E9. The holdings include microfilm copies of early newspapers from about 1880 to the present; biographical sketches of 625 Nova Scotians; indexed family histories; and a great many general books on genealogy. The records of early census returns and newspapers are on microfilm and may be borrowed through the inter-library loan system.

Pictou-Antigonish Regional Library, Civic Buildings, New Glasgow, NS B2H 5E3. Here you will find an extensive collection of cemetery records covering nearly all the cemeteries in Pictou County. They are in 61 volumes and are indexed by cemetery. Other holdings include the 1838 census for the county (Maxwellton is missing); records of county marriages, 1825–38; records of deaths, 1864–77; and books of newspaper clippings. You will also find early newspapers at the nearby Pictou County Historical Society, 85 Alexander Street, New Glasgow, NS B2H 2S5.

Hector Centre Trust, PO Box 1210, Pictou, NS B0K 1H0. This is the main centre for genealogical research in the county. The 1871 Census is published, and is for sale; the *Eastern Chronicle* is being indexed from 1843 until well into this century, and so is the *Pictou Advocate*, which started in 1895. There are also a number of family papers, maps, genealogies, cemetery listings, and local histories.

South Shore Regional Library, PO Box 34, Bridgewater, NS B4V 2W6. This is a growing source of genealogical information. The collection began with published genealogies of local interest, but since 1981 it has included census returns for the three counties of Lunenburg, Queens, and Shelburne, cemetery records, school attendance lists, and other items of general information for the three counties since 1758.

| Other Sources

There are a number of other genealogical sources scattered throughout the province. These are listed below, but I have not included information about their holdings. They are each concerned with a particular area, and basically their information is the same: census returns, cemetery inscriptions, school attendance returns, and local genealogies. There are variations on this, but if a particular source listed for your area of interest is there, you must write to them for more detailed information. Please don't forget the return postage!

Acadian Museum, PO Box 98, Chéticamp, NS B0E 1H0
Admiral Digby Library, PO Box 938, Digby, NS B0V 1A0
Annapolis Valley Macdonald Museum, PO Box 925, Middleton,
    NS B0P 1X0
Archelaus Smith Museum, PO Box 190, Clark's Harbour,
    NS B0W 1P0
Beaton Institute, University College of Cape Breton, PO Box 5300,
    Sydney, NS B1P 6L2
Bedford Heritage, PO Box 704, Bedford, NS B4A 3H5
Burning Bush Museum, 9 Prince Street, Pictou, NS B0K 1H0
Canso Historical Society, RR #1, Hazel Hill, Canso, NS B0H 1H0
Centre Acadien de l'Université Ste. Anne, Church Point,
    NS B0W 1M0
Chapel Hill Historical Society, PO Box 70, Shag Harbour,
    NS B0W 3B0
Cold Harbour Rural Heritage Society, RR #1, Bissett Road,
    Dartmouth, NS B2W 3X7
Cumberland County Museum, 150 Church Street, Amherst,
    NS B4H 3C4
Desbrisay Museum, PO Box 353, Bridgewater, NS B4V 2W9
Fortress of Louisbourg, PO Box 160, Louisbourg, NS B0A 1M0
Heritage Association of Antigonish, PO Box 1492, Antigonish,
    NS B2G 2L7
Heritage Society of District 14 (Halifax County), PO Box 14,
    Waverley, NS B0N 2S0
Kings County Historical Society (Genealogical Committee),
    Berwick, NS B0P 1E0
Lake Ainslie Historical Society, East Lake Ainslie, NS B0E 3M0
La Société St. Pierre, PO Box 430, Chéticamp, NS B0E 1H0
Le Musée Acadien, Pubnico, NS B0W 2M0
North Cumberland Historical Society, RR #3, Pugwash,
    NS B0K 1L0
North Queens Heritage Society, RR #1, South Brookfield,
    NS B0T 1X0
North Shore Archives Society, Tatamagouche, NS B0K 1V0
Nova Scotia Highland Village, PO Box 58, Iona, NS B0A 1L0

Old Court House Museum, PO Box 232, Guysborough,
  NS B0H 1N0
Old St. Edward's Church, Deep Brook, NS B0S 1J0
Parkdale–Maplewood Museum, RR #1, Barss Corner, NS B0R 1A0
Port Hastings Historical Society, PO Box 115, Port Hastings,
  NS B0E 2T0
Queens County Museum, PO Box 1078, Liverpool, NS B0T 1K0
Shelburne County Museum, PO Box 39, Shelburne, NS B0T 1W0
South Rawdon Museum, RR #1, Mount Uniacke, NS B0N 1Z0
Sunrise Trail Museum, RR #2, Tatamagouche, NS B0K 1V0
Tupperville School Museum, RR #3, Bridgetown, NS B0S 1C0
Vaughan Memorial Library, Acadia University, Wolfville,
  NS B0P 1X0
West Hants Historical Society, 140 Chestnut Street, Windsor,
  NS B0N 2T0
Whycocomagh Historical Society, PO Box 171, Whycocomagh,
  NS B0E 3M0
Wolfville Historical Society Museum, PO Box 38, Wolfville,
  NS B0P 1X0
Yarmouth County Historical Society, PO Box 39, Yarmouth,
  NS B5A 4B1

One last word about Nova Scotia. The records are extremely good—if a little scattered—but if you are as determined as your Nova Scotian ancestors, you will be very successful in your search.

Do not forget the vast resources of the LDS Church—read all about them in Chapter 4, and then make contact with the nearest LDS Family History Library, at PO Box 414, Hampton, NB E0G 1Z0, or 1660 Manawagonish Road, Saint John, NB E2M 3Y3.

(The Church has recently copied the Genealogical File of the Beaton Institute of Cape Breton College. This information was received as this edition went to press and no further details were available.)

CHAPTER 16
Ontario

The area that is now Ontario was originally the home of several Indian tribes — Huron, Iroquois, Ojibwa, Cree, to mention a few. Étienne Brûlé explored southern Ontario in 1610–12, Henry Hudson sailed into the bay that now bears his name in 1611, and Samuel de Champlain reached Lake Huron in 1615. Behind them came other explorers, missionaries, trappers, and fur-traders, and the stage was set for the bitter rivalry of the British and the French in the heart of the continent. However, permanent settlements were hard to maintain because of constant Iroquois attacks.

In the 1690s the Hudson's Bay Company set up trading-posts and a fort in the Bay area, and started its steady push southward into southern Ontario and Manitoba. The French, too, established their trading-posts, and the fight for political and commercial control of what is now Ontario took place at the same time as similar rivalry in the Atlantic provinces.

The conflict ended when the Treaty of Paris in 1763 forced France to cede control of its colonies in North America. In 1774 the British government attached Ontario to Québec. The latter was, of course, predominantly French-speaking, and the union was intended to create an English-speaking majority in the whole area of English Canada. When the Loyalists poured across the border at the end of the American Revolution, they were given land grants in the Niagara region, along the north shore of Lake Ontario, and the areas south and west of Montréal. Within a year or so there was a strong demand by the

UEL for the creation of an independent English-speaking, self-governing province, free of French influence in the areas of law, religion, and land tenure. The Constitutional Act of 1791 split Québec into Lower Canada (present-day Québec) and Upper Canada (Ontario), with the Ottawa River as the boundary line.

After the Napoleonic Wars in Europe, which had their own North American echo in the War of 1812 with the Americans, many settlers arrived from Great Britain and Europe. The tight control over Ontario by the Family Compact led to a radical rebellion in 1837 which was soon put down. However, the British government sent over Lord Durham to investigate the grievances of the population. He recommended that the two provinces should be joined again and granted full self-government under the Crown. Accordingly, Upper and Lower Canada joined in 1841 and became known as Canada West and Canada East—often abbreviated in genealogical records as CW and CE.

The union soon proved unworkable and in 1867 the Dominion of Canada was formed, with the two provinces of Ontario and Québec joining with New Brunswick and Nova Scotia to form a confederation.

Ontario has become the area of greatest settlement in Canada, and you will find more details on the great migrations in Chapter 3. British and Germans formed the majority of the early settlers, but since the Second World War, Ontario's inhabitants have been drawn from almost every country in the world.

| Civil Registration

The registration of births, marriages, and deaths started in Ontario on 1 July 1869, but the public was slow to obey the law for the usual reasons: "What is it to do with the government?", "They will use it to make us pay more taxes", "I'm not walking five miles in the snow to tell 'em I've got a new son", and so on. The records are not complete before about 1885. It has been stated by officials of the Registrar General's office that "by 1880 there were still only sixty per cent of deaths, seventy per cent of births, and ninety per cent of marriages being recorded." The records are in the custody of the Registrar General, Macdonald Block, Parliament Buildings, Toronto, ON M7A 1Y5. There is no public access, but a search will be made for a fee. You will have to obtain an application form from the office, complete it, mail it, and then wait for three or four weeks for a reply. Be sure, in your application, that you state the reason for your request, and ask for a *full* certificate. The fee you pay includes a five-year search — two years on each side of the date you gave, if necessary.

Within the office all records are indexed alphabetically by year for the whole province. This means that if your ancestor was Thomas Pearson and he was born in 1890 in Ontario, the officials might find six people with the same name born in that year, and would have no means of deciding which of them was the one you wanted. You must, therefore, try to come up with a date, or at least the month, a middle name (if there was one), and the place in which the event occurred. Other information will be helpful: maiden name if a married woman, next of kin, first name of parent, and so on. The more detail you can give, the more information you will get. One unfortunate fact is that before 1905 the names of parents do not appear on the death certificate.

It would be helpful if the department would give the public access to the indexes, as is done, for example, in Great Britain. According to the minister concerned, a similar system for Ontario is being considered. If indexes were available in the larger libraries and archives, the cost to the taxpayer would not show any increase, and the work of the staff would be reduced, with a consequent saving in manpower.

Recently the government created a problem for itself when it introduced the Change of Name Act, 1986. Apparently, although for centuries in most countries of the Western world a woman has automatically assumed the surname of her husband, this action had no basis in law. I have often thought that the most visible sign of a male-dominated world was the fact that a woman gave up the use of her own surname upon marriage. Nowadays, quite a few women want to hyphenate their name to that of their husband upon marriage, or retain their own name, alone. After the recent law was passed and change-of-name applications were made, the applicant was issued with a brand-new birth certificate in her new name.

This led to a great many protests, and, as a result, the new birth certificate bears both the old and the new name, and the original entry in the Registrar General's Office also now shows both the old and the new name. Just as well, as otherwise ancestor-hunting in 2089 might be a little difficult!

| The Provincial Archives of Ontario

The Archives are located at 77 Grenville Street, Toronto, ON M7A 2R9. Praise be, there is a fresh wind blowing along the corridors and into the vaults of this 84-year-old institution! There is a new and energetic Provincial Archivist, with new ideas and increased financing from the provincial government. Changes were badly needed and changes are being made—not all at once, but there is a new climate, and the results are becoming evident.

For example, the Ontario Archives have long been ill-famed for not providing access to their microfilmed records through the inter-library loan system. This was not caused by lack of will but by lack of money. The simple fact is that the Archives could only afford one positive copy of each microfilm, and as these were in constant use in the Reading Room, their use was restricted to the premises.

New resources, in both staff and funding, have now been provided, and already many high-priority negatives are having an additional positive copy prepared for inter-library loan purposes. By the time you read this, the first loan should already have been made.

The inter-library loan of books is a different matter. Quite rightly, the Archives remain reluctant to risk allowing valuable and fragile books to leave the premises, because many could not be replaced, nor could they withstand mailing and photocopying. However, the Archives is working closely with the Canadian Institute of Historic Microproduction in their program to microfiche all pre-1900 publications. All the early and rare material of the Archives will become available on microfiche subscribed to by many libraries. For other material, the Archives can supply photo-copies—provided the process will not damage the document, and there are no copyright restrictions. The main holdings of the Archives are listed below:

Vital Statistics

These deal mainly with the period *before* 1869 when civil registration officially started. They include church registers, marriage records, bonds, and licences. Most of them are now on microfilm, but some are still in manuscript form.

Marriage Bonds

These were only prepared for civil marriages which would be performed by licence. A bond was basically a financial guarantee that no impediment to the marriage existed. The bond included names of the engaged couple, place of residence, and date of issue. The posting of a bond was usually followed by a marriage within a few days, but sometimes the marriage did not take place, and in that case the cancellation was usually entered on the filed copy of the bond. The period covered was 1803–45. It is necessary to consult the microfilmed index according to surname. There are three microfilm reels covering, respectively, Hester Abbott–Richard Grant, Robert Grant–Thomas Patterson, Ann Patterson–Charles Zeins.

District Marriage Registers

These registers date from 1831 (with some scattered entries dating back to the early 1800s) and were compulsory for dissenting denominations, which had only been given the right to perform marriages in that year. Most of the district registers are indexed, and the following districts are available on microfilm for the dates given. It is not possible to list every place included in a particular district, and in any case the boundaries appear to have been a little elastic! An additional complication is that the area of a district grew or shrank from time to time. It is wiser to consult the Archives about a particular place and its district in a particular year than to go wading through the entries for one district and then discover it was the wrong one.

Bathurst, 1831–48	London, 1833–55
Brock, 1839–58	Newcastle, 1839–51
Colborne, 1831–48	Ottawa, 1816–53
Gore, 1842–55	Prince Edward, 1833–46
Home, 1816–50	Talbot, 1838–57
Huron, 1841–49	Victoria, 1839–58
Johnstown, 1801–50	

Some of these have been published, and copies are in the Archives and also in the library of the Ontario Genealogical Society. The information contained consists of names, place, date, denomination, and witnesses. Understand that you will not find Anglican or Catholic marriages listed in these records.

County Marriage Registers (1858–69)

These registers are for *all* denominations, and include name, age, residence, birthplace, parents' names, date, place, denomination, and witnesses' names. The originals and microfilm copies are in the Ontario Archives. The majority have also been published and indexed by Generation Press, 172 King Henry's Blvd., Agincourt, ON M1T 2V6. Brant, Bruce, Carleton, Dundas, Durham, Elgin, Frontenac, Grey, Haldimand, Halton, Hastings, Huron, Kent, Kingston City, Lambton, Lanark, Leeds & Grenville, Lennox & Addington, Lincoln, Middlesex, Norfolk, Northumberland, Ontario, Oxford, Peel, Perth, Peterborough, Prince Edward, Simcoe, Stormont, Toronto City, Victoria, Waterloo, Welland, Wellington, Wentworth and York. (All started in 1858 and ended in 1869 when civil registration started, except for Bruce (1896), Frontenac (1934), Huron (1909), Leeds & Grenville (1896), Peel (1887), and Wellington (1891).)

There are some other marriage records often overlooked. In the early years of the province, a justice of the peace was permitted to perform a marriage ceremony for a man and woman who lived more than eighteen miles from a clergyman. These records are in the Provincial Archives as well. There are also some odds and ends of marriage records which were handed over to the Archives by the Registrar General for the period before 1869.

Church Registers

Most of these are listed a little later, but the few held by PAO are:

Anglican

Delaware	BM	1834–47
Fort Albany	BMD	1859–1966
Moose Factory	BMD	1780–1894
Penetanguishene	B	1835– M 1836– D 1837–
West Gwillimbury	BD	1849–

(includes Bradford, Coulson, and Middleton)

Baptist

Picton	BM	1817, 1826, 1832
Fredericksburg	BMD	1826–31

Catholic

Glengarry	BMD	1805–37
St. Andrews West	BMD	1837–61

Quaker

York County	BD	1803

United Church

Amherstburg	P	M 1837
Appleton	PM	*See* Carleton Place
Beckwith	PM	*See* Carleton Place
Bond Head	P	B 1822–
Carleton Place	UC	M 1834–55
Cornwall	P	BMD 1833–
Drummondville	P	B 1822–44
King Township	P	M 1859–
London	P	M 1835–50
Moravian Town	MO	B 1800
Wilton	M	M 1858

| Wills

The Archives hold microfilmed copies of Ontario wills (1785–1900) which were donated by the LDS Church.

The estate (or probate) files are divided into three categories:

Records of the Surrogate Clerk

These are vital when the place of residence of a dead person at the date of death is unknown. The records cover the whole of the province and date from 1859 to 1967. There is a microfilm index that will point the way to the appropriate volume. The books are on microfilm up to 1923, but after that date the original must be checked. The main information the book gives you is the county in which the deceased was living when he or she died. Then you must consult the Surrogate Court Index Books.

Records of the Surrogate Court and the Probate Court

Two courts were established in 1793. The Surrogate Court was responsible for granting probate of an estate of a dead individual whose property was located in a single district and did not involve a large amount of money. The Probate Court was responsible for estates in two or more districts and valued at five pounds or over. In 1858 the Probate Court was abolished. An index covers the period of its existence (1793–1858). The Surrogate Court then had sole jurisdiction over all estates.

A Surrogate Court Office exists in each county and district; therefore the records are arranged on this basis. They are on microfilm and are indexed to 1900. There is a card index to lead you to the correct microfilm reel. The Archives also hold original files from 1900 to 1948. Records of wills since then are almost all in the Surrogate Courts. The latter are located in the various courthouses in the county capitals:

Brant, 1852–1900	Lincoln, 1795–1900
Bruce, 1867–1900	Middlesex, 1846–1900
Carleton, 1840–1900	Norfolk, 1800–1900
Dufferin, 1881–99	Oxford, 1841–1902
Elgin, 1859–1900	Peel, 1867–1905
Essex, 1785–1900	Perth, 1853–1900
Frontenac, 1814–1900	Peterborough, 1842–1900
Grey, 1859–1900	Prescott–Russell, 1823–1900
Haldimand, 1846–1900	Prince Edward, 1859–1900
Halton, 1851–1928	Renfrew, 1867–1900
Hastings, 1840–1900	Simcoe, 1843–1900
Huron, 1855–1900	Victoria, 1863–1900
Kent, 1851–1900	Waterloo, 1853–1900
Lambton, 1854–1900	Welland, 1856–1900
Lanark, 1848–1914	Wellington, 1840–1900
Leeds–Grenville, 1786–1900	Wentworth, 1816–1900
Lennox/Addington, 1865–1900	York, 1825–1900

Many of the above have been published by Generation Press (see page 203) and are indexed for 1859–1900.

London District Surrogate Court Registry (1800–39)

I must include a special paragraph about the records of this registry. Although they are on microfilm in the PAO, there is quite a story to be told. In 1846 a fire destroyed the files in the Registry Office in London back to 1839, and it was subsequently believed that, in fact, all the files back to 1800 had been burnt. However, the files for the period 1800–39 had never been lodged with the later ones (for reasons too involved to explain now) and they were actually still in a Land Registry Office in Simcoe. There they stayed, neatly packed away in dusty old metal boxes, until 1972. In that year the moving of the office to another location led to a house-cleaning operation and the files were discovered. They are now on microfilm in the D. B. Weldon Library in the University of Western Ontario, in London. There are also copies in the PAO, the Elgin County Library, the London Public Library, and the Donly Museum in Simcoe. They can, of course, be borrowed through the inter-library loan system. In 1987 an alphabetical index was published in the Ontario Genealogical Society journal *Families*, Vol. 26, No. 4, as part of an article by Guy St. Denis, of the D. B. Weldon Library. I wonder how many more precious records are left undiscovered in other dusty vaults in Ontario?

| Land Records

This is probably the largest collection of genealogical interest in the Archives. The various sections are:

> Computerized Land Records Index
> Index to Land Patents
> Abstract Index to Deeds
> Township Papers
> Land Petitions
> Orders in Council
> Letters (Surveyor General)
> Letters (Fiats and Warrants)
> Locations Registers
> Military Land Grants (1901–22)
> Heirs and Devisee Commission
> Atlas and Map Collection
> Canada Company Papers

These will be dealt with later in this chapter, as we are at present dealing with the Archives, and many of the land records are inextricably connected with other locations and other offices.

Genealogical Collections

There are a number of collections in the Private Manuscripts Section which are of value to the ancestor-hunter:

Perkins Bull Collection
This contains family histories and family trees, mainly in the Peel County area. Part of it is on microfilm and the finding-aid in the Archives will give you a good idea whether or not the information is of interest to you.

Genealogies Collection
This is a collection of various family histories and genealogies donated to the Archives. It is card-indexed by surname.

High-Treason Register
If your ancestor fought on the wrong side in the War of 1812, you will probably find a great deal of information about him if he was charged with high treason.

Ewan Macdonald Papers
This collection contains genealogical charts and work-sheets on various families in the Glengarry area.

F. D. McLennan Collection
This also contains genealogical information about the same area.

Peter Robinson Papers
This collection contains information about the organized settlement of Irish families in the Peterborough area by Peter Robinson in the 1820s. It is available on microfilm.

Education Records

This is a miscellaneous collection of attendance lists at grammar schools (1854–71), and various reports on teachers between 1850 and 1932. The information is geographically scattered, but if you know for sure that your ancestor was a schoolteacher, this section should be explored. There is a good finding-aid which can point you in the right direction.

| Immigration Records

These records are from 1867 to 1902. Earlier records are in the National Archives in Ottawa. Don't raise your hopes too high about this collection. It is a grab-bag of bits and pieces, with many gaps.

| Newspaper Collection

The Archives have a large collection of early Ontario newspapers which are worth checking for vital statistics (BMD) and obituaries. Many of them have been microfilmed and are card-indexed. Please note that in addition to these there are very many early newspapers in local archives and libraries all over the province. Some details of these will be given under Libraries later in this chapter, but you should also consult *Checklist of Indexes to Canadian Newspapers*, published by the National Library of Canada in 1987 and obtainable by inter-library loan.

| Secondary Sources

The Archives' Library has a large collection of local histories, county and city directories, voters' lists, journals of genealogical and historical societies, etc. Some of this material is on microfilm.

You are very lucky in Ontario because the Archives house the largest collection of genealogical material among all the ten provinces, and you will find over the next couple of years that access to all the vast holdings will be steadily improving. It will be to your advantage at present to arrange, if you can, to pay a personal visit. Be sure you make a list of the items in which you are interested, find out before you go about hours of opening, and arm yourself with pencils and a notebook. If you are driving, you will be wise to park further away than on Grenville Street—there are problems!

| Censuses

These will be among your most important sources of information, but unfortunately they are not always reliable. The family details given to the enumerator may not be correct. So much depends on the individual and the accuracy of his knowledge (and so much depends on the enumerator and his handwriting!). As you will already know, the Canada-wide censuses available are those for 1851, 1861, 1871, 1881, and 1891. There was an Ontario Census in 1842, but it only named the head of the household, and not all returns have survived. Those that are available on microfilm from the National Archives, and that can also be found in archives and libraries serving a particular area, are:

Albion (York)
Aldborough (London)
Alnwick (Newcastle)
Ancaster (Gore)
Ashfield (Huron)
Augusta (Grenville)
Barton (Gore)
Bastard (Leeds)
Bathurst (Lanark)
Bayham (London)
Beckwith (Lanark)
Beverley (Gore)
Big Creek (Gore)
Binbrook (Gore)
Brantford (Gore)
Caledon (York)
Caledonia (Ottawa)
Cambridge (Ottawa)
Canborough (Haldimand)
Caradoc (London)
Carleton (Carleton)
Cartwright (Durham)
Cavan (Newcastle)
Cayuga (Haldimand)
Clarence (Ottawa)
Clarke (Durham)
Clinton (Lincoln)
Cobourg (Northumberland)
Cramahe (Northumberland)
Crosby (Leeds)
Cumberland (Ottawa)
Dalhousie (Lanark)
Darling (Lanark)
Darlington (Durham)
Delaware (London)

Denwick (London)
Dorchester (London)
Drummond (Lanark)
Dumfries (Gore)
Ekfrid (London)
Elizabethtown (Leeds)
Esquesing (Gore)
Essa (Simcoe)
Etobicoke (York)
Fitzroy (Carleton)
Flos (Simcoe)
Gainsborough (Lincoln)
Georgina (York)
Glanford (Gore)
Goulbourn (Carleton)
Gower (Grenville)
Haldimand (Newcastle)
Hamilton (City)
Hope (Newcastle)
Horton (Renfrew)
Huntley (Carleton)
King (York)
Kingston (City)
Kitley (Leeds)
Lanark (Lanark)
Lansdowne (Leeds)
Lavant (Lanark)
Leeds (Leeds)
Lobo (London)
London (City)
Longueuil (Ottawa)
McNab (Renfrew)
Malahide (London)
Manvers (Durham)
Mara (York)

Markham (York)
Medonte (Simcoe)
Monaghan (Northumberland)
Mosa (London)
Mulmur (Simcoe)
Murray (Newcastle)
Nassagaweya (Gore)
Nelson (Gore)
Nepean (Carleton)
Niagara (Lincoln)
Orillia (Simcoe)
Oro (Simcoe)
Osgoode (Russell)
Oxford (Grenville)
Pakenham (Renfrew)
Percy (Newcastle)
Pickering (York)
Plantagenet (Ottawa)
Puslinch (Gore)
Rainham (Haldimand)
Rama (York)
Reach (York)
Ross (Renfrew)

Russell (Ottawa)
Scarborough (York)
Scott (York)
Seymour (Newcastle)
Sherbrooke (Lanark)
Sherbrooke Forest (Haldimand)
Southwold (London)
Stamford (Lincoln)
Tay (Simcoe)
Thorold (Lincoln)
Torbolton (Carleton)
Toronto (City)
Townsend (Norfolk)
Trafalgar (Gore)
Vespra (Simcoe)
Wainfleet (Lincoln)
Walpole (Haldimand)
Wawanosh (Huron)
Westmeath (Renfrew)
Westminster (London)
Willoughby (Lincoln)
Wolford (Grenville)
Yarmouth (London)

Note: These returns give only the name of the head of the household, are not always complete, and are microfilmed by district, so many places will appear on the same microfilm. There were some other censuses before 1842 in scattered locations, and information about these can be obtained from the NAC, the PAO, and local archives and libraries, or branches of the Ontario Genealogical Society. (Example: The Leeds & Grenville Branch of the Ontario Genealogical Society has indexed Augusta Township censuses for 1796, 1806, 1813, 1823, and 1824.)

| Land Grants and Records

Before 1867, land grants were made by the colonial government, but in that year of Confederation the responsibility passed to the provinces. In order to obtain a grant of land a settler had to make a formal written application, known as a petition. As I mentioned earlier, the petition often provides genealogical information. In order to bolster his chances of getting a grant, the petitioner would indulge in a bit of family history: give details of his place of origin and date of arrival in Canada, and the names of his wife and children and their ages. He would explain how hard-working he was, possibly include a character reference from a clergyman, and say how he needed the grant to provide food and shelter for his family.

Searching the land records is now much easier since the *Abstract Books* were microfilmed by the LDS Church, and a copy given to the Provincial Archives of Ontario. All you now need to start a search is a surname. A microfilm of the Land Petitions can be borrowed from the National Archives. The period covered is 1764–1867, and the index is on 27 reels of microfilm.

There is also the computerized Land Records Index (1780–1914) with two different alphabetical listings: one by the applicant's name and one by township or city. The information on which this index is based comes from the Crown Land Papers, the Canada Company Papers, and the Peter Robinson Papers. The latter two sources are from the company concerned with settlement in the early 1800s in Upper Canada (Ontario), and the records of the organized settlement by Peter Robinson in 1825 in the Peterborough area. Only the initial ownership is recorded. It also includes grants to United Empire Loyalists and to veterans of the South African War.

Changes in ownership are recorded in the various Land Registry Offices. The books are called Abstract Indexes to Deeds, and a page is devoted to each piece of land and the various transactions over the years — usually filed by concession number and lot number in each township, or by a town lot within a city. Very few changes have been made in township boundaries over the years. When there were changes, they were usually caused by the establishment of a self-governing village. The establishment of the Village of Lakefield in 1875 and its removal from Smith Township is an example. If you do not know the lot and concession, you can usually find this out by searching an early directory, such as the 1837 York County Directory, or by referring to an historical atlas of a county. This usually lists the name of each inhabitant with the lot and concession number.

When you have this information, you can then visit the Land Registry Office for the county, and for a fee of $4 you can obtain details of all the transactions of the land since the original grant or sale. When you visit a Registry Office, you must realize that its primary purpose is to provide facilities for legal checks on land ownership and not to help the ancestor-hunter. Be prepared to be treated accordingly. You will get very little help or advice from the overworked clerks behind the counter and you will be competing for space with an army of law clerks and law students.

You will eventually find a wealth of information about the piece of land. My own house was built in 1841, and I found full information about the original purchase of the land by the Canada Company from the Crown in 1829 (it was part of a parcel of 131 acres), followed by a succession of sixteen owners down to my wife and myself.

Many of the Abstract Indexes are also available on microfilm in the Family History Libraries of the LDS Church, and in other local libraries.

I list below the locations of the Land Registry Offices in the province. If you cannot identify a particular one as being the one you need for your particular search, I suggest you write to the Director of Land Registration, 393 University Avenue, Toronto, ON M5G 1E6.

There are 65 Land Registry Offices and each one has an official number, which appears in brackets after the name:

Sault Ste. Marie (1)	Milton (20)	Oshawa (40)
Brantford (2)	Belleville (21)	Woodstock (41)
Walkerton (3)	Goderich (22)	Parry Sound (42)
Ottawa (4)	Kenora (23)	Brampton (43)
Ottawa (5)	Chatham (24)	Stratford (44)
Cochrane (6)	Sarnia (25)	Peterborough (45)
Orangeville (7)	Almonte (26)	L'Orignal (46)
Morrisburg (8)	Perth (27)	Picton (47)
Port Hope (9)	Brockville (28)	Fort Frances (48)
Bowmanville (10)	Napanee (29)	Pembroke (49)
St. Thomas (11)	St. Catharines (30)	Russell (50)
Windsor (12)	Gore Bay (31)	Barrie (51)
Kingston (13)	London (33)	Cornwall (52)
Alexandria (14)	Glencoe (34)	Sudbury (53)
Prescott (15)	Bracebridge (35)	Haileybury (54)
Owen Sound (16)	North Bay (36)	Thunder Bay (55)
Durham (17)	Simcoe (37)	Lindsay (57)
Cayuga (18)	Colborne (38)	Kitchener (58)
Minden (19)	Cobourg (39)	Welland (59)

Arthur (60)	Toronto (63)	Toronto (66)
Guelph (61)	Toronto (64)	Cambridge (67)
Hamilton (62)	Newmarket (65)	

Note: An excellent book, *Land Records in Ontario Registry Offices*, by David and Jean McFall, was published by the Ontario Genealogical Society in 1984. It is now out of date so far as the names and locations of Registry Offices are concerned, and also the fee basis has been changed.

Other miscellaneous documents and land records in the Provincial Archives include:

Land Record Copy Books
These contain copies of deeds, mortgages, wills, liens, etc., affecting legal title to land. From 1797 to 1846 the registers are by county, and from 1846 to 1866 by city, town, township, and village. From 1866 to 1955 the registers included other items such as power of attorney, probate administration, etc. As well as in the Archives, there are microfilm copies in each Registry Office.

Upper Canada Land Petitions
These records, mentioned above, are in the NAC, but the PAO have copies on microfilm. They are indexed by surname, but it is wise to check every possible variation in the spelling of your name.

Patents
These were confirmation of land ownership granted to a settler after he or she had fulfilled their obligations in respect of the land: clearance, building, road work, rights of way, etc. These are also in the PAO on microfilm and are indexed by surname from 1795 to 1825, and by township to 1850.

Other records in the PAO include letters about land received by the Surveyor General, 1786–1905 (indexed by name and on microfilm); Fiats and Warrants for special groups (United Empire Loyalists, Peter Robinson Settlement, military grants, etc. Microfilmed. These included grants to volunteers in the Fenian skirmishes, and to the South African War veterans. There is an alphabetical index.)

There are also the records of the Heirs and Devisee Commission which was in being between 1805 and 1911. It sat at intervals to review claims to land by heirs.

I mentioned the value of historical atlases in finding the concession and lot number of ancestral land, and I have also pointed out that most of these atlases give the names of the settlers on the various lots. Copies of the atlases can be found not only in the Archives of Ontario but in local archives and in most libraries of any size. Set out below you will find what I hope is a complete list with dates:

Addington (*see* Frontenac, Lennox, and Addington)
Brant, 1875
Bruce (*see* Grey and Bruce)
Carleton, 1879
Dundas (*see* Stormont, Dundas, and Glengarry)
Durham (*see* Northumberland and Durham)
Elgin, 1877
Essex and Kent, 1881
Glengarry (*see* Stormont, Dundas, and Glengarry)
Frontenac, Lennox, and Addington, 1878
Grey and Bruce, 1880
Haldimand, 1879
Halton, 1877
Hastings and Prince Edward, 1878
Huron, 1879
Kent (*see* Essex and Kent)
Lambton, 1880
Lanark
Leeds and Grenville, 1861
Lennox (*see* Frontenac, Lennox, and Addington)
Lincoln and Welland, 1876
Middlesex, 1878
Muskoka and Parry Sound, 1879
Norfolk, 1877
Northumberland and Durham, 1878
Ontario, 1877
Oxford, 1876
Peel, 1877
Perth, 1879
Peterborough, 1875 (this also covers the period from 1825. It is not
    strictly an historical atlas because it is a modern reconstruction
    [1975] based on early histories and records, and on family
    papers of early settlers, and it is produced by the County
    Historical Society.)
Prince Edward (*see* Hastings and Prince Edward)

Renfrew, 1881
Simcoe, 1881
Stormont, Dundas, and Glengarry, 1879
Waterloo, 1877
Wellington, 1877
York, 1878

Township Papers

These records in the PAO are often overlooked. It is a pity, because (a) they may provide genealogical information and (b) few records bring you so close to your ancestors. The papers are not indexed, but they are filed in folders alphabetically by township. They consist of letters written by settlers to the government about the land they have been granted and have either occupied or visited. Basically, they are letters of complaint — complaints about misrepresentation or disputes with neighbours. If your settler ancestor had no complaints, you will not find a letter. If he or she did, you may find such complaints as, "The land was described to me as being 80 per cent arable and 20 per cent swamp—the reverse is true," or, "according to the land description my eastern boundary runs along a creek. My neighbour insists the creek is twenty yards inside his property and denies me the use of the water." Apart from information of this kind, which will give you an insight into your ancestor's problems, the letter is interesting because it is a hand-written original, and you can get a photo-copy and know exactly what your great-grandfather's handwriting looked like.

Remember that you will only find a letter if your ancestor had a problem. You may find a hundred letters in the folder and you will have to search through them, because they are in no kind of order.

| Genealogical Society

The Ontario Genealogical Society is located at Suite 253, 40 Orchard View Boulevard, Toronto, ON M4R 1B9. It is the giant among Canadian societies, with more than 5000 members and 27 branches covering almost every area of the province. It was founded in 1961, and ever since then its growth has been quite spectacular.

The OGS and its branches have two major projects at the present time:

1. The transcribing and indexing of tombstone inscriptions

from all Ontario cemeteries. Nearly 4000 of these have been completed, but there are still about 1000 to go! The target date for completion is November 1991. If you live in the province and would like to help, perhaps the job could be finished by 1990!

2. The indexing of the 1871 Census for the whole of the province. These indexes are being published on a county basis, and ten are already in print; it is estimated that another twenty volumes will be needed.

If your ancestors first settled in Ontario, I urge you to join the branch operating in their particular area. If you live in your area of ancestral settlement, you will be able to attend meetings, meet other members, and take part in all the many activities of the branch. If you live far away, it is still worth your while to join, because you will receive the OGS and local branch publications and will be kept up to date with all new developments in genealogy. You will also be able to place two free queries a year in *Families*, the OGS magazine. This may well produce information and solve an apparently unsolvable problem.

The very large OGS library holdings are housed at the North York Public Library, Canadiana Department, 5120 Yonge Street, North York, ON M2W 5N9. The hours are 0900 to 2030 Monday to Thursday, 0900 to 1800 on Friday, and 0900 to 1700 on Saturday. Books are available for reference only and may not be taken out.

The branches of the OGS are listed below. Their main projects are the two listed above, but some have already completed these and are already turning their eyes in other directions. Almost every branch has its own publications, such as leaflets and booklets of indexes for individual cemeteries, local censuses, church registers, indexes to BMD notices in local newspapers, etc. By writing to the branch (enclosing return postage) you can get a list of its publications and information about membership. Do not expect the branch to undertake searching for you or provide immediate information about your family.

The full list of OGS branches is:

Brant County: PO Box 2181, Brantford, ON N3T 5Y6
Bruce & Grey: PO Box 66, Owen Sound, ON N4K 5P1
Elgin County: PO Box 416, St. Thomas, ON N5P 3V2
Essex County: PO Box 2, Station A, Windsor, ON N9A 6J5
Halton-Peel: PO Box 373, Oakville, ON L6J 5A8

Hamilton: PO Box 904, Hamilton, ON L8N 3P6
Huron County: PO Box 469, Goderich, ON N7A 5C7
Kawartha: PO Box 162, Peterborough, ON K9J 6Y8
Kent County: PO Box 964, Chatham, ON N7M 5L3
Kingston: PO Box 1394, Kingston, ON K7L 5C6
Lambton County: PO Box 2857, Sarnia, ON N7T 7W1
Leeds & Grenville: PO Box 536, Brockville, ON K6V 5V7
London: PO Box 871, Station B, London, ON N6A 6Z3
Niagara Peninsula: PO Box 2224, St. Catharines, ON L2M 6P6
Nipissing: PO Box 93, North Bay, ON P1B 8G8
Norfolk County: PO Box 145, Delhi, ON N4B 2W9
Ottawa: PO Box 8346, Ottawa, ON K1G 3H8
Oxford County: PO Box 1092, Woodstock, ON N4S 8A5
Perth County: PO Box 9, Stratford, ON N6A 6S8
Quinte: PO Box 301, Bloomfield, ON K0K 1G0
Sault Ste. Marie: PO Box 1203, Sault Ste. Marie, ON P6A 6N1
Simcoe County: PO Box 892, Barrie, ON L4M 4Y6
Sudbury: c/o Public Library, 200 Brady Street, Sudbury, ON
  P3E 5K3
Thunder Bay: PO Box 373, Station F, Thunder Bay, ON P7C 4V9
Toronto (York County): PO Box 147, Station Z, Toronto, ON
  M5N 2Z3
Waterloo-Wellington: PO Box 603, Kitchener, ON N2G 4A2
Whitby-Oshawa: PO Box 174, Whitby, ON L1N 5S1

There are also genealogical groups not affiliated with OGS. They are located in Cobourg, Cornwall, Haldimand County (Simcoe), Lanark County (Perth), Parry Sound, Upper Ottawa Valley (Pembroke), and in Vermilion. There is also an Historical Society with genealogical interests in Osgoode Township (Vernon). For further information about them, consult the nearest Public Library. The library location is given in brackets where it differs from the title of the group.

The latest information about individual branch projects, apart from the cemetery recording and the indexing of the 1871 Census, is given below. If a branch is not listed it simply means that no information has been received. Its members may be so busy with new projects they have no time to provide any details for the book!

As with all organizations there is great variety from branch to branch so far as activity is concerned. Most of them have now completed the two major projects I mentioned earlier—or, if not, they are well on the way to doing so. Many are now starting other projects and all of them need more help from members. If you have some time to spare, do please play your part in recording our history.

Brant: 1869 directories of local townships are being indexed, as well as voters' lists, school attendance records, and BMD entries in local churches.

Bruce & Grey: Complete cemetery listings for Bruce County are available and Grey is nearly finished. The indexed 1871 Census has been published. On-going projects include a Surname Collection, which is not yet published but is available in the Owen Sound Public Library.

Elgin: This branch operates in two sections—Elgin and West Elgin —and both have projects under way recording assessment rolls, and copying local church registers.

Essex: Although the cemetery recording is not complete, the branch is busy sorting and cataloguing the Bacon-Vaughan Papers, a large collection donated to it and dealing mainly with early French settlers.

Halton-Peel: The branch has completed the cemetery recording and is now copying BMD entries in local church registers.

Hamilton: Major projects include cemetery recording, indexing Baptist BMD notices, and local funeral home records.

Huron: The branch has indexed the 1871 Census and is working hard to complete the recording of cemetery inscriptions in the vicinity.

Kawartha: The branch has now published BMD extracts from the Peterborough and Cobourg newspapers, and is also publishing township maps of Victoria County. Work on cemetery records is not complete but is proceeding rapidly.

Kent: The Kent branch is recording pioneer farms in the county, their ownership and location. It is also recording BMD entries in local churches and pre-1871 census returns for the area.

Kingston: The main on-going projects are to complete and publish the records of Lennox and Addington cemeteries; to index pre-1871 census returns; and to copy BMD entries from local church registers.

Lambton: The 1851 Census return for Lambton has already been published, as have the cemetery records. There is considerable research into early settlers and their families, and in listing lot owners in eleven of the townships.

Leeds & Grenville: The cemetery listings are almost complete and the branch is now planning the recording of BMD entries in local church registers.

London: All the cemeteries in Middlesex County have been indexed and published. Present projects include recording all names on city maps from about 1878; indexing funeral-home records; and indexing a local census of 1854. Many completed early records are available on microfiche.

Niagara: Sixty per cent of the cemetery records have been published, with more to follow shortly. An inventory is being made of church records in preparation for copying. Publications already available include indexing of local census returns dating back to 1828.

Nipissing: Apart from the continuing work on cemetery records (many of which have been published) the branch is now indexing BMD registers of North Bay churches, and BMD notices in the *North Bay Nugget*.

Norfolk: Formed in November 1987. On-going projects are cemetery registers (several already published); and church registers including the Dundas Catholic Mission one for 1840–53.

Ottawa: Ongoing projects include cemetery recording and expanding the branch library (housed in the City of Ottawa Archives).

Oxford: The branch is now working on local church records, and has almost completed the photo-copying of many Tweedsmuir local histories (see also under Woodstock Public Library).

Perth: No information supplied.

Quinte: The branch has recorded all the cemetery inscriptions in Prince Edward County, and is now copying BMD registers in the churches in Seymour Township.

Sault Ste. Marie: Work on the cemetery records is nearly complete, and the branch is indexing BMD notices in *The Daily Star* and the *Bruce Mines Spectator* from 1901 to 1925. Census returns up to 1891 have been indexed and published, and local baptisms in Methodist churches from 1860 to 1880 are ready for publication.

Simcoe: The branch is still working on indexing the 1871 Census, and has also published a large number of cemetery records. Its next project will be work on BMD entries in area churches.

Sudbury: The branch is still concentrating on copying and publishing local cemetery inscriptions.

Thunder Bay: No information supplied.

Toronto: No information supplied.

Waterloo-Wellington: Most of the cemetery records have now been published and the branch is working on BMD entries in local churches.

Whitby-Oshawa: The branch has copied and published nearly all the cemetery records for the southern part of Durham Region. BMD records have been copied in Bowmanville and Darlington; the Bowmanville Burial Book from 1857 (10,000 entries) and other miscellaneous BMD entries from various circuits have also been copied.

From all this you can appreciate the constant activity in the various branches, *and* the need for more people to help get the various projects completed.

| Church Registers

The following parishes of the Anglican Church in Ontario were in existence *before* civil registration of births, marriages, and deaths in 1869. The parishes are listed alphabetically under the name of each diocese:

DIOCESE OF HURON: Adelaide, Amherstburg, Auburn, Bayfield, Beachville, Belmont, Berlin, Bervie, Biddulph, Brantford, Brooke, Burford, Carlisle, Chatham, Dresden, Eastwood, Edwardsburg, Exeter, Florence, Froomfield, Galt, Goderich, Greenock, Hanover, Harrietsville, Hillsboro, Holmes Hill, Howick, Ingersoll, Katesville, Kincardine, Kingsville, Lambeth, London, McGillivray, Meaford, Metcalfe, Mitchell, Mohawk, Moore, Morpeth, Mount Pleasant, Oneida Chapel, Otterville, Owen Sound, Parish, Pine River, Port Albert, Port Burwell, Port Dover, Port Rowan, Port Stanley, Proton, St. Thomas, Sandwich, Sarnia, Simcoe, Southampton, Stratford, Strathroy, Thamesford, Thorndale, Tyrconnell, Vienna, Vittoria, Walkerton, Walpole Island, Wardsville, Warwick, Westminster, Wilderness, Wilmot, Windsor, Wisbeach, Woodstock, Zorra.
DIOCESE OF ONTARIO: Adolphustown and Fredericksburg, Almonte, Amherst Island, Arnprior, Ashton, Barriefield, Bath, Beachburg, Belleville, Brockville, Carleton Place, Carrying Place, Clark's Mills, Cornwall, Cumberland, Douglas, Finch, Fitzroy, Franktown, Gananoque, Hawkesbury, Hillier, Horton, Huntley, Kemptville, Killery, Kingston, Lanark, Leeds, Loughborough, Lyn, Madoc, Maitland, March, Marysburgh, Matilda, Merrickville, Mountain, Napanee, Nepean, Newboro, New Edinburgh, North Augusta,

North Gower, Osgoode, Osnabruck, Ottawa, Pembroke, Perth, Picton, Portsmouth, Prescott, Richmond, Roslyn, Shannonville, Smiths Falls, Stirling, Tamworth, Trenton, Tyendinaga, Waterloo, Williamsburg, Wolfe Island.

DIOCESE OF TORONTO: Amherst Island, Ancaster and Dundas, Arthur, Barrie and Shanty Bay, Barriefield, Barton and Glandford, Bath, Belleville, Berkeley and Chester, Bowmanville, Brampton, Brock, Brockville, Camden and Sheffield, Carleton Place, Carrying Place, Cartwright and Manvers, Cavan, Charlestown, Chippawa and Stamford, Clarke, Cobourg, Collingwood, Cornwall, Credit and Sydenham, Darlington, Douro, Dunnville, Elora, Emily, Etobicoke, Fenelon Falls, Fergus, Fitzroy and Pakenham, Fort Erie, Franktown, Fredericksburg and Adolphustown, Gananoque, Garden River, Georgetown and Norval, Georgina, Glenallan, Goulbourn and Huntley, Grafton and Colborne, Grantham, Grimsby, Guelph, Hamilton, Kemptville, Kingston, Lakefield, Lamb's Point, Lindsay, Lloydtown and Albion, Louth, Manetoahning, March, Markham, Merrickville, Metcalfe and Osgoode, Milton and Hornby, Minto, Mono and Orangeville, Morrisburg, Mountain, Napanee, Newborough and Leeds, Newmarket, Niagara, Northport and Sophiasburg, Oak Ridges, Oakville and Palermo, Orillia, Osnabruck, Otonabee, Ottawa, Pembroke, Penetanguishene, Perrytown, Perth, Peterborough, Pickering, Picton, Port Hope, Portsmouth, Port Trent, Prescott and Maitland, Reach, Rice Lake, Richmond, Rockton and Beverley, Rockwood, St. Catharines, Saltfleet and Binbrook, Scarborough, Seymour, Smiths Falls, Stewarttown, Stirling, Streetsville, Sydenham and Frontenac, Tecumseth, Thornhill and Vaughan, Thorold and Port Robinson, Toronto, Tyendinaga, Walpole, Watertown, Welland, Wellington, Wellington Square, West Gwillimbury, West Hawkesbury, Weston, Whitby, Wolfe Island, Woodbridge, York, York Mills.

Note: You will notice some duplication of names of parishes between the latter two dioceses; this is caused by boundary changes.

The following parishes of the Catholic Church in Ontario were in existence *before* civil registration in 1869. The parishes are listed alphabetically under the name of each diocese:

DIOCESE OF ALEXANDRIA: Alexandria, Cornwall, Lancaster, St. Andrew's West, Williamstown.

DIOCESE OF HAMILTON: Hamilton (St. Mary), Acton, Arthur, Brantford, Burlington, Carlsruhe, Dundas, Formosa, Guelph, Hespeler, Macton, Maryhill, Mount Forest, New Hamburg, Oakville, Owen Sound, Paris, Riversdale, St. Agatha, St. Clement's, Teeswater.

DIOCESE OF KINGSTON: Cathedral, Belleville, Brockville, Centreville, Erinsville, Kemptville, Marysville, Morrisburg, Napanee, Perth, Picton, Prescott, Read, Smiths Falls, Stanleyville, Stoco, Toledo, Westport, Wolfe Island.

DIOCESE OF LONDON: Cathedral, Ashfield, Belle River, Chatham, Corunna, Goderich, Ingersoll, Kinkora, La Salette, Lucan, Maidstone, Merlin, Mount Carmel, Pain Court, Perth, Petrolia, River Canard, St. Columban (Dublin), St. Joseph (Zurich), St. Peter's (Kent), St. Thomas (Elgin), Sarnia, Stoney Point, Stratford, Tecumseh, Thamesville, Tilbury, Windsor (Assumption, St. Alphonsus).

DIOCESE OF OTTAWA: Cathedral, St. Joseph, St. Patrick, Almonte, Corkery, Curran, Embrun, Fallowfield, Fitzroy Harbour, L'Orignal, Orléans, Pakenham, Richmond, St. Eugène, South Gloucester, South March.

DIOCESE OF PEMBROKE: Cathedral, Arnprior, Brudenell, Chapeau, Ile-de-Grand-Calumet, La Passe, Mattawa, Mount St. Patrick, Portage du Fort, Quyon, Renfrew. (This diocese includes part of Québec.)

DIOCESE OF PETERBOROUGH: Bowmanville, Cobourg, Douro, Downeyville, Hastings, Lindsay, Port Hope.

DIOCESE OF ST. CATHARINES: Cathedral, St. Mary, Caledonia, Fort Erie, Grimsby, Niagara Falls, Niagara-on-the-Lake, Port Colborne, Thorold.

DIOCESE OF NORTH BAY: Gardem River.

DIOCESE OF THUNDER BAY: Holy Family, Gull Bay, Lake Head.

DIOCESE OF TORONTO: Cathedral, St. Basil, St. Joseph (Highland Creek), St. Mary, St. Patrick, St. Paul, Beaverton, Bradford, Colgan, Collingwood, Lafontaine, Markham, Mississauga, Newmarket, Orillia, Oshawa, Penetanguishene, Phelpston, Pickering, Richmond Hill, Stayner, Thornhill, Uptergrove, Whitby, Wildfield.

I give below the locations of church registers of the various denominations held by the various archives: governmental, ecclesiastical, university, library, and museum. The lists are as complete and up-to-date as I can make them—based on information supplied by the various organizations concerned and my own research. Having said that, I must also say that these lists can only be taken as a guide, because the situation is changing so rapidly. A number of registers are in the process of being microfilmed at this moment, and no listing is available; many church archives have collected original registers for the purpose of microfilming them and cannot even list them or advise when the microfilming will be done; a number of registers are being microfilmed by local libraries, archives, and historical and genealogical societies.

In the Anglican Church in particular, the pace of change has quickened to such a degree that it is no longer possible to keep abreast of developments. The Church itself has recognised the need for detailed information about church records and registers and has now published its *Guide to the Archives of the Ecclesiastical Province of Ontario*, at 365 pages (Generation Press, Agincourt, 1990). In view of this, I have decided *not* to list in these pages the locations of Anglican registers in the Province since the *Guide* is readily available in all major libraries and through inter-library loan. It will be updated from time to time. The scope of the *Guide* is so wide, however, that a detailed description of the contents is necessary, so that you may know just what is included and what is not.

The entries represent the complete holdings of the seven dioceses in Ontario, and of North-Western Québec, parts of which are included in this province for administrative convenience. The list was compiled up to October 1, 1989 and includes selected holdings of Wycliffe and Trinity Colleges.

There are, of course, many items of no direct genealogical value in the *Guide*—records of administration, personal papers of various Bishops, well-known clergy, and prominent laity. There are also miscellaneous records of early missionaries. If your ancestors were prominent in church affairs you may find mention of them among the personal papers. Above all in importance to you are parish records; it is under this general heading that you will find church registers.

Within each diocese you will find administrative records; details of officers and committees; diocesan organisations such as Anglican Church Women, and Young People's Association; papers and documents; and church registers. For the latter, outside dates are given but large gaps are shown by multiple sets of dates, and doubtful dates are given in square brackets.

For all other denominations, you will find the register locations still listed in the following pages, since none of the other churches have plans to publish a guide, nor are they transferring registers to church archives on a scale similar to that of the Anglicans.

There are many pitfalls and possibilities of error ahead of you when you start to consult parish registers. I have covered many of these on pages 62–65 so far as church registers generally are concerned, but Ontario has its own peculiarities. In western Provinces — because of much later settlement — the oddities are not so great because authorities had their baptism of fire in Ontario.

Here are some of the things you must bear in mind when you work with Ontario registers (and to a lesser degree those of other Provinces):

(1) Remember that many places have changed their names a number of times over the years. If, for example, you know that your great-grandfather settled in Beaver Creek in 1855 and you cannot find Beaver Creek on a map, don't give up. Write to the Archives of Ontario for information. The odds are good that an archivist there will be able to tell you that Beaver Creek became Knott's Landing in 1884.

(2) All your problems are not necessarily solved. You find that Knott's Landing registers may be in the original church, or in the Diocesan Archives, or in the Archives of Ontario, or in the local Public Library.

(3) Let us assume that you are lucky: the registers are still in the local church. You pay it a visit, meet the local parson, and he lets you settle down with the registers.

You soon find the entry for grandmother's marriage in 1896 —and that is all you do find. No mention of the baptism of their eight children, including your own father! You know they were all born in Knott's Landing—you have the exact dates in your family Bible. What could have happened?

(4) You ask the clergyman for help. He tells you the parish boundaries were re-drawn in 1897 and the area where your family had settled was transferred to the neighbouring parish of Mapleville. So where are the Mapleville registers? Your friendly clergyman tells you that the Mapleville church burnt down in 1910 and was not rebuilt. He does not know more than that.

(5) Back to square one. You check with the Anglican Church archives and find they have the Mapleville registers from 1865 up to the year of the fire. So all is well and you find all the records for which you are searching.

However, that is only one scenario — there are others. You might have found that your ancestors attended Mapleville church for a couple of years and then stopped going because they did not like the parson, or it was too far away from the farm — so they went back to the church in Knott's Landing.

On the other hand, grandfather could have changed his religion — it often happened. Perhaps he became a Presbyterian or a Methodist. There were some pretty strange religions and sects about in those days and you may have to do some checking.

A book published by the National Archives in Ottawa giving details of censuses between 1666 and 1891 lists such religions as The Bible Church, Episcopal Methodists, Free Presbyterians, Methodist Episcopal, Reformed Presbyterian, United Presbyterian, and Wesleyan Methodists. Add to these a number of others I have found in my own research—Primitive Methodists, True Methodists, Bible Christians, New Connection Methodists, Fundamental Baptists, etc., etc. You will also find that, quite often, they will be referred to by their initials, so you will have to work out the meaning of RP, UP, FB, TM, and so on.

You may also find that your surname was changed by your grandfather or great-grandfather. This does not happen very often with Anglo-Saxon or Scots or Irish names — except for a great deal of spelling differences from generation to generation — but it is much more likely with European names. Often they were hard to pronounce and great-grandfather may have got fed up with spelling his name of Pryzyborski and changed it to Price, and so all his children were baptised under the new name.

While we are talking about names, let me remind you once more that a century or so ago our ancestors were not always able to read or write or spell. This is no reflection on them or their mental ability. Education was not free, generally speaking, and if grandfather was a blacksmith or a plowman or a stableman he did not need to read or write anyway. This meant that entries in church registers were made by the clergyman and spelt as they sounded to him. In this way the good French name of Rousseau became Rusaw, Dickinson or Dickson became Dixon, MacKay became Mackie, and so on.

All these various obstacles I have mentioned must be borne in mind if your search for, or in, church registers is to be successful.

You will find the addresses of the Anglican and Catholic dioceses and all other church bodies in Chapter 7.

Before referring to any of the church registers listed below, I suggest you reread the explanatory notes in Chapter 7.

Baptist

Church	Dates	Archives
Barford Township	M 1842–44	BAP
Binbrook	M 1859–	BAP
Breadalbane	M 1858–	BAP
Brockville First	M 1862–	BAP
Drumbo	M 1857–	BAP
Dundas	M 1858–	BAP
Hartford	MD 1783–	NAC
Kingston	M 1858–	BAP
Kitchener (German)	MD 1855–61	NAC
Picton	BM 1817, 1826, 1832	PAO
St. Thomas	M 1858	BAP
Toronto	M 1830–39	BAP
Waterford	M 1858–	BAP
Woodstock	M 1844–74	BAP
York Mills	MD 1832–	BAP

Catholic

The policy of the Catholic Church appears to be to have no policy. According to information received from various Archdioceses and Dioceses, there is infinite variation in the attitude of the Church to the preservation of registers. Some have microfilmed early registers and then returned the originals to the church; in some cases, genealogists have no access to the diocesan copies, in other cases they do; many Dioceses have not microfilmed the registers or taken custody of them; others have retained the originals after microfilming and given copies to the local church and the Provincial Archives. There are several other variations so I must make it clear you have to check with each particular Diocese to discover the policy for your area of interest. You will find addresses on page 69.

Although the Catholic Church was originally the most conservative of them all, it has now completely changed its attitude with respect to copying. The Archdiocese of Toronto has allowed the LDS Church to microfilm all records of baptism and marriage from the beginning of each parish up to 1910. The earliest records began in 1833. Whenever the registers contained death records, they too were microfilmed. In addition, the Archdiocese microfilmed the same records, and they are to be updated every five years. They have now been updated to December 1987.

The microfilms are stored in the archives of the Archdiocese and a copy is kept in the parish. However, some parishes do not have microfilm-readers, and so application must be made in such cases to the Church Archives, 355 Church Street, Toronto, ON M5B 1Z8. The registers may be consulted up to 1910.

Other Catholic archdioceses and dioceses are now doing the same thing in other areas. It is left to the local Ordinary of a diocese to decide whether the LDS Church should be permitted to do the microfilming, or whether the diocese should undertake this work itself. I know that some will still not grant permission under any circumstance but will insist that each parish handcopy its registers and lodge the copy in the Diocesan Chancery Office. This means that outside Toronto you will have to check the policy of the Bishop in the diocese in which you are interested.

So far as Toronto is concerned, the archives of the Archdiocese also have copies of burials in St. Paul's Cemetery (1849–57) and St. Michael's Cemetery (1855–1985); published marriage banns of 1849 for St. Paul's Church; listing of the headstones in Potter's Field Cemetery, 1826–55; listing of tombstones in Midland, Ontario, St. Patrick's Cemetery, Toronto Gore (also known as Grantville, Gribben, and Wildfield), and St. Patrick's Cemetery, Caledonia. Finally, two odd bits of information that may solve problems for someone: BMD in "township above York", 1830–33, and baptisms in the Niagara District, 1851–52.

Church	Dates	Archives
Alexandria	M 1858–69	NAC
Centreville	BMD 1846–	NAC
Dwyer Hill	*See* Richmond	NAC
Embrun	BMD 1841–	NAC
Glengarry	BMD 1805–37	PAO
Goulbourn	*See* Richmond	NAC

Kemptville	BMD 1844–68	NAC
Kent County	B 1802– M 1806– D 1803–	PAO
Kitley Township	BM 1835–	NAC
Niagara-on-the-Lake	BMD 1827–	PAO
Ottawa	BMD 1858–	NAC
Perth	BMD 1823–	NAC
Richmond	BMD 1836–	NAC
St. Andrews West	BMD 1837–61	PAO

Lutheran

Church	Dates	Archives
Cambridge	BMD 1834–	NAC
Fredericksburg	BMD 1826–31	PAO
Lennox & Addington	BM 1791–1850	PAO
Morrisburg (St. John)	BMD 1840–	NAC
Morrisburg (St. Lawrence)	BMD 1826–	NAC
Morrisburg (St. Paul)	BMD 1840–	NAC
Morrisburg (St. Peter)	BMD 1858–	NAC
Osnabruck	BD 1837–53	NAC
Preston	*See* Cambridge	NAC
Williamsburg	BMD 1843–	NAC

Society of Friends (Quakers)

Sects: H = Hicksite; O = Orthodox (also see page 77)

Church	Dates	Archives
Newmarket (Yonge Street) (H)	BD 1803–66 M 1804–40, 1859	UWO
Pelham (H)	M 1845–	UWO
Pickering (O)	M 1844–	UWO
Pickering (H)	BM 1829– D 1829–66	UWO
West Lake (H)	M 1855–	UWO
West Lake (O)	M 1859–	UWO
Yarmouth (O)	BD 1803–	UWO
York County (H)	BD 1803–	PAO

United Church and Associated Denominations

Please note that the various denominations listed below in this section are not necessarily "associated" theologically, and I do not intend to suggest they are. It is simply that they have more in common than not—and since a change of religion was quite common, you may well need to check the registers and records of several of these denominations. Changes were usually made between the various Nonconformist religions: Methodist to Wesleyan, Methodist to United Church, for example, rather than Methodist to Anglican or Catholic. You might also reread Chapter 7 on churches and religions to recall the various splits and schisms, and also the formation of the United Church in 1925. Abbreviations for the various denominations in this section are given on p. xvi.

Church	Denomination	Dates	Archives
Aberfoyle	EUB	*See* Morriston	UCA
Acton	P	BMD 1857–	PAO
Agincourt	UC	BD 1830–57 M 1848–	UCA
Ailsa Craig	P	B 1869–	PAO
Allan Park	P	B 1862–3	UCA
Almonte	UC	BMD 1833–	NAC
Amherstburg	P	M 1837–	PAO
Amherst Island	P	M 1800–41	NAC
Ancaster	P	*See* Dundas	NAC
Annan	M	B 1864–9	UCA
Ashbury	UC	BMD 1858–	NAC
Avonton	P	BM 1859–	PAO
Bastard Township	CS	BMD 1846–	NAC
Bay of Quinte	P	BMD 1800–41	PAO
Beamsville	C	B 1824–35	UCA
Beckwith	P	B 1822– MD 1834–	UCA
Bell's Corners	M	M 1858–	UCA
Bobcaygeon	M	M 1858–	UCA
Bolton	ME	M 1860–3	UCA
Bond Head	P	B 1822–	PAO
Bothwell	M	B 1861–	UCA
Bowmanville	P	BMD 1853–	UCA
Brampton	P	M 1858–	UCA
Brant	PM	M 1858–	UCA
Brinston	ME	B 1844–54	UCA
Brockville	P	BM 1812–	UCA
Caledon	C	B 1866–	UCA
Caledon	P	B 1866 only	UCA
Caledonia	P	M 1853–	UCA
Camlachie	P	B 1860–	PAO
Canboro	ME	M 1853–	UCA
Cannington	WM	B 1832–41	UCA

Church	Denomination	Dates	Archives
Carleton Place	UC	M 1834–55	PAO
Carleton Place	M	B 1829–43	UCA
Carp	UC	BMD 1858–	UCA
Chatham	M	M 1858–	UCA
Chippewa	P	B 1847–	PAO
Claremont	M	B 1868–	UCA
Clayton	UC	BMD 1805–	NAC
Cobourg	M	M 1867–	UCA
Collingwood	P	B 1856–61	UCA
Cornwall	P	BMD 1831–57	NAC
Cumberland	P	BMD 1844–	OCA
Don Mills	M	M 1868–	UCA
Dorchester	P	M 1858–	UCA
Drummondville West	P	B 1822–44	PAO
Dundas	P	M 1848–52	NAC
Dunnville	P	B 1846– M 1858–	PAO
Eastern District	WM	BM 1833–57	NAC
Easton's Corners	M	BMD 1858–	OCA
Eden Mills	P	B 1862–	PAO
Elizabethtown	P	BMD 1846–	NAC
Elora	P	B 1837– M 1856–	PAO
Ernestown	P	BMD 1800–41	NAC
Ernestown	M	BMD 1855–9	NAC
Fergus	P	B 1845–	PAO
Finch	P	B 1845–	PAO
Fingal	P	B 1861–	PAO
Flamborough West	P	B 1847–	PAO
Fort Frances	WM	B 1840–	UCA
Franktown	P	B 1823– M 1834–55 D 1863–	UCA
Galt	P	BM 1833– D 1853–	PAO
Galt	WM	BM 1854–60	NAC
Georgetown	C	M.1858–	UCA
Glencoe	P	B 1842–53	UCA
Gorrie	M	B 1862–	UCA
Guelph	P	B 1868–	UCA
Guelph	PM	M 1858–	UCA
Gwillimbury West	P	M 1857–	UCA
Hallowell Circuit	M	B 1836–8	PAK
Hamilton (B. Stone)	P	B 1842–50 D 1841–3	UCA
Hamilton (St. Andrew)	P	B 1833–68 M 1834–60 D 1841–67	PAK

Hamilton (St. Andrew)	WM	B 1840–57 M 1842–8	UCA
Hamilton (Knox)	P	BMD 1834–68	PAK
Hamilton (Knox)	C	B 1848–	UCA
Harrington	P	M 1859–	PAK
Hawkesbury	M	BMD 1853–	OCA
Horton–McNab (Renfrew)	P	BM 1841–83	UCA
Ingersoll	P	BMD 1846–62	UCA
Inglewood	P	M 1857–	UCA
Innisfil & Essa	P	B 1856–	PAK
Kemble	P	B 1868–	UCA
Kincardine	P	B 1865– M 1859	PAO
King Township	P	M 1859–	PAO
Kingston	P	BM 1821–69	PAO
Kingston	M	M 1831–50	UCA
Kingston	C	B 1849– M 1858–	UCA
Kirkhill	CS	*See* Lochiel	NAC
Kitchener	P	BM 1857–	PAO
Laurel	PM	B 1852–	UCA
Lochiel	CS	BMD 1820–	NAC
Lochiel	C	M 1833–44	NAC
Lochwinnoch	P	B 1867–	NAC
London	MNC	M 1865–	UCA
London	C	M 1862–	UCA
London	P	M 1835–50	PAO
London Circuit	PM	B 1861– M 1858–	UCA
L'Orignal	P	*See* Dundas	NAC
Lucan	P	B 1869–	UCA
Lunenburg	P	*See* Osnabruck	NAC
Malahide	ME	B 1822– M 1833– D 1829–	UCA
Malcolm	P	B 1854–67	UCA
Mallorytown	ME	B 1859–68 D 1866–	UCA
Malton	P	M 1858–69	UCA
Maple	P	B 1833–61 M 1860–	PAO
Markham	P	M 1840– D 1854–6	UCA
Markham	PM	B 1868– M 1857–	UCA
Mayfield	UC	B 1832–	UCA
Meaford	C	M 1862–	UCA
Middleville	P	B 1858–65	UCA
Milton	WM	M 1858–	UCA
Milverton	M	M 1860–	UCA
Mimico	P	BMD 1827–60	PAO
Mississauga	M	M 1857–	UCA

Church	Denomination	Dates	Archives
Mitchell	P	B 1856–	PAO
Moraviantown	MO	B 1800–	PAO
Morriston	EUB	M 1862–	UCA
Mountain	P	B 1864– M 1858–	OCA
Napanee	M	B 1854 only	UCA
Napanee	P	M 1853–	UCA
Nelson Circuit	M	B 1832–43	UCA
New Hamburg	MEN	BMD 1863–	MA
Newmarket	P	M 1858–	PAO
Niagara Circuit	ME	B 1795–1855 M 1835–55	UCA
Niagara Falls	P	M 1857–	UCA
Niagara-on-the-Lake	P	BMD 1817–22, 1830	PAO
North Augusta	M	M 1858–	OCA
North Gower	P	B 1835–	OCA
North Gower	M	M 1859–	OCA
Norval	P	B 1852–	PAO
Orangeville	P	M 1859–	UCA
Osnabruck	FP	BMD 1848–	NAC
Osnabruck	P	B 1852–	NAC
Ottawa (Bytown)	P	BMD 1829–	NAC
Ottawa (Bytown)	C	BM 1859–	OCA
Owen Sound	P	B 1856– M 1856–7	UCA
Pakenham	UC	BMD 1840–	NAC
Pembroke	M	B 1841–	NAC
Perth	WM	M 1858–	NAC
Perth	P	BMD 1817–	NAC
Perth	FP	BMD 1858–	NAC
Peterborough	P	M 1834–57	NAC
Playfair	M	M 1859–	UCA
Port Dalhousie	UC	B 1855–63 D 1853–5	UCA
Port Dover	P	M 1858–	PAK
Port Elgin	UC	M 1868–	UCA
Prescott	P	B 1825– M 1834–68 D 1852–7	PAK
Preston	P	BM 1856–	PAO
Ramsay	P	B 1795–1835	PAK
Riceville	ME	B 1864– M 1858–	UCA
Riceville	UC	B 1844–	OCA
Rideau Circuit	ME	B 1824–43	UCA
Rockwood Circuit	WM	BMD 1861–	UCA

Romney–Glenwood	P	M 1859–	UCA
Russell	P	B 1859–	OCA
Scarborough	P	B 1796–	PAO
Seaforth	P	B 1865–	UCA
Shannonville	P	M 1858–	UCA
Shelburne	ME	B 1864– M 1858–	UCA
Springville	P	B 1854–	UCA
Stratford	P	B 1849– M 1839–	PAO
Sydenham	ME	B 1839–49	UCA
Toronto (Alice Street)	PM	B 1869– M 1858–	UCA
Toronto (Bay Street)	PM	B 1832–	UCA
Toronto (Bond)	UC	B 1863– M 1858–	UCA
Toronto (Carlton)	PM	B 1869–	UCA
Toronto (Cooke's)	P	M 1858–	UCA
Toronto (Elm)	M	M 1865–	UCA
Toronto (George)	BWM	B 1842–51 M 1833–51	UCA
Toronto (Gould)	P	MD 1865–	UCA
Toronto (Knox)	P	B 1823–38 M 1826–31	UCA
Toronto (Zion)	C	B 1840–54	UCA
Trafalgar	C	B 1840–54	UCA
Vaughan	P	B 1845–	PAK
Vaughan	UP	B 1847–	PAK
Warkworth	M	BM 1856–67	UCA
Waterdown	NMC	M 1858–	UCA
Wellandport	P	B 1860–	PAK
Whitby	M	B 1848–57 M 1864–	UCA
Wiarton	P	B 1822–	PAO
Williamsburg	P	BM 1779–1810 D 1811–7	NAC
Williamstown	P	BMD 1779–	NAC
Wilton	M	M 1858–	PAO
Wolfe Island	M	B 1855–	UCA
Wolfe Island	P	M 1862– D 1856–	UCA
Woodstock	P	BM 1858–	PAO
Eastern Circuit	Misc.	M 1831–65	UCA
Marriage Certificates	ME	M 1849–80	UCA

1. Wesleyan Methodist registers are available by inter-library loan for 1825–1910.
2. Methodist Circuit registers from 1792.

| Civil Registers

District	Dates	Archives
Alexandria	M 1858–69	NAC
Alexandria (Lochiel)	BMD 1862–	NAC
Alnwick	M 1858–82	NAC
Amherstburg	B 1826, 1845–62	NAC
Avondale	D 1871–	PAO
Ayr	BMD 1836–61	NAC
Baden	BMD 1836–60	NAC
Bathurst District	M 1816–69	NAC
Berlin (Kitchener)	B 1836–60 M 1854–5 D 1855, 1860	NAC
Eastern District	M 1831–65	NAC
Essex County	B 1826, 1845–62	NAC
Goderich	D 1866–	UWO
Grenville	D 1769–	NAC
Johnstown	M 1801–51	NAC
Lochiel Township	BMD 1862–	NAC
London District	M 1784–1833	NAC
Middlesex County	M 1784–1833	NAC
Ottawa	M 1859–69	NAC
Peterborough County	M 1859–73	NAC
Norfolk County	M 1810–13, 1826, 1832–50	NAC
Roxborough, Kenyon, and Maxwell	D 1813–	NAC
Waterloo County	BMD 1836–61	NAC

Notes:

1. Many church registers listed for a particular place also include nearby villages and settlements.

2. Circuits may include as many as twenty places.

3. Civil registers often include odds and ends from local church registers.

| Libraries

So far as Ontario is concerned, and for people across Canada of Ontario descent, this is probably the most important section of the book. For the first time in this volume the genealogical holdings of important libraries in all provinces are listed. Ontario leads the way in the number of public libraries with genealogical holdings, and this is reflected in the quantity of the listings in this section.

Libraries, collectively, are making a tremendous contribution to the research of genealogists, and to our knowledge of the history of the area in which they are located. Librarians, moved by their own efficiency and enthusiasm, and aided by members of local genealogical societies and by individuals, are creating local archives and centres of genealogical and historical knowledge. The public library is no longer just a place to go to borrow a book. Unfortunately the ancestor-hunter is unaware of the information just awaiting him or her in a library. I hope the sections that follow will open new areas of research for anyone tracing ancestry.

Throughout this whole book, library holdings in all provinces are mentioned, but Ontario leads the way in the number of such libraries because of its early history, its population, and the widespread activities of its genealogical society and branches. Its records, of course, are of interest not only to people living in Ontario but also to people in all provinces whose family origins were in Upper Canada.

The libraries are listed alphabetically. Not all libraries are included — a few were not prepared to help in providing this valuable information for genealogists. In these cases, where I know genealogical collections do exist, I give the name of the chief executive officer of the library and suggest you write directly to him or her and ask for the information you need about that particular area. Be sure you enclose a stamped, self-addressed envelope.

Alliston: Public Library, PO Box 1199, Alliston, ON L0M 1A0. The books about local history in the library are:

A History of Alliston & Vicinity, S. Ellis, 1984
The Review of Tosorontio, 1850–1950
History of Alliston & Area, L. Gallaugher, 1977
St. James Church, Colgan, South Adjala, 1825–1965
History of Burns United Church, 1865–1965
The Story of SS #8, Tosorontio, 1894–1966
Grant Family History, E. Banting, 1985
From Armagh to Essa (The Flynns, 1870–1973)
Cemetery Inscriptions, Tecumseth & West Gwillimbury
Local History of Peel, York, and Durham

Thompsonville: History of the Church & Community
Palgrave United Church & Community
Life on the Old Plank Road (Highway 88)
Tweedsmuir History—Alliston

Barrie: Public Library, 37 Mulcaster Street, Barrie, ON L4M 3M2.
The library does not have a genealogical collection because the area is served by the Simcoe County Archives (details at the end of this section). However, it does have an index to local newspapers, a printed index to BMD in newspapers from 1847 to 1900 (this is an ongoing project), local histories for Simcoe County, and local censuses on microfilm, 1842–91. The main concern of the library is collecting material on Barrie and the townships of Oro, Essa, Vespra, and Innisfil. This includes books, atlases, maps, newspapers, cemetery listings, church histories, family histories of Barrie and the county, school yearbooks, and photographs.

Bath: Public Library, PO Box 400, Bath, ON K0H 1G0.
The library has the 1851 Census return of the township of Ernestown, an index to Loyalist graves in the Quinte area, a history of Bath United Church, a history of St. John's Anglican Church, the Tweedsmuir history of Millhaven, and a book about the Bradshaw family.

Belleville: Public Library, 223 Pinnacle Street, Belleville, ON K8N 3A7.
The library has a very good genealogical collection, as one would expect in such an early-settled and historically-minded area. There are early directories for Belleville from 1857, and from 1860 for Hastings County. There are telephone directories on microfilm from 1883, published records of BMD from various locations and Loyalist graves in the Bay of Quinte. There are some cemetery records, early Methodist records from the circuits of Smith's Creek, the Bay of Quinte, and Napanee, and a number of registers of BMD by clergymen in various locations in the area (please check with the library for more detailed information about the dates and places covered). There is also a great deal of Loyalist information: muster rolls of the King's Royal Regiment, Loyalist Claims, land grants, Loyalist family histories, etc.

There are cemetery records from Belleville, Dungannon, Hungerford, Huntingdon, Lake, Limerick, Madoc, Marmora, Mayo, Monteagle, Rawdon, Sidney, Seymour, Napanee (Hay

Bay), and Thurlow. Please note that in some places—Rawdon, for example—there are several cemeteries of various denominations as well as pioneer and farm ones.

The library has indexed census returns for 1851–91 on microfilm. The land records include Copy Books (Hastings), 1800–1954, the Ontario Archives Land Records Index, and lists of Crown Grants, 1787–98. There are Township Papers on microfilm for Hungerford, Huntingdon, Rawdon, Sidney, and Thurlow, and many local histories. There are over a hundred family histories—too many to list—so please check with the library about your particular family (enclosing return postage). You will also find indexed microfilms of local newspapers from 1856 to date.

Bracebridge: Public Library, 94 Manitoba Street, Bracebridge, ON P0B 1C0.

The library holds a large number of books about local history—too many to list—and some of the books are:

> *Early Days in Muskoka*, G.W. Boyer, 1970
> *Notes and Sketches in the History of Parry Sound*, S. Brunton, 1969
> *Muskoka & Haliburton, 1615–1875*, F. B. Murray, 1963
> *Huntsville—A Brief Centennial History*, H. E. Rice, 1964
> *Family History of Thomas Rosewarne*, P. and W. Rosewarne, 1968
> *History of the Sheas*, B. Shea, 1967
> *Redmond Thomas Scrapbooks*, Redmond Thomas, 1969

Brampton: Public Library, 65 Queen Street East, Brampton, ON L6W 3L6.

The local-history collection chronicles the history of Brampton and the former townships of Chinguacousy and Toronto Gore. It contains voters' lists, assessment rolls, family and place-name indexes, grave registers and cemetery records, local newspapers from 1867 to date, books, newspaper clippings, maps, photographs, and filmstrips. The library is also the repository for the Halton–Peel branch of the OGS (Ontario Genealogical Society). Material on microfilm can be borrowed by inter-library loan (except for the holdings of the OGS branch).

Brantford: Public Library, 75 George Street, Brantford, ON N3T 2Y3.

Books in this library include:

Tracing Your Family Tree in Brant County, A. Files, 1981
BMD from the Christian Messenger (*Brantford*), 1854–64
Haldimand County Marriages, 1803–56, W. Yeager, 1983
Index to 1871 Census of Brantford & Brant County

There are also a large number of genealogical books of general interest.

The holdings contain local newspapers on microfilm: the *Brant County Herald*, 1857–58, the *Brantford Courier*, 1884–1918, and the *Brantford Expositor*, 1852 to date; the census returns on microfilm for the area served by the library and many counties much further away.

1842: Eastern District to Western District, and Townsend Township.

1851: Counties of Addington, Brant, Bruce, Carleton, Elgin, Haldimand, Lincoln, Norfolk, Northumberland, Oxford, Waterloo, Welland, and Wentworth.

1861: Brant, Durham, Elgin, Essex, Grey, Haldimand, Halton, Lennox and Addington, Lincoln, Middlesex, Norfolk, Northumberland, Ontario, Oxford, Victoria, Waterloo, Welland, Wentworth, and York.

Census returns are also available for local areas for the period 1871–91. There are also city and county directories from 1851 to the present; cemetery records from 44 graveyards; maps and historical atlases from the neighbouring counties from 1875; and a great many books of local history. Books about specific families include Bell, Best, Bingham, Birkett, Buchner, Burtch, Carr, Duncombe, Fairchild, Fonger, Franklin, Good, Harvie, Knill, Lang, McMichael, Malcolm, Mathews, Moore, Mulholland, Rosebrugh, Rushton, Switzer, Terhune, Vansickle, Walker, Weylie, Wilkes, and Wood. There are also a great many church histories that contain details of prominent members of the congregation over the years. Finally, there are scrapbooks, county marriage registers, land record indexes, and a number of Tweedsmuir Histories of townships.

Brockville: Public Library, PO Box 100, 21 George Street, Brockville, ON K6V 5T7.

The library holds books about a number of local families: Andress, Booth, Carr, Cossitt, Dunn, Kincaid, Malloney, Shipman, Throop and Truesdell. There are a number of cemetery records from Augusta and Elizabethtown townships and Leeds

County; some local census returns dating back to 1796; and, of course, the regular censuses for the area from 1861 to 1891. There is a Tweedsmuir History of Lyn. Brockville newspapers on microfilm are:

The Gazette, 1828–32
Recorder, 1830–76
Evening Recorder, 1830–1918 (with gaps)
Recorder and Times, 1918 to date
Weekly Recorder, 1830–1957 (with gaps)
Times, 1882–1910

Burlington: Public Library, 2331 New Street, Burlington, ON L7R 1J4.
Books of local genealogical interest in the library are:

From Pathway to Skyway, C. Emery and B. Ford, 1967
Burlington: Suburb to City, R. Keast, 1981
Burlington Area Cemeteries, S. Littlewood, 1977

The cemetery records include Brandt, Colling, and Kilbride; there is the 1877 atlas of Halton County; indexes to local newspapers; the Tweedsmuir Histories of Aldershot, Campbellville, and Halton; and various church histories. There are family histories for Allen, Easton, Freeman, Gage, Gallagher, Jones, Lindley, Pettit, etc. The census returns on microfilm for 1851–91 cover the whole Halton area; the Halton County marriage registers for 1869–73 are available, as are marriage registers for Bathurst, Brock, Gore, and Home, districts. The collection of family papers includes Bates, Blanshard, Brant, Davis, Fonger, Peart, and Springer.
Cambridge: Public Library, 20 Grand Avenue North, Cambridge, ON N1S 2K6.
The library provides minimal information about its holdings. They include indexed BMD notices from local newspapers: *Galt Dumfries Reformer*, 1849–92; *Galt Reporter*, 1857–1959 (with gaps); *Hespeler Herald*, 1902–47. Cambridge is the result of the merger of Galt, Preston, and Hespeler. For local-history purposes the libraries of the three districts are still divided, although the main collection is in the central branch in Galt. According to Ryan Taylor in his book *Family Research in Waterloo & Wellington Counties*, minimal staff assistance is available. The same remark applies to the Preston and

Hespeler branches, where the records can be seen by appointment only.

Chatham: Public Library, 120 Queen Street, Chatham, ON N7M 2G6.

The holdings of the library which serves Kent County are: Chatham and Kent County newspapers from 1841 to date, indexed by name and subject; directories from 1880 for the county and from 1876 for Chatham; cemetery transcriptions for the county, arranged by township, and indexed; census returns on microfilm for the 1851–91 censuses for the counties of Kent, Essex, and Lambton—these are indexed to 1871. There are also Kent County marriage registers, 1857–69; Crown Land first patentees for Kent County, indexed; a reprint of the *1881 Historical Atlas* of the counties of Essex and Kent; similar atlases for the surrounding counties; a listing of Kent County century farms and owners—this includes some detailed family histories.

There are also land record indexes; papers of the Kent Historical Society; death notices of Ontario, 1810–49; marriage notices, 1813–54, and a later supplement; death notices from various church newspapers; and marriage bonds, 1803–34.

Three books of considerable local value are:

> *The History of the Negro Community in Chatham, 1787–1865,* John K. Farrell, 1955
> *Blacks in Buxton and Chatham, 1830–90,* J. M. Walton, 1979
> *Some Irish Pioneers in Kent County,* Joseph Kearns

Cobourg: Public Library, 18 Chapel Street, Cobourg, ON K9A 1H9.

The constant aim of the library is to obtain more material for the local-history collection, particularly for Cobourg and the township of Hamilton in Northumberland County. It already has an index of censuses and assessment records—1842, 1851–91 for the former, and 1846/7, 1856, and 1859 for the latter—for the city of Cobourg. The indexes for the censuses in the township are much more detailed and valuable, since they include many years not covered by the Canada-wide census. These date from 1797 on an almost yearly basis up to 1842 and include lists of settlers, militia rolls, and church records of membership. The assessment records are complete from 1807 to 1847 and are indexed—a great help to ancestor-hunters seeking an exact location for their family in the township.

Books of interest to genealogists are:

The Church of St. Peter, Cobourg
The History of Trinity United Church, Cobourg (1805–1985)
Index of Cobourg Names in the Registry Office Abstract Index,
1800–60
Births, Marriages and Deaths in the Cobourg Star, *1831–1849*
(1200 indexed surnames)
Early Cobourg, P. Climo, 1985
Cobourg, 1837–1987
Cobourg, 1798–1948, E. Guillet, 1948

A great many names of early settlers are mentioned in these books and in others on the shelves of the library. There is also a book about the counties of Northumberland and Durham covering the period 1767–1967—a mass of information about early settlement. Local newspapers on microfilm include:

Cobourg Star, 1831–49
Cobourg Star, Sentinel, and World, 1848–1900 (indexed)
Cobourg World, 1901–11 (indexed)
Cobourg World, 1912–48 (indexed to 1919 ongoing)
Cobourg Star, 1966 to present (indexed 1985 to date)

Cemetery transcripts are those of Union, St. Peter (Anglican), and St. Michael (Catholic) cemeteries. There are also indexed transcripts for the two townships of Hamilton and Haldimand. Early city directories are also available from 1851.
Collingwood: Public Library, 100 Second Street, Collingwood, ON L9Y 1E5.
The library holds a collection of books about the history of Simcoe, Bruce, and Grey counties; early directories and atlases; a card index for BMD in Collingwood newspapers from 1882; a good collection of transcripts from local cemeteries; census returns on microfilm for the area from 1851 to 1891; and a growing collection of family histories, including Brock, Campbell, Carter, Clark, Elworthy, Jardine, Johns, Lougheed, Metheral, Robertson, Sheffield, Shiply, Smart, Telfer, Trott, and Wensley.
Cornwall: Public Library, PO Box 939, 208-2nd Street East, Cornwall, ON K6H 5V1.
This library has a great deal of material covering nearly all aspects of genealogical research. The microfilmed census

records cover the local counties of Glengarry, Russell, and Stormont but also ones further afield such as Frontenac, Prince Edward, and several others. The years covered are from 1851 to 1891; all, of course, are on microfilm. Local parish registers include:

Trinity Anglican Church, Cornwall, BMD 1803–49
St. Raphael's Catholic Church, Glengarry, BMD 1805–31
Kemptville Catholic Mission, BMD 1844–74 (indexed)
Williamstown Presbyterian (including Glengarry & Stormont), BMD 1784–
Osnabruck and Lunenburg (Stormont County) Presbyterian, BMD 1852–1909
Eastern District of Ontario, 1831–1865, certified marriages in Church of Scotland, Lutheran, Congregational, Baptist, Independent, Methodist, Mennonite, Tunker, Presbyterian, and Moravian Churches, 1831–65 (indexed)
Johnstown District, register of marriages, 1801–50 (indexed)
Presbyterian Church (St. Johns), Cornwall, B 1915–76, M 1896–1981, D 1954–69

Newspapers on microfilm:

Cornwall Reporter, 1876–79
The Freeholder, 1883–1932
Cornwall Standard, 1886–1932
Standard–Freeholder, 1932 to date

(There are some missing years.)

Cemetery transcripts: Some 48 of these were transcribed in 1965, and they include a number of small farm or pioneer cemeteries very often overlooked.

There are over 250 books on the shelves which can be described as of genealogical value, a number of them histories of churches of various denominations in which many people are mentioned by name. The many family histories include Barkley, Bulger, Cameron, Campbell, Carkner, Casselman, Countryman, Dillabough, Durant, Hickey, Hyndman, Kennedy, Ketcheson, Kyle, McCormick, MacDiarmid, MacDonell, MacGillivray, McIntosh, MacLean, Munro, Newell, Robertson, Ross, Salmon, Van Allen, Warner, etc. (most of the Scots names refer to families in Glengarry). There is an extraordinary number of local histories covering almost all centres of population in the area. It should be noted that both the books about churches and some of the local histories include details of church registers not published elsewhere. If your ancestors came from this area, you should make every effort to spend at least one day at the library, which is very well and clearly organized with a very helpful and friendly staff.

Deep River: Public Library, Alder Crescent, Deep River, ON K0J 1P0.

The collection here is small but it is growing, and it reflects the great enthusiasm of the librarian and the local residents. The holdings include abstracts from the *Renfrew Mercury*, 1871–1915 (indexed); cemetery records from St. Andrew's United Church at Chalk River, St. Narcissus Catholic Cemetery at Mackey, the Catholic Cemetery at Stonecliffe, and the Protestant and the Catholic cemeteries at Deux Rivières. There is also a list of North Renfrew County burials for Deep River, Point Alexander, and Rapide des Joachims (Québec).

Dundas: Public Library, 18 Ogilvie Street, Dundas, ON L9H 2S2.

Books on the history of Dundas available in the library are:

The Dundas Heritage, I. D. Brown and A. W. Brink, 1970
Dundas, 1947–73, L. Button and J. Don, 1982
The Wheels of Progress, O. Newcombe, 1972
History of the Town of Dundas, T. R. Woodhouse, 1965

The collection of genealogical material includes scrapbooks of newspaper clippings from the *Dundas Star*, 1939–44; high school yearbooks from 1950; atlases of Wentworth County; assessment rolls from 1837 for the townships of Beverley, Binbrook, East Flamborough, Glanford, West Flamborough, and Dundas. There are census returns on microfilm for 1851–91 for Dundas and the various townships surrounding it in Wentworth County.

The following newspapers are in the library and are card-indexed to 1948, and from 1977 onward:

Dundas Star, 1893–1979
Dundas True Banner, 1859–85
Gore Gazette, 1827–29
Star Journal, 1979–
Valley Journal, 1973–79

There are Tweedsmuir Histories for Orkney and Strabane; Dundas directories from 1928; church histories; and family histories for Aikman, Betzner, Lennard, Morden, Olmstead, and Pillow. Local histories are plentiful — too many to list — but information as to the existence of one for a particular district can be obtained from the library.

Elliot Lake: Public Library, 1 Mary Walk, Elliot Lake, ON P5A 1Z9.

This library and this town—neither of which existed a few years ago—are making great efforts to build a genealogical collection, but their resources are limited. The holdings include newspaper clippings from *The Standard*, 1956–60; a copy of the 1871 Census return for this area of Algoma, and some books of local history.

Exeter: Public Library, 330 Main Street, Exeter, ON N0M 1S0.

Local histories in the library include:

A History of Tuckersmith, I. Campbell
History of Exeter, L. Joseph
Kippen and Its Families, R. Workman
St. Joseph, J. Wooden
Huron County Settlement, J. Scott

There is also an Historical Atlas of 1879, showing farms and names of early settlers; newspapers on microfilm (*Exeter Times*, 1873–1924; *Exeter Advocate*, 1887–1926; and *Exeter Times-Advocate*, 1927 to date); cemetery records for various townships in Huron County: Ashfield, Hay, Howick, Hullett, Morris, Stephen, Tuckersmith, Usborne, and East and West Wawonosh. In addition there is an index of BMD in Exeter and area for 1873–93 by M. Aitken, and a history of the Monteith family by J. E. Monteith.

Fergus: Public Library, 190 St. Andrew Street West, Fergus, ON N1M 1N5.

Although this library was established in 1835 and is in one of the early settled areas of Ontario, it does not have any genealogical material except for a few books on local history. Very fortunately for people of Fergus descent there are the magnificent libraries in Guelph and Kitchener, and the Wellington County Museum and Archives — all three with a wealth of material about the general area.

The library's local-history books include:

Fergus, A. E. Byerly, 1934
Melville Church, H. Templin and J. M. Imlah, 1945
Pioneer Days in Nichol, A. W. Wright, 1924
Twelve Townships of Wellington County, H. I. Mack, 1977
History of Elora, R. Allen, 1982
Early History of Elora, J. R. Connon, 1930

Gananoque: Public Library, 100 Park Street, Gananoque, ON K7G 2Y5.
The library has the *Gananoque Reporter* indexed by surname and subject (1860–1923). It is on paper to 1930 but will be on microfilm to 1987 by the time you read this; there are township papers for Leeds and Lansdowne (indexed), and cemetery records for St. John's Catholic, Willowbank, Gananoque (being indexed). Outside Gananoque there are cemetery records for St. John's (Anglican), Oak Leaf (Anglican), Olivet Church, Lillies Baptist, Lansdowne (Ebenezer), the Cross — all in Leeds and Lansdowne. Also the South Crosby cemeteries of Briar Hill, Clear Lake, Crosby, Knowlton, Ripley, St. Columbanus. Other cemeteries include Allen, Barber, Brewers Mills, Dulcemaine, Herald Angel, Jelly's, Lake Eloida, Marble Rock, Pinegrove Methodist, Plum Hollow Baptist, Rowsome Place, Sand Bay, Sand Hill Presbyterian, St. Barnaby's, Staffords, and Washburn. Family histories in the library include Landon, and general histories of many families on Howe Island, and in Leeds and Grenville.
Goderich: Public Library, 52 Montreal Street, Goderich, ON N7A 2G4.
The library has a number of useful books on local history — never neglect such items, because your own family may be mentioned:

The Settlement of Huron County, J. Scott, 1966
Huron Gazetteer & Directory, 1869
Memories of Goderich, D. Wallace, 1977
Goderich Township Families, A. Lobb, 1985
Colborne Connections, 1836–1986, S. Hazlitt, 1987
County Marriage Registers, 1858–69 (Vol. 4)
Huron County Historical Notes (leaflet)

In addition, the library holdings include Huron Assessment Rolls, 1842–48; censuses for 1848, 1850, 1851–91; microfilms of local newspapers: *Signal* (1848–1936), *Star* (1868–1937 —

1891–6 missing), *Signal–Star* (1937 to date), *Lucknow Sentinel* (1875 to date); Huron County Surrogate Court records, 1855–1967. Also Tweedsmuir Histories for Goderich, Hensall, Hurondale, and Lakelet.

Grimsby: Public Library, 25 Adelaide Street, Grimsby, ON L3M 1X2.

There are unindexed microfilms of Lincoln County censuses for 1828, 1851–91; assessment rolls for 1875–1976; an incomplete file of the weekly newspaper (*The Independent*) from 1885 to 1945 (unindexed), and a complete run from 1946 to date, also unindexed. There are three local history books available:

> *Grimsby, 1876–1976*
> *Grimbsy and District*, 1901
> *Annals of the Forty* (10 vols.), 1950 (Vols. 3–10 give details of
> pre-1840 families)

Guelph: Public Library, 100 Norfolk Street, Guelph, ON N1H 4J6.

This is another library with a special dedication to genealogical research, and the moving spirit on the staff is Linda Kearns, the Local History Archivist and Librarian. Within the past ten years the library has re-microfilmed the newspaper collection (covering 130 years) and added censuses, assessment rolls, Tweedsmuir Histories, city directories, telephone books, and manuscript material. There is a considerable amount of information about local families—too much to list, but specific inquiries about a particular family will be answered, provided you cover the return postage. Some idea of the attitude towards ancestor-hunters and the efforts being made to build up an outstanding collection are the facts that 200 mail queries were answered in 1987 and 1400 people used the genealogical resources at the library. The materials available are listed below.

Books of major importance to genealogists researching in the Guelph area are:

> *Annals of the Town of Guelph, 1827–77*, C. A. Burrows, 1877
> *Guelph Mercury: Centennial Edition*, 1927
> *Mercury History of Guelph* (scrapbook), 1866
> *History of Guelph*, L. A. Johnson, 1977
> *Incidents of Pioneer Days in Guelph and Bruce*, D. Kennedy,
> 1903

Twelve Townships of Wellington County, H. Mack, 1977
Family Research in Waterloo & Wellington Counties, R. Taylor, 1986
A Brief Sketch of the Early History of Guelph, R. Thompson, 1877

There are also a number of books about various clubs and institutions, local regiments, schools, and municipal records. The family histories include Crowe, Goldie, Higinbotham, McCrae, Nichol, and Shutt. There are county and city directories on microfilm dating back to 1852, and historical atlases for Waterloo and Wellington (1881 and 1887), and Wellington (1906). These contain details of local families and farm locations. The library holds newspapers on microfilm and manuscript from 1840 up to date.

The census records include the Gore District (parts of Waterloo, Brant, and Wentworth) for 1818–1845; the 1851 Canada West Census for Wellington County (Guelph is missing); and the regular censuses for the area for the period 1861–91. There is also the computerized Land Records Index on microfilm. This gives details of land records in the Provincial Archives. No documents are held in the library. There is a small photographic collection dating back to the late 1800s.

There is also a collection of Tweedsmuir Histories — these are histories of mainly rural areas written by local branches of the Women's Institute — of Alma, Arkell, Badenoch, Brock Road, Eden Crest, Ennotville, Eramosa, Morriston, Mosborough, Riverside, Royal, Speedside, and West End. They contain much information about local families. All are on microfilm and may be borrowed through inter-library loan.

Hamilton: Public Library, 55 York Boulevard, Hamilton, ON L8R 3K1.

This is another outstanding library with which Ontario is blessed. The Special Collections Department has a great deal of material about the Hamilton–Wentworth Region, and a fair amount of it is indexed. The library indexes local newspapers, clippings, photographs, books, and a great deal more. The staff will deal with research queries by mail and charge an escalating fee depending on the degree of difficulty. If the question is too involved, you will be referred to the local OGS Branch.

The microfilms cover the following areas: assessment rolls for Barton Township, Hamilton, Dundas, and Wentworth County; telephone books from 1879; indexed funeral-home records from 1851 onwards; Tweedsmuir Histories for Blackheath, Cainsville, Copetown, Greensville, Hamilton area, Maggie Johnson, Mountsberg, North Brant, Oakland, Orkney, Rockton, Sandusk, Springvale, Strabane, and Wentworth South. There is a nominal index for the War of 1812 (claims for losses), Gore and Hamilton Gaol Registers (1833–67), Hamilton Orphan Asylum (1848–1914), militia records from 1837, various scrapbooks for the mid-1800s, city directories from 1853, and family papers of Bury, Case, Crowell Smith, Houghton, Macnab, Newburn, Robinson, and Turner.

The newspaper collection is probably the most widespread of any library in Ontario — too many to list. The records start in 1824 and continue up to date. Hamilton must have set some kind of record for the number of local publications—newspapers and journals—because the library list totals 74; the area newspapers total 19 and include some for Ancaster, Burlington, Dundas, Gore, Grand River, Halton, Stoney Creek, and Waterdown. From even further afield there nearly 100 newspapers represented from outside the Hamilton area.

There are municipal records from the Township of Beverley, the Police Village of Lynden, Binbrook Township, East Flamborough, Waterdown, Glanford, West Flamborough, and Hamilton City Council. The picture collection includes more than ten thousand photographs and drawings of people, places, and events; maps and surveys of Hamilton and area dating back to 1791; plus a variety of business and professional records. The censuses from 1842 are in microfilm up to 1891, plus a number of BMD registers from Wentworth County and very many records of cemetery inscriptions and voters' lists.

Huntsville: Public Library, PO Box 1029, 7 Minerva Street, Huntsville, ON P0A 1K0.

This library has only very limited genealogical material, but it does have a good collection of local history books covering Algonquin Park, Bracebridge, Gravenhurst, Huntsville, Muskoka, Parry Sound, Port Carling, and Port Sydney, and several church histories including Sand Lake and Norway Point. There is a genealogical group in Huntsville that may be of some help: Muskoka–Parry Sound Genealogy Group, PO Box 2857, Huntsville, ON P0A 1K0.

Kingston: Public Library, 130 Johnson Street, Kingston, ON K7L 1X8.

No information available, beyond the fact it has census and cemetery records. (CEO Arnold Maizen.)

Kitchener: Public Library, 85 Queen Street North, Kitchener, ON N2H 2H1.

This is yet another first-rate and beautifully organized library — the area served by the Guelph, Hamilton, and Kitchener libraries is, indeed, very fortunate. The genealogical resources of the Kitchener Library (and other neighbouring libraries, museums, and archives) are described in great detail in Ryan Taylor's superb book *Family Research in Waterloo and Wellington Counties*, published by the Ontario Genealogical Society in 1986. If your ancestors came from this area, get this book — borrow it or buy it but get it! It's good! The details I give below are taken with permission from the book, since the author is in charge of the Grace Schmidt Room of Local History in the library:

Censuses for Waterloo and Wellington counties for the period 1824–91 are in the library on microfilm, but only 1851 is indexed at the moment. The places covered by the early censuses (1824–42) are Dumfries, Eramosa, Erin, Garafraxa, Guelph, Nichol, Puslinch, Waterloo Township, Wilmot, and Woolwich. A great many places in the area of the two counties have changed their names over the years and you will find details in Ryan Taylor's book — it is vital that you check this before researching census returns. Local histories in the library include such places as Arthur, Ayr, Breslau, Clifford, Dumfries, Eden Mills, Elmira, Elora, Eramosa, Erin, Fergus, Galt, Garafraxa, Guelph, Harriston, Hespeler, Hillsburgh, Kitchener, Maryborough, Maryhill, Minto, Morriston, Mount Forest, New Dundee, Nichol, Petersburg, Puslinch, St. Agatha, St. Jacobs, Waterloo, Wellesley, and Wilmot. The library also holds early directories from 1864 and atlases from 1877. There are many earlier maps of smaller places which give the names of early settlers and details of the land on which they lived. There is a full list of these places in the Taylor book. There are over 70 of these in the library and they are an invaluable source of important information if your ancestor was an early settler in the area.

The library has a good newspaper collection. Indexes for BMD are included in the collection. So far as the Kitchener Library is concerned, the following are available:

Ayr News, 1904–60, 1962 to date
Elmira Signet, 1893, 1900–82. Not complete
Galt Weekly Reformer, 1898–99, 1903–12
Galt Dumfries Reformer, 1849–63, 1867–97
Galt Reporter, 1857–59, 1888, 1912–17, 1919–22, 1923–57, 1967–71
Hespeler Herald, 1919–49
(Kitchener) *Kanada-Museum* (German language), 1835–40
(Kitchener) *Deutsche-Kanadier* (German), 1841–64. Not complete
(Kitchener) *Berlin Telegraph,* 1856–64, 1898–1922. Not complete
(Kitchener) *Berliner Journal* (German), 1859–1920
(Kitchener) *Berlin Daily News,* 1878–79
(Kitchener) *Freie Presse* (German), 1886–87
(Kitchener) *Deutsche Zeitung* (German), 1891–99
(Kitchener) *Record* (now *Kitchener-Waterloo Record*), 1893 to date
(New Hamburg) *Hamburger Beobachter* (German), 1855–56
(New Hamburg) *Neu-Hamburger Neutrale* (German), 1855–57
(New Hamburg) *Kanadisches Volksblatt* (German), 1865–66
New Hamburg Independent, 1917 to date
Preston Times, 1948–58, 1966–69
(Walkerton) *Glocke* (German), 1883–87, 1889–98
(Waterloo) *Der Morgenstern* (German), 1839–41
Waterloo Sentinel, 1909–12
Waterloo Chronicle, 1868–69, 1922–29, 1932 to date
Wellesley Maple Leaf, 1900–04, 1906–08

The Tweedsmuir Histories created by the local Women's Institutes can be a wonderful source of family and farm information. The library has them for the following places — most are on microfilm:

WATERLOO COUNTY: Ayr, Bloomingdale, Branchton, Bridgeport, Central Dumfries, Centreville, Dorking, Elmdale, Grand River, Haysville, Helena, Feasby, Hespeler, Jubilee, Laura Rose (Galt), Lexington, Linwood, Little's Corners, Maple Grove (Kossuth), Mill Creek, New Dundee, New Hamburg, Preston, Rummelhardt, St. Jacobs, Wellesley, Winterbourne, Woolwich (Elmira).

WELLINGTON COUNTY: Alma, Arkell, Arthur, Badenoch, Beehive, Belwood, Brock Road, Carry On (Palmerston), Clifford, Coningsby, Conn, Cumnock, Damascus, Drayton, Drew, Eden Crest, Elora, Ennotville, Eramosa, Erin, Farewell (Mount Forest), Fergus, Greenbush (Harriston), Greenock, Hillsborough,

Little Ireland (Minto), Living Springs (W. Garafraxa), Mimosa, Moorefield, Morriston, Mosborough, Northgate, Palmerston, Ponsonby, Puslinch, Riverside, Rock-a-Long (Rockwood), Rothsay, Royal, Speedside, Teviotdale, Utoka, and Westend.

I will not attempt to list the cemetery records because the number copied is enormous—over 240, and more to come. They are all listed in Ryan Taylor's book.

You will also find in the same book nearly thirty pages of church records and registers of all denominations, and these also I am omitting because of lack of space.

Since Ryan Taylor's book was published, the library has indexed Wesleyan Methodist baptisms for Waterloo and Wellington counties covering the period from 1835 onwards. These are not well known, and I was asked to mention this new addition to the holdings. The library also holds a number of family histories; names are not available, but information can be obtained from the library about a specific surname.

Lanark: Public Library, George Street, Lanark, ON K0G 1K0.

The library has limited genealogical information but it has the following books of local interest:

Lanark Legacy, H. Brown
Pioneer History of the County of Lanark, J. McGill
The Ireton Family Tree, M. Ireton
Historical Atlas of Lanark & Renfrew Counties, 1880
St. Paul's Church, Lanark, J. C. Hanson

Leamington: Public Library, 1 John Street, Leamington, ON N8H 1H1.

Books of genealogical interest on the library shelves are:

Biographical Record of the County of Essex, Beers, 1905
Biographical Record of the County of Kent, Beers, 1904
Leamington's Heritage, F. S. Snell, 1974
A History of Leamington, L. Newland, 1947
Leamington and Its Churches, A. M. Robertson, 1902

The library also has on microfilm the issues of the *Leamington Post* from 1907 to date; Historical Atlases of Essex and Kent, and Lambton; cemetery lists from Albuna (Mersea), Fairview (Ruthven), Graceland and Fox Family (Gosfield South), Lakeview, Kingsville (abandoned), Ruthven United and Kenyon

Point (Gosfield South). In addition there are books and manuscripts about some local families: Bruner, Cowlthorpe (or Colthorp), De Laurier, Kinsley, Malott, McDonald, Reid, and a book including several families (Coatsworth, Fox, Friend, Iler, McCormick, Malotte, Scratch, Shepley, Wigle, and Wilkinson), all early settlers in Essex County.

Lennox & Addington: Public Library, PO Box 400, Bath, ON K0H 1G0.

See entry under Bath.

Lindsay: Public Library, 190 Kent Street West, Lindsay, ON K9V 2Y6.

No information available. (CEO Moti Tahiliani.)

London: Public Library, 305 Queens Avenue, London, ON N6B 3L7.

This is another outstanding library with a very good genealogical collection and, in particular, one of the best collections of family histories in the country. This will be so useful to ancestor-hunters in the London area that I wish I could list all the names, because it covers a wide area, not only London. I can only suggest you contact the library (with the usual self-addressed envelope) for information about a particular family.

The library has a number of indexed microfilms of area newspapers, including the following:

The Age, Strathroy, 1870–1900
Dispatch, Strathroy, 1890–99
Dutton Enterprise, 1881–89
Glencoe Transcript, 1873–1914
Gore Gazette, 1827–29
London Advertiser, 1864–1936
London Free Press, 1849 to date
London Gazette, 1836–42
Oxford Star, 1848–49
Parkhill Gazette, 1893–1911
St. Thomas Liberal, 1832–33
St. Thomas Standard, 1844–46
Western Dispatch, 1879–90
Western Globe, 1845–51

There are also indexes to local-history scrapbooks (Elgin, Middlesex, Norfolk, and Oxford counties); the Seaborn Collection (indexed), which consists of diaries, clippings, memoirs, etc., of Dr. Edwin Seaborn. In the London Room of the library you will find a collection of data about settlers who lived in the county before 1880. This is an ongoing project of the London Branch of the OGS. There is also a collection of cemetery records for the counties of Elgin, Middlesex, Norfolk and Oxford; an index of names appearing in the *London Free Press*, 1849–1861; and a card index to the same newspaper for BMD for the period 1862–80. There are also, of course, copies of church registers, histories of several churches, and the usual microfilm records of census returns and land transactions.

Madoc: Public Library, 20 Davidson Street, Madoc, ON K0K 2K0.

This is a good example of a small library gradually building up a good genealogical collection. It has schoolhouse histories of various one-room schools; a Tweedsmuir History of Madoc on microfilm; family histories for Gawley, Holmes, Ketcheson, and Orr; local newspapers (*Madoc Mercury* and *Madoc Review*) on microfilm or microfiche, from 1863 to date, but with some issues missing. Indexing of BMD has recently started. There is a growing list of cemetery records: Greenwood, Hazzard's, Lakeview, Queensborough, White Lake, White Lake Pioneer, and five family cemeteries: Haggerty, Mitts (Lilac), Reid, Venn-Collins, and Wood.

Markdale: Public Library, 21 Main Street East, Markdale, ON N0C 1H0.

Family history books and manuscripts include Armstrong, Bellamy, Benson, Benthem, Blakely, Boyd, Carefoot, Christoe, Clayton, Coleman, Elliot, Flesher, Ford, Hamilton, Haskett, Heard, Henry, Irving, Irwin, Lever, Lucas, McFarland, McLeod, McTavish, Mann, Mercer, Moffat, Moore, Munshaw, Murdoch, Pickell, Piper, Richardson, Ritchie, Rutledge, Sproule, Stewart, Strain, Taylor, Thibaudeau, Thompson, Thurston, Trimble, Turnbull, and Wright. There are microfilmed editions of the *Markdale Standard*, 1880–1986, with an index of obituaries. There is also a number of books of genealogical interest, including:

Markdale and Flesherton: A Written Heritage, Markdale, 1979. (This was a co-operative effort of the public libraries of the two towns, and of the Grey County Historical Society. It is of great value, because it gives details of some 80 local families.)

William Armstrong & His Descendants, 1846–1979, P. Armstrong, 1979.
(Another "must" for anyone with ancestral roots in the area because it, too, gives details of more than 50 families.)
Alexander Irwin and His Descendants, 1859–1986, P. Armstrong, 1987
Pioneers of the Queen's Bush (The Williams Family), F. A. Fee, 1984

All the above books are of major importance so far as much information of early settlers is concerned.

This coverage of early settlers and settlement is quite outstanding, and compensates to some extent for the lack of other material. Basically, the emphasis is on settlers and settlement and not on genealogy, but that may change.

Markham: Public Library, Thornhill Community Centre Library, 7755 Bayview Avenue, Thornhill, ON L3T 4P1.

The old village of Markham gives its name to a greatly expanded area and the library system is trying hard to keep up with the population explosion in the district. Its genealogical resources are very limited and consist mainly of a few local-history scrapbooks and some local-history books:

A New History of the County of Grey, T. A. Davidson, 1972
Thornhill: From Wilderness to Urban Village, H. J. Easton, 1975
German Pioneers of Toronto and Markham Township, 1976
Markham, 1793–1900 (Markham Historical Society), 1979

Marmora: Public Library, Marmora, ON K0K 2M0.

There are no genealogical sources in this library, but several local people do have information about local families such as Bleecker, Bonter, Hawley, Kerr, McCoy, McNairn, and Nobe, and contact can be made through the librarian (Mrs. Ruby McCoy).

Meaford: Public Library, 15 Trowbridge Street, Meaford, ON N0H 1Y0.

The most important holding of the library is the Frank Harding Collection of 400 family trees of Meaford families. Other holdings are the Canada West Census of 1851 for the general area around Meaford, and the Canada-wide censuses for the years between 1861 and 1891. Books on the shelves of genealogical interest include:

A History of the County of Grey, 1931
History of the Schools of St. Vincent Township, 1847–1967
A History of Collingwood Township, 1979
The History of Owen Sound, M. M. Croft, 1980
History of Sydenham Township, 1967
The History of the County of Bruce, N. Robertson, 1960
History of Derby Township, 1839–1972, 1972
Perpetual Pioneers (The Seaman Family), K. Weaver, 1984
Knights: From Generation to Generation, n.a.

The library also has on microfilm the local newspapers: the
Meaford Monitor from 1869 to 1900 and the *Meaford Mirror*
from 1886 to 1897.
Midland: Public Library, 320 King Street, Midland, ON
L4R 3M6.
Books on the shelves of interest to those with ancestors in the
Midland area are:

Midland and Her Pioneers, G. R. Osborne, 1939
Midland's Past Inhabitants (Tombstone Inscriptions), S. M.
    Gianetto
Midland's Yesteryears, E. Shushan
Penetanguishene, 1875–1975, n.a.
Migration of Voyageurs from Drummond Island in 1828, A. C.
    Osborne

The other material available is voters' lists for Midland
(1913, 1919), Flos Township (1889), Tay (1891), Tiny (1882–95);
the Canadian Census for the area for 1861 and 1871; and cemetery inscriptions from

St. Ann's Catholic Cemetery, Penetanguishene
St. John's Anglican Cemetery, Tay Township
St. Michael's Catholic Cemetery, Orillia
St. Mary's Catholic Cemetery, Victoria Harbour
Union Cemetery, Victoria Harbour

There are also a few books about the history of local churches
in Elmvale, Midland, and Penetanguishene.
Nepean: Public Library, 16 Rowley Avenue, Nepean, ON
K2G 1L9.
Most of the reference material of the library is located at the
Merivale Road Branch, 1541 Merivale Road, Nepean, ON

K2G 3J4. Only very limited information about the genealogical holdings is available, and if the details given below are
not sufficient, I suggest you write directly to the library (CEO
David Weismuller). The material available includes County
Marriage Registers of Ontario, 1858–69; death notices from
the *Christian Guardian*, 1836–60; Land Records Index; and a
number of books about United Empire Loyalists generally.
Newcastle: Public Library, 62 Temperance Street, Bowmanville, ON L1C 3A8.
The library has an index of local newspapers, BMD records,
census returns, and a number of books on local history.
New Hamburg: Public Library, 145 Huron Street, New Hamburg, ON N0B 2G0.
This district is in the heart of the German settlements in
Waterloo and Wellington, and a great deal of genealogical
information about New Hamburg is included in the holdings
of the Kitchener and Waterloo libraries and the Wellington
County Archives. In the library itself you will find the following: Waterloo Historical Society magazines, 1913–87; historical atlases for Waterloo and Wellington counties, 1881, 1887
(as you know, these often contain names of early settlers and
details of the land they occupied); a plan of the village of Hamburg (1854); and a collection of newspaper clippings and photographs from the *New Hamburg Independent*.
The books of genealogical interest that are available are:

Holy Family Church, New Hamburg, 1883–1983
Petersburg School, Wilmot, 1836–1936
The Story of Waterloo County, B. Moyer, 1971
History of the County of Perth, 1825–1902, W. Johnstone
Little Paradise: German Canadians of Waterloo County, 1800–
1975
A History of Kitchener, W. V. Uttley, 1975
Amish Settlement in the Township of Wilmot
New Hamburg Historical Notes
Pioneer Settlement of S. W. Wilmot
Family History of Jonas Shantz and Hannah (Snyder), 1710–
1980
The Family: Puddicombe, Martlon, Tye, Macdonald, Thoms, E.
Thoms
Murner Genealogy, R. M. Connell, 1976
St. Peter's Lutheran Church: A History

Niagara-on-the-Lake: Public Library, Rear 26 Queen Street, Niagara-on-the-Lake, ON L0S 1J0.
The library is the repository for the book collection of the Niagara Historical Society. As you can imagine, this is a large one, and it is not possible to list all the books. Those about specific families are Bolton, Booth, Calder, Cawthra, Coe, Coleman, Crysler, Dampson, Dempster, Drake, Fairchild, Fitzpatrick, Fraser, Gage, Johnson, Johnston, Keefer, Kingsmill, Lampman, Landis, Merriman, Mills, Nelson, Osborn, Prentice, Regehr, Russell, Sebor, Secord, Stein, Stone, Talbot, Thompson, Van Every, Warner, Woodruff, Wright.
The library was kind enough to supply me with a complete list of the microfilm holdings of the Niagara Historical Resource Centre and this is an embarrassment of riches, since there is no way in which I can list even a part of this tremendous collection. I can simply tell you it includes municipal records, military records, school lists, business and commercial records, publications and records of the Niagara Historical Society back into the nineteenth century, census returns from 1842, including a special one of Niagara in 1867, copies of local newspapers from 1799, Surrogate Court records for Lincoln County, land records, copies of British military records from the National Archives in Ottawa, etc.
There are also some church registers:

Eight Mile Creek Church, Grantham, BMD 1849–1928
St. Andrews Presbyterian Church, BMD 1830 to date
St. Georges Anglican, Homer, BMD 1877–1944
St. John's Anglican, Virgil, BMD 1895–1954
St. Mark's Anglican, BMD 1826–1979
St. Vincent-de-Paul Catholic, BMD 1856–1975
Various Methodist Circuit Registers, 1859–1938

Niagara Falls: Public Library, 4848 Victoria Street, Niagara Falls, ON L2E 4C5.
The holdings of the library are:
Censuses of Niagara, 1782, 1783, 1787 (Loyalist), 1828, 1850, and the Canadian censuses for the area for the period 1851–1871 (this is being indexed); land records; early atlases and maps for Bertie, Newark, Niagara, and the counties of Lincoln and Welland. Indexed extracts are available for the following newspapers:

Farmer's Journal (Welland), 1826–30
Niagara Chronicle, 1844–54
Niagara Gleaner, 1823–35
Niagara Reporter, 1833–42
Niagara Spectator, 1816–19

There are also some church registers and records:

Chippewa Presbyterian Church, BMD 1842–1923
Drummondville Presbyterian, BMD 1843–1901
Holy Trinity Church, Chippewa, BMD 1840–1920 (incomplete)
Immaculé Conception (Catholic), BMD 1924–85
Sacré Coeur, Welland (Catholic), MD 1919–84
St. Anthony of Padua (Niagara), B 1955–85
St. Jean-de-Brébeuf (Catholic), BMD 1951–83
St. Paul's Anglican (Fort Erie), BMD 1836–44

You will also find baptismal records for the following:

Fort George, 1821–27
Grimsby (general), 1817–22
Niagara (general), 1792–1832
Presbyterian Church, Newark, 1781–1814
St. Andrew's Niagara, 1830–33
St. Andrews United, 1856–94
St. Mark's Anglican, Niagara, 1832–40
St. Paul's, Fort Erie, 1849–52

In addition, there are a number of records of marriages — registers and licences — and death and burial notices for various nearby areas. An extraordinary number of cemetery inscriptions have been copied and indexed; detailed information about a particular locality can be obtained from the library (include self-addressed envelope, please).

Finally, there are muster rolls of militia regiments, voters' lists, early directories, assessment rolls, and a special section devoted to United Empire Loyalists. There are also nearly a hundred family histories, ranging from Bastedo to Woolley, and a great many histories of local towns and townships which include a great deal of family information.

Oakville: Public Library, 120 Navy Street, Oakville, ON L6J 2Z4.

The books of genealogical value on the shelves are:

Oakville: A Small Town, 1900–30
Historical Atlas of Halton County, 1877
Index to the 1871 Census (Halton-Peel)
Research in Halton/Peel, J. and R. Speers
History of St. John's United Church, 1832–1972, E. Wilson

There are census returns on microfilm for the immediate area for 1842 and 1851–91, and for the Trafalgar–Gore District for 1816–49; Tweedsmuir Histories for Halton and Hornby; assessment rolls for Trafalgar Township; the private papers of a number of local families; high school registers; and church histories.

There is also a names index for over 20,000 individuals from 1800 to 1900; indexes to the local newspaper from 1850 to date; early maps of Oakville; indexed newspaper clippings; and early directories and telephone books. There is also—and this is most useful—a list of people using the library for genealogical research and the name of the family they are researching. There are local registrations of BMD for the period 1869–95 for Oakville, and other registers for Bathurst, Haldimand, and Halton.

The church registers in the library are Knox Presbyterian Church, BMD 1850–63; Palermo United Church, BMD 1959–72; and Trafalgar Church, BMD 1901–56.

Orangeville: Public Library, 144 Broadway Avenue, Orangeville, ON L9W 1J9.
No information available. (CEO Mrs. V. Wingfield-Digby.)

Orillia: Public Library, 36 Mississauga Street West, Orillia, ON L3V 3A6.
No information available. (CEO Katherine D. McKinnon.)

Oshawa: Public Library, 65 Bagot Street, Oshawa, ON L1H 1N2.
The library refers inquirers to *Bibliography of Ontario History, 1976–86*, published by Laurentian University; *Bibliography of Ontario History pre-1976*, published by the University of Toronto Press, and *Local History of the Regional Municipalities of Peel, York, and Durham*, published in 1980 by the Central Ontario Regional Library System. If you are unable to obtain these books, I suggest you write directly to the CEO, Miss R. P. Brooking, at the library.

Ottawa: Public Library, 120 Metcalfe Street, Ottawa, ON K1P 5M2.
The only book in the library of local genealogical interest is *Tracing Your Ottawa Family*, B. S. Elliott, 1980. You will also

find early directories from 1861 to date for Ottawa, and from 1837 for Hull; the Ottawa-Hull telephone directories from 1878 to date; library scrapbooks of biographical clippings from Ottawa newspapers from 1939 to 1975, with a few dating back to 1911; census returns for the Ottawa-Hull region for 1842 and 1851–91; a card index of Ottawa-area BMD as reported in the *Ottawa Journal* from 1885 to 1920. There are also a number of family histories, the majority of which are not connected with Ottawa. If your own ancestors settled in Ottawa (or Bytown as it was), I suggest you contact the library for more specific information (the usual self-addressed envelope please).

Owen Sound: Public Library, 824-1st Avenue West, Owen Sound, ON N4K 4K4.

The holdings of the library concentrate in the main on the counties of Grey and Bruce. There is a surname collection (mainly obituaries) which is based on the local newspapers, and has been compiled by the Bruce–Grey Branch of the OGS. However, there are also BMD taken from the *Chesley Enterprise*, the *Port Elgin Times*, and the *Wiarton Echo* from 1879 to 1900. There are Bell Telephone directories from 1866; a directory of Owen Sound for 1892; a great many local histories; voters' lists from 1976; a great many oral-history tapes of memoirs and reminiscences; and a great deal of information about settlement, and settler families, in the townships of Artemesia, Bentinck, Collingwood, Derby, Egremont, Glenelg, Keppel, Osprey, Proton, St. Vincent, Sarawak, and Sydenham. In Bruce County the townships are Albemarle, Amabel, Arran, Brant, Bruce, Carrick, Culross, Eastnor, Elderslie, Greenock, Huron, Kincardine, St. Edmund, Saugeen. One interesting collection, which I have not found anywhere else, is a collection of family Bibles; the following families are included: Arnold, Brower, Campbell, Daniels, Eaton, Foster, Geddes, Gordon, Hayes, Mathers, McAllister, McCosh, Nesbit, Price, Reid, Rodgers, Smith, Sparrow, and Stewart. Individual family histories in the library number nearly 200—too many to list, unfortunately.

Parry Sound: Public Library, 29 Mary Street, Parry Sound, ON P2A 1E3.

Many years ago I was impressed by a project of senior-citizen groups in the area who got together and transcribed all the tombstones of all the cemeteries in the Parry Sound area, and published it in 1974. It is of tremendous help to people with ancestral roots in the area, and its existence is comparatively unknown; another collective project in the late 1960s was that of the Historical Society, which produced *Notes and Sketches on the History of Parry Sound* — another book of required reading for descendants of the early settlers, many of whom, of course, later migrated to the West, where they went down in history as "The Parry Sounders". Two other books of value are *Along Memory Lane* (2 volumes, with No. 3 on the way) by Edith MacFie, covering the period 1868–1980, and the *East Georgian Bay Historical Journal (Muskoka, Parry Sound, & Simcoe)*, edited by Gail Lucas. For a general history of the area there is *A History of Parry Sound* by Agnes Wing. In addition to these, there are a number of family histories produced by the local genealogical organization; they include Beatty, Foot, Gibson, Johnson, Miller, Miner, Newburn, Oastler, Pearce, Radforth, Spring, Starkey, and Wilkinson.

Pembroke: Public Library, 237 Victoria Street, Pembroke, ON K8A 4K5.

The genealogical holdings of the library are concentrated on the immediate area of the county of Renfrew and of Pembroke itself. There is good coverage of history books about local townships: Admaston, Alice and Fraser, Bromley, Griffith, Macnab, Matawatchan, Westmeath, and, of course, Pembroke itself. Local newspapers available on microfilm include the *Pembroke Observer*, 1855 to date (with some issues missing); the *Pembroke Standard*, 1910–26; and the *Pembroke Bulletin*, 1934–55. Printed family histories include Biesenthal, Humphries, Nielke, Raddatz, Tennant, Woermke, and a general book, *Family Histories*, about various families in the Pembroke area. The early directories are not all that early, and date only from 1925. There are several church histories: Wesley United Church (1835–1935) and Calvin Church (1849–1949); these histories can often provide genealogical information if your ancestor was active in a particular church.

Perth: Union Public Library, 30 Herriott Street, Perth, ON K7H 1T2.

This library was destroyed by fire in 1980 and is slowly rebuilding its local-history and genealogical holdings. It has some books about early settlement and families: Perth, the county of Lanark, South Elmsley, the Presbyterians of Lanark County, the 1817 Census of Perth, a history of Pakenham.

Peterborough: Public Library, 345 Aylmer Street North, Peterborough, ON K9H 3V7.

The main section of the library of interest to the ancestor-hunter is the "Peterborough Collection" of very early histories of the area, and the library also houses the collection of the Kawartha Branch of the Ontario Genealogical Society. Neither of these collections is available on inter-library loan.

The library has available Tweedsmuir Histories for Baillieboro, Millbrook, and Roseneath, as well as a number of local histories for various villages in the area. Family histories include Burnham, Kidd, Logan, Macdonald, Rogers, Stock, Strickland, and some others with little connection with the district. There is a collection of documents of the Peter Robinson colonization of the area in 1825. You will also find a great deal of family information in the Peterborough Museum and Archives, and a visit there is essential if you are doing family research in the Peterborough area. The library has census returns for Hastings, Northumberland, Peterborough, and Victoria counties for 1842 and the period 1851–1891. In addition, it has on microfilm the assessment rolls of the Newcastle District for 1819–40, and the North Monaghan municipal records for 1852–86. It has the following newspapers on microfilm:

Morning Times, 1895–1914
Peterborough Examiner, 1858 to date
Peterborough Review, 1854–1920
Peterborough Times, 1872–84
Weekly Dispatch, 1846–52

There is also the Dobbin Index to early newspapers — with errors! As well there are early directories of the city and county dating back to 1858, and early historical atlases for a large number of counties—and not only the ones adjacent to the city.
Port Colborne: Public Library, 310 King Street, Port Colborne, ON L3K 4H1.
The library has a limited genealogical collection, but it is growing: books about local families (Carter, Fehrman, Sherk, Skinner, Weaver, and Zimmerman); city directories from 1942; a pioneer file of 20,000 records of local BMD; the *Welland–Port Colborne Evening Tribune* and its predecessors on microfilm from the 1880s (indexed); and some cemetery and census records for the area.
Port Hope: Public Library, 31 Queen Street, Port Hope, ON L1A 2Y8.
This library is not prepared to supply information about its genealogical holdings because its "material is not well organized", and I suggest you write directly to Victoria Owen, the

Chief Librarian, with any queries you may have. Be sure you include return postage.

Richmond Hill: Public Library, 24 Wright Street, Richmond Hill, ON L4C 4A1.

The library is not able to supply information about its holdings, except to refer inquirers to a book by Patricia Hart entitled *Local History of the Regional Municipalities of Peel, York, and Durham; an annotated listing of published materials located in the regional municipalities.* It does have files on these families: Armstrong, Arnold, Atkinson, Baker, Barker, Brodie, Burv, Button, Cameron, Davis, De Chalus, De Puisay, Doane, Dooks, Gamble, Hartman, Hopper, Hunt, Innes, Johnston, Klinck, Kurtz, Langstaff, Leece, Lloyd, Lund, MacDonald, McKenzie, McMillan, Marsh, Miner, Moran, Palmer, Purdy, Quantz, Reaman, Richmond, Riel, St. George, Sanderson, Shaw, Steel, Stong, Switzer, Teal, Trench, Trombauvev, Van der Burgh, Villier, Webster, Wellman, White, Willson, and Wright.

Rideau: North Gower Public Library, PO Box 280, North Gower, ON K0A 2T0.

The library does not have a large genealogical collection, but it does have a Hyland Family History, and an indexed list of the transcriptions of the sixteen cemeteries within the township.

St. Catharines: Public Library, 54 Church Street, St. Catharines, ON L2R 7K2.

The library has over five thousand books of local history and genealogy, plus 1100 microfilm reels. The collection of census records includes *indexed* returns for the following areas:

Elgin, 1842, 1851, 1861, 1871
Halton/Peel, 1871
Huron, 1871
Lambton, 1861
Norfolk, 1861
St. Catharines, 1861
Welland, 1851

Other holdings include a name index (BMD taken from many different sources); a large number of family histories; county marriage registers on microfilm; marriage bonds on microfilm, 1803–46; early Canadian marriages in Erie County, 1840–90; cemetery transcriptions for the counties of Lincoln and Welland; wills for the same two counties on microfilm, 1794–1900; funeral-home records (Hulse & English), indexed, 1859-66; voters' lists for St. Catharines, 1907 to date (incomplete); records of some local churches; Tweedsmuir Histories for Grantham Township and Port Dalhousie.

There are local newspapers on microfilm: the *St. Catharines Standard*, 1891 to date, and a number of others scattered around the Niagara Peninsula. There are indexes for the *St. Catharines Constitutional*, 1861–71, and the *Thorold Post*, 1875–76.

St. Thomas: Public Library, 153 Curtis Street, St. Thomas, ON N5P 3Z7.

The library is also the repository for the book collection of the Elgin County Branch of the Ontario Genealogical Society. It is hoped that this latter library can be integrated into the main collection and made available to the general public. At present the St. Thomas Library holds a number of family histories: Campbell, Caswell, Charlton, Corless, Duncombe, Foster, Gilbert, Hunter, Johnstone, Monteith, Newell, Penhale, Tisdale, and Willson. There are many more in the OGS collection.

The library has on microfilm St. Thomas newspapers from 1832 (with many missing issues), and newspapers in Aylmer and Rodney. There are city directories from 1865 to date, but some are missing. Tweedsmuir Histories are available for Belmont, Lyons, Middlemarch, North Yarmouth, Rodney, South Yarmouth, and Wallacetown. Many of the biographical books are indexed, and the local newspaper is indexed up to 1920. BMD records in two churches have also been indexed: Old St. Thomas Church and Trinity Church. There are also local marriage registers for 1853–73.

Sarnia: Public Library, 124 Christina Street South, Sarnia, ON N7T 2M6.

The library holdings include cemetery records from Lambton County; indexed census returns for the period 1851–91, partially indexed; indexed lists of BMD notices from the *Sarnia Observer* from 1853 to date, together with indexed obituaries, and the same information from the *Sarnia Gazette* from 1960 to date.

The library has a number of local histories in which the names of early settlers and settlements are mentioned:

Biographical Record of the County of Lambton, J. H. Beers
Benjamin Zavitz & Esther Augustine and Descendants, H. Clark
Beauchamp Genealogy, 1600–1987, D. B. Cook
Duchesne Genealogy, 1620–1987, D. B. Cook

A History of Lambton, J. T. Elford
Thomas McIlveen & Louisa Aitkin, P. Depew
History of the Village of Mooretown, I. Finlayson
History of Blackwell Church & Community, C. Phelps
Lambton's Hundred Years, V. Lauriston
Robbins Family History, Anna Mason
Forest Free Press BMD Index, 1898–1907, E. Nielsen
Index of Marriages (Plympton Township), 1833–60, E. Nielsen
Records of Joseph Lang Family, M. Bauer & M. Guenther

Sault Ste. Marie: Public Library, 50 East Street, Sault Ste. Marie, ON P6A 3C3.
The library's microfilmed census returns include those for 1842, 1848, 1850, and the period 1851–91. The 1861 Census is the first to include "The Soo", but it is listed under Algoma; there is a city directory available from 1901 to date; and voters' lists for 1891, and from 1956 to date. The library has on microfilm copies of the *Sault Star* from 1901 to date, and it has been indexed for BMD notices up to 1925 by the Sault Ste. Marie Branch of the Ontario Genealogical Society. The Branch has also indexed the BMD notices in the *North Shore Sentinel* from 1971 to 1982. This latter newspaper is a weekly which circulates along the shore from Echo Bay to Blind River. There are no historical atlases for the Algoma District, but the library does have an atlas of the city that was published in 1888.

There are early Bell Telephone directories dating from 1902 to 1979 (1945 and 1946 are missing); there are some Tweedsmuir Histories; and, most precious of all, there are the transcriptions of over 70 cemetery tombstones—a gift from the local genealogical branch and a priceless asset in a very scattered area.

Finally there are local histories not only of Sault Ste. Marie but of other nearby areas of early settlement — Algoma, Kirkland Lake, Manitoulin Island, Sudbury, Thunder Bay, Wawa — and of one or two churches in the area.

Smiths Falls: Public Library, 81 Beckwith Street North, Smiths Falls, ON K7A 2B9.
The library has a number of books about local families, including Bowman, Bruce, Dillabough, Frost, King, Livingstone, McKenzie, Metcalfe, Moran, Phillips, and Rathwell. It also has BMD notices and some cemetery inscriptions.

Stayner: Public Library, 201 Huron Street, Stayner, ON L0M 1S0.

The holdings of this library are limited because it is so near the Simcoe County Archives (see below). There is a collection of newspaper clippings; local municipal registers of BMD from 1896; and a small book collection of local families (Blair, Doner, Sage) and local places (New Flos, Nottawasaga, Stayner, and Sunnidale).

Stratford: Public Library, 19 St. Andrew Street, Stratford, ON N5A 1A2.

According to the library, all the genealogical material for Stratford is located in the Stratford–Perth Archives, 24 St. Andrew Street, Stratford, ON N5A 1A2. Unfortunately the archives are not prepared to give details of their holdings. I regret my inability to obtain any information, because I have seen their collection and know how good it is. I can only suggest you write directly to the Archivist for details of material of interest to you.

The only material in the library consists of newspapers on microfilm covering the period from 1855 (*Stratford Beacon*) up to the present day (*Beacon-Herald*). Other newspapers included are the *Beacon Daily*, *Daily Herald*, *Evening Beacon*, *Evening Herald*, *Perth Herald*, *Stratford Times*, and *Weekly Herald*.

Sudbury: Public Library, 200 Brady Street, Sudbury, ON P3E 5K3.

The library has an excellent genealogical and local-history collection. There are biographical scrapbooks; obituaries from the *Sudbury Star* since 1960 (indexed); family histories for Caswell, Merlin, and Merry; local histories for Blind River, Bruce Mines, Cartier, Capreol, Chapleau, Cochrane, Cockburn Island, Copper Cliff, French River, Hagar, Haileybury, Hornepayne, Kagawong, Kirkland Lake, Kirkwood, Larchwood, McGregor Bay, Michipicoten, Nickel Centre, Onaping Falls, Thessalon, Timmins, Walden, and Wawa. There are also books about ethnic communities in the area—Finnish and Polish. The church histories (which include BMD) are from Algoma, Capreol, Chelmsford, St. Charles, Sudbury, Thessalon, and Walford.

There are also voters' lists from McKim (1889) and Sudbury (1930–87); Bell Telephone directories from 1904 to date; city directories for Sudbury from 1911; and an index to the *Sudbury Star* from 1910 (there are more newspapers on microfilm in the Department of History, Laurentian University). Finally, there are over 200 oral-history tapes and clippings from *Le Voyageur* (the local French-language newspaper), which started in 1987 to print a weekly genealogical column that contains a great deal of local family history.

Tillsonburg: Public Library, 2 Library Lane, Tillsonburg, ON N4G 3P9.

The library has an index to BMD notices in the *Tillsonburg News* from 1863 to 1924; and local family histories (Beck, Bennett, Dresser, Gibson, Knight, McCaffrey, Marchant, Oatman, Parson, Pollard, and Tilson).

Toronto: Metropolitan Toronto Reference Library, 789 Yonge Street, Toronto, ON M4W 2G8.

The holdings of this remarkable library are too great to list in any detail but the main items are:

Biographical Index: This is taken from Toronto newspapers and unindexed books of local interest.

The Sands Collection: This is a collection of published items of local historical interest arranged by place.

Toronto Star Scrapbooks: A card-index file to a microfiche collection of local historical articles in the *Star*.

City Directories: These cover the period from 1833 to the present date.

Telephone Directories: There are on microfilm or microfiche from 1879.

The library is attempting to collect all available printed sources, including cemetery records, census indexes, and family histories. At the present time it does not have any Ontario nominal censuses, except for York County.

Trenton: Public Library, 18 Albert Street, Trenton, ON K8V 4S3.

No information available. (CEO Dorothy L. Davies.)

Whitby: Public Library, 405 Dundas Street West, Whitby, ON L1N 6A1.

The library is the repository for the Whitby–Oshawa Branch of the Ontario Genealogical Society and its holdings and publications. This includes transcriptions of most of the cemeteries in Ontario County, and a number of local and family histories. The library has also several scrapbooks about Whitby history, indexes to the local newspapers from 1850 (with many gaps), and census records for the county from 1842 and national censuses for the period 1851–91. The Land Record Index and the Registry Office deeds are both available on microfilm.

Circulating books of genealogical value include:

The Beaverton Story (multiple authorship)
Bowmanville: A Retrospect, L. and M. Hamlin
History of Bowmanville, J. T. Coleman
Oshawa, Canada's Motor City, M. M. Hood
The Pickering Story, W. A. McKay
The Ontario Village of Brougham, R. A. Miller
The Story of Uxbridge, F. H. Moore
Townships of Darlington & Clarke, J. Squair
The Village of Pickering, 1800–1970
Past Years in Pickering, W. Wood
Whitby Centennial, 1855–1955
A History of Clarke Township, H. Schmid and S. Rutherford
A Place Called Solina, M. Fraser
From Paths to Planes (Claremont), L. M. Gauslin
Brooklin (Tweedsmuir History)
History of the County of Ontario, 1615–1875, L. A. Johnson

There are also a number of family histories: Anderson, Barclay, Bengough, Dryden, Frost, Fuller, Greenwood, Gould, Ham, Hare, Mackey, Newman, Perry, Stillwell.

(There is also the Whitby Archives, 416 Centre Street, Whitby, ON L1N 4W2, holding records from Whitby, Ashburn, Brooklin, and Myrtle from 1801: BMD notices, obituaries, family records, photographs, etc.)

Waterloo: Public Library, 25 Albert Street, Waterloo, ON N2L 5E2.

This library, overshadowed more than a little by the County Archives and the Kitchener and Guelph libraries, is in a state of transition and growth. It has a small local-history collection and is planning to expand it. The collection consists of books of local history, memoirs, and some government documents. There is now a Local History Room, and it is hoped that with this additional space, local groups of various kinds may deposit their collections there.

The family histories the library holds at present are: Eby, Foot, Good, Martin, Putnam, Read, Ritter, Schaus, Schmidt, Sherk, Shuh, and Weber. There is also a biographical history of Waterloo Township by Ezra Eby which contains information about a number of early settled families.

Windsor: Public Library, 850 Ouellette Avenue, Windsor, ON N9A 4M9.

A section of this library is devoted to municipal archives, not all of which are of genealogical value, unless your ancestor was a prominent personality in the city or its nearby district. It does have some family papers and records of local clubs dating back to 1738. The main library has published *How To Trace Your Roots in Essex County*, which sets out in some fifty pages details of the genealogical holdings of the library and other locations.

There are local histories for the black community of Essex County (1885–1960), French families of the Detroit River Region, Amherstburg, Belle River, Colchester North, Harrow, Kingsville, Leamington, Leamington–Mersea, Pelee Island, Rochester, Sandwich, Sandwich South, Tecumseh, Walkerville, and the Jews of Windsor and Essex County.

Family histories available include the following families: Asselstine, Baby, Baillargeon, Bogardus, Bondy, Bradt, Casgrain, Cesire, Cowell, Denis de Larounde, Denomme, Desjardins, Donnelly, Drouillard, Ducharme, Fuller, Goyeau, Imeson, Kendall, Knight, Labute, Langlois, Lassaline, Lauzon, Letourneau, Lucier, McLerie, Maillou, Masse, Meston, Oatman, Ouellette, Paquin, Pare, Pouget, Taffelmeyer, Trembley, Trudelle, and Wigle.

There are many local newspapers on microfilm dating as far back as 1831; census records from 1851 to 1891 for Windsor and the surrounding counties; voters' lists for the city, 1930–82; histories of a number of local churches; and cemetery inscriptions provided by the Essex County Branch of the Ontario Genealogical Society. There are also scrapbooks and historical atlases for the counties of Essex and Kent.

The Essex County records at the library include family histories for Ballard, Beausoleil, Gouin, Hyland, Jacob, Lesperance, Letourneau, Maycock, and Senessacsues; telephone directories since 1884; and BMD notices from local newspapers from 1883. There are census returns for the county which are indexed for 1851, and a number of parish registers.

All this information is set out in much more detail in the library publication mentioned above.

Woodstock: Public Library, 445 Hunter Street, Woodstock, ON N4S 4G7.

The library's published genealogies are: Austin, Bray, Buchner, Burtch, Cain, Carr, Carroll, Climo, Cody, Corless–Brooks, Crawford, Dundass, Fewster, Flewelling, Gardhouse, Garner, Gunn, Hatch, Holmes, Kelly, Kipp, Jickling, Lampman, Lamport, Lapp, McCorquodale, McKay, Parson, Pelton, Plaskett, Sage, Smale–Kennedy, Thornton, Treffry. There are census returns from 1851 to 1891 with indexes for 1851 and 1871;

births and baptisms for Woodstock and Oxford County from 1859 to 1900; cemetery recordings by the Oxford County Branch of the Ontario Genealogical Society; and two very important records if your ancestors were early settlers: Oaths of Allegiance, Oxford County, 1800–34, and Naturalization Registers for the same county, 1828–49. There are the usual lists of land grants; assessment rolls from 1812; early directories from 1852; historic maps from 1798; and a number of miscellaneous local marriage records from 1784. Other sources of information in the area are the Woodstock Museum, 466 Dundas Street, Woodstock, ON N4S 1C4, and the Norwich and District Archives, RR #3 Norwich, ON N0J 1P0.

| Archives

Various local archives have been mentioned earlier in this chapter, but there are others that should be listed; space does not permit complete coverage, and you should always check with the local public library in your area of interest as to the existence of a local archive.

St. Lawrence Parks Commission, Upper Canada Village, PO Box 740, Morrisburg, ON K0C 1X0. This is often overlooked as a source of genealogical information. The librarian, Jack Schecter, has asked me to make a few comments about the library. The best time to send in a query (stamped, self-addressed envelope please!) is during the winter, when time is available. When there are questions that cannot be answered, he refers the inquirer to a local genealogist, the local branch of the Ontario Genealogical Society, or an appropriate museum or archives. Some questions cannot be answered because they are outside the time period 1783–1867, or because the inquirer does not give enough basic information, or because a prolonged and detailed search is requested. The Upper Canada Village Reference Library is a specialized one, supporting the historical programs of the village. Among the holdings you will find the following: censuses on microfilm for the counties from Prince Edward east to the Québec border (1861–71); pre-Confederation newspapers from Brockville, Cornwall, Hallowell, Kingston, Montréal, Ottawa, Perth, and Picton; Surrogate Court records of Stormont, Dundas, and Glengarry, 1801–71; Anglican Church registers of Williamsburg, Matilda, Osnabruck, and Edwardsburg, 1788–1886; Lutheran registers of

Morrisburg and Williamsburg, 1823–1972; and computerized land records. All the above records are on microfilm or microfiche.

There are a number of books of general genealogical information, and early maps of adjoining counties dating back to 1861. There is a large collection of early newspapers on microfilm from Brockville (1830–68), Cornwall (1835–85), Gananoque (1860–62, 1872–1904), Hallowell (1830–34), Kingston (1810–58), Ottawa (1846–60), Perth (1834–67), Picton (1860–63), Prescott (1850–61), St. Lawrence (Ogdensburg, N.Y.) (1817–57), Smiths Falls (1831–77). The family histories include Ault, Campbell, Carman, Hickey, Hoople, McCormick, Myers, Robinson, Shaver, and Shea; not all of these are local families. There are a number of genealogy files with notes referring to families with local connections, and several local histories.

Simcoe County Archives, RR #2, Minesing, ON L0L 1Y0. These archives have two claims to fame — they are the first county archives in Ontario, and, in my opinion, they are still among the very best. They are not solely concerned with genealogy, and the collection includes many municipal records, as well as business records, and the papers of clubs and associations. The genealogical records include census returns for the county for 1861–91; the land patent book for Simcoe County; tax assessment rolls, 1858–1912; pre-1869 marriage registers on microfilm and BMD from 1869 to 1873; early directories from 1866; and a growing number of genealogical records of local families. The newspaper collection dates from 1847 and is indexed; and the Simcoe County Branch of the Ontario Genealogical Society has recorded a number of tombstones in the cemeteries in the county.

The archives make a charge of $10 for a two-hour search — with no guarantee of success.

Wellington County Museum and Archives, RR #1, Fergus, ON N1M 2W3. I am envious of people with ancestral roots in this area of Ontario—not only do they have the superb genealogical collections of Kitchener, Guelph, and Cambridge, but they also have the enthusiastic and hard-working members of the Waterloo–Wellington Branch of the Ontario Genealogical Society, and — above all — the holdings and assistance and facilities of the County Museum and Archives! That we could all be so lucky!

This is another case of an embarrassment of riches—so many treasures to describe and not enough space to do them justice.

If your roots are here, make the Museum and Archives your first call and pick the brains of a remarkable young woman, the Archivist, Bonnie Callen. The holdings include early directories dating back to 1867; local newspapers on microfilm from most of the towns and townships in the county, and dating back in some cases to 1842 and in others to 1891.

There are 18 municipalities in the county: Arthur, Clifford, Drayton, Elora, Eramosa, Erin, Fergus, Guelph, Harriston, Maryborough, Mount Forest, Nichol, Palmerston, Peel, Pilkington, Puslinch, West Garafraxa, and West Luther. Every one of these areas, with one exception, has at least one history book about it on the shelves, and in some cases there are several — all invaluable, because many local families are mentioned. The lone exception appears to be Pilkington, and I hope one is being written about that place too! There are over 600 family histories and 9000 photographs of people and places.

Raleigh Township Museum, North Buxton, ON N0P 1W0. This museum (established in 1967) is devoted to records of black slave settlements in the Chatham area in the mid-1800s.

Region of Peel Archives, 9 Wellington Street East, Brampton, ON L6W 1Y1. These archives include much MS material for the district, including scrapbooks, Tweedsmuir histories, directories, and maps. There is also an index to the Brampton Conservator, 1876–89, and several glass negatives from local photographic studios.

Please bear a couple of things in mind about the various library collections I have described:

1. Many of the records listed are on microfilm or microfiche and may be borrowed through inter-library loan. All you need to do is visit your nearest public library with a microfilm-viewer and ask them to borrow the particular microfilm for you. I suggest it will be wise the check its availability with the distant library first.

2. Books may also be borrowed at the discretion of the lending library (rare and delicate books will not be available, and others are not always available on loan), depending very much on the demand by people visiting the library in person.

3. There are still treasures to be found in tiny libraries in obscure parts of the province; if the library in your place of interest is not listed here, or has not been prepared to supply information, write directly to it. Be sure that in all your corre-

spondence you enclose a self-addressed stamped envelope, and be patient—you are not the only person writing for information.

One final word as we leave the bountiful records of Ontario: do not forget the resources of the LDS Church. In Chapter 4 I listed the addresses of the various LDS Family History Centres in the province. If you plan to visit one of these libraries—and I hope you do—it is wise to telephone ahead of time and reserve a microfilm-reader. The space is usually limited and you do not want to find your journey has been wasted. As I mentioned, the main source of information is the International Genealogical Index, with its 85 million names, but there are many other records of value to you. The volunteer staff in the centres are always friendly and helpful. They will not search for you, but they will point you in the right direction and will make no attempt to convert you to their religion.

Ontario Genealogical Card Index

This index in the Archives of Ontario has recently been copied by the LDS Church. It covers the period 1780–1869 and consists of 43,000 cards of personal names extracted from many different sources — cemetery records, family histories, marriages, wills, land records, etc.

CHAPTER 17
Prince Edward Island

On July 1, 1534, Jacques Cartier first landed on the North Shore and claimed the island for the King of France. In 1603 Samuel de Champlain named it Île St. Jean. There was no permanent settlement on the island until 1719—the occasional temporary residents were fishermen and traders. Development of the island was hampered by the constant state of war between Great Britain and France. The latter country had no great interest in the island except as a supply base for the fortress of Louisbourg.

In 1710 there was some movement into the island by Acadians, but they found that all the land had been granted by the King to various individuals and none was available for them. Most of them had left by 1716, but in 1719 the French tried again, and a small settlement was established at a site named Port La Joie, located in the area of what is now the capital, Charlottetown. The next year three ships brought three hundred emigrants from France. There was still little development, and a census in 1728 recorded 76 males, 51 females, and 156 children, plus 125 fishermen and 14 domestic servants. Many of the original settlers of 1720 must have moved to the mainland or into Québec, since the fishermen were transients.

By 1740 there were 450 settlers located at Malpeque,

Pisquid, Port La Joie, St. Peters, Savage Harbour, Tracadie, and Trois-Rivières. In 1745 the British landed — actually, most of the invaders were from New England. They rounded up the settlers, destroyed the settlements, and garrisoned the island until 1748. In that year a peace treaty restored the island to France. By this time there were over 700 settlers, mostly Acadians. By 1755 another 2000 had arrived from the mainland; they no longer felt very secure because of the probability of a British attack on Louisbourg.

In 1758 the British returned to the island, and this time they stayed. It was renamed St. John Island and was administered as part of Nova Scotia. Many Acadians fled to France or to Québec — except for the settlers at Malpeque. The latter were lucky, since the British left them alone because of the distance from Port La Joie and the lack of any direct land communication. The Acadians of Malpeque are the ancestors of nearly all the Acadians on the island today. In 1763 it was officially annexed to Nova Scotia. Port La Joie was renamed Charlottetown, and the first organized settlement of the island took place.

Lt.-Col. Robert Stewart brought sixty families from Argyll, in Scotland, and established them on Lot 18, while Sir James Montgomery brought a similar number to Lot 34, the former location being by Richmond Bay and the latter in Covehead and Stanhope. The island became a separate colony in 1769. Real development of the area was impossible, because most of the land had been granted in lots to absentee landlords in England and practically no freehold land was available. The original grants had been made on condition that the owners would organize parties of settlers from Great Britain, but only a few of them observed the rules, and then only on a very limited scale. The remainder let their land lie idle, though there was a certain amount of "squatting" in various areas.

In 1779 only 19 of the 67 lots had any settlers. In 1797 a survey discovered that on 23 lots totalling half a million acres there were no residents at all, and on another 12 lots totalling 400,000 acres there was only 36 families.

In 1799 the colony was renamed Prince Edward Island, and at that time the rights of the absentee landlord were abrogated and steady development started. In 1803 Lord Selkirk organized an emigration from Scotland of some 800 settlers on to the two lots he owned, and probably half of the present inhabitants are descended from these hardy adventurers, plus others of English, French, and Irish descent.

The colony refused to enter Confederation in 1867, but did so in 1873, when it became part of the Dominion of Canada.

| Civil Registration

This started in the province in 1906 so far as births and deaths are concerned. The marriage records date back to 1787, but there are gaps between 1813 and 1824. The custodian of the records is the Director, Department of Vital Statistics, Rochford Street, Charlottetown, PE C1A 7N8. The Department is unique among similar offices in Canada in that it has copied all known existing church records for baptisms from 1885 to 1905. Some 110 churches were involved in the project. It must be noted that the BMD records since 1885 are described as "confidential", and information will be given only to individuals giving proof of direct descent. Be sure you ask for a "full certificate" for "genealogical purposes". It will cost you a little more, but the extra information will make it worth while.

The Department has transferred the indexed baptismal records for the period before 1885 to the P.E.I. Museum and Heritage Foundation (more about this organization later). These pre-1885 records are also on microfilm at the Provincial Archives. You should bear in mind that they are based on church registers and so are not necessarily complete. Many church records have been lost and others were never kept. The Marriage Books for 1833–1905 were also transferred, while the earlier ones were sent to the Provincial Archives, where they are being indexed.

There are two problems to consider at this point. The Department's decisions as to which records go to the Archives and which to the Foundation appear to be arbitrary, in that they do not follow a pattern. The other problem is that in spite of the transfers the Department is still stating in letters, "We have some birth records dating back to 1840, and some marriage records dating back to 1886."

| Provincial Archives

These are known as the Public Archives of Prince Edward Island and are located in the Coles Building, Richmond Street, Charlottetown, PE C1A 7M4. The archives were created in

1964 to "acquire, preserve, and conserve records of P.E.I.'s historic past". In actual fact, in spite of the very small area of the province, you will find genealogical records in various places, and the Public Archives do not have the majority of them. You will find early maps, land-lease records, newspapers, school lists, pre-1832 marriage bonds from the counties, marriage licences (1787–1900), census records (with that for 1881 on microfilm), and some microfilmed church registers.

There are the personal papers of prominent individuals and leading island families, diaries, account books, letters, etc. These may well be of interest if your ancestors took a very prominent part in the development of the province. For example, there are the Palmer Family Papers, 1800–72, and these mention many other families and individuals besides the Palmers.

Over eighty different newspapers have been published in PEI since 1787 and the Archives have many of these, either as originals or on microfilm. There are also a number of church registers on microfilm, and you will find details of these later in this chapter. Other holdings include land registry records, 1769–1900; wills, 1807–1900; cemetery transcripts; telephone directories, 1930–52; provincial and city directories from 1864; and a number of family genealogies.

The Prince Edward Island Museum and Heritage Foundation, 2 Kent Street, Charlottetown, PE C1A 1M6, is a publicly and privately funded organization that has the main collection of genealogical records in the province. The holdings are basically divided into four sections:

1. *Family Files:* This is a big collection of family records and research by individuals and includes both published and unpublished material. The Foundation has not checked the accuracy of the research that produced all the family information, and so the records should be accepted on that basis, and checked by you.

2. *The Kindex:* This is a very useful cross-index of the names and addresses of people searching a particular surname. This should be your first check with the Foundation, since you may well discover someone else is checking, or has already checked, your family.

3. *Vital Statistics:* These are records transferred from the Department concerned. They include baptismal records from some churches dating back before 1885. There are also marriage books from 1832 to 1932, but they may be far too fragile

for you to use. However, microfilm copies are available in the Public Archives and are being indexed, as are a small collection of death or burial records.

4. *The Master Name Index:* This is by far the most important possession of the Foundation. It is an alphabetical card index of names of individuals that have appeared in print for whatever reason; there are over half a million cards.

The names are taken from a variety of sources:

(a) Census Returns for PEI for 1798, 1841, 1861, 1871, 1881, 1891. The census for 1848 for Charlottetown, Royalty, and Lot 31 is also included.

(b) Marriage Bonds and Licences (1814–46), from the collection in the Public Archives. These are indexed under the names of both the bride and the groom. The Marriage Record Books (1832–1923) have also been indexed.

(c) Inquest Records (1787–1846), from the Public Archives. These give the name of the deceased, as well as the witnesses and the jurors.

(d) Petitions (1770–1837). These are demands for roads, bridges, and land.

(e) The Belfast Book of Records, kept by a Presbyterian minister in Belfast, PEI, from 1888 to 1906.

(f) Patrons and settlers listed in an 1880 atlas.

(g) All names included in a business directory of PEI for 1864.

(h) Passenger lists from all known genuine lists. These exist for *Lovely Nellie* (1775), *Jane* (1790), *Lucy* (1790), *Elizabeth, Ann, Humphrey, Isle of Skye, Rambler,* and *Spencer* in 1806, and the *Lulan* in 1848.

(i) The Royal Kalendar. A list of burials in St. Paul's Anglican church, Charlottetown, from 1805 to 1823.

(j) The Charlottetown MS. A list of mid-nineteenth-century families (mainly from the city) with dates of birth, and sometimes marriage and death. Origin is unknown, and its accuracy cannot be guaranteed.

(k) Newspapers. At least one newspaper has been indexed for each year from 1787 to 1919 and onwards.

(l) Meacham's 1880 Atlas, showing settlers' names and locations.

(m) Cemeteries. Most of the tombstones in the province have been transcribed by the Genealogical Society, and these are indexed.

(n) Burial Records, 1869–1961, from St. Peter's Anglican church, Charlottetown.

(o) Funeral-home records from Alberton, Charlottetown, Hunter River, and Kensington.

(p) Penelope Cundall's Birthday Book. A record of people's names and birthdays compiled between 1836 and 1915.

(q) School Registers from Milton (1860), Kingsboro (1889), and Red Point (1895).

A major source of information for the Index is the steady flow of local histories being published; at least forty of these have been included, and more are published each year. Up to 1981, sixty were included; since then another forty have been added.

There are other sources being included all the time, and with each addition this Index becomes more and more valuable. However, don't be too disappointed if your ancestor is not included — his or her name may never have appeared in print, the original author of a book or document may have made an omission, or the card may just have been misfiled.

The Foundation has produced a number of publications, and a list can be obtained from the address above. It includes not only their own publications but most of the local histories mentioned above. When you write for the list, please pay for the return postage — and remember, it has 16 pages, so send two dollars!

| Census Returns

I have already given details of the location of these. Remember that 1841 and 1861 give only the name of the head of the household; 1861 is missing for a few areas; and only a very few returns for 1871 have survived. 1881 and 1891 are complete, and the Foundation has them completely indexed by now.

| Wills

There is one Probate Office for the province. Since 1960 it has been a division of the Supreme Court. You can find wills from the late 1700s. They are located in the Law Courts, Charlottetown, PE C1A 7N8.

| Land Records

All pre-1900 records are in the Public Archives. Those since
then are with the Registrar of Deeds, PO Box 2000, Kent
Street, Charlottetown, PE C1A 7N8. You may have some difficulty here: the main function of the office is providing information for lawyers, and ancestor-hunters do not find the
welcome mat out for them!

| PEI Genealogical Society

PO Box 2744, Charlottetown, PE C1A 8C4. The Society has
no staff, and does no research; all the genealogical material is
at the Museum and Heritage Foundation mentioned earlier.

The most recent — and most important — project of the Society has been the microfilming of all the cards in the Master
Name Index. This was a tremendous task when you realize that
the Index is contained in 285 drawers and required 68 rolls of
microfilm. These rolls are available on sale from the Foundation. If, for example, you want to buy one listing all entries for
your particular surname, the Foundation will quote you a price
based on the number of entries. If your name is rare, one roll
will be enough, but if it is common, you may need two or three.

| Church Registers

As mentioned above, the Department of Vital Statistics has
transferred the indexed baptismal records for the period prior
to 1886 to the Museum and Heritage Foundation, with microfilm copies to the Public Archives. They are not separated by
denomination, as in some cases this does not appear. The dates
shown are the starting dates of the registers:

ST. JOHN'S ANGLICAN CHURCH, 1837: includes Brookfield, Cherry
Valley, Milton, North and South Winsloe, North River, North
Wiltshire, Riverside, Rustico, and Wheatley River.
UNITED CHURCH WINSLOE PASTORAL CHARGE, 1800: includes Glasgow
Road, Highfield, Prince Town Road, and Winsloe.
UNITED CHURCH, YORK, 1806: includes Bedford, Black River,
Brackley, Dunstaffnage, East Royalty, French Fort, Grand
Tracadie, Harrington, Marshfield, North Rustico, Pleasant Grove,
St. Peter's Road, Suffolk, Ten Mile House, Union Road, West
Covehead, and York.

ST. JOHN UNITED CHURCH, MOUNT STEWART, 1871: includes East St. Peter's, Mount Stewart, and West St. Peter's.

UNITED CHURCH, CORNWALL, 1857: includes Brackley Point Road, Clyde River, Kingston, Little York, Meadowbank, New Dominion, Nine Mile Creek, Rocky Point, Tracadie Road, Union Road, West River, Wiltshire, and Winsloe Road.

BREADALBANE UNITED, 1845: includes Breadalbane, Hartsville, Hunter River, North Granville, Pleasant Valley, Rose Valley, and Stanley Bridge.

KIRK OF ST. JAMES, CHARLOTTETOWN, 1849

ST. PETER'S CATHEDRAL, CHARLOTTETOWN, 1836: includes Charlottetown, Cherry Valley, George Town, Keppoch, Little Sands, Little York, Morell, New Glasgow, North River, Southport, and Winsloe Road.

TRINITY UNITED CHURCH, CHARLOTTETOWN, 1836: includes Grace Church records, and First Methodist, Charlottetown.

GEORGETOWN ANGLICAN CHURCH, 1842: includes Cardigan, Darnley, Georgetown, Harmony, Malpeque, Montague, Morell, Murray Harbour, New Perth, Peakes Station, St. Peters Road, Souris, and Sturgeon.

FREE CHURCH OF SCOTLAND, 1868: includes Albany, Birch Hill, Brooklyn, Carleton Point, Central Bedeque, Freetown, Kinross, Mount Albion, Mount Mellick, Murray Harbour, Murray River, Pleasant Valley, Pownal, Seal River, Searletown, Summerside, Tryon, Vernon River, Wilmot Creek, and Wood Island.

ST. PAUL'S ANGLICAN CHURCH, 1777: includes Keppoch, Marshfield, Milton, Morell, Mount Edward Road, New Glasgow, North Wiltshire, Saint John (NB), Souris, Southport, and Vernon River.

ZION PRESBYTERIAN CHURCH, 1868

POWNAL UNITED CHURCH, 1856: includes Albany Plains, Alexandra, Baltic Road, Birch Hill, Bunbury-Clifton, Cherry Valley, Hillsborough River, Lots 48, 49, 50, Millview, Mount Albion, Mount Herbert, Orwell, Pownal, Roseneath, Southport, Squaw Bay, Vernon River, and Village Green.

MARSHFIELD PRESBYTERIAN, 1862

UNITED CHURCH, MONTAGUE, 1828: includes Georgetown, Methodist Church (Montague), Montague, and Valleyfield.

ST. DAVID'S UNITED CHURCH, GEORGETOWN, 1854: includes Albany, Alliston, Cambridge, Georgetown, Milltown Cross, and Sturgeon.

PRESBYTERIAN CHURCH, BELFAST, 1823: includes Eldon, Flat River, Garfield, Mount Buchanan, Newtown Cross, Ocean View, Orwell Cove, Pinette, Point Prim, Rosebury, and Souris.

WOOD ISLANDS PRESBYTERIAN, 1851

UNITED CHURCH, HAMPTON AND CRAPAUD, 1831: includes Appin Road, Bedeque, Bonshaw, DeSable, Tryon, and Victoria.

ST. JOHN'S ANGLICAN CHURCH, CRAPAUD, 1843: includes Albany, Borden, Breadalbane, Crapaud, Emerald, Granville, Hampton, Long Creek, Springfield, Victoria, and Westmoreland.

UNITED CHURCH, BEDEQUE, 1843: includes Albany, Augustin Cove, Bedeque, Borden, Cape Traverse, Carleton, Central and Lower Bedeque, Chilton, Fernwood, Searletown, South Shore, and Tryon.

UNITED CHURCH, NORTH BEDEQUE, 1826: includes Freetown, Lower Bedeque, North Bedeque, Travellers Rest, and Wilmot Valley.

ST. MARY'S ANGLICAN CHURCH, SUMMERSIDE, 1865: includes Miscouche, St. Eleanors, Sherbrooke, Summerside, and Travellers Rest.

ST. MARK'S ANGLICAN CHURCH, KENSINGTON, 1821: includes New London and St. Eleanors.

KENSINGTON PRESBYTERIAN CHURCH, 1855: includes Breadalbane, French River, Grahams Road, Granville, Indian River, Kensington, Long River, New London, Norboro, Springfield, Spring Valley, and Summerfield.

UNITED CHURCH OF MARGATE, 1860: includes Baltic, Burlington, Cavendish, Clinton, Darnley, French River, Granville, Long River, Malpeque, Margate, New London, Norboro, Pleasant Valley, Searletown, Sea View, South Freetown, and Stanley Bridge.

ST. AUGUSTINE'S RC CHURCH, SOUTH RUSTICO, 1817

ST. ANN'S, HOPE RIVER, 1881

BIDEFORD UNITED CHURCH, 1875: includes Conway, Egmont Circuit, Enmore River, Lot 14, Lot 16, Sheep River, Tyne Valley, Union Corner, and territory from Miscouche to Mount Pleasant.

ST. DUNSTAN'S BASILICA, CHARLOTTETOWN, 1830

ST. PATRICK'S CHURCH, FORT AUGUSTUS, 1854

ST. JOACHIM'S, VERNON RIVER, 1837

ST. MICHAEL'S, IONA, 1868

ST. GEORGES, ST. GEORGES, 1836

ST. MARY'S CHURCH, SOURIS, 1864

ST. ALEXIS, ROLLO BAY, 1847

ST. COLUMBA, ST. COLUMBA, 1836

ST. JAMES, GEORGETOWN, 1855

ST. PAUL'S CHURCH, STURGEON, 1867

ST. ANN'S RC, LOT 65 (no starting date given)

ST. JOSEPH'S PARISH, KELLY CROSS (no starting date given)

ST. PETER'S RC CHURCH, SEVEN MILE BAY, 1846

ST. MALACHY'S RC CHURCH, KINKORA (SW BEDEQUE), 1860

ST. PAUL'S RC CHURCH, SUMMERSIDE, 1854

TRINITY UNITED CHURCH, SUMMERSIDE, 1866

ANGLICAN CHURCH, PORT HILL, 1842

ST. BONAVENTURE RC CHURCH, TRACADIE, 1845

ST. ANDREWS RC CHURCH, ST. ANDREWS, 1856

ST. LAWRENCE RC CHURCH, MORELL, 1881

ST. TERESA RC CHURCH, ST. TERESA (CARDIGAN PARISH), 1868

PRESBYTERIAN CHURCH, MURRAY HARBOUR NORTH, 1876

ST. JOHN THE BAPTIST, MISCOUCHE, 1817

ST. MARY'S RC CHURCH, INDIAN RIVER, 1838

ST. PATRICK'S RC CHURCH, GRAND RIVER, 1878

ST. ANNE'S RC CHURCH, LENNOX ISLAND, 1842

NOTRE DAME DU MONT CARMEL, 1820

ST. PETERS BAY RC CHURCH, 1850

ST. FRANCIS DE SALES (LITTLE POND PARISH), 1865–85

ST. MARGARETS RC CHURCH, ST. MARGARETS, 1881–85

ST. JACQUES RC CHURCH, EGMONT BAY, 1821

ST. MARY'S CHURCH, BRAE, LOT 9, 1833

ST. BRIGID'S PARISH, 1876

IMMACULATE CONCEPTION, WELLINGTON PARISH, 1884–85

ST. ANTHONY CHURCH, BLOOMFIELD PARISH, 1839–86

WEST CAPE UNITED CHURCH records (at O'Leary), 1847

SACRED HEART CHURCH, ALBERTON, 1879

ST. PETER'S ANGLICAN CHURCH, ALBERTON, 1859

UNITED CHURCH, ALBERTON, 1895

STS. SIMON AND JUDE RC CHURCH, TIGNISH, 1831

IMMACULATE CONCEPTION CHURCH, PALMER ROAD, 1882

ST. MARK'S RC CHURCH, LOT 7, BURTON, 1871

ST. MICHAEL'S PARISH (LAUNCHING), 1840

In addition to the above, the following original registers or microfilm copies are held in various archives:

Church	Denomination	Dates	Archives
Alberton	A	BMD 1859–	PEA
Alexandra	B	BMD 1843–73	MBA
Belfast	B	BMD 1822–	MBA
Belfast (St. Johns)	P	B 1823–49	NAC
Breadalbane	UC	BMD 1845–	PEA
Cascumpeque	CA	BMD 1839–68	NAC
Charlottetown (St. James)	P	BMD 1849–	PEA
Charlottetown (Cathedral)	A	BMD 1869–	PEA
Charlottetown (Trinity)	UC	MBD 1836–	PEA
Cornwall	UC	BMD 1857–1886	PEA
Georgetown	A	BMD 1842–	PEA

Church	Denomination	Dates	Archives
Malpeque	CA	BMD 1817–35	NAC
Mont Carmel	CA	BMD 1844–	AAM
North River	B	BMD 1865–	MBA
Palmer Road	CA	BMD 1878–90	AAM
Port Hill	A	BMD 1842–	PEA
Port La Joie		*See* St. Pierre-du-Nord	
Rustico	CA	BMD 1812–24	PEA
St. Pierre-du-Nord (Notre Dame)	CA	BMD 1724–58	NAC
St. Pierre-du-Nord (St. Pierre)	CA	BMD 1721–24, 1749–58	PEA
Tignish	CA	BMD 1844–69	PEA
Lot 10	B	BMD 1885–	MBA
Belfast (Pictou County)	A	B 1823–49	ANS

Notes:

1. Registers may be in more than one archive (for example, St. Pierre-du-Nord is in both NAC and PEA).

2. Belfast contains records for part of Pictou County, Nova Scotia.

3. Baptists do not practise infant baptism, so baptismal dates cannot be related to birth dates.

There is no Anglican Church Diocese for Prince Edward Island — it is part of the Diocese of Nova Scotia. The archives are in the Diocesan Centre, 5732 College Street, Halifax, NS B3H 1X3.

The following Anglican parishes were in existence on the island before civil registration started:

Alberton, Charlottetown (Cathedral), Charlottetown (St. Paul), Cherry Valley, Crapaud, Georgetown, Milton, New London, Port Hill, Springfield, and Summerside. Please bear in mind that the Anglican parishes in the province are often "multi-point" parishes — that is, there are usually several congregations, each with its own church, within one parish. Any further information as to which *churches* existed before 1906 can be obtained from the Diocesan Church Society, PO Box 101, Summerside, PE C1N 4P6.

The headquarters of the Catholic Diocese of Charlottetown can be contacted at PO Box 907, Charlottetown, PE C1A 7L9. The parishes in existence before civil registration are:

Alberton, Bloomfield, Brac, Cardigan Bridge, Charlottetown (Cathedral), Corran Ban, Cove Head, East Point, Egmont Bay, Fort Augustus, Georgetown, Grand River, Hope River, Indian River, Kelly's Cross, Kinkora, Lennox Island, Lot 7, Lot 11, Miscouche, Morell, Mount Carmel, Palmer Road, Rollo Bay, Rustico, St. Andrews, St. Charles, St. George, St. Margaret, St. Peter, St. Teresa, Seven Mile Bay, Souris, Sturgeon, Summerfield, Summerside, Tignish, Trassad, Tyrone, Vernon River, and Wellington.

| Libraries

The Confederation Centre Library
Box 1000, Charlottetown, PE C1A 8B5 (located on Queen Street). This library has a collection of books and leaflets, maps, and early directories, and newspaper and census records on microfilm. It also has wills from 1800 to 1900 on microfilm and these may be borrowed through inter-library loan.

The Church of Jesus Christ of Latter-Day Saints (the LDS Church) is not represented on the island. The nearest LDS Church Family History Library can be contacted at PO Box 414, Hampton, NB E0G 1Z0. Do not neglect the vast records and resources of this church. You will find more information about it in Chapter 4.

At this point you will have realized what a wealth of genealogical information is available in Prince Edward Island — even if it is not as centralized as it might be. The Museum and Heritage Foundation, with limited staff and money, is very helpful to ancestor-hunters; if you have experienced this, do please give a donation over and above any fee you may be charged. It really will assist both the work of the organization and fellow genealogists who come after you!

CHAPTER 18
Québec

In 1534 Jacques Cartier planted a cross on a hill in the Gaspé, and the next year sailed up the St. Lawrence. In 1608 Samuel de Champlain built a trading-post on the site of present-day Québec City, and from here the French penetrated almost the entire North American continent. The colony was named New France in 1663, and a long struggle followed between the British and the French for the control of the area. This ended in 1759 when the British defeated the French on the Plains of Abraham, and the Treaty of Paris in 1763 gave the whole of New France to Great Britain.

In 1774 the British government, faced with continuing unrest among the French inhabitants, passed the Québec Act, which allowed the colony to continue its feudal system of land tenure, and to retain its language, religion, laws, and social customs. At this time the colony of New France stretched from the Atlantic to the Niagara region and Lake Superior.

After the American Revolution the English-speaking area was detached to form the colony of Upper Canada and what is now Québec became Lower Canada. The concessions made by the British in 1774 were not enough, and in 1837 Louis Papineau led a revolt. In the same year William Lyon Mackenzie led a similar rebellion in Upper Canada. Neither uprising was successful, but the events led to changes in the political system. Parliamentary government was established and Upper and Lower Canada were rejoined, and Québec became known as Canada East. The name often appears in genealogical sources as CE.

In 1867 Canada East became the province of Québec and joined with three other provinces — New Brunswick, Nova Scotia, and Ontario — to form the Dominion of Canada.

At one time the high birth-rate in Québec was described as *la revanche du berceau* — the revenge of the cradle — but this is no longer true, although a great majority of Québécois are French-speaking.

One genealogical problem in Québec is the small number of French surnames compared with other provinces; this makes ancestor-hunting difficult without knowledge of a location in the province, and even that is no guarantee of success. The problem is caused, of course, by the fact that so many Québécois are descended from the early settlers. On the plus side is the fact that the French are far more knowledgeable about their ancestry than the British are; and that an oral family-history tradition has survived for many generations.

There are other problems in ancestor-hunting in Québec for people of both British and French descent: records are scattered, many are not indexed, there are few genealogical collections in local public libraries, and — for Anglos — there is the language problem. This, of course, is also a problem for people of French-Canadian descent who cannot speak the language of their ancestors.

Let us talk for a moment about language. If you are corresponding with government departments, you can write in English — but you may sometimes receive a reply in French! This can be overcome with a good two-way dictionary. If you are writing for information to a local priest, or to an historical society, it will speed your reply if you can write in French. You can probably find a friend or relative, or a local schoolteacher, who will write a letter for you, and then translate the reply if you cannot use a dictionary. If you cannot find anyone to help, write in English — in any case, remember a letter in good English is better than a letter in bad French. Do start your letter with the words "I regret my inability to write to you in French." Oh, I know, you may object to saying this, but this is officially a bilingual country. Anyway, it will help you get a reply to your query.

When you are writing to the priest of a small town or village, there are a couple of things to remember. One, you are not the only ancestor-hunter writing to him. Two, he will have little time or money available. Be sure you pay the return postage, make a small donation to church funds, and are polite. There is no law that says he must reply to you.

As a priest in Québec once said to me, "I get over a hundred letters a year — mostly in English — and no one sends me a stamp. I have a large parish, many old or sick people I visit each week, no secretary, and no spare money. I used to reply to letters—in my bad English—but now I do not. This troubles my conscience, but what else can I do?"

I should mention at the outset the standard work of reference for French family history, and its later additions. This is the 7-volume *Dictionary of French Canadian Families (Dictionnaire généalogique des familles canadiennes)* by l'Abbé C. Tanguay. This monumental work was first published in the period 1871–90 and was reprinted in 1975. It was subsequently followed by two more books: *Complément au dictionnaire généalogique Tanguay* by Arthur Leboeuf, published by the Société Généalogique canadienne-française in 1957 and 1977 in Montréal; and *Dictionnaire généalogique des familles du Québec* by René Jetté, published in 1983. This also was published by the Montréal University Press, using the same database mentioned above.

These three works are unique in their detailed coverage of French-Canadian family origins and it is essential you consult them at the start of your research. They can be borrowed through inter-library loan, and as far as Tanguay is concerned you simply request the loan of the volume containing your family name.

| Civil Registration

Registration of baptisms, marriages, and deaths started in Québec in 1622. This was done by local Catholic priests. *In theory* one copy was kept in the church and another sent to the office of the Prothonotary of the Superior Court of each judicial district. *In fact* this was not always done until the early eighteenth century. In 1760 the same procedure was introduced for Protestants.

Civil registration, as we know it today, only came into effect in Québec in 1926 — for the benefit of families without any church affiliation or membership. All marriages had to take place in a church until 1969, when civil ceremonies were permitted. It was also necessary to register all births at a church, but now this can be done in the local city hall or municipal office.

The registration of Protestant marriages applied originally to the Anglican Church alone, but in later years other denominations were permitted to baptize, marry, and bury their members, and keep records in the same way as the Catholics and the Anglicans. This permission was granted on a local basis in various places and on various dates. It is not possible, for example, to state categorically that Baptists were permitted to do so in 1832. This was so in the city of Montréal, but in other smaller places they had to wait longer.

Basically, most of the Protestant denominations were included between 1830 and 1850. The various regional archives in Québec have lists of Protestant registers in their custody up to 1875. They are indexed under the heading "Non-Catholic" and are not divided into separate denominations. Since 1875 the registers have been held in the Palais de Justice (Courthouses) in the various judicial districts, with copies in the individual churches or in church archives. This will be set out in detail later in the section on church registers.

The parish registers up to 1876 have been microfilmed by the LDS Church and are available at any LDS Church Family History Library. A word of warning here: if you find gaps in a microfilmed register, or fail to find an entry known to be there, you should check the originals in the provincial archives or courthouses. Copies are only as good as the copier, and errors and omissions are not unknown.

In order to get a copy of a certificate in Québec, it is almost essential to know in which parish your ancestor lived at the time of birth, marriage, or death. If you know the parish, it is fairly easy to find out the judicial district. If you have difficulty, you should write to the Registrar General, Registre de la Population, 1279 Boulevard Charest Ouest, Québec Cité, PQ G1N 2C9, and ask for the address of the judicial district that includes the parish in which you are interested. Then, armed with this knowledge, you can write to the Palais de Justice for a copy of the certificate you want. Be sure you ask for a *full* copy and not an extract.

The National Archives of Québec (Archives Nationales de Québec)

The Archives are located at 1210 avenue du Séminaire, CP 10450, Sainte Foy, PQ G1V 4N1. There are also regional centres of the National Archives in various places in the province. Each of these is responsible for the documents deriving from its own area. As a result, there is an ongoing process of sending such records from the central archives to the regional ones, and at the same time a process of indexing many of them. On top of all this, many government records over 100 years old are also being transferred to the regional archives.

If you are planning a personal visit to one of these regional centres, you will be wise to write or telephone to find out whether the records you want are actually there and are available. This does not apply to Québec and Montréal centres, which appear to be well organized and keeping ahead of their acquisitions. If a personal visit is not possible, records and books already on microfilm or microfiche may be borrowed through the inter-library loan system and inspected in your nearest library with facilities for viewing. Nearly all civil registers and records are now available on microfilm or microfiche.

The addresses of the regional archive centres are:

Chicoutimi: 930 rue Jacques-Cartier Est, Chicoutimi, PQ G7H 2A9
Hull: 170 rue Hôtel-de-Ville, Hull, PQ J8X 4C2
Montréal: 1945 rue Mullins, Montréal, PQ H3K 1N9
Québec: 1210 avenue du Séminaire, Québec, PQ G1V 4N1
Rimouski: 337 rue Moreault, Rimouski, PQ G5L 1P4
Rouyn–Noranda: rue du Terminus Ouest, Rouyn–Noranda,
    PQ J9X 2P3
Sept-Îles: 649 boulevard Laure, Sept-Îles, PQ G4R 1X8
Sherbrooke: 740 rue Galt Ouest, Sherbrooke, PQ J1H 1Z3
Trois-Rivières: 225 rue des Forges, Trois-Rivières, PQ G9A 2G7

There are also civil archives (archives civiles) and courthouses (palais de justice) located in each judicial district. Their holdings include birth, marriage, and death records from 1900 to date, and these are indexed. Earlier records are in the regional centres listed above.

The locations of the civil archives are:

Alma, Amos, Arthabaska, Baie-Comeau, Campbell's Bay, Chibougamau, Chicoutimi, Cowansville, Drummondville, Hâvre-Aubert, Hull, Joliette, Lac Mégantic, La Malbaie, La Sarre, La Tuque, Longueuil, Mont-Laurier, Montmagny, Montréal, New-Carlisle, Percé, Québec, Rimouski, Rivière-du-Loup, Roberval, Rouyn–Noranda, St. Hyacinthe, St. Jean, St. Jérôme, St. Joseph, Sept-Îles, Shawinigan, Sherbrooke, Sorel, Thetford-Mines, Trois-Rivières, Val d'Or, Valleyfield, and Ville-Marie.

Note: It may be necessary to obtain a permit in advance to do a personal search in various archives in Québec. If the documents you need are in the local courthouse (palais de justice) and are defined as "legal", permission must first be obtained from the Directeur-général des greffes, Ministère de la Justice, 1200 rue de l'Église, Sainte-Foy, PQ G1V 4N1.

Although it has been established that all records more than a century old are to be transferred to the National Archives, this has not yet been done in all cases. It should be evident to you by now that record-keeping in Québec is in a state of flux —be guided accordingly.

The holdings of the National Archives are so vast that books have been written about just one source of information in them. The holdings listed below all contain genealogical information, but their value varies according to the geographical location and the ancestral social background:

The Period of New France (1608–1763)

Judicial and notarial documents, 1638–1759 (Collection de pièces judiciaires et notariales): These contain dossiers, documents, court records, seigneurial records, judgments, inquests, and a collection of notarial papers from 44 different notaries.

Documents of administration of Trois-Rivières, 1646–1759 (Documents de la juridiction): The twenty volumes contain details of criminal and civil proceedings in the area.

Seigneurial Courts, 1662–1760 (Cours Seigneuriales): Details of judgments on land ownership and transfers of property for the seigneuries of Batiscan, Beauport, Beaupré, Cap de la Madeleine, Champlain, and Rivière-du-Sud.

Registers of the Sovereign Council, 1663–1760 (Conseil Souverain): Records of Council meetings, judgments, deliberations, registrations of official acts, letters patent of societies, letters of ennoblement, and other records of seigneurs.

Notices and censuses, 1723–58 (Aveux et dénombrements): When making their official homage to the King of France, the seigneurs had also to describe their territory, its development, and the heads of households of their tenants. Details are also given of transfers of property. These records cover the districts of Cap St. Ignace, Île d'Orléans, Montréal, Portneuf, St. Sulpice, Sillery, Tremblay, and Varennes.

The Period of Lower Canada and Québec

Civil State, 1765–1895 (État Civil): Among the records in this section are electoral lists (poll-books) for 1814–36.

Seigneuries, 1716–1862: These records include censuses of certain seigneuries for the period 1777–99.

Provincial Secretary's records, 1768–1893 (Secrétaire Provincial): These include lists of carters (charretiers), pedlars (colporteurs), bakers (boulangers), and innkeepers (taverniers) from 1807 to 1812, and from 1814 to 1840; and lists of inns and taverns, 1818–46.

Army and Militia, 1834–71 (Armée et Milice): Lists of officers and militiamen.

Land grants for military service, 1812–51 (Demandes de terres): Applications and grants in alphabetical order.

There are also notarial records which are more specific in their genealogical value:

Marriage contracts (Contrats de mariage): These date from 1636, but there are not a great many before the eighteenth century. There are lists of over thirty thousand contracts for the judicial districts of Montmagny, Montréal, and Trois-Rivières. These are indexed. In addition, lists of such contracts for Québec City and Charlevoix have been published and are obtainable through the inter-library loan system:

Inventaire des contrats de mariage du régime français by P. G. Roy, 1937. 6 volumes.
Inventaire des contrats de mariage au greffe de Charlevoix by Éloi-Gérard, 1943.

Marriage contracts can provide a lot of genealogical information. The prospective bride and groom would usually visit a local notary a few days or a couple of weeks before the wedding, accompanied by close relatives of both families. The contract records the names and residences of such witnesses. Of course, the contract could be annulled before the wedding, and this annulment would then be recorded on the original document.

Inheritance records (Partages de biens): These date from 1634 and give very full details of names and residences of deceased persons and their heirs — giving ages and relationships.

Orphan records (Tutelles et curatelles): These started in 1637 and give names, addresses, ages, names of parents and other close relatives, and their residences.

Inventories (Inventaires après décès): These also date from 1637 and continue until the middle 1850s. They record the personal and real estate of the deceased, with full details of family members. If the items were later sold by auction, or by individual purchase, the notary recorded each item sold, the name of the successful bidder or purchaser, and the price obtained. Usually heirs were allowed to bid first on the best pieces.

Donations (Donations entre vifs): These records are unique to Québec. It was the custom for elderly people, when they felt that death was approaching, to divide the property they had inherited from their parents among their own children.

Cemetery records (Registres de cimetières): These lists date from about 1740 and give names, places, and dates.

Poll-books (Listes électorales): These contain the names, occupations, and residences of voters from 1815 onwards.

Court records (Cours civiles): These date from 1651 and give the names and addresses of persons engaged in litigation in the Bailiff's Court (Cour du Bailliage); in the Court of Common Pleas (Plaidoyers communs); and the Superior Court (Conseil Supérieur). These records often include wills (if in dispute) and marriage contracts (if causing litigation).

Indenture records (Engagements): These date from the early days of settlement and give many details about immigrants who arrived from France as indentured servants or apprentices to settlers already resident in New France. They often give — apart from name and date of arrival — the place of origin in France.

Lists of early colonists (Listes des colons): These come from many different sources and cover the period from 1608 to 1700. They give names, year and place of marriage, date of arrival, and place of origin in France.

In addition to all the above there are thousands of family

dossiers, and family papers. An alphabetical list has been published (*L'État Général des Archives Publiques et Privées du Québec*, 1968).

| Censuses (Recensements)

These have been held in parts of Québec from 1666 onward. Many have been indexed and published, others are on microfilm, and the details are given below:

1666, 1667: Cover most of what is now Québec. Indexed.
1678: Census of the area of Sillery. This was only for the seigneurie of Sillery and was taken by the Jesuit fathers. Indexed.
1681: Census of Québec. Indexed.
1716: Census of Québec City. Indexed.
1731: Census of the seigneurie of Montréal taken by the Seminary of St. Sulpice. Indexed.
1741: Census of Montréal.
1744: Census of Québec City. Indexed.
1760: Census of Three Rivers (Trois-Rivières). Indexed.
1762: Census of Québec.
1762: Census of Montréal and Three Rivers (Trois-Rivières).
1765: Census of Montréal and Three Rivers (Trois-Rivières).
1773: Census of the English population of Québec.
1781: Census of the seigneurie of St. Sulpice taken by the Seminary. Indexed.
1792, 1795, 1798, 1805: Censuses of the parish of Québec.
1815: Census of Québec City.
1818: Census of Québec City. Indexed.
1825: Census of Montréal. Indexed.

From 1666 to 1681 every member of the household is listed. In the later years only the head of the family was listed. From 1851 to 1891 inclusive all family members were included. Please note that many of the early censuses were not official, complete, or accurate. Nearly all are on microfilm and may be borrowed through the inter-library loan system from the National Archives of Canada, from the various Québec archives, and some from the LDS Church. Some of the indexes were published privately, or remain in manuscript form, and for these you should check with archives in Québec.

| Wills

Because of the French attitude to property and possessions, wills of early settlers are more common than in other provinces. However, this advantage is nullified by the fact that the original will was kept by the notary concerned. When he died, the wills were transferred to his successor, but if the practice died with him, the wills were sent to the local Palais de Justice. A record of such transfers is kept by the Board of Notaries (Chambre des Notaires) — the professional association. Wills over 100 years old are now in the various regional archives and are being indexed. Wills less than 100 years old (except for the exceptions mentioned above) are still in the offices of the notaries and are not open to public search unless the information is required because of a legal dispute.

For further information regarding wills and their whereabouts you must write to the Board of Notaries (Chambre des Notaires), c/o the Minister of Justice (Directeur-général des Greffes), 225 est Grande Allée, Québec, PQ G1R 5G5. Alternatively, the local genealogical or historical society may have information about the location of the wills drawn up by a particular local notary.

| Land Records

Under French rule the seigneurial system was the method of land ownership and settlement. All the land belonged to the King of France, who granted large areas to the seigneurs or to the Catholic Church. In return, they accepted responsibility for settling the land, building roads, and establishing grist mills. The church was responsible for building hospitals and schools. The settlers, or *habitants*, undertook to clear and cultivate the land, and maintain the nearby roads and rights of way. This system continued from 1626 until its abolition in 1854.

Montréal was a seigneury granted to the Order of the Sulpicians in 1663, and as a result the Order holds records up to 1854 in its office at 116 rue Notre Dame Ouest in Montréal.

The names and addresses of the Registry Offices (Bureaux d'enregistrement) are given below. The various offices retain custody of land records and documents:

Abitibi: 891 3e rue Ouest, Amos, PQ J9T 2T4

Argenteuil: 505 Béthanie, CP 337, Lachute, PQ J8H 3X5

Arthabaska: 800 boulevard des Bois-Francs sud, Arthabaska,
PQ G6P 5W5

Bagot: 51 Lemonde, CP 210, St. Liboire, PQ J0H 1R0

Beauce: 111 de la Station, CP 458, Beauceville, PQ G0S 1A0

Beauharnois: 150 chemin St. Louis, Beauharnois, PQ J6N 2H9

Bellechasse: 23 avenue Chanoine-Audet, CP 130, St. Raphael,
PQ G0R 4C0

Berthier: 180 Champlain, CP 299, Berthierville, PQ J0K 1A0

Bonaventure (1): Palais de Justice, CP 250, New Carlisle,
PQ G0C 1Z0

Bonaventure (2): 17 Lacroix, CP 599, Carleton, PQ G0C 1J0

Brome: 15 Chemin St. Paul, CP 40, Knowlton, PQ J03 1V0

Chambly: 2555 boulevard Roland-Therrien, Longueuil,
PQ J4M 2J4

Champlain: 211 de l'Eglise, CP 9, Ste. Geneviève-de-Batiscan,
PQ G0X 2R0

Charlevoix (1): 237 St. Etienne, CP 1810, La Malbaie, PQ G0T 1J0

Charlevoix (2): 4 St. Jean-Baptiste, CP 250, Baie-St. Paul,
PQ G0A 1B0

Châteauguay: 164 St. Joseph, Ste. Martine, PQ J0S 1V0

Chicoutimi: Palais de Justice, 224 Racine Est, Chicoutimi,
PQ G7H 5C5

Coaticook: Édifice de l'Hôtel de Ville, 150 Child, Coaticook,
PQ J1A 2B3

Compton: 89 du Parc, CP 459, Cookshire, PQ J0B 1M0

Deux-Montagnes: 140 St. Eustache, Place Duchesne, St. Eustache,
PQ J7R 2K9

Dorchester: 115 Langevin, CP 99, Ste. Hénédine, PQ G0S 2R0

Drummond: Palais de Justice, 1680 boulevard St. Joseph,
Drummondville, PQ J2C 2G5

Gaspé: Palais de Justice, CP 128, Percé, PQ G0C 2L0

Gatineau: 266 Notre-Dame, Maniwaki, PQ J9E 2J8

Hull: 170 de l'Hôtel de Ville, Hull, PQ J8X 4C2

Huntingdon: 25 King, CP 129, Huntingdon, PQ J0S 1H0

Iberville: 380 4e Avenue, Iberville, PQ J2X 1W9

Îles-de-la-Madeleine: Palais de Justice, Îles-de-la-Madeleine,
PQ G0B 1J0

Joliette: 577 Notre Dame, Joliette, PQ J6E 3H8

Kamouraska: 395 Chapleau, CP 577, St. Pascal, PQ G0L 3Y0

Labelle: 440 boulevard Paquette, Mont Laurier, PQ J9L 1K8

Lac St. Jean: 725 boulevard Harvey Ouest, Alma, PQ G8B 1P5

Lac St. Jean Ouest: 1221 boulevard St. Dominique, Roberval,
   PQ G8H 3B8
Laprairie: 214 St. Ignace, La Prairie, PQ J5R 1E5
l'Assomption: 300 Dorval, CP 631, L'Assomption, PQ J0K 1G0
La Tuque: 290 St. Joseph, La Tuque, PQ G9X 3Z8
Laval: 155 boulevard Je-Me-Souviens, Laval, PQ H7L 1V6
Lévis: 6 route Trans-Canada Ouest, Local 34, Lévis, PQ G6V 4Z2
L'Islet: 14 avenue Gaspé Ouest, CP 578, St. Jean-Port-Joli,
   PQ G0R 3G0
Lotbinière: 6296 Principale, CP 218, Ste. Croix, PQ G0S 2H0
Maskinongé: 121 Petite Rivière, Louiseville, PQ J5V 2H3
Matane: 750 de Phare Ouest, Matane, PQ G4W 3W8
Matapédia: 29 boulevard St. Benoît, CP 1508, Amqui, PQ G0J 1B0
Missisquoi: 1 Principale, CP 300, Bedford, PQ J0J 1A0
Montcalm: 1532 Albert, CP 190, Ste. Julienne, PQ J0K 2T0
Montmagny: 25 boulevard Taché Ouest, Montmagny, PQ G5V 2Z9
Montmorency: 7007 avenue Royale, Ange-Gardien, PQ G0A 2K0
Montréal: Palais de Justice, 1 Notre Dame Est, Montréal,
   PQ H1Y 1B6
Napierville: 361 St. Jacques, CP 368, Napierville, PQ J0J 1L0
Nicolet (1): 3050 avenue Nicolas-Perreault, Bécancour,
   PQ G0X 1B0
Nicolet (2): Palais de Justice, 395 Monseigneur Courchesne,
   Nicolet, PQ J0G 1E0
Papineau: 266 Viger, CP 320, Papineauville, PQ J0V 1R0
Pontiac: 159 John, CP 310, Campbell's Bay, PQ J0X 1K0
Portneuf: 185 Route 138, Cap-Santé, PQ G0A 1L0
Québec: Palais de Justice, 300 Jean-Lesage, Québec, PQ G1K 8K6
Richelieu: Maison du Québec, 46 Charlotte, Sorel, PQ J3P 6N5
Richmond: 746 Principale nord, CP 490, Richmond, PQ J0B 2H0
Rimouski: 337 Moreault, Rimouski, PQ G5L 1P4
Rouville: 1601 Edmond-Guillet, CP 1080, Marieville, PQ J0L 1J0
Rouyn–Noranda: 2 avenue du Palais, Rouyn–Noranda,
   PQ J9X 2N9
Saguenay: Palais de Justice, 71 Mance, Baie-Comeau,
   PQ G4Z 1N2
Ste. Anne-des-Monts: 10 boulevard Ste. Anne, CP 517, Ste. Anne-
   des-Monts, PQ G0E 2G0
St. Hyacinthe: 3100 boulevard Laframboise, St. Hyacinthe,
   PQ J2S 4Z4
St. Jean: 320 du Séminaire, St. Jean-sur-Richelieu, PQ J3B 5K9
Sept-Îles: Palais de Justice, 425 Laure, Sept-Îles, PQ G4R 1X6
Shawinigan: 212 6e Rue, CP 608, Shawinigan, PQ G9N 6V6

Shefford: 77 Principale, CP 99, Granby, PQ J2G 8E2
Sherbrooke: 375 King Ouest, CP 634, Sherbrooke, PQ J1H 5K5
Stanstead: 100 chemin Dufferin, CP 240, Stanstead Plain,
 PQ J0B 3E0
Témiscamingue: 8 St. Gabriel nord, CP 757, Ville-Marie,
 PQ J0Z 3W0
Témiscouata: 65a Iberville, Rivière-du-Loup, PQ G5R 1H2
Terrebonne: 85 de Martigny Ouest, St. Jérôme, PQ J7Y 3R8
Thetford: 693 St. Alphonse Ouest, CP 244, Thetford-Mines,
 PQ G6G 5S5
Trois-Rivières: 878 de Tonnancourt, Trois-Rivières, PQ G9A 4P8
Vaudreuil: 420 Roche, Vaudreuil, PQ J7V 2N1
Verchères: 461 St. Joseph, Ste. Julie, PQ J0L 2C0
Yamaska: 400 Notre-Dame, CP 29, St. François-du-Lac,
 PQ J0G 1M0

Access to *applications* for land grants in Québec is easy now
that the indexes to them have been microfilmed by the
National Archives for the period 1637–1841. All you need to
start is the surname of the individual. Once you know this,
you can apply for the correct microfilm reel through the inter-
library loan system. There are 18 reels covering the alphabetical list of names. For example, if the name you are looking
for is GEOFFRION, you will find this in No. 7, which starts with
the name GABANA and ends with the name HALL. The index
will give you the reel number; you apply for that, and when
it arrives at your library you will find all the information
about the land holdings of everyone named GEOFFRION.
Of course, it helps if you know that his first name was Pierre
and that he was granted land in the county of Kamouraska!
Otherwise, Geoffrion being a not uncommon name, you will
have a fair amount of elimination to do. However, let us
assume that you do have reasonably specific information about
him and that you will then be able to read all the details about
his land set out quite clearly for you.

The British system was by Crown grants, and these were
issued to settlers from 1700 to 1890. Land grants given under
both the French and the British régimes may be found in the
National Archives of Québec from 1626 to 1890.

Petitions

Starting in 1764, all settlers applying for free land had to sub-
mit a petition. In return for the land, the settler had to clear
it and build a dwelling. When this had been done, he was given

clear title to the land. Free grants were discontinued in 1827 except for those who qualified by military service.

The indexes to the Petitions, arranged by counties, and then listed alphabetically within the county, are to be found in the archives under the headings:

Lower Canada Land Petition Index, 1737–1867

Index to Land Grants in Québec, 1637–1841

Deeds of Sale

Records of purchase, sale, and transfer are in the local Registry Offices (Bureaux d'enregistrement) or in the Provincial Archives up to 1875.

Genealogical Societies

There are a limited number of these in the province, but there are a number of Historical and Genealogical Societies, and a great many Historical Societies. This, I think, is the reason so few public libraries have any genealogical holdings. I list the genealogical societies below (it may not be a complete list because I have heard rumours of some societies in places not listed but have been unable to obtain definite information).

The addresses given are correct at the time this book was printed, but circumstances change, officers depart, organizations go into suspended animation. There is no Provincial Genealogical Society to knit all the others together. If you do have some difficulty in contacting a particular society that I list, I suggest you ask the Québec Family History Society (La Société de l'Histoire des Familles du Québec) for up-to-date information. Be sure you send a stamped self-addressed envelope with your query. The Society is the first one listed below:

The Québec Family History Society

PO Box 1026, Pointe Claire, PQ H9S 4H9.

This was formed in 1977 to study genealogy among English-speaking people in the province. It holds regular monthly meetings from September to May in the Maison du Brasseur, 2901 boulevard St. Joseph, Lachine. It is the only society concerned with Anglophone Québecers. If your English-speaking ancestors came from the province, it will be well worth while to become a member, even if you live outside Québec. Membership means you have use of the library (including the microfilm collection), you can put genealogical queries in the quarterly journal, and you can use — by correspondence — the

Society's microfiche copy of the International Genealogical Index (IGI).

The main ongoing projects of the Society are:

1. A directory of the location of Cemetery Grave Lists in and near the province. The current edition lists 800 cemeteries. These are the smaller old Protestant ones in Québec, eastern Ontario, the Plattsburg area of New York State, northern Vermont and New Hampshire, and Newfoundland. The directory is indexed alphabetically by county and name, and by name alone.

2. Increasing the Society library of cemetery inscriptions.

3. Developing more *details* of sources for research in Québec.

The Society does not undertake genealogical research, but it will send you a list of approved researchers. It has its offices and library at the Somerlea Centre, 250-48th Avenue, Lachine, PQ. This may not be a permanent address and so all correspondence should be sent to PO Box 1026, Pointe Claire, PQ H9S 4H9.

Société de généalogie de Québec

CP 9066, Sainte-Foy, PQ G1V 4A8.

This society has been in existence since 1961. It has no branches or chapters. The main project at the moment is compiling marriage data covering the parishes in the counties of Rivière-du-Loup, Témiscouata, and Kamouraska. The Society has a magazine published ten times a year, several reproductions of old maps on sale, and many books of marriages in various areas. A list of these can be obtained from the Society by sending a stamped self-addressed envelope.

La Société Généalogique Canadienne-Française

CP 335, Station Place d'Armes, Montréal, PQ H2Y 3H1.

This society has no branches, either. Its library is located at 3300 boulevard Rosemont. They have an ongoing project of publishing marriage records, and so far these include those of Notre Dame des Anges de Cartierville, St. Jacques de Montréal, marriages of Catholics and of Protestants of the county of Iberville, St. Édouard de Montréal, St. François de Sales de l'Île Jésus, etc.

Société de généalogie des Cantons de l'Est

CP 635, Sherbrooke, PQ.

This society is located at 1215 rue Kitchener, Sherbrooke, PQ J1H 3L1. Among their publications is a record of Protestant marriages in the Judicial District of St. François from 1879, and Catholic marriages from thirteen of the various counties in the area served by the Society: Abitibi, Arthabaska, Compton, Drummondville, Frontenac, Mégantic, Nicolet, Richmond, Sherbrooke, Stanstead, Témiscamingue, Wolfe, Yamaska.

Quite apart from all these genealogical and historical societies which I am about to list for you, do not neglect the Eastern Townships' Research Centre at Bishop's University in Lennoxville, and the large Special Collection in the University Library. So far as the historical societies are concerned, do not make the mistake of assuming their marriage records are only Catholic; many of them include Protestant marriages as well.

Other French-Canadian genealogical societies in addition to those I mention above are:

Batiscan et son histoire,
  CP 67, Batiscan, PQ G0X 1A0.
Beaurepaire–Beaconsfield Historical Society,
  303 Beaconsfield Boulevard, Beaconsfield, PQ H9W 4A7.
Brome County Historical Society,
  PO Box 690, Knowlton, PQ G1R 4S6.
Centre de généalogie Madeleine
  CP 244, Havre-Aubert, I. M., PQ G0B 1J0.
Comité historique de St. Prosper,
  CP 4, St. Prosper-de-Champlain, PQ G0X 3A0.
Compton County Historical Society,
  RR #5, Cookshire, PQ J0B 1M9.
Hudson Historical Society,
  PO Box 802, Hudson, PQ J0P 1H0.
Lennoxville Ascot Historical Society,
  CP 61, Lennoxville, PQ J1M 2A3.
Megantic County Historical Society,
  PO Box 86, Inverness, PQ G0S 1K6.
Missisquoi Historical Society,
  PO Box 186, Stanbridge, PQ J0J 2H0.
Richmond County Historical Society,
  PO Box 280, Melbourne, PQ J0B 2B0.
Société de généalogie de la Mauricie et Bois Francs,
  CP 901, Trois-Rivières, PQ G9A 5K2.
Société de généalogie de Lanaudière,
  CP 221, Joliette, PQ J6E 3Z6.
Société de généalogie de l'Est du Québec,
  CP 253, Rimouski, PQ G5L 7C1.

Société de généalogie de l'Outaouais,
CP 2025, succ. B, Hull, PQ J8X 3Z2.
Société de généalogie de St. Benoît,
St. Benoît de Packington, PQ G0L 1Z0.
Société de généalogie de Salaberry–Valleyfield,
75 St. Jean Baptiste, Valleyfield, PQ J6T 1Z6.
Société de généalogie des Laurentides,
CP 131, St. Jérôme, PQ J7Z 5T7.
Société d'histoire d'Amos,
CP 626, Amos, PQ J9T 3X2.
Société d'histoire de Beloeil–Mont St. Hilaire,
CP 12, Beloeil, PQ J3G 4S8.
Société d'histoire de Charlevoix,
CP 748, Clermont, PQ G0T 1B0.
Société d'histoire de Deux-Montagnes,
CP 204, St. Eustache, PQ J7R 4K6.
Société d'histoire de la Seigneurie de Chambly,
CP 142, Chambly, PQ J3L 4B1.
Société d'histoire de l'Île Jésus,
5495 boulevard St. Martin ouest, Laval, PQ H7W 3S6.
Société d'histoire de Longueuil,
CP 175, succ. A, Longueuil, PQ J4H 3W6.
Société d'histoire de Louiseville,
CP 172, Louiseville, PQ J5V 2L6.
Société d'histoire de Matagami,
CP 160, Matagami, PQ J0Y 2A0.
Société d'histoire de Montarville,
1651 rue Beaubien, St. Bruno, PQ J3V 2V8.
Société d'histoire de Noyan,
CP 8, Noyan, PQ J0J 1B0.
Société d'histoire de Pointe-Bleue,
406 Amisk, Pointe-Bleue, PQ G0W 2H0.
Société d'histoire de Pointe-Calumet,
206 49e Avenue, Pointe-Calumet, PQ J0H 1G0.
Société d'histoire de St. Hubert,
CP 24, St. Hubert, PQ J3Y 5S9.
Société d'histoire des Îles de la Madeleine,
CP 8, Bassin, PQ G0B 1A0.
Société d'histoire des Îles Percées, Boucherville,
CP 234, Boucherville, PQ J4B 5J6.
Société d'histoire des Mille-Îles,
CP 315, Ste. Thérèse, PQ J7E 4J4.

Société d'histoire de Val d'Or,
600 73 rue Val d'Or, Val d'Or, PQ J9P 3P3.
Société d'histoire d'Oka,
CP 999, Oka, PQ J0N 1E0.
Société d'histoire du Cap-de-la-Madeleine,
CP 212, Cap-de-la-Madeleine, PQ G8T 7W2.
Société d'histoire du Haut-Richelieu,
203 rue Jacques-Cartier nord, Saint Jean, PQ J3B 6Z4.
Société d'histoire du Haut St. Laurent,
CP 193, Contrecoeur, PQ J0L 1C0.
Société d'histoire du Témiscamingue,
CP 1022, Ville-Marie, PQ J0Z 3W0.
Société d'histoire et archéologie des Monts,
CP 1192, Ste-Anne-des-Monts, PQ G0E 2G0.
Société d'histoire et de généalogie de Dolbeau,
1150 boulevard Wallberg, Dolbeau, PQ G8L 2P9.
Société d'histoire et de généalogie de Matane,
CP 608, Matane, PQ G4W 3P6.
Société d'histoire et de généalogie de Rivière-du-Loup,
67 rue Durocher, Rivière-du-Loup, PQ G5R 1J8.
Société d'histoire et de généalogie de St. Prosper,
CP 4, St. Prosper, PQ G0X 3A0.
Société d'histoire Mouillepied,
31 rue Lorne, Saint-Lambert, PQ J4P 2G7.
Société d'histoire régionale de Lévis,
CP 1303, Station Notre Dame, Lévis, PQ G6V 6Z8.
Société du patrimoine et de généalogie de Rouyn–Noranda,
CP 308, Rouyn, PQ J9X 5C3.
Société du patrimoine et de généalogie du Canton Nédelec,
623 route 101, Nédelec, PQ G0Z 2Z0.
Société généalogique de la Côte-Nord,
649 boulevard Laure, Sept-Îles, PQ G4R 1X8.
Société généalogique de la Presqu'île,
137 rue Ste. Catherine, St. Polycarpe, PQ J0P 1X0.
Société généalogique du K.R.T.,
258 avenue Sirois, St. Épiphane, PQ G0L 2X0.
Société généalogique du Saguenay,
CP 814, Chicoutimi, PQ G7H 5E8.
Société généalogique et historique de Trois-Pistoles,
CP 1478, Trois-Pistoles, PQ G0L 4K0.
Société historique Cavelier de la Salle,
CP 231, Succ. Champlain, La Salle, PQ H8P 3J1.

Société historique d'Alma,
54 St. Joseph, Alma, PQ G8B 3E4.
Société historique de Brossard,
2840 Rue Malo, Brossard, PQ J4Y 1B3.
Société historique de Cabano,
CP 464, Cabano, PQ G0L 1E0.
Société historique de Charlesbourg,
270, 56e Rue ouest, Charlesbourg, PQ G1H 4Z6.
Société historique de la Gaspésie,
CP 680, Gaspé, PQ G0C 2L0.
Société historique de la Gatineau,
Old Chelsea, PQ J0X 1N0.
Société historique de la Pointe-aux-Trembles,
1879-7e Avenue, Pointe-aux-Trembles, PQ H1B 4J9.
Société historique de Lotbinière,
428 rang St. Eustache, Lotbinière, PQ G0S 1S0.
Société historique de Pierreville,
104 Maurault, Pierreville, PQ J0G 1J0.
Société historique de Rigaud,
CP 1335, Rigaud, PQ J0P 1P0.
Société historique de St. Constant,
CP 159, St. Constant, PQ J0L 1X0.
Société historique des Quatre Lieux,
CP 1, St. Césaire, PQ J0L 1T0.
Société historique du Bout de l'Île,
38 rue Oxford, Baie d'Urfé, PQ H9X 2T5.
Société historique du Cap-Rouge,
4473 St. Félix, Cap Rouge, PQ G0A 1K0.
Société historique et généalogique de Ste. Julienne,
2482 place Rivet, Ste. Julienne, PQ J0K 2T0.
Société historique Lanoraie et Dautray,
360 rue Notre-Dame, Lanoraie, PQ J0K 1E0.
Société historique Odanak,
Odanak, PQ J0G 1H0.
Société historique Pierre-de-Saurel,
145 rue Georges, Sorel, PQ J3P 1C7.
Westmount Historical Association,
4575 rue Sherbrooke ouest, Westmount, PQ H3Z 1G1.

It is understood that most of the historical societies have genealogical material — cemetery lists, marriages, census returns, published and manuscript family histories — and usually have available a leaflet describing their documents. With the limited number of genealogical societies, you will find the historical societies of great value.

| Church Registers

Anglican

There are two dioceses of this denomination in the province and their names are given below, together with the parishes in each one:

MONTREAL

Abbotsford, Alymer and Hull, Bedford, Berthier, Brome, Buckingham, Chambly, Christieville, Clarenceville and St. Thomas, Clarendon, Coteau du Lac, Cowansville and Churchville, Dunham and West Dunham, Edwardstown and St. Rémi, Frost Village, Gore, Granby and North Shefford, Grenville, Hemmingford, Huntingdon, Île aux Noix, Kildare and Ramsay, Lachine, Lacolle and Sherrington, Laprairie and Longueuil, Mascouche and Terrebonne, Milton, Montréal, New Glasgow, Onslow, Ormstown, Potton, Rawdon, Rougemont and West Farnham, Russelltown, Sabrevois, St. Andrew, St. Armand, St. Hyacinthe, St. Johns, St. Martin, Ste. Thérèse, Shefford and Waterloo, Sorel, Stanbridge East, Sutton, Vaudreuil.

QUÉBEC

Bury, Cape Cove and Percé, Compton and Waterville, Danville and Trout Brook, Drummondville and Lower Durham, Dudswell and South Ham, Durham Upper, Eaton, Frampton and Cranbourne and Standon, Gaspé Basin and Little Gaspé, Hatley and Coaticook, Hopetown, Ireland and Inverness, Kingsey and Spooner's Pond, Leeds and Lamby's Mill, Lennoxville, Lake Beauport and Stoneham, Magdalen Islands, Nicolet, New Carlisle and Paspebiac, Point Lévis and New Liverpool, Portneuf and Bourg Louis, Québec, Richmond and Melbourne and Ely, Rivière du Loup, Sandy Beach and Malbaie, Sherbrooke, St. Sylvester and Cumberland Mills, Stanstead, Trois-Rivières, Valcartier.

There are three other Anglican Dioceses which, although their headquarters are located outside the province, have responsibility for some areas of Québec:

OTTAWA: This diocese includes part of the county of Papineau, and the counties of Gatineau, Hull, and Pontiac.
MOOSONEE: This includes the area of Québec bordering on James Bay.
THE ARCTIC: This includes the area of northern Québec.

The addresses of these five dioceses are given in Chapter 7. Basically, the Anglican registers before 1875 are now in the various archives. When a church closes, the registers are sent to the Diocesan Office, and a second copy goes to the archives.

United Church

Most churches retain their own registers. If a church closes, the registers are sent to the Church Centre, 3480 Décarie Boulevard, Montréal, PQ H4A 3J5. The archives there cover all the province except the Gaspé. Some of the registers for the latter area are located at Pine Hill Divinity Hall, Franklin Street, Halifax, NS B3H 3S5.

Baptist

A small number of registers are located in various archives, and details are given later in this chapter.

Presbyterian

The same comments apply.

Catholic

There are 64 dioceses of the Catholic Church in Canada, and 21 of them are in the province. With limitations on space, it is not possible to list every parish. I therefore have simply listed the various dioceses. If you wish to contact any of them regarding the registers they may hold, you will find the diocesan addresses in Chapter 7.

The names of the dioceses are:

Amos, Baie Comeau, Chicoutimi, Gaspé, Gatineau–Hull, Joliette, Mont-Laurier, Montréal, Nicolet, Québec, Rimouski, Rouyn–Noranda, Ste. Anne-de-la-Pocatière, St. Hyacinthe, St. Jean, St. Jérôme, Sherbrooke, Trois-Rivières, and Valleyfield. There are also the Greek Melkite Catholic Diocese of Montréal, and the Slovak (Byzantine) Catholic Diocese of Montréal.

In the chapters on the other provinces I gave details of church registers of various denominations that preceded the start of civil registration. There is no point in doing this in Québec since civil registration did not start until 1926, and therefore practically all registers were in existence before that year.

The National Archives in Ottawa hold original or microfilm copies of Québec church registers of all denominations. Exact details can be found in *Checklist of Parish Registers (Répertoire de registres paroissiaux)* published by the National Archives. The cost is $12, but most large libraries will have a copy in their reference section. The list of registers in the NAC is on a county basis and includes civil registers for various places as well as church registers:

Argenteuil County: Grenville, St. André d'Argenteuil, St. André Est.

Beauharnois: Beauharnois.

Berthier: Berthier, Île Dupas, Lanoraie, Lavaltrie, St. Antoine de Lavaltrie.

Bonaventure: Restigouche.

Brome: Allen's Corner, East Farnham, Farnham Township, Potton Township.

Chambly: Boucherville, Chambly, Fort Chambly, Fort St. Louis, Longueuil.

Champlain: Batiscan, Cap-de-la-Madeleine.

Châteauguay: Bassin-de-Châteauguay, Châteauguay, St-Joachim-de-Châteauguay, Sault-St-Louis.

Deux-Montagnes: Lac des Deux Montagnes, L'Annonciation, Oka, St. Benoît, St. Eustache, St. Hermas, Ste. Scholastique.

Gaspé-est: Pabos.

Gatineau: Aylmer, Chelsea, Denholm Township, Eardley Township, Hull, Hull Township, Lac-Ste-Marie, Lapêche, Masham, Ottawa County, Rivière-à-Lapêche, Ste-Cécile-de-Masham, Wakefield, Wakefield Township, Wright County.

Hull: Gatineau, Ottawa County, Templeton, Templeton Township, Wright County.

Huntingdon: St. Régis.

Île-de-Montréal: Bout-de-l'Île, Lachine, La Pointe Olivier, Longue Pointe, Montréal, Pointe-aux-Trembles, Pointe-Claire, Ste-Anne-de-Bellevue, Ste-Anne-du-Bout-de-l'Île, St. Laurent, Sault-au-Récollet, Ville-Marie.

Île-Jésus: Île-Jésus County, Laval, Ste. Rose.

Kamouraska: Kamouraska County, St-André-de-Kamouraska, St-Louis-de-Kamouraska.

La Prairie: La Prairie.

L'Assomption: Îles Bouchard, Lachenaie, L'Assomption, Repentigny, St. Sulpice.

Laval: Ste-Rose-de-Laval.

Lévis: Lévis.

L'Islet: St-Roche-des-Aulnaies.

Maskinongé: Louiseville, Rivière-du-Loup.

Missisquoi: Dunham Township, St. Armand-Ouest.

Montmagny: Cap-St-Ignace, Pointe-à-Lacaille.

Montmorency: Côte de Beaupré, Ste. Anne de Beaupré, Château-Richer, L'Ange-Gardien.

Papineau: Buckingham, Buckingham Township, Montebello, Notre-Dame-de-Bon-Secours, Ottawa County, Petite-Nation, Portland Township, Wright County.

Pontiac: Bristol, Bristol Township, Bryson Township, Calumet Island, Campbell's Bay, Charteris, Clarendon Township, Fort Coulonge, Grand Calumet Island, Isle des Allumettes, Leslie Township, Litchfield Township, Mansfield Township, North Clarendon, North Onslow, Onslow Township, Ottawa County, Pontiac County, Portage-du-Fort, Quyon, Shawville, Starks Corners, Thorne Township, Wright County, Wyman.

Portneuf: Deschambault, Lachevrotière.

Québec: Québec.

Richelieu: Fort William Henry, L'Enfant-Jésus-de-Sorel, Ste-Anne-de-Sorel, St. Gabriel Lalemant, St-Joseph-de-Sorel, St. Ours, St-Pierre-de-Sorel, St. Robert, St-Roch-de-Richelieu, Ste. Victoire, Sorel, Seigneurie de Sorel, Tracy.

St. Jean: Fort St. Jean.

St. Maurice: Trois-Rivières.

Soulanges: Côte-St-Georges, Côteau-du-Lac, Rivière-Beaudette.

Terrebonne: Ste-Anne-des-Plaines, St-Louis-de-Terrebonne, Terrebonne.

Vaudreuil: Rigaud, Ste-Madeleine-de-Rigaud, St-Michel-de-Vaudreuil.

Verchères: Contrecoeur, Fort St. Louis, Varennes, Verchères.

Yamaska: St-François-du-Lac.

In addition, there are copies in the original churches, in the offices of the prothonotaries, and in the various regional archives. The Central Library, 1210 Sherbrooke Street East,

Montréal, PQ H2L 1L9, also has microfilms of every Catholic parish register from 1621 to 1877.

Another vital source of information in Québec is marriage bonds. These have been published and are also on microfilm in various libraries, as well as in the National Archives, Ottawa, and the various Québec regional archives:

Marriage Records for Various Counties or Parishes

County of Kamouraska, 1867–1978
County of La Prairie, 1751–1972
County of Missisquoi, 1846–1968
County of Napierville, 1823–1970
County of Pontiac, 1836–1973
County of Portneuf, 1679–1950
County of St. Jean, 1828–1950
County of Shefford, 1846–1968
Coeur Immaculé de Marie (Montréal), 1946–79
L'Enfant Jésus de la Pointe-aux-Trembles, 1674–1975
Mission d'Aylmer, 1841–51
Notre Dame de Jacques Cartier, 1901–81
Notre Dame de Montréal, 1642–1850
Notre Dame de Pitié, 1945–80
Notre Dame de Trois-Pistoles, 1713–1979
Notre Dame de Verdun, 1899–1977
Region of Drummondville, 1863–1950
Rivière-des-Prairies (Montréal), 1687–1970
Sacré-Coeur de Jésus, 1917–1981
Ste. Anne-de-la-Pocatière, 1715–1972
Ste. Camille (Bellechasse County), 1902–75
Ste. Clothilde (Châteauguay County), 1885–1974
Ste. Cunegonde (Montréal), 1874–1978
St. Cyrille de l'Islet, 1865–1976
St. Denis-de-la-Bouteillerie, 1841–1978
Ste. Dorothée, 1869–1970
St. Elzéar-de-Laval, 1900–70
St. Eugene-de-l'Islet, 1868–1976
Ste. Flore (St. Maurice County), 1867–1977
St. François d'Assise, 1914–80
St. François d'Assise de la Longue-Pointe, 1724–1975
St. Gabriel, 1938–78
St. Gervais (Bellechasse County), 1780–1973
St. Jean (Port Joli), 1779–1980

St. Jean Berchmans (Montréal), 1908–75
St. Joseph de Burlington (Vermont), 1834–1930
St. Léonard de Port Maurice (Montréal), 1886–1977
Ste. Martine (Châteauguay County), 1823–1972
St. Maurice (Champlain County), 1844–1973
St. Moïse, 1873–1978
Ste. Nerée (Bellechasse County), 1883–1971
St. Noël, 1944–78
St. Ours, 1750–1975
St. Paul (Montréal), 1874–1979
St. Paul de Grand-Mère, 1899–1977
St. Philémon (Bellechasse County), 1886–1975
St. Philippe de Néri, 1870–1978
St. Pierre-aux-Liens (Montréal), 1898–1975
St. Raphaël (Bellechasse County), 1851–1974
St. Roch de Québec, 1901–81
Ste. Sabine (Bellechasse County), 1906–75
Ste. Vierge (Dorval), 1895–1975
St. Zéphirin-de-Stadacona, 1896–1979
Sault-au-Récollet, 1736–1970

Marriage Contracts (Contrats de Mariage)

Until 1970 a man and woman who were married in Québec were "in community of property", and for this reason it was the usual practice for engaged couples to enter into a formal marriage contract prepared by a notary. These contracts are in the various regional archives, filed by names and date of signing of the document, and covering the period from 1636 to 1874. Those since the latter date are in the local Registry Offices. Since 1970, marriage contracts are scarce, because the law now directs that couples keep pre-marriage assets but divide equally those acquired during the marriage. This makes a formal contract unnecessary.

Loiselle Marriage Index

This covers the province from 1642 to 1963, indexing one million records of 520 parishes. The names of the parents and their place of marriage are also given. The records, prepared over many years by Père Antoine Loiselle, are in the National Archives and the regional archives, and are on microfilm.

Obituaries

A number of these have been published and are in the same locations as the marriage records. They are given below by parish. Please note that these are being published frequently, so that even if your parish of interest is not listed, you should check with the appropriate regional archives:

Berthier-sur-Mer, 1710–1977
Notre Dame du Rosaire, 1889–1974
St. Anselme, 1830–1976
Ste. Camille (Bellechasse), 1902–75
St. Gervais (Bellechasse), 1780–1973
St. Henri (Lévis), 1766–1957
St. Michel, 1733–1974
St. Moïse, 1873–1978
Ste. Nerée (Bellechasse), 1883–1971
St. Noël, 1944–78
St. Paul, 1868–1974
St. Philémon (Bellechasse), 1886–1975
St. Pierre-du-Sud, 1740–1974
St. Raphaël (Bellechasse), 1851–1974
Ste. Sabine (Bellechasse), 1906–75

Another valuable source of information is a computerized demographic study being undertaken by the University of Montréal. Entries are being made from parish registers of old Québec, from notarial returns of the period, and from census returns. Its coverage starts in 1621 and will continue until 1765. The undertaking began in 1980, and at present thirty volumes have appeared—half the final number expected. The title of the study is *Le répertoire des actes de baptême, mariage, sépulture et des recensements du Québec ancien*. It is being edited by Hubert Charbonneau and Jacques Legaré, and the publisher is the University of Montreal Press (Les Presses de l'Université de Montréal). It is, of course, entirely in French, but an English "Key to the Repertory" is available. For more information about other books of value you must turn to the Bibliography.

| Directories and Newspapers

Do not neglect these as a vital source of information. Directories of Montréal exist from 1842 and of Québec City from 1848. They can be found in regional archives and in local libraries. Major libraries also have newspapers dating back to 1750; these include notices of births, marriages, and deaths, and obituaries of prominent people in the area served by the particular newspaper. The National Archives in Ottawa have a name and subject index of entries in the *Gazette du Québec* from 1764 to 1823.

There is also a directory of available newspapers and their locations in various archives and libraries. It is *Les Journaux du Québec de 1764 à 1964* by André Beaulieu and Jean Hamelin. It was published in 1967 by Laval University Press and is available through the inter-library loan system.

Bell Canada has also made its contribution to the great ancestor-hunt! It has donated to the National Archives of Canada and the National Archives of Québec microfilm copies of every telephone directory published in the province. The earliest was that for Montréal which appeared in 1879.

Be sure you make full use of all the records of the Church of Jesus Christ of Latter-Day Saints (the LDS Church, or the Mormons). Read Chapter 4 and you will soon realize what a vast collection of genealogical information is available for those of us who are not members of the church, nor are likely to be. Just be grateful for the generosity of the church in making all their records available for everyone. There are two main centres of the LDS Church in Québec:

470 Gilford, Montréal, PQ H2J 1N3
6666 Terrebonne, Montréal, PQ H4B 1B8

| Montréal Central Library

1210 rue Sherbrooke Est, Montréal, PQ H2L 1L9.
I have left to the end a brief account of all the material in this library, which is fast becoming the main centre for genealogical research in the province. This development has been concentrated on the past decade. Earlier in this chapter I mentioned the fact that the library held all the Catholic church registers on microfilm, but this is only a minute part of their general collection. The library also has:

The non-Catholic registers up to 1879 for all the parishes of the province (remember that the term non-Catholic means exactly that, and the registers include not only Protestant records but

Jewish as well, not only Anglican Church but Baptist and Congregationalist and Unitarian, and so on).

All the church registers for the parishes of the Moncton Archdiocese of the Catholic Church; this covers the great majority of the *Acadian* parishes.

Censuses of all the provinces on microfilm from 1825 to 1891.

The Loiselle Marriage Index (1642–1963) mentioned earlier, but also the supplement containing the records of a further 169,000 marriages — giving a total of over 719,000 marriages recorded.

The equally valuable Rivest Card File, an alphabetical list by the name of the *wife* containing over 100,000 names.

The Fabien Card File, with more than a quarter of a million names for the Outaouais region and Prince Edward Island.

Federal election lists for the province, 1935–79.

Land papers for the province.

Notarial papers — lists of deeds processed by a notary (répertoires chronologiques) and the indexes of public notaries; these are on 3000 microfiche, just to give you some idea of the quantity of records involved!

Telephone books for the province, 1880–1979.

City directories for Montréal, 1842–1978.

Marriage records — more than a thousand books of marriages in Québec, and in parts of New Brunswick, Ontario, and the New England States.

Family and parish histories — over 1000 family histories and 4000 parish histories, mainly for the province.

Genealogical dictionaries — all the main ones mentioned earlier: Tanguay, Drouin, and Jetté.

The ongoing projects of the library include:

The Pontbriand Card File, containing over a million marriages for the province.

Records of border points of entry from the United States, 1908–18.

Indexes for all the U.S. censuses.

Adding to the value of the notarial papers by microfilming the texts of the various deeds. This is a monumental undertaking and one not attempted elsewhere.

A consolidated index to all deaths in the province, 1926–85.

Church registers for areas of French-Canadian colonization in other Canadian provinces and in the United States.

Note: Some, but not all, of the records listed on microfilm may be borrowed through inter-library loan. It is suggested you check with the Library first before putting in a request through your own library.

In addition to all the above, there are, of course, many thousands of volumes in the library, many of which are of genealogical value. The collection is built around that of Philéas Gagnon (1854–1915), who sold his library to the city in 1910.

The Library staff are particularly helpful to ancestor-hunters. Obviously, if it is practicable for you to travel to Montréal, a couple of days in the Library will be of great benefit to you, but, failing that, you should check into the availability of inter-library loan of microfilms, or request a simple check of an uncomplicated inquiry, or make contact with a genealogical society. In all these instances write a clear, concise letter and cover the return postage. Do not expect the staff to do lengthy research for you — you will not be the only person writing!

CHAPTER 19
Saskatchewan

The people of Saskatchewan have their roots in many different countries; fewer than fifty per cent are of British and Irish descent. The French established trading-posts in the area in the mid-1700s, and they were soon followed by Scots and English traders in 1763, when the end of the Seven Years War transferred the control of Canada from France to England. By 1820 there was a score of posts and forts in the northern part of what is now Saskatchewan. The history of the Northwest Territories—from which the province was eventually created—is also the story of the Hudson's Bay and North West companies and of the railways.

In 1821 the two great trading companies merged under the name of "the Bay", and the number of trading-posts was reduced. The Company divided the area for administrative purposes into several districts, including Athabaska, Cumberland, English River, and Saskatchewan. It was at about this time that the first Anglican Church mission was established at Lac La Ronge. The Oblate Fathers of the Catholic Church arrived in 1845, and so did the first Grey Nuns. They were followed by Wesleyan missionaries.

After the formation of the Dominion of Canada in 1867 — consisting of Upper and Lower Canada (Ontario and Québec), Nova Scotia, and New Brunswick—the government negotiated an agreement with the Hudson's Bay Company under which the Company received £300,000 and retained a block of land surrounding each trading-post, plus five per cent of land in each township as it was surveyed. In return, the Company surrendered its claim to the millions of acres it owned in the area now to be known as the Northwest Territories. The area that would eventually become the province of Saskatchewan would now be administered by a lieutenant-governor instead of by the all-powerful Company.

In 1873 a council for the Northwest Territories was established, and in 1877 the administrative centre was set up in what is now Battleford (then Telegraph Flat). In 1882 the government in Ottawa divided the southern part of the Northwest Territories into four districts: Alberta, Assiniboia, Athabaska, and Saskatchewan.

The Canadian Pacific Railway reached Moose Jaw in the same year. At this time development was rapid: cattle-ranching started in Battleford; there was a grist mill in Prince Albert; and newspapers were published in Battleford, Prince Albert, Regina, and Saskatoon.

Until 1885 the population was almost entirely Indian, Métis, French, and British. Then immigrants from the United States and Europe started to arrive. From the United States settlers of Hungarian origin established themselves at Esterhazy, named after their leader, Count Paul Esterhazy. Soon afterwards, Swedish settlers crossed the border on the south and established a colony at New Sweden. Other small settlements came into being: Germans in Langenburg, Icelanders in the Qu'Appelle Valley at Tantallon, Germans and Romanians near Balgonie, Germans and Austrians at Ebenezer, and Danes in Yorkton.

The railway from Regina to Prince Albert via Saskatoon was completed in 1890. This brought in German-speaking Mennonite settlers from Russia, as well as French and Ukrainians. In 1899 over 7000 Doukhobors from Russia settled in three colonies near Yorkton and Prince Albert. In 1903 the Rev. I. M. Barr brought 1500 settlers from England to settle in the Lloydminster and Saskatoon areas. There was also greatly increased immigration from the United States at this time, owing to assistance from the railways, the organization of the Saskatchewan Valley Land Company, and the drive and enthusiasm of Clifford Sifton, the Secretary of the Interior in Ottawa. The longest journey made by immigrants at this time was that of two hundred Welsh settlers in Patagonia. They left Argentina (where they had settled thirty years earlier) in 1902 and settled in the Saltcoats area.

In 1905 the provinces of Alberta and Saskatchewan were established and the area of the Northwest Territories was reduced to its present size — Manitoba (which had previously been known as the Red River Settlement) had been detached to form a separate province in 1870.

(For much of the above information I am indebted to *Saskatchewan: The History of a Province* by Jim Wright. Published by McClelland & Stewart, 1955, Toronto.)

| Civil Registration

Immediately after the province was established, the official registration of births, marriages, and deaths came into effect. However, registration in Saskatchewan is not as simple and as easy as you would expect. On the plus side is the fact that under the laws of the Northwest Territories (of which the area of Saskatchewan had formed a part) the registration of marriages had commenced in 1878, and of births and deaths in 1888. On the minus side is the fact that the new provincial government — for some reason unknown — had difficulty in establishing a proper system of registration; as a result, the records between 1905 and 1920 have many omissions. People born in the province after 1905 and trying to prove their age in order to qualify for the Old Age Pension have had problems. You will, too, and, like them, you must be prepared to search other records such as church registers, land titles, wills, school attendance lists, and local-history books.

The records are in the custody of the Division of Vital Statistics, Department of Health, 3475 Albert Street, Regina, SK S4S 6X6. Records relating to living persons will not be released, except to the person concerned. Information about deceased individuals will be released upon *proof* of identify. So, when you apply for information, you will have to supply this proof and complete a long official form which the Division will send you.

The information contained in the various registrations has varied over the years. For example, the table below shows the basic information required in 1889 plus further questions asked from time to time:

Births

1889: Name, date, place, sex, name of father, maiden name of mother.

1898: Birthplace of parents (usually just the Canadian province or territory, or the country of origin).

1916: Age of parents, and number of children born so far to mother.

Marriages

1899: Name, age, residence, religion, birthplace of both parties, place and date of event, names of witnesses, name of officiating clergyman, name of parents of bride and groom.

1900: Religion of clergyman.

1916: Maiden name of mothers.

1920: Birthplaces of fathers.

1947: Birthplaces of mothers.

Deaths

1889: Name, date, place, sex, birthplace, age, occupation.

1898: Marital status.

1916: Residence, name and birthplace of father, maiden name and birthplace of mother.

1920: Date of birth.

1947: Name of husband or maiden name of wife.

When you apply for a certificate, be sure you request a *full* certificate and state that it is required for genealogical purposes. If you do not do this, you will receive a bare minimum of information. Be prepared to wait at least four weeks for a reply.

| Provincial Archives

Saskatchewan's archives are split between the two largest cities of the province, Regina and Saskatoon. The reason appears to be to provide access in these two main centres, and at the two universities. I must admit I hope that Alberta does not follow with Calgary and Edmonton, or British Columbia with Vancouver and Victoria, since this division of archives does cause problems and delay research. As early as 1937 the University of Saskatchewan set up an Historic Public Records Office in Saskatoon, and in 1945 the provincial government established a similar office in Regina.

Basically, the Regina office houses material from the south of the province, and Saskatoon material from the north.

Having told you that, I must also tell you that, although Regina is the capital of the province, the governmental records are, generally speaking, in Saskatoon. Documents needed for genealogical research can be transferred on request from one office to another. This can be time-consuming for the genealogist — particularly when you find that the record you need to inspect in Saskatoon has just been transferred on a temporary basis to Regina!

The two addresses for you to remember are:

1. Saskatchewan Archives Board, Library Building, University of Regina, Regina, SK   S4S 0A2.

2. Saskatchewan Archives Board, Murray Memorial Building, University of Saskatchewan, Saskatoon, SK   S7N 0W0.

The division of records I mentioned above needs some clarification:

The records of the Supreme Court of Saskatchewan, the Court of Appeal, the Court of King's Bench, and the District Courts — all prior to 1931 — are in the Saskatoon Office, with two exceptions: those of the Saskatoon Judicial District are still in the Saskatoon Court House and those of the Regina District are in the Regina Archives Office.

The original files of the Homestead records — of importance to many genealogists — are in the Saskatoon Office, with copies in the Regina Office. The records of both offices have been microfilmed by the LDS Church.

So far as church registers are concerned, the Archives Board is unable to provide any information about its holdings. It states it has custody of some 7000 church records of various kinds from various denominations, but less than one per cent pre-date the official date of the start of civil registration. This seems a little doubtful, but certainly settlement in the province started later than in any other. There was no settlement at all in the Regina area before 1882, and the only major settlements at that time were in the vicinity of Prince Albert and Battleford.

I have been able to put together a partial list of registers held in the Archives, but this was obtained from unofficial sources and is not complete. If you do not find the place of your ancestral settlement listed, I suggest you write to the Archives Board for information. Let us hope that eventually an official list may be made available. You should also write to the nearest headquarters of the particular denomination; I list these as well.

The church registers known to be in the Regina Office of the Archives Board are:

Church	Denomination	Dates
Asissippe	A	BMD 1876–94
Duck Lake (St. Laurent)	CA	BMD 1871–96
Duck Lake (St. Michael)	CA	BMD 1894–1927
Duck Lake (St. Sacrement)	CA	BMD 1870–93
English River	A	M 1857–71 D 1850–89
Nepowewin	A	BMD 1853–91
Qu'Appelle	CA	BMD 1888–
Prince Albert (St. Mary)	A	B 1875–91
Rupert's Land (Diocese)	A	BM 1813–90
St. Catherine's	A	D 1884–87
Stanley	A	D 1850–89
Stanley (Trinity)	A	M 1847–78
Wolseley	CA	BMD 1883–

The following registers are held by the National Archives, 395 Wellington Street, Ottawa, ON K1A 0N3, and are available on microfilm through inter-library loan:

Balgonie	CA	B 1827–1932 M 1872–1915
		D 1899–1916
Carlton House (Fort Pelly)	A	BMD 1828–29
Cumberland House	A	BMD 1828–29
Fort Ile-à-la-Crosse	A	BMD 1820–41
Neudorf	EL	BMD 1894–1961
Swarthmore	Q	BMD 1836–1929

Addresses of religious headquarters that may be of help with further information about location of other registers:

Anglican
DIOCESE OF QU'APPELLE, 1501 College Avenue, Regina, SK S4P 1B8
DIOCESE OF SASKATCHEWAN, PO Box 1088, Prince Albert, SK S6V 5S6
DIOCESE OF SASKATOON, PO Box 1965, Saskatoon, SK S7K 3S5
Baptist
BAPTIST ARCHIVES, McMaster Divinity College, Hamilton, ON L8S 4K1

Catholic

DIOCESE OF GRAVELBOURG, PO Box 690, Gravelbourg, SK S0H 1X0

DIOCESE OF PRINCE ALBERT, 1415-4th Avenue West, Prince Albert, SK S6V 5H1

DIOCESE OF REGINA, 3225-13th Avenue, Regina, SK S4T 1P5

DIOCESE OF SASKATOON, 106-5th Avenue North, Saskatoon, SK S7K 2N7

DIOCESE OF SASKATOON (UKRAINIAN CATHOLIC), 866 Saskatchewan Crescent East, Saskatoon, SK S7N 0L4

Lutheran

EVANGELICAL LUTHERAN CHURCH (SASKATCHEWAN SYNOD), 707-601 Spadina Crescent East, Saskatoon, SK S7K 3G8

LUTHERAN CHURCH-MISSOURI SYNOD (MANITOBA-SASKATCHEWAN OFFICE), 1927 Grant Drive, Regina, SK S4S 4V6

Mennonite

MENNONITE HERITAGE CENTRE ARCHIVES, 600 Shaftesbury Boulevard, Winnipeg, MB R3P 0M4

United Church

SASKATCHEWAN CONFERENCE, ST. ANDREW'S COLLEGE, 1121 College Drive, Saskatoon, SK S7N 0W3. (This includes Congregational, Methodist, and Presbyterian; independent churches of the latter denomination which did not join the United Church are represented by the Presbyterian Synod of Saskatchewan, 2127 Albert Street, Regina, SK S4P 2V1.)

All the above information—while designed to help you—is more than a little complicated, but blame it all on the lack of a list from the Archives Board. You face one more complication: because of the late and scattered settlement of the province, and the consequent scarcity of early churches and chapels, you may have to chase your Protestant ancestor through several different denominations.

| Census Returns

The first Canadian census to include parts of what is now Saskatchewan is that of 1881, and it was for the "North-Western Territory". The only other year open to public search since then is 1891. The Saskatchewan Archives Board has copies of both censuses in its two offices, and the 1881 Census is indexed.

The 1881 Census includes Battleford and Qu'Appelle. The former place also includes Frog Lake, Lac La Biche, Livingstone, Long Lake, Saddle Lake, Victoria Mission, and White Fish Lake. The 1891 Census adds to this list Batoche, Carleton, Duck Lake, Fort-à-la-Corne, Fort Pitt, Grandin, Green Lake, Lake Winnipeg, Prince Albert, Red Deer Hill, Regina, St. Laurent, Saskatoon, and Stobart.

Microfilm copies of the above returns are in the National Archives in Ottawa, and may be borrowed through your nearest local library with a microfilm-viewer.

| Wills

Wills that have been probated are kept on file at the Courthouse in the centre where the probate was granted. A will probated before 1958 will be found at the judicial centre nearest the place of residence of the deceased.

After 1958 the law was changed so that any judicial centre could grant probate regardless of the place of residence. The Surrogate Court at the Courthouse in Regina has a central index covering all the wills probated in all the judicial centres in the province. A small fee is charged for a search by the Registrar.

The addresses of the judicial centres in the province are listed below (all correspondence should be addressed to The Sheriff–Local Registrar, the Courthouse):

Assiniboia, SK S0H 0B0	Moosomin, SK S0G 3N0
Battleford, SK S0M 0E0	Prince Albert, SK S6V 4W7
Estevan, SK S4A 0W5	Regina, SK S4P 3E4
Gravelbourg, SK S0H 1X0	Saskatoon, SK S7K 3G7
Humboldt, SK S0K 2A0	Shaunavon, SK S0N 2M0
Kerrobert, SK S0L 1R0	Swift Current, SK S9H 0J4
Melfort, SK S0E 1A0	Weyburn, SK S4H 0L4
Melville, SK S0A 2P0	Wynyard, SK S0A 4T0
Moose Jaw, SK S6H 4P1	Yorkton, SK S3N 0C2

As I mention elsewhere in the book, do not count too much on discovering the will of Great-grandfather. Remember that the average early settler was not too blessed with this world's goods, and if he had nothing to leave, he or she would not make a will. Another explanation for the lack of a will could be that he or she died suddenly, or was killed in an accident long before they had thought about dying. Finally, allow for the fact that in a close-knit family the allocation of possessions might well have been made before Mother or Father died—everyone knew who was to get what, so why waste money on a lawyer?

Land Titles

You can often learn a great deal about your ancestor and his immediate family by checking land records. Apart from the Homestead records already mentioned, there are the regular land titles to be investigated: the sale and transfer of real estate. There are eight Land Registration Districts which have records of land transactions since the province was formed in 1905. Records before that date are in the Land Titles Office in Regina. The records are open for public inspection and you can search them yourself, or pay a small fee for the staff of the office to search for you. The offices are located in Battleford, Humboldt, Moose Jaw, Prince Albert, Regina, Saskatoon, Swift Current, and Yorkton. The postal codes for these offices are the same as those listed above under Wills. If you have only a vague idea of the particular area in which your ancestor owned land, you should contact the Archives Office at Saskatoon—they have alphabetical indexes available.

Genealogical Societies

The Saskatchewan Genealogical Society is a very active, energetic, and efficient one, with a number of branches, a tremendous library, and many ongoing projects. The mailing address for the Society is PO Box 1894, Regina, SK S4P 3E1. Branches are located in the following places in the province: Battleford, Biggar, Border (Lloydminster), Central Butte, Craik, Estevan, Grasslands (Hazenmore), Grenfell, Kindersley, Moose Jaw, Pangman, Prince Albert, Radville, Regina, Saskatoon, South East (Carnduff & Oxbow), Swift Current, Triangle (Kipling), West Central (Eston), Weyburn, and Yorkton.

I am not listing postal addresses, since these have a habit of changing when the secretary does; I suggest instead that you write to the branch secretary care of the address of the Society HQ above. Be sure you always cover return postage!

The main library and offices are located at 1870 Lorne Street, Regina. Open Monday to Friday, 0900 to 1630 hours. The library is the largest genealogical library in Canada which mails books to its members. The collection is made up of books, maps, and microfilm/microfiche records. The library is open to the public but only members of the Society may borrow and use the microfilm/microfiche collection.

The Society has the following projects on an ongoing basis:

1. Surname file: Information supplied by individual members who wish to share information with others searching the same name.

2. Cemeteries: This includes locating cemeteries in Saskatchewan, and copying and indexing the inscriptions. (Over 100,000 names on microfilm.)

3. Obituaries: A collection of obituaries from newspapers throughout the province.

4. Periodical index: Major articles in the fifty periodicals and newspapers purchased by the Society.

5. Census index: The Society is indexing the 1891 Census for the Northwest Territories—not only for those parts now in Saskatchewan, but also for the area now in the provinces of Manitoba and Ontario.

6. General reference: Answering questions by telephone or mail from members or others seeking information. A fee is charged for these services. (The sources that will be checked include Homestead Index, Obituary Index, Cemetery Index, and Newspaper Index. If this produces results, the search will be extended into other areas.)

What makes the Saskatchewan Genealogical Society so unusual is that its library records are not confined to the province. For instance, it has the Indirect Hamburg Passenger List Index for 1855–1910 and the actual lists for 1882–1910. As you will know, this records those emigrants from Hamburg who did not sail directly over the ocean but proceeded via other countries such as England, France, Ireland, etc. Other records on file include the Ontario Computerized Land Records Index, the Griffith Valuation Index from Ireland, and the Loiselle and Rivest Marriage Indexes from Québec.

It is impossible to list all the books of reference about each province held in the Society library, or even the names of over 400 cemeteries recorded on film with indexes of names. There are over 200 family histories; there are books and manuscripts about such subjects as Greek Catholic records in Hungary, Palatine Church Visitations, Angus Monumental Inscriptions (Scotland), East Prussians from Russia, records of Galician

Mennonites, Black Sea Germans in the Dakotas — the list is almost endless, and it seems impossible that this Society was only founded twenty years ago.

| Libraries

Public libraries continue to develop into local archives, and are no longer just a place to borrow a book. This is true of Saskatchewan — the Becker Collection of material on Germans in Eastern Europe is in the University of Saskatchewan Library, and you will also find there extensive collections of French-Canadian genealogical information. It is, however, in the smaller public libraries that great developments are taking place:

There are over 300 local public libraries in the province, and though not all have genealogical collections, here are the details of some of them:

Estevan Public Library, 1037-2nd Street, Estevan, SK S4A 0L8. Here you will find local parish registers and the cemetery records of the city. These include the little-known Jewish cemetery at Hirsch, to the east of Estevan. Books on local history and settlement include *A Walk Through Time*; *Estevan: The Power Centre*; *Estevan, 1890–1980*; *The History of Alameda and District*; *Cambria, 1902–77*; *The Saga of the Souris Valley*; and many other books and manuscripts about the area.

North Battleford Library, 1392-101st Street, North Battleford, SK S9A 1A2. This library, as befits an early centre of settlement in the province, has a good genealogical collection and a very helpful library staff. The collection includes early directories, early telephone directories, and local newspapers on microfilm. These are:

North Battleford News, 1905, 1909–53
North Battleford Optimist, 1943–53
News Optimist, 1953–88
Battlefords Press, 1906–49
Battlefords Telegraph, 1980–88
Saskatchewan Herald, 1878–1938
The Little Joker (Battleford), 1888
The Guide (Industrial School), 1895–99

The book collection contains many books about local places and people—at 85, too many to list—but if your ancestor came from a small place near the Battlefords, the odds are there is a book about the settlement, and the possibility that your forebear is mentioned.

Moose Jaw Public Library, 461 Langdon Crescent, Moose Jaw, SK S6H 0X6. Here you will find local histories and obituaries since 1968, and burial indexes for Rosedale Cemetery.

Regina Public Library, 2311-12th Avenue, Regina, SK S4P 3Z5. The Prairie History Room at this library is a treasure-house of local history, with over a thousand published works about early settlement and pioneer families in every part of the province. There is a computerized finding-aid to these histories which is frequently updated. There are also some 250 local histories from Alberta and Manitoba. The Room also has the LDS Church Family Registry and accepts registrations for that service.

There is also an index to the *Regina Leader* and the *Leader-Post*, which, combined, cover the years from 1883 to 1981. The library has copies of Regina directories from 1909, and — on microfilm—directories of the Northwest Territories from 1884 to 1909. So far as census returns are concerned, there are indexes to the 1881 Census for Manitoba and the Northwest Territories, and microfilms of both the 1881 and the 1891 censuses for the Territories should be available by the time you read this.

There are plans for additional indexing in the near future. This may include biographical notes about Regina personalities, indexes to Hudson's Bay records, and an alphabetical listing of those who fought or served in the uprising of 1885. All this is in the future, but today those of you of Saskatchewan descent are blessed with superb public-library systems and — probably — one of the best genealogical societies in North America.

Saskatoon Public Library, 311-23rd Street East, Saskatoon, SK S7K 0J6. The Local History Room of this library may not match that of Regina, but just a sampling of the available records here will prove that Saskatoon does not lag far behind. There are published directories of Saskatoon from 1908 to 1988, and very many published histories of Sasktoon and its early settlement and pioneer families; even more important, in many ways, to the ancestor-hunter are the many published and manuscript memoirs and reminiscences of early Saskatoon settlers. There is an indexed collection of newspaper clippings, and general information about Saskatoon people.

There are over 400 published books relating to the local history of towns, villages, and school districts, and most of these include family histories of local residents.

The many family histories may include the story of your own family. I list the names below, but you will notice many of them are fairly common, so please don't jump to the immediate conclusion that it must be *your* family. You will find the histories of Elliott, Fowler, Gareau, Hauer, Lamport, MacMillan, Molder, Morrison, Pederson, Sarauer, VanCleave, Vinnard, Walliser, Wicks, and Woodward.

As always, I must remind you never to neglect the resources and records of the LDS Church. There is a Family History Library in Saskatoon—mailing address: PO Box 7347, Saskatoon, SK S7K 4J3.

| Church Registers

Anglican
The following parishes of the Anglican Church were in existence in Saskatchewan before civil registration of births, marriages, and deaths (1888):

DIOCESE OF QU'APPELLE: Cannington, Churchbridge, Fort Qu'Appelle, Grenfell, Moose Jaw, Moosomin, Qu'Appelle Station, Regina, Souris, Sumner, and Whitewood.

DIOCESE OF SASKATCHEWAN: Battleford, Bresaylor, Cumberland, Holy Trinity, La Corne, Onion Lake, Pelican Narrows, St. Alban's, St. Augustine, St. Cyprian's, St. David's, St. Mary's, St. Paul and St. Catherine, Sandy Lake, Saskatoon, and Stanley.

Catholic
The following parishes of the Catholic Church were in existence in Saskatchewan before civil registration in 1888:

DIOCESE OF PRINCE ALBERT: Cathedral, Aldma, Batoche, Delmas, Duck Lake, Green Lake, Onion Lake, St. Laurent.

DIOCESE OF REGINA: St. Mary's.

CHAPTER 20
The Yukon and Northwest Territories

This area was first explored for the Hudson's Bay Company in the 1840s. As a result, trading-posts were established on the Yukon River. The Canadian government acquired the area in 1870 as part of the purchase of the Hudson's Bay Company land. After this the region was administered as part of the Northwest Territories. In the 1890s gold was discovered, and at one period more than thirty thousand hopeful prospectors were roaming the territory.

The Yukon was made a separate district in 1895 and became a territory in 1898. The capital was originally at Dawson but was transferred to Whitehorse in 1952.

Civil Registration

Records date back to 1896 and are in the custody of the Registrar General, PO Box 2703, Whitehorse, YT Y1A 2C6. There is no public access, but searches will be made for a small fee.

Territorial Archives

The Yukon Archives (postal address as above) hold the following genealogical material:

Manuscripts

These are private papers of individuals and families associated with the development of the territory: diaries, letters, scrapbooks, account books, etc.

Photographs

This collection is partially indexed and contains early prints, negatives, slides, and postcards.

Directories

These date back to 1901 (A-M only, in this case) and are held at irregular dates since then. There are also telephone directories since 1956.

Search Files

These contain alphabetical biographies, newspaper clippings, etc., about well-known Yukon personalities.

Newspapers

These are on microfilm for the following:

Dawson News, 1899–1953
Klondike Nugget, 1898–1903
Morning World, 1904–08
Yukon Sun, 1901–04

Funeral Records

This is an alphabetical index to Dawson funeral-home records, 1898–1907. Information includes name, age, date, and cause of death. Occasionally a country of origin is stated.

Private Collections

1. *Craig Family Collection:* Contains an alphabetical list of people leaving Dawson in 1898–1907, including name of intended destination; a Yukon Order of Pioneers membership list for 1897–1949; a list of Yukoners leaving in 1908–20; and a list of deaths in 1898–1955.

2. *Faulkner Collection:* This includes a list of government employees in 1898–1911, and a 1905 voters' list.

3. *McLennan Collection:* This has the Dawson school registers for 1903–04 for Section 8 below Discovery along Bonanza Creek.

Hospital Records
These are subject to restriction but cover the period 1900–31, and birth records from 1933 to 1951. There are some deaths, 1898–1903.

School Records
St. Mary's School, Dawson, 1899–1966.

Marriage Licences
These are held for the period 1901–17.

Tax Records
Dawson City tax returns, 1902–59.

Cemetery Records
Whitehorse 6th Avenue Cemetery, 1904–65.

| Dawson Museum

PO Box 303, Dawson City, YT Y0B 1G0.
Resources here include newspapers from 1898 onwards; people cards (brief biographies); business directories, 1901–24; Catholic Church records for Dawson (indexed); death records, 1898–1937; and voters' lists for 1904, 1917, and 1938. There is also a large library of local histories, both published and in manuscript form. A genealogy service is offered — 30 minutes' search for free, and a small fee for longer periods.

| Libraries

There are public libraries in a number of places in the Yukon, but few have any genealogical records. However, they can provide a great deal of local knowledge about families and individuals. They are located in:
Beaver Creek, Burwash, Carcross, Carmacks, Dawson, Destruction Bay, Elsa, Faro, Haines, Keno Hill, Mayo, Old Crow, Pelly Crossing, Ross River, Tagish, Teslin, Tungsten, Watson Lake, and Whitehorse.

Church Registers

The National Archives, in Ottawa, have on microfilm the registers of St. Mary's, Dawson, for BMD 1898–1956.

The Yukon Archives have the following Anglican registers. Please note that the parishes named also include in their registers a number of very small communities within the general area. Fuller information can be obtained from the Diocese of Yukon, PO Box 4247, Whitehorse, YT Y1A 3T3:

Atlin, BD 1899–1962
Carcross, BMD 1884–1948
Carmacks, BMD 1899–1981
Dawson, BMD 1897–1960
Elsa, BMD 1883–1957
Haines, BMD 1909–69
Old Crow, BMD 1883–1966
Teslin, BMD 1923–64
Whitehorse, BMD 1901–70

Cemetery Records

The Dawson City Museum holds these for the following cemeteries: Hillside, Jewish, Masonic, New Catholic, New Public, Old Catholic, RCMP, 3rd Avenue Cemetery, and West Dawson.

The **Northwest Territories** occupy more than a third of the total land mass of Canada, and at one time were even larger. Yellowknife has been the capital since 1967; before that the Territories were administered from Ottawa. They are divided into three districts; the southern ones are Keewatin and Mackenzie, and the northern one Franklin.

Sir Martin Frobisher and Henry Hudson were the first explorers in the region. The fur trade in the area was developed by the North West Company, operating out of Montréal in competition with the Hudson's Bay Company. In 1821 the HBC absorbed the smaller company. In 1870 the whole of the Northwest Territories was sold by the Company to the Canadian government. Part of the Territories was then added to Ontario and Québec. Manitoba was created out of the Territories in 1870, and Alberta and Saskatchewan in 1905. Earlier in the nineteenth century British Columbia had also been a part of the region, but Vancouver Island was ceded in 1849, and the lower mainland in 1858. Both became Crown Colonies. The present boundaries of the Northwest Territories were set in 1912.

The various settlements of the original Northwest Territories are mostly included in the western provinces and the Yukon Territory. Archives do exist, but permanent European settlement is too recent to be of interest to the genealogist.

CHAPTER 21
Writing a Family History

Suppose you've done the research, met some friends, tramped through graveyards; what do you *do* with the information? Write it down, of course. In this chapter I'll give you an example of what can be done with the information you've gathered.

I am often asked the difference between a family tree and a family history. Another question is the difference between family history and genealogy. The latter question arises more frequently now that the LDS Church is substituting family history for genealogy in most of its activities. I do not mind this a bit: genealogy (usually mispronounced geneology) is a complicated word, and I much prefer family history as a clear description of the hobby of ancestor-hunting.

There is, however, a considerable difference between a family tree and a family history. A family tree is a chart that shows your actual descent from your ancestors in a clear and easily understandable format — an example of this was given in Chapter 2. A family history is an account of your family and your ancestral background set out in narrative form. It enables you to go into much greater detail about your ancestors and their lives and surroundings over the centuries than does a family tree. The latter can, of course, take any one of several forms. The example I gave was concerned with your *direct* ancestral line. A variation would be if you wished to include all your own living relatives. Some people are more concerned with finding all their existing cousins than they are with trying to trace back the family over several centuries. Which route you take is for you to decide. Most genealogical or family history societies have for sale a variety of forms and books for recording information to fit your own requirements. A more recent development is the use of personal computers to store information about all the offshoots of the family tree. The LDS Church has at least one program for sale.

There are no forms for recording a family history, and none are required. I think the simplest explanation is for me to set out below the earlier part of a Baxter family history I wrote some years ago after I finished tracing back that side of my ancestry. As the result of detailed research into the social history of the district where the Baxters originated, I was able to include information about their way of life over the years; details about the sheep they raised, the food they ate, the clothes they wore; and the reason they eventually left the ancestral dale.

This is something that anyone can do by buying or borrowing books. It is, in fact, something you *should* do if you really want to know about the people who formed you — it will put leaves on the bare branches of the family tree. For me, it was not enough to have traced my family back for nearly eight centuries — I was not content with dates of birth, marriage, and death. I wanted to really get to know them as men and women — to find out how they lived, so that I could get a clear picture in my mind of these ordinary mortals whose names appeared in my family tree. To paraphrase the famous prayer of Sir Francis Drake: "It is not the roots and the tree which yieldeth the true glory but rather the leaves which adorn the branches."

| The Baxters of Swindale and Morecambe

Swindale is a remote dead-end valley, or dale, located in the old county of Westmorland in north-west England. It is now merged with the county of Cumberland to form the new county of Cumbria. Swindale is located west of Shap Fell and almost midway between the towns of Kendal and Penrith. The wild and mountainous country was first populated by the Beaker people from Yorkshire and Northumberland who settled in the dales in 2000 BC. They were farmers, and were followed in 300 BC by the Celts — another farming people from Ireland. Two centuries later the Brigantes moved into the area from the east, followed in AD 100 by the invading Romans from the south.

The Romans built their hill forts and roads, fought frequently with invaders from the north, and finally departed in AD 410. The Cymry then moved in from the north (Cumbria is named after them) and in 600 the warlike Angles from the eastern Kingdom of Northumbria occupied the area. The name Westmorland orginated at this time when the district was called Westmaringaland — "the land of the western border" — by the Angles.

In AD 850 the first Vikings appeared, coming not from the east but from Ireland. They came as refugees, fleeing from attacks by other Viking bands in a civil war raging in that troubled island. From 950 to 1032 Westmorland was part of Scotland. It reverted to England in 1032, but in 1066 (the year of the Norman Conquest of England) the Scots again seized control.

As a result of these many invasions and settlements, the place names of Westmorland include Celtic, Roman, Viking, Scots, and Norman words. There are also a few names of Saxon origin. In 1092, according to the *Anglo-Saxon Chronicle*, "William II marched north to Carlisle with a large army, re-established the fortress and built the castle, garrisoning it with his own men, and afterwards returned to the south, and sent thither very many peasants with their wives and stock to dwell there to till the ground." Since the name Baxter was originally Baecestre — a Saxon word for baker — the first of the family to settle in Westmorland may well have been one of the Saxons brought there by the son of William the Conqueror.

The first mention of a Baxter in the area was in 1195 when John le Bacastre owned land at Helton Flechan (between Bampton and Askham) at the foot of Swindale, and now known simply as Helton. This name is an Angle one meaning "the farmstead by the hill". Just above Helton is a grove of trees still known as "Baxters' Rash" — another word brought in by the Angles. In 1252 another John Bacastre owned land in Helton, and the same name appears in 1284 and in 1340. In the latter year John Baxter (note the gradual change in spelling from Norman French to English) is on record as owning a carucate of land in Helton. (A carucate was as much land as could be tilled with one plough and eight oxen in a year.)

A few years earlier, in 1303, a William le Bakester, "a free tenant", held half a carucate at Castlerigg, some ten miles to the north-west, and paid four pence per annum to the Manor of Derwentwater. This was part of the vast estates of the Radcliffe family (Earls of Derwentwater). Most land in Westmorland (separated from Cumberland in 1190 and reunited with it in 1975) was held on a tenure which, though not technically freehold, gave the occupier security of succession. The land was poor, and the local economy depended on the rearing and grazing of sheep and cattle, and the production of wool.

In 1362 John Baxter, of Helton Flechan, and his wife, Beatrice, were mentioned in the will of Sir Thomas Lengleys when he left them forty sheep. From this date until the present day, the family records are complete. Soon after, in 1366, a Thomas Baxter was living at Cliburn, about seven miles north-west of Helton, and with him was Joan, widow of his brother Walter. The third brother was the John I have already mentioned. The family was spreading out in the district.

In 1469 the family had moved the few miles from Helton to Bampton, and by 1496 they had prospered with the raising of sheep and the marketing of wool, and had built Bampton Hall, in the centre of their 167 acres of land. The John Baxter who built the Hall married Elizabeth Lowther in 1450. She was the daughter of Sir Hugh, one of Henry V's knights at the Battle of Agincourt. Her mother was Margaret de Derwentwater. This marriage allied the Baxters with the two most powerful families in Westmorland. John Baxter's grandson — another John — cemented the alliance still more by marrying Mary Lowther, daughter of Sir John and his wife Mary (née Curwen). His brother, Henry, married another Mary Curwen, and the next most powerful family were linked by blood to the Baxters.

The family were now well-to-do "statesmen" with other neighbouring families such as the Lowthers and the Gibsons. At this point I should explain the origin of the term "statesmen" as it applied to yeoman farmers owning their own land in the Lake District of England. Originally they were free men, but after the Conquest they found themselves tenants of their new Norman lords. They kept far more of their independence than the unfortunate "villeins" in other counties, who became serfs. This was because the farmers in the Lakeland dales held their land by Border Tenure. This meant they retained the land as their own in return for their promise of military service in repelling any Scots invasion. The Normans, and their successors, who were constantly threatened by the warlike Scots, continued this arrangement.

One attempt was made in 1605 to end Border Tenure and transfer ownership of the land to James I and the great lords. There was a trial in the courts and the decision was that the lands were "estates of inheritance", quite apart from the promise of Border service, and so the "estatesmen", or "statesmen", came into existence. They were their own masters: each farm was a separate, independent estate, and each family raised or made its own food and clothing. The fluctuations of the market and the economy did not affect them at all directly.

In Swindale it was a particularly idyllic existence. They prospered with the wool trade; they were not affected by the plagues of 1208, 1268, 1319, or by the Black Death of 1348, and they were untroubled by the Scots border raids, since the main thrusts of the attacks were to the east and west of the remote dale. The Scots came south to Penrith, and then went either by way of Mardale and Windermere, or via Shap and Kendal — in both cases they left Swindale quiet and peaceful in the middle!

For this reason the houses were not fortified as were more exposed ones — there is no evidence of any pele towers in the dale, whereas on the main invasion routes they abounded. Bampton Hall is built of local slate (though now covered with stucco), low to the ground, and has two storeys. The house still stands, but additions and alterations have changed its appearance over the centuries.

The next generation after the builder of the Hall was headed by yet another John (1520–94)—the Baxters showed little enterprise in the selection of first names. He brought "brass" and not "class" into the family when he married Isabel Wilkinson, whose family had a small but prosperous iron foundry at Pennybridge.

This generation knew peaceful days, whereas the previous ones had a long-established feud with their neighbours, the Gibsons of Bampton Grange. On 1 May 1469 the two families signed a bond in which they agreed their disputes should be arbitrated by Sir Thomas Curwen and Thomas Sanford. Part of the document is missing and so the cause of the trouble is unknown. Probably it was a dispute over boundaries, or grazing rights for the sheep. Each statesman had his own area on the fells and crags for grazing, and this was called a stint. The Herdwick sheep raised in this area were reputed to know their own stints, and to observe the boundaries—perhaps in this case the Baxters and the Gibsons were too trusting!

The Herdwick sheep that the Baxters bred were the toughest

of all the hill breeds, braving the highest crags in the depth of winter for the sake of some minor nibbling. The Baxter stints, both owned and rented, covered eighteen square miles of Mardale and Swindale Commons, and this area, according to informed calculations, could support 1500 sheep. In the spring the yows were brought down for the lambing. In June the shearing took place. There were ten clippers at work and each could shear ten sheep an hour. In November the yows were brought down from the fells again for mating. One tup could serve fifty yows. The tup was smeared with red smit, or grease-paint, and if a yow showed no sign of this, it was clear she had not been mated, and she was set aside to have the job completed. The smit came in a variety of colours to establish ownership among the sheep-farmers. The Baxters' dye was red, the Gibsons' green, and so on, and all the colours used were registered.

Between 1500 and 1600 the selling-price of wool multiplied five times, but wages and production costs remained stable. This was probably the most profitable period in history for the wool trade. The average sheep produced 21 pounds. The selling-price per stone (14 pounds) was five shillings in 1600, seven shillings in 1700, and ten shillings in 1800; with a flock of 1500, this represented a good income for the Baxter family. Once a year, buyers from Ghent in the Low Countries would cross the North Sea to Newcastle-upon-Tyne, rent pack-horses, and then head over the hills to the Lake District to buy the wool from the farmers.

The son of the Baxter-Wilkinson marriage — a William this time — married Janet Holm in 1565. She was the daughter of another wealthy local family. He was part owner of coal mines near Whitehaven, and his acreage in Swindale now totalled over 1200, quite apart from the enormous fell area over which the Baxters had their grazing rights.

The next generation saw a parting of the ways in the family. The Baxter-Holm marriage produced five sons and one daughter. The latter married Thomas Curwen, and the five sons farmed the ancestral land. The eldest—inevitably another John —lived at Bampton Hall, while the others had farms at Tailbert, Bomby, Swindalefoot, and Swindalehead. History does not record whether the son who farmed the latter was bothered by the Swindale Boggle. This was the ghost of a woman in flowing white robes who haunted the fells in that area. She was supposed to have been a woman who starved to death in a cottage near the farm.

There may have been a Baxter house at the extreme head of the dale, even beyond Swindalehead Farm. It was possibly built before Bampton Hall. The ruins of the two-storey house still remain, and experts have estimated the date of the building as about 1400. It appears on old maps as High Swindalehead House, but so far no definite information can be found about it. It had a large floor area measuring sixty feet by forty feet, and several outbuildings.

In 1600 the youngest of the five sons, James, married Mabel, daughter and heiress of Sir James Preston, of Ackenthwaite, near the border with Lancashire. He farmed a large estate there after his marriage, and died in 1677, aged 101 — the first, and so far the last, centenarian in the Baxter family.

The eldest son of the Baxter–Preston marriage, Richard (1646–1720), married Elizabeth, daughter of Thomas Gibson, of Bampton Grange, his second cousin. The Baxter–Gibson feud had probably had its final burial when Janet Baxter, of Bampton Hall, married Thomas Gibson in 1592.

Westmorland had a dialect and a language all its own. A ram was a tup, a ewe a yow, a growing lamb a hogg, a two-year-old a twinter, and a gelded ram a wether. The farmers also had a system of counting of unknown origin: 1 = yan, 2 = tan, 3 = tethera, 4 = methera, 5 = pimp, 6 = sethera, 7 = lethera, 8 = hovera, 9 = dothera, 10 = dick, 11 = yan-a-dick, 12 = tan-a-dick, 13 = tethera-dick, 14 = methera-dick, 15 = bumfit, 16 = yan-a-bumfit, 17 = tan-a-bumfit, 18 = tethera-bumfit, 19 = methera-bumfit, 20 = gigot . . . and so on.

Meanwhile, back in Swindale, the family continued to prosper. In 1703 Thomas Baxter, then the leading man in the area, gave 300 acres as an endowment to finance the building of a free school. The indenture reads:

> Thomas Baxter, in consideration of his great affection towards the inhabitants of Swindale, and to promote virtue and piety by learning and good discipline, grants a messuage of 260 acres 3 rods 33 perches at Wasdale Foot in his manor of Hardendale, and another 31 acres 2 rods 9 perches in the manor of Crosby Ravensworth, that the trustees may build a school-house on some part of my lands at Bampton, and make convenient desks and seats, and maintain a well qualified person to teach the English and Latin tongues, etc.

The school was built near the chapel in Swindale, and over the next century and a half the school produced many graduates who went out into the world to become clergymen, lawyers, and architects. It was said in Westmorland at that time, "In Bampton they drive the plough in Latin, and shear the sheep in Greek." Seven years after the school was built, Thomas provided a free library. He was obviously far ahead of his time—for a tiny village in a lost dale to have such facilities in 1710 was unique. More than any of my ancestors, he is the one I would most like to have known. What was this man like? Why did a sheep-farmer and landowner develop a taste for the classical languages? Had he travelled a great deal in Europe? Was he influenced by some friend, or were there others like him in the area? These are questions that will never be answered but they remain in my mind to tantalize me!

The Baxters were mentioned by Nicholson and Burn in their book in 1777: "This Mr. Baxter and his forefathers from time immemorial have been called Kings of Swindale, living as it were in another world, and having no one near them greater than themselves."

The family remained in Swindale until 1796, when the estates were sold to the Earl of Lonsdale, the head of the Lowther family. The Herdwick sheep are still on the fells, but the only memorial to the proud Baxters is a short lane beside Bampton Hall still called "Baxters' Lane", although no one living near by knew why until I told them!

There is more to the family history, of course, bringing it down to the present day, but it is dull reading, and I think I have told you enough to show what can be discovered about the life of one's ancestors. There is so much for you to find out, and so much information is available if you research carefully. If your ancestors were immigrants into Canada and you discover the date, then by delving into the history of the place from which they came you can find out why they came. The answers are there waiting for you to discover.

I wondered why my own ancestors had left Swindale in 1796. I discovered that the reason was a rather surprising one. In the winter the family members — men, women, and children — would comb and card the wool, and, with a hand-loom, turn it into homespun cloth. In the spring they would sell it to buyers from Lancaster who came around the Lakeland farms. This extra income made all the difference to a large family, since the wool trade was no longer profitable because of the supply of cheap cotton. The year 1796 saw the invention of the spinning-jenny, and this led to the establishment of mills where one worker could supervise the operation of twenty looms. There was no longer a market for homespun cloth; the younger family members went into the mills in Kendal and Lancaster, or as far afield as Manchester, and only the older people were left on the farm. That is why the Baxters left the land and why I am not raising sheep in that lonely, lost valley of my ancestors!

BIBLIOGRAPHY

This is not a complete list of all books about genealogy in Canada. It does not include any books written about families, individuals, or localities (apart from provinces and territories). It does list the books I have found most useful in thirty-five years of research in Canada. For information about books written about a particular area you should contact the local genealogical or historical society, the various archives, or the local public library. Actually, you will find a number of books in this category mentioned in the text as being held by local libraries, or published by genealogical societies. In the following pages you will find books listed under Canada (general) and under each of the provinces:

Canada (General)
Bagnell, K. *The Little Immigrants.* Toronto, 1980.
Birkett, P. *Checklist of Parish Registers* (NAC). Ottawa, 1987.
Boyer, C. *Ship Passenger Lists* (USA). Newhall, CA, 1978.*
Bruce, R. M. *The Loyalist Trail.* Kingston, 1965.
Burrow, S., and Gaudet, F. *Checklist of Indexes to Canadian Newspapers* (NAC). Ottawa, 1987.
Campbell, W. *The Scotsman in Eastern Canada.* Toronto, 1911.
DeMarce, V. *German Military Settlers in Canada.* Sparta, WI, 1984.
Dorland, A. G. *History of Friends (Quakers) in Canada.* Newmarket [n.d.]
Epp, F. *Mennonites in Canada (1786–1920).* Toronto, 1974.
Fitch, E. R. *The Baptists of Canada.* Toronto, 1911.
Gellner, J. *The Czechs and Slovaks in Canada.* Toronto, 1968.
Gingerich, H. R., and Kreider, R. *Amish and Amish Mennonite Genealogy.* Gordonville, PA, 1986.
Guillet, E. *The Great Migration.* Toronto, 1963.
Gutteridge, P. *Canadian Genealogical Resources.* Surrey, BC, 1987.
Hillman, T. A. *Census Returns* (NAC). Ottawa, 1987.
Ivison, S., and Rosser, F. *The Baptists in Upper & Lower Canada.* Toronto, 1956.
Kaminow, J. and M. *List of Emigrants to America (1718–59).* New York, 1964.*
Lancour, A. H. *Ship's Passenger Lists (1538–1825).* New York, 1963.*
McKenzie, D. A. *Death Notices from* Christian Guardian (2 vols.: 1836–50, 1851–60). Lambertville, NJ, 1982, 1984.

Mika, N. and H. *United Empire Loyalists.* Belleville, ON, 1976.

Momryk, M. *Archival Sources — Polish Canadians* (NAC). Ottawa, 1987.

Moore, C. *The Loyalists.* Toronto, 1984.

Sprague, D., and Frye, R. *The Genealogy of the First Métis Nation.* Winnipeg, 1983.

Tapper, L. F. *Archival Sources — Canadian Jewry* (NAC). Ottawa, 1987.

Tepper, M. *New World Immigrants.* Baltimore, MD, 1979.

Whyte, D. *Scottish Emigrants to the U.S.A.* Edinburgh, 1972.*

———. *Emigrants from Scotland to Canada.* Edinburgh, 1986.

———. *The Old United Empire Loyalist List.* Baltimore, MD, 1976.

———. *Union List of Manuscripts in Canadian Repositories* (NAC) (with later supplements). Ottawa, 1975.

———. *Union List of Canadian Newspapers in Canadian Repositories* (NAC). Ottawa, 1977.

*These books refer to emigrants to the USA but many continued on to Canada from the port of disembarkation.

Alberta

Blue, J. *Alberta Past and Present.* Chicago, 1924.

Cashman, A. W. *History of Western Canada.* Edmonton, 1971.

Kaye, V. *Early Ukrainian Settlements (1895–1900).* Toronto, 1964.

Liddell, K. *This Is Alberta.* Toronto, 1952.

MacGregor, J. *A History of Alberta.* Edmonton, 1972.

Macrae, A. *History of the Province of Alberta.* Calgary, 1912.

Morton, A. *History of the Canadian West.* Toronto, 1973.

Ricker, M. B. *Alberta.* Toronto, 1949.

Stanley, G. F. G. *The Birth of Western Canada to 1870.* Toronto, 1960.

Strathern, G. *Alberta, 1854–1979.* Calgary, 1980.

British Columbia

Bancroft, H. *History of British Columbia.* San Raphael, CA, 1888.

Begg, A. *History of British Columbia.* Toronto, 1972.

Griffin, H. *British Columbia: The People's Early Story.* Toronto, 1958.

Johnson, P. *Canada's Pacific Province.* Toronto, 1966.

Maine, L. *Index to 1881 BC Census.* Vancouver, 1981.

Ormsby, M. *British Columbia: A History.* Toronto, 1958.

Pethick, D. *British Columbia Recalled.* Saanich, BC, 1974.

Manitoba

Bryce, G. *A History of Manitoba.* Toronto, 1906.

Healy, W. J. *Winnipeg's Early Days.* Winnipeg, 1927.

Jackson, J. A. *Centennial History of Manitoba.* Toronto, 1970.

Lorne, W. M. *Index to 1881 Census of Manitoba.* Vancouver, 1984.
Morton, W. L. *Manitoba: The Birth of a Province.* Altona, MB, 1965.
——. *Manitoba: A History.* Toronto, 1957.
Paterson, E. *Pioneers & Early Citizens of Manitoba.* Winnipeg, 1971.
Schaefer, P. *The Mennonites of Russia.* Altona, MB, 1946.
Stokes, K. R. *Marriage and Death Notices from Manitoba Newspapers.* Winnipeg, 1986.

New Brunswick
Bill, I. E. *The Baptists of the Maritimes.* Saint John, 1880.
Fellows, R. *Researching Your Ancestors in New Brunswick.* Fredericton, 1979.
Hannay, J. *History of New Brunswick.* Saint John, 1909.
MacNutt, W. S. *New Brunswick: A History, 1784–1867.* Toronto, 1963.
Maxwell, L. *Outline of the History of Central New Brunswick.* Sackville, 1937.
Taylor, H. *New Brunswick History: Secondary Sources.* Fredericton, 1975.
Wright, E. *The Loyalists of New Brunswick.* Fredericton, 1955.

Newfoundland
Devine, P. K. *Notable Events in the History of Newfoundland.* St. John's, 1900.
Glover, R. S. *Bristol and America.* Bristol, 1931.
Harvey, M. *A Short History of Newfoundland.* London, 1890.
Howard, M. *Vital Statistics from Newfoundland Newspapers.* Saint John, 1980.
Matthews, K. *Who Was Who in the Fishing Industry* (1660–1840). St. John's, 1971.
Prowse, D. W. *A History of Newfoundland.* St. John's, 1971.

Acadia
Arsenault, B. *Histoire et généalogie des Acadiens.* Québec, 1965.
Bernard, A. *Histoire de la survivance acadienne.* Montréal, 1935.
Blanchard, H. *Histoire des Acadiens de l'Île du Prince-Édouard.* Moncton, 1927.
de Ville, W. *Acadian Church Records, 1679–1757.* New Orleans, 1985.
Doughty, A. *The Acadian Exiles.* Toronto, 1920.
Gaudet, P. *Acadian Genealogy and Notes.* Ottawa, 1906.
Griffiths, N. *The Acadians: Creation of a People.* Toronto, 1973.
Leblanc, E. *Les Acadiens.* Montréal, 1963.
Rieder, M. *The Acadiens in France, 1762–1776.* Metairie, LA, 1967.

Nova Scotia

Bell, W. *Foreign Protestants and the Settlement of Nova Scotia.* Toronto, 1961.

Dunn, C. *Highland Settler.* Toronto, 1953.

Gilroy, M. *Loyalists and Land Settlement in Nova Scotia.* Halifax, 1937.

Haliburton, T. *History of Nova Scotia, 1829.* Belleville, 1973.

Peterson, T. *The Loyalist Guide.* Halifax, 1983.

Punch, T. Genealogical Research in Nova Scotia. Halifax, 1978.

Rawlyk, G. *Nova Scotia and Massachusetts.* Montréal, 1973.

Saunders, E. M. *The Baptists of the Maritimes.* Halifax, 1941.

Stark, J. *The Loyalists of Massachusetts.* Boston, MA, 1907.

Ontario

Anglican Church. *Guide to the Holdings of the Ecclesiastical Province of Ontario.* Toronto, 1990.

Caniff, W. *Settlement of Upper Canada.* Belleville, ON 1971.

Chadwick, E. M. *Ontarian Families.* Lambertville, NJ, 1983.

Cowan, H. *British Emigration to North America.* Toronto, 1967.

Craig, G. *Upper Canada.* Toronto, 1963.

Crowder, N. K. *Indexes to Ontario Census Records.* Toronto, 1987.

Fretz, J. W. *Mennonites in Ontario.* Waterloo, 1982.

Gates, L. *Land Policies of Upper Canada.* Toronto, 1968.

Guillet, E. *The Valley of the Trent.* Toronto, 1957.

Keffer, M. *Some Ontario References and Sources.* Toronto, 1978.

McFall, D. and J. *Land Records in Ontario Registry Offices.* Toronto, 1984.

Merriman, B. *Genealogy in Ontario.* Toronto, 1988.

Ontario Genealogical Society (Toronto Branch). *Directory of Cemeteries (Toronto & York).* Toronto, 1989.

Reid, W. D. *Loyalists of Ontario.* Lambertville, NJ, 1973.

——. *Marriage Notices of Ontario* (1813–54). Lambertville, NJ, 1985.

Ronnow, V. (ed.). *Inventory of Cemeteries in Ontario.* Toronto, 1987.

Prince Edward Island

Callbeck, L. *The Cradle of Confederation.* Fredericton, 1964.

Campbell, D. *History of Prince Edward Island.* Charlottetown, 1875.

Clark, A. *Three Centuries and the Island.* Toronto, 1959.

Greenhill, B. *Westcountrymen in Prince Edward Island.* Toronto, 1967.

Stewart, J. *Canada's Smallest Province.* Charlottetown, 1973.

Warburton, A. *A History of Prince Edward Island.* Saint John, 1923.

Warren, W. H. *A Century of Baptist History on Prince Edward Island.* Charlottetown, 1920.

Québec

Charbonneau, H., and Legaré, J. *Le répertoire des actes de baptême, mariage, sépulture, et des recensements du Québec ancien.* Montréal, 1980.

Dionne, N.-E. *Canadiens français: les origines des familles émigrées de France, d'Espagne, et de Suisse.* Québec, 1914.

Drouin (Institut). *Dictionnaire national des Canadiens français, 1608–1760.* Montréal, 1975.

Gingras, R. *Précis du généalogiste amateur.* Québec, 1973.

Grégoire, J. *A la recherche de nos ancêtres.* Montréal, 1957.

Jenkins, K. *Montréal Island: City of the St. Lawrence.* New York, 1966.

Jetté, R. *Dictionnaire généalogique des familles du Québec.* Montréal, 1983.

Langelier, C. *List of lands granted by the Crown in the Province of Québec, 1763–1890.* Ottawa, 1891.

Leboeuf, J. A. *Complément au dictionnaire généalogique Tanguay.* Montréal, 1977.

Poulin, J.-P. *Premiers colons du début de la colonie.* Montréal, 1960.

Roy, A. *Bibliographie de généalogies et histoires de famille.* Montréal, 1940.

Roy, P.-G. *Inventaire des contrats de mariages du régime français conservés aux Archives Judiciaires de Québec.* Beauceville, 1941.

——. *Inventaire des testaments, donations, et inventaires du régime français conservés aux Archives Judiciaires du Québec.* Beauceville, 1941.

——, et Roy, A. *Inventaires des greffes des notaires du régime français.* Beauceville, 1943.

Tanguay, C. *Dictionnaire généalogique des familles canadiennes.* Montréal, 1871 (reprinted 1975).

Saskatchewan

Black, N. *History of Saskatchewan.* Regina, 1913.

Hande, D'Arcy. *Exploring Family History in Saskatchewan.* Saskatoon, 1986.

Hawkes, J. *The Story of Saskatchewan.* Chicago, 1924.

Rempel, D. D. *Family Chronicle* (Mennonite). Saskatoon, 1973.

Wright, J. *Saskatchewan.* Toronto, 1955.

INDEX